Scripture Sevens

DAILY MEDITATIONS MAKING UP
52 WEEKLY STUDIES ON
SOME OF THE BEAUTIFUL GROUPS
OF SEVEN FOUND IN THE SCRIPTURES

COMPILED AND EDITED BY PHIL COULSON

JOHN RITCHIE LTD
CHRISTIAN PUBLICATIONS

ISBN 1 904064 28 0

SCRIPTURE SEVENS
Copyright © 2005 John Ritchie Ltd.
40 Beansburn, Kilmarnock, Scotland

Contents

Preface

The thought of such a book as this arose during a long train journey in India. In the company, and with the help, of my esteemed brother in the Lord, Michael Browne, I began to draw up a list of distinct groups of seven found in the Scriptures. By the end of that particular journey it was evident that plenty of material was there for profitable study and, over the ensuing months, the list grew. The sequence of events that led to the compilation of this book was, we trust, of the Lord's arrangement, and certainly the desire of the contributors and publishers is that it will be used for His glory.

Before the advent of electronic communication, word processing and typesetting, the production of this volume would have taken a very long time. As it is, from conception to availability on the shelf has taken little more than one year, even though no fewer than 43 contributors have been involved. Rarely, if ever, has a compilation of such a broad range of written ministry from such a large number of brethren been bound between two covers. That in itself is a great pity, for imagine the wealth of teaching that might have been preserved had the technology been available to our forebears.

Together, those of us who read this book are indebted to the busy men who have somehow found the time to prepare and write the material it contains. The contributors were requested to imagine their articles being read by a wide audience, from parents reading together with their children in their daily devotions, to the elderly saint at the fireside who is looking for encouragement and cheer from the Scriptures. It can be asserted with confidence that every reader will glean something for their soul from the wide range of ministry presented by the contributors. The subjects covered span the Scriptures from Genesis through to Revelation, from Old Testament characters and types through to New Testament doctrine and practical exhortation.

But the clear emphasis and theme that links all the articles is Christ, the Son of the living God, the effulgence of divine glory, the One who took upon Him the form of a servant and was made in the likeness of men. That ministry of

Christ, so vital for our souls, is the intent of this volume of meditations. What is the spiritual need of the reader? A ministry of Christ will meet it. The glories of His deity, His humanity, His moral beauty as He walked amongst men; the wisdom and the sweetness of His words; the tenderness and compassion of His ministry to the poor and unloved; the depths of His sufferings and shame at Calvary; the mighty victory of His resurrection out from among the dead; His ascension and exaltation at the Father's right hand in heaven; the lovely titles that He bears and the blessed fulness of His ministry to His loved ones today. He is our Saviour, Redeemer, Mediator, High Priest and Lover of our souls. He is our God! How much we need a ministry of Christ!

What must it have been to hear Him expound in all the Scriptures the things concerning Himself? That which the Saviour so beautifully ministered to the favoured pair on the road to Emmaus, the Spirit of God now ministers to the hearts of the redeemed. Through our meditation upon Christ and His word the Holy Spirit will reveal the glories of the Saviour, and it is to provoke such meditation that this compilation of Scripture Sevens has been published.

Phil Coulson

"Delight thyself in Him; delight is free;
And He will give thee all thy heart's desire.
Give in to Him and He'll give all to thee;
The more thou giv'st the more thou shalt acquire
    If thou delight in Him.

Journey with Him that separated path;
Follow His steps toward that cross of shame;
Know thou the pleasure that His service hath;
Live for the honour of His precious Name.
    Journey, my soul, with Him.

Please thou the Lord; let men say what they will,
Men who forget the Listener unseen.
Thou shalt remain all undisturbed and still,
Like mountain peak above the storm serene
    If thou but please the Lord".

(I. Y. Ewan)

Week 1

7 FEATURES OF THE PERFECT SERVANT IN ISAIAH 42

Introduction

Jehovah has had a multitude of servants, several of whom He specifically refers to as "My servant". Examples of these are, "My servant Abraham" (Gen 26:24); "My servant Moses" (Num 12:7); "My servant Caleb" (Num 14:24); "My servant David" (2 Sam 7:5); "My servant Job" (Job 1:8); "My servant Isaiah" (Isa 20:3). Of course there were so many others, in both Old Testament and New, men who enjoyed the high privilege of being "servants of the most high God" (Dan 3:26; Acts 16:17).

With all of these servants however, great though they were, there were human failings. They served God well, and served their generations well too, but none could be described as a perfect servant. Then He came, of whom our chapter speaks, "My Servant, whom I uphold … in whom my soul delighteth". With Him there was no failure. There was no lapse in His service. There was no disappointment. Jehovah had found, for the first time, a Perfect Servant.

The chapter opens abruptly, "Behold My Servant". The servant whom we are asked to contemplate is not named or identified, yet none who know Him and love Him ever think of asking, "Lord, which servant?" There is but one servant who served in the unbroken faithfulness as outlined in the verses which follow. As Delitzsch remarks in his scholarly style, "In Isaiah 41:8 this epithet was applied to the nation, which had been chosen as the servant and for the service of Jehovah. But the servant of Jehovah who is presented to us here is distinct from Israel, and has so strong an individuality and such marked personal features, that the expression cannot possibly be merely a personified collective. Nor can the prophet himself be intended; for what is here affirmed of this servant of Jehovah goes infinitely beyond anything to which a prophet was ever called, or of which a man was ever capable. It must therefore be the future Christ".

The seven features of the Servant which are detailed in this passage are seven reasons for Jehovah's pleasure in Him. He came to do the will of God, He did it, He did it perfectly, and He delighted to do it. It is our joy to contemplate Him, the Perfect Servant.

Day 1

SUBMISSIVENESS

Isaiah 42:1

"Behold My servant". That He who was the eternal Son of God, the Son of the Father, should be content to be called "My servant", is submissiveness indeed. In the Jewish household everyone knew that sons were not servants and servants were not sons. Even the prodigal knew that. On returning to his father's house he had planned to say, "I am no more worthy to be called thy son, make me as one of thy hired servants" (Luke 15:19). He never did get to saying that, but it had been his intention, for he knew that there was a dignity in sonship to which he had not risen in his behaviour, and he would now be content with the lowly status of servant.

Jehovah however could say of the Saviour, "My beloved Son, in whom I have found my delight" (Matt 3:17 JND), and could also say, "My servant, in whom my soul delighteth". Our Lord was the Beloved Son and the Perfect Servant. He lived and served for the pleasure of the Father and in this Servant-Son the Father had found His delight. All His life was devoted to that service. As He came into the world He said, "Lo, I come to do thy will O God" (Ps 40:7-8; Heb 10:9). During His ministry He could say, "My meat is to do the will of Him that sent me" (John 4:34), and on His last evening on earth He said, "Not my will, but thine, be done" (Luke 22:42). His was a life unreservedly and entirely consecrated to doing the will of God. He was indeed the unique Son but in beautiful submissiveness was willing to be Jehovah's Servant.

By His submissiveness the Lord Jesus has added a new dimension to sonship and He has added a new dignity to service. His saints then, in the wake of His blessed example, can rejoice in that they are sons of God indeed, but can joy too in the privilege of service.

Characteristically, the Saviour taught these things not only by word of mouth but also by example. What He preached He had already practised! He could say, "I am among you as He that serveth" (Luke 22:27). And this was not words only. He who wore the garments of glory in eternity was willing to wear the swaddling clothes of a lowly humanity (Ps 104:1-2; Luke 2:7). He whose train had filled the temple wrapped Himself in a linen towel, a slave's apron (Isa 6:1; John 13:4), and by His gracious example has taught us the greatness of voluntary humility and submissiveness. Is it really to be wondered at that Jehovah should say to us, "Behold My servant"!

Day 2

FAITHFULNESS

Isaiah 42:1

"Behold My servant … in whom my soul delighteth". The word "faithfulness" may not be specifically mentioned in this verse but it must surely be implied that if the very heart of Jehovah had found unmitigated delight in His Servant, then there must have been constant faithfulness in His service. In a world of failure and sin, where there was unbelief and unfaithfulness even in the chosen nation, there lived one Perfect Servant who was, as one has written "Faithful amidst unfaithfulness; 'midst darkness only light".

On two occasions a voice from heaven fused together this expression from Isaiah 42:1 and another from Psalm 2:7, declaring, "My Son … my delight"! The first of these occasions was at the end of thirty years of quiet service in Nazareth. No miracle; no parable; no public ministry at all, but just faithful devotion to His Father's business (Luke 2:49). In holy retrospect, in divine appreciation of those years of faithfulness, the Father proclaims, "This is my beloved Son, in whom I have found my delight" (Matt 3:17 JND).

Three busy years of ministry then followed, with journeys throughout Galilee, Judea, and Samaria, and at the end of these years the Father speaks again. The words are the same, "This is my beloved Son, in whom I have found my delight" (Matt 17:5 JND). So it was, that at the close of the hidden years in Nazareth, as at the end of the busy years of public ministry, the Father acknowledges from an opened heaven the faithfulness of the Perfect Servant.

Observe too, that on that first occasion our Lord was at Bethabara in the south of the land, perhaps not too distant from the northern shore of the Dead Sea. But on the second occasion He was on the Mount of Transfiguration, which was almost certainly Mount Hermon, on the northernmost border of Israel. It seems as though that, from north to south, for the entire length of the land, Jehovah would have the nation, and the world, to know that He had found delight in a Man. There has been on earth a Servant who was a Perfect Servant, living and serving, in obscurity as in publicity, in uninterrupted faithfulness.

When that public ministry began, the Saviour delivered what is now familiarly called 'The Sermon on the Mount', recorded for us in Matthew 5,

6, and 7. Perhaps a most profitable way to read these chapters is to see them as an exposition of the exemplary life of the Saviour Himself. For thirty years He had lived out all those features which He outlines in the Sermon. He now expects the same from the children of the kingdom, who should take character from the King.

Day 3

FRUITFULNESS

Isaiah 42:1

"I have put my Spirit upon Him". This is the central one of three similar expressions concerning Christ and the Holy Spirit in this prophecy. Compare Isaiah 11:2, "the spirit of the Lord shall rest upon him" and Isaiah 61:1, "The Spirit of the Lord God is upon me". The Perfect Servant of Jehovah lived and served in unbroken communion with the Holy Spirit. Divine Persons were in gracious harmony in the Servant's ministry. In the meat offering of Leviticus 2 three different words are used to describe the application of the oil to the offering. Sometimes flour and oil were "mingled". Sometimes the offering was "anointed" with oil. At other times the oil was "poured" upon the offering, thus saturating it. How beautifully expressive are these early pictures of Him who was miraculously conceived in the womb of the virgin by the operation of the Spirit, who was publicly anointed at His baptism when the Spirit in bodily form as a gentle dove rested upon Him, and whose entire ministry was in the power of the same Spirit.

All this being so, it may well be expected that we should find in Him that nine-fold fruit of the Spirit of which Paul speaks in Galatians 5:22-23. We are not disappointed when we read the Gospels looking for this fruitfulness in the life of the Perfect Servant. There was love, joy, and peace. There was longsuffering, gentleness, and goodness. There was faith, meekness, and temperance, perfect self-control. These were all in perfect balance in Him. There was not more love than joy. There was not more gentleness than goodness, nor more faith than meekness. There was no imbalance in that fruitful ministry.

This fruitfulness was the fulfilment of an early prophecy that went forth concerning Joseph. That much-loved son of Jacob was to become, in the picturesque language of the East, "A fruitful bough by a well, whose branches run over the wall" (Gen 49:22). Loved by his father but rejected by his brethren, Joseph was to be blessed by God and become a foreshadowing of our heavenly Joseph. How literally was it all fulfilled, when one memorable day Jesus sat on a well at Sychar, near to a parcel of ground which Jacob had given to his son Joseph (John 4:5). The Lord Jesus, Perfect Servant that He was, although weary, thirsty, and hungry, saw the need of a poor Samaritan woman who came to draw water. As a fruitful bough His branches ran over the wall of Judaism carrying the refreshing fruit of salvation to a thirsty Gentile soul.

And so it is still, as His Gospel reaches out to poor Gentile sinners everywhere, bearing salvation to all.

Day 4

QUIETNESS

Isaiah 42:2

Since there are no contradictions or discrepancies in our Bible, two verses in this chapter require comment and explanation. Verse 2 says, "He shall not cry", but verse 13 states explicitly, "He shall cry, yea roar". As with many other perceived problems, the answer is really very simple. The two expressions belong to two different phases of our Lord's ministry. The second, in verse 13, refers to a coming day when, as a warrior King, He will appear in glory. Like a man of war He will vanquish His enemies. It is a shout of triumph here. The first expression, however, belongs to the time of His gracious ministry when, in a beautiful quietness, He moved among men dispensing blessing.

"He shall not cry". The Lord Jesus knew nothing of the raucous cry of the street vendor. This is the cheapest and most primitive form of advertising. It is the loud attracting of attention to oneself. It is the cry of the street market, noisily calling to the passer-by to come and buy. The Saviour was never characterised by such publicity of self, but rather the reverse was true, as will be seen often in the Gospels.

Early in His ministry the demons recognised Him. They saw beyond the guise of the Carpenter of Nazareth and acknowledged Him as the Holy One of God. He forbade them to tell! (Mark 1:24, 34). He would not attract attention to Himself. In the same chapter He similarly commands the healed leper to say nothing to any man (v.44). How often throughout the Gospels does that word occur, "Tell no man". It will be found some eight times in Matthew, Mark, and Luke, in various situations.

When He healed the poor man who was deaf and had a speech impediment there was great astonishment, but "He charged them that they should tell no man" (Mark 7:36).

When, at Caesarea Philippi, He confirmed the great confession of His disciples that He was indeed the Christ, "He charged them that they should tell no man" (Mark 8:30).

When, in the house of Jairus, He raised their little daughter from the dead, He spoke to the astonished parents and "charged them that they should tell no man" (Luke 8:56).

It was so again when, on the Holy Mount, the Mount of Transfiguration, they saw His glory. With the same words "He charged them that they should tell no man (Mark 9:9).

Such was the quiet dignity that characterised the Perfect Servant during all His sojourn here. He came quietly into the world at Bethlehem. He spent thirty silent years in Nazareth. He moved graciously among men for three busy years.

A ministry of quietness indeed!

Day 5

GENTLENESS

Isaiah 42:3

"A bruised reed shall He not break, and the smoking flax shall He not quench". The vocabulary is very beautiful and the verse is often quoted, but what exactly is "a bruised reed" and what is "the smoking flax"?

With the latter there is really no problem. Here is pictured the smouldering wick of the Eastern oil lamp. Doubtless at one time it burned brightly and the flame was smokeless and clear. But now it is not burning as it should be, and indeed not as it had been. What is the remedy? Well, men might say, the wick in itself is of little value. It is but a piece of flax, dispensable and replaceable. Cast it aside and get another. So it may be with many a believer. Once clear and bright in testimony for the Saviour, but now for whatever causes, not burning brightly any more. Men might be tempted to discard such, but not the Perfect Servant. He will gently tend and carefully trim the smoking flax and restore the willing backslider to useful service again.

But what then is a bruised reed? There are several explanations and the following is offered for consideration. Perhaps all are familiar with the idea of a little shepherd boy sitting in the midst of the flock while the sheep and lambs graze peacefully around him. To pass the hours as he sits and watches he cuts down a hollow reed. Patiently he cuts holes along the length of the reed at skilfully measured intervals until he has a primitive wind instrument. Now he can produce a melody while he sits with his flock.

Suddenly an emergency among the sheep demands his immediate attention. He jumps to his feet, hastily, abruptly, and in the process the reed is bruised. Returning to it he picks it up again, but sadly it will not now produce the melody as before. What will he do? Well, it is only a reed and there are plenty more around him. Intelligence says, discard it and get another.

There are bruised reeds among believers today, men and women overtaken by failure, whose lives and testimonies have been blighted. The backslider is not a happy person. Many, like poor Peter, weep bitter tears as they lament their failure, and, regrettably, some would discard them. Not so the Perfect Servant! He will not break the bruised reed. He will not quench the smouldering flax. Gently He would rekindle the flame of testimony and mend the bruised life so that once again there should be sweet melody for His pleasure and glory.

How zealously should every servant, in his dealings with the saints, emulate the gentleness of the Lord Jesus.

Day 6

STEADFASTNESS

Isaiah 42:4

"He shall not fail". What a varied ministry was that of Jehovah's Perfect Servant! He ministered to a variety of people, with a variety of needs, in a variety of places. But whatever the time, whatever the task, whatever the circumstances, He did not, could not, fail. Nothing could deflect Him from the path of the will of God.

Notice the changing circumstances in the opening chapter of the Gospel of Mark, the Gospel of the Perfect Servant. He stands in the river; He departs to the wilderness; He returns to the seashore; He is in the synagogue; then in a fisherman's cottage; now back to the wilderness again. But wherever He is, whatever He does, it is always true, "He shall not fail". His was a ministry of steadfast determination to do always and only those things that pleased the Father.

In that same first chapter of Mark, such a variety of need presents itself to Him. There is a man with an unclean spirit, a woman with a fever, a multitude with many diseases, and a poor man full of leprosy. Throughout the chapters which follow there is more demon possession, more disease and deformity, men that are deaf and some who are dumb. There is a raging storm on the lake, frightening even those experienced Galilean fishermen, a hungry multitude needing to be fed, and a little girl in the cold grasp of death. Such need! How will the Perfect Servant cope with it? "He shall not fail". Neither demons, disease, death, or the deep can deter Him. He will not deviate from His determination to live and serve for Jehovah's pleasure.

Eighteen miracles are crowded into the first eleven chapters of Mark's Gospel. These, with a series of parables and a lengthy prophetic discourse on the Mount of Olives, engage Him almost until the Passover. Then, the sorrow of Gethsemane, the blasphemy of the high priest's palace, the mockery of the Roman judgment hall, the agony of Golgotha, and the solitude of the tomb.

How many a servant would have faltered, and failed, but He walked and served and suffered resolutely. It was the will of God for Him. He had come to do that, and whatever the cost, He would do it. He did the will of God; He did it perfectly; and He delighted to do it. At the end of a busy life He could say, "I have glorified Thee on the earth" (John 17:4).

Well might we enter Mark's Gospel with that word ringing in our ears and in our hearts, "He shall not fail", and then see it so accurately fulfilled throughout every succeeding chapter. His was a steadfast ministry indeed.

Day 7

RIGHTEOUSNESS

Isaiah 42:6; 19-21

"Jehovah is well pleased for His righteousness sake". What a delightful tribute to the Perfect Servant! Men may not have recognised Him, regarded Him, or appreciated all that He was and all that He did, but Jehovah was well pleased, and said so more than once from the opened heavens.

That righteous ministry of Jehovah's Servant was characterised by complete impartiality. He ministered to all who needed Him and, as Simeon said, He was "A light to lighten the Gentiles and the glory of my people Israel". Did Simeon have this verse 6 in mind? "A covenant for the people … a light of the Gentiles". Jehovah had called Him in righteousness and the righteous ministry to which He was called demanded the impartiality which is here suggested. Well He knew, in His omniscience, that Jew and Gentile would eventually be joined in His cruel rejection, but here in verse 6 they are together the objects of His gracious ministry of blessing.

It is well known that among men in general, and even among the servants of God, there is a human tendency to be distracted from a straight path. There is a natural weakness which can easily be influenced and biased in one direction or another. This was never true of the Perfect Servant and perhaps this is the explanation of the strange expression in verses 19-20. "Who is blind as he that is perfect, and blind as the Lord's servant?" He sees many things, but does not observe; he opens his ears, but does not hear! Jehovah's Perfect Servant is blind and deaf to all distracting sights and sounds. Our Lord Jesus sojourned for thirty-three years in this world and served resolutely. During three years of busy public ministry there were many who would have influenced Him if they could, but none could move Him from a path of righteousness.

He was full of grace and truth in perfect balance. In one chapter He could be a gracious guest at a wedding and then purge the temple with a whip of small cords (John 2). He could talk with a learned theologian of Israel, and He could converse freely with a poor disadvantaged woman of Samaria (John 3-4). Whether men or women, rich or poor, learned or illiterate, Jew or Greek, did not matter to Him, for His impartial righteous ministry reached out to all who needed Him. He lived only for the blessing of the people and the glory of God and could not be deflected.

Considering the virtues of the Perfect Servant we cannot wonder that Jehovah should say, "Behold My Servant". He desires that others should join Him in holy contemplation of the Servant who never failed.

JIM FLANIGAN

Week 2

7 DESCRIPTIONS IN SCRIPTURE
OF THE MANNA

Introduction

"Command that these stones be made bread" (Matt 4:3) were the tempter's words to the incarnate Son of God in the wilderness. The need was present, even pressing, for the Lord Jesus had not eaten for forty days. That he was capable of the miracle demanded is beyond doubt. The Lord gave his reason for refusing the evil one's suggestion by quoting Scripture, "man shall not live by bread alone, but by every word that proceedeth out of the mouth of God" (Matt 4:4).

By answering in this way the Saviour not only leaves us a valuable example of how to resist the devil, but reveals that, as a man in the wilderness, he will be completely dependant upon his God to meet his needs. The passage quoted by the Lord is found in Deuteronomy 8. "He … suffered thee to hunger, and fed thee with manna … that he might make thee know that man doth not live by bread only, but by every word that proceedeth out of the mouth of the Lord doth man live" (Deut 8:3).

Food to meet our physical need is important. Without it we become weak and eventually die. Similarly, we dare not neglect our spiritual diet. Reading John's Gospel chapter 6 we are left in no doubt that what the manna was to the Israelites physically, Christ is to the Christian spiritually. Words like "I am the bread which came down from heaven" (John 6:41) make this abundantly clear. Thus our study of the manna must bring Christ before us. We find that there are seven names given to the manna in Scripture and that each one sets before us a different aspect of His lovely person. We will look at them in the order in which they occur.

1. Bread from heaven (Exod 16:4).
2. Manna (Exod 16:15).
3. Light bread (Num 21:5).
4. Corn of heaven (Ps 78:24).
5. Angels' food (Ps 78:25).
6. Spiritual meat (1 Cor 10:3).
7. Hidden manna (Rev 2:17).

Each of these names brings before us a particular aspect of the one of whom they speak and will lead us to consider other things that we are told about the manna. We trust that this in turn will lead to an increased appreciation of our Lord Jesus Christ.

Day 1

"BREAD FROM HEAVEN"

Exodus 16:4

The Jews, we read in John 6:41, murmured at him, because He said, "I am the bread which came down from heaven." Murmur they may, but the fact remained that the Lord Jesus had said that the manna – the "bread from heaven" – pictured Himself, thus claiming to be far more than they were willing to accept. In this, the first name given to the manna, we are taught something of Christ incarnate.

The first reference to bread in our Bible is found in Genesis 3:19, "In the sweat of thy face thou shalt eat bread", bread that must be wrested from an unwilling, cursed earth. Sin has made it so. But come now to Exodus 16; see a weary, growling people in a waste, howling wilderness. Despite having so recently witnessed God's power they are murmuring against Him. Not having reached Sinai they have not yet placed themselves under law, which can only bring the judgement they deserve, so God is still dealing with them in grace. Hear then the gracious words of Jehovah, "I will rain bread from heaven for you" (Exod 16:4). Not now bread reaped from an unwilling earth, but bread rained from an unstinting heaven. What a picture of the incarnation of our blessed Lord Jesus Christ!

To Bethlehem – the House of Bread – came the Bread of God. "O little town of Bethlehem, so still we see thee lie". Manna-like He came, softly and pure as the dew upon which it fell, "so silently, so silently, the mighty gift is given". Small it was, the word means 'very small', speaking of the humility of Christ. The God who has been described as "a circle whose centre is everywhere and whose circumference is nowhere" is found "wrapped in swaddling clothes and laid in a manger". "Lo, within the manger lies, He who built the starry skies". Jerusalem expected someone grander – Christ in glory. Bethlehem witnessed one who could hardly have been lowlier – Christ in grace. Pharaoh refused to humble himself (Exod 10:3), Nebuchadnezzar had to be driven from his palace (Dan 4:33), yet He who rightfully occupied the highest place voluntarily took the lowest place. "Being found in fashion as a man, he humbled himself, and became obedient unto death, even the death of the cross" (Phil 2:8).

Daily, for their very life depended on it, the children of Israel fed on the bread from heaven. How we need to feed on the down-stooping humility of Christ. How appropriately we sing, "Bread of Heaven, feed us till we want no more". Want no more of earth's glory, earth's pride, earth's place. The more I am occupied with the Bread from Heaven, the less I will value the best of earth.

Day 2

"MANNA"

Exodus 16:15

'Bread from Heaven' is a title given by God. 'Manna' is what men called that heavenly bread. Manna means 'what is it', which is what the people said when they saw it. Moses had to tell them "this is the bread which the Lord hath given you to eat" (Exod 16:15). So, although bread had been promised, "in the evening flesh … in the morning bread" (Exod 16:8), the time detailed and the word partially fulfilled in the giving of the quails, still they did not recognise the promised bread for what it was when it came.

It is not difficult to see the parallel with the coming of the Lord Jesus Christ. Prophecy after prophecy had been given. The time, the place, the manner of his coming had all been foretold, yet when he came so few recognised him. Even after thirty years John the Baptist, his prophesied forerunner, had to say "there standeth one among you, whom ye know not" (John 1:26). If the God-given title 'bread from heaven' speaks of Christ incarnate, surely the man-given title 'manna', tells us of Christ unrecognised.

"He was in the world, and the world was made by him, and the world knew him not" (John 1:10). "Is not this Jesus, the son of Joseph, whose father and mother we know? How is it then that he saith, 'I came down from heaven'?" (John 6:42). These, and many other verses, speak of the unrecognised Christ. Although His words, "never man spake like this man" (John 7:46); His works "we never saw it on this fashion" (Mark 2:12); His walk "who did no sin" (1 Pet 2:22), all testified very clearly to who He was, He was generally unrecognised.

No one likes to feel unappreciated; we all like to feel that our efforts in the service of the Lord are recognised, at least by our fellow Christians. A veteran thing" (Rom 7:18). We should take to heart what the hymn writer meant when he said "Not what I am, O Lord, but what Thou art, this, this alone can be my soul's true rest". Feeding upon the corn of heaven – meditating on the fruitfulness of Christ, on the daily delight he brought to His Father – we will find worship rising in our heart to God for Him. And we will be glad that such worship is acceptable to our God because of what we are in Him.

Day 5

"ANGELS' FOOD"

Psalm 78:17-40

"Men did eat angels' food", literally translated, is "every one did eat the bread of the mighty". Nowhere else in Scripture is the word used here translated as 'angels'. Perhaps the expression is not intended to convey that manna was the food of angels, but that food suitable for those who would be mighty for God was provided, not for a select few, but for all.

It is instructive to see that the word for wilderness in verse 17 of this psalm is not the usual word but a word meaning dry, thirsty, or barren. So we are taught that in the very place where reliance on natural food could only result in starvation and utter weakness, God provided food capable of making the people mighty for Him. Typically, then, Christ is seen as food to spiritually strengthen all the people of God in a world where, naturally, there is nothing to sustain them.

It is important to note that the manna was provided for everyone. It was not only the priests, Levites or the leaders that needed strength for the way. Everyone did. We need to be aware that, whoever we are, whatever we seek to do for God, it is vital to feed on Christ.

The manna had to be gathered early because, when exposed to the heat of the sun, it melted. To gather manna had to be a priority each day. Many things claim first place in our lives, and the result is that this number-one priority can get pushed down the list for the day, even though we know in our heart that we should first spend time with God and His Word. Later, in the heat of the day, when trials and pressures come our way, when perfectly legitimate things demand our attention, we find that the heat has melted the manna. We cannot find the spiritual sustenance that we need and we discover, to our dismay, just how weak we are.

Angels are ministering spirits, mighty in the service of God and "greater in power and might" than men (2 Pet 2:11). We can understand why King James' translators followed the Septuagint version of Psalm 78 in rendering 'mighty ones' angels. Acceptance of their translation does not really change the truth conveyed. He was "seen of angels" (1 Tim 3:16), not as in Isaiah 6:1, a sovereign on the throne, but as a servant upon the earth and a sufferer upon the cross.

What food for angels! What strength for service, not for angels only but for all! How each one of us needs to hear the angel's word to Elijah every day "arise and eat; because the journey is too great for thee" (1 Kings 19:7).

Day 6

"SPIRITUAL MEAT"

1 Corinthians 10:3

It has been well said that there are no short-cuts to spirituality. Spiritual growth, like natural growth, takes time. There are, however, many short-cuts to carnality. 'By-path meadow' is never far away for any one of us. Just as natural growth requires natural food, so spiritual growth requires spiritual food. I am what I eat. Our diet becomes part of us. It is therefore essential that we eat sensibly in the spiritual as well as the natural realm. Occupation with Christ produces likeness to Christ, and increased likeness to Christ is the essence of spiritual growth. We have already seen that feeding on the manna means occupation with Christ.

Spiritual food produces spiritual features. Manna had first to be gathered, and we do this by prayerful reading of the Word. Then it had to be prepared. Thus we meditate on what we read, allowing the Spirit of God to reveal Christ to our heart. But manna merely gathered and prepared would have done the Israelite no good at all, it had to be eaten. For us this means that we allow the Spirit not only to reveal Christ to us but to reproduce Christ in us.

The manna was small, picturing for us the humility of Christ. If I am really feeding on this spiritual food I will not be a proud person, easily offended and insisting on my rights, but I will rather look not on my own things but "also on the things of others" (Phil 2:4).

The manna was round, telling us of the One who is eternal having come into time. So, feeding on the manna, I will not be living for this world, but rather for eternity. Its whiteness speaks to us of His absolute purity. As I feed on this, I will be like the man of 1 John 3:3 who "purifieth himself even as He is pure".

The manna was sweet (Exod 16:31). If I am sour in spirit I can hardly be feeding on Christ. It had the appearance (Num 11:7 margin) of bdellium, most likely signifying the lustre of a pearl. How often we feel that our lives and testimony are dull and dim, lacking that spiritual lustre that we ought to display! May it be because we are not feeding on Christ as we should? Gesenius renders Numbers 11:8 "sweet cakes made with oil", and oil is ever the emblem of the Spirit of God.

Every true believer wants to be more spiritual and, although there are no short-cuts by which we may become so, there is a way which never fails to take us in the right direction. To tread that path we will require that spiritual food which is freely provided in the Scriptures – Christ.

and renewing of the Holy Ghost" (Titus 3:5). They are, indeed, "clean every whit" (John 13:10). However, they need the daily cleansing of the feet (their walk is in view) that comes through reading, meditating upon and applying the word of God. They have an obligation towards each other in this matter: "If I then, your Lord and Master, have washed your feet; ye also ought to wash one another's feet (John 13:14).

Day 5

SERVING THE HOUSE – THE TABLE OF SHEWBREAD

Exodus 25:23-30; Leviticus 24:5-9

Today's meditation takes the reader into the thrilling atmosphere of the Holy Place, "the first tabernacle" (Heb 9:6). It was a place of infinite beauty, where the air was impregnated with the smell of incense. No ray of natural light was permitted to enter and it was here that the priests were found "accomplishing the service of God" (Heb 9:6). Three of the seven vessels were placed in it and they direct the believer's gaze into heaven, where Christ is (Heb 9:24).

The table of shewbread speaks of fellowship and communion. It was made of shittim (or acacia) wood, overlaid with pure gold, indicating that communion with God was only possible because He took upon Himself flesh. It was the same height as the mercy seat, suggesting that fellowship and communion are on the basis of Christ's atoning work on the cross.

Primarily, the table stood before the Lord (Exod 25:30). Shewbread means "face bread, bread of the presence" and therefore portrays Christ as the One who is always fit to appear before the face of God. The twelve loaves were made of fine flour, declaring His perfection and purity. They contained no leaven (evil) or honey (natural sweetness) but they were covered with pure frankincense, pointing to His fragrant life. He spoke of Himself as "the true bread … the bread of God … the bread of life" (John 6:32-35). Bread is the product of fine flour being taken and "baked (bruised)" (Lev 24:5). The Lord Jesus went on to refer to His own death by saying, "The bread that I will give is my flesh, which I will give for the life of the world" (John 6:51).

The shewbread was the only food on the table and it was replaced with fresh loaves each Sabbath. That which was removed became the food of the priests. God graciously allows His people to share in the perfect satisfaction He finds in His Son. All believers today are priests and therefore have the privilege of feeding daily on Christ as revealed to them in the Scriptures. The two crowns of gold prevented the loaves from falling off the table and the vessels from its border during the wilderness journeys. They, along with the staves and rings for transporting the table, testify to the truth that Christ is ever-present, and able, to sustain and keep his people as they journey through this barren world. He will never fail them, no matter how hard the journey becomes. The twelve loaves (one for each tribe), sprinkled with frankincense, assure them that they are seen as one in heaven, because they are accepted in all the beauty and fragrance of Christ.

Day 6

SERVING THE HOUSE – THE GOLDEN CANDLESTICK

Exodus 25:31-39; Leviticus 24:1-4; Numbers 8:1-4

An encounter with a man who was born blind led the Lord Jesus to declare to His disciples, "As long as I am in the world, I am the light of the world" (John 9:5). On another occasion, He called them to Him and told them, "Ye are the light of the world (Matt 5:14). Both truths are displayed in the beautiful candlestick, which was beaten out of a talent of pure gold.

As Christ's deity is displayed in the candlestick, wood was absent and no measurements were given. He is seen in its central stem. It was higher and more ornate than the other branches, speaking of His pre-eminence. The "beaten gold" (Num 8:4) and "pure olive oil beaten" (Lev 24:2) serve as solemn reminders of His sufferings and death. However, the almond bowls (recalling Aaron's rod that budded), knops (buds) and flowers witness to His glorious resurrection. The oil, a picture of the Holy Spirit, depicts Him as the One of whom Peter declared, "God anointed Jesus of Nazareth with the Holy Ghost and with power" (Acts 10:38).

The primary purpose of the candlestick was to throw light upon itself (Num 8:2). The Lord Jesus said of the Holy Spirit, "He shall not speak of himself … he shall glorify me" (John 16:13-14). However, it also cast light on the table of shewbread, signifying that Christ and His people are seen in the light of the lamps. The lamps were for the night season and therefore they burned "from the evening unto the morning before the Lord continually" (Lev 24:3). There will be no candlestick in the millennial temple, because the Sun of righteousness will "arise with healing in his wings" (Mal 4:2). Of the future holy Jerusalem, John reveals that "the glory of God did lighten it, and the Lamb is the light thereof" (Rev 21:23).

Six other branches, which were integral to the candlestick, came out of its shaft. Shaft means 'thigh' (Gen 24:2) or 'loins' (Gen 46:26), teaching that the church came out of Christ and cannot be severed from Him: "For both he that sanctifieth and they who are sanctified are all of one" (Heb 2:11). The beaten gold, the almond bowls, knops and flowers indicate that it is the product of His death and resurrection.

Christ is no longer in the world and therefore there is a need for spirit-filled believers today to "shine as lights in the world" (Phil 2:15). No provision was made for carrying the candlestick, emphasising that it is the Holy Spirit that leads and true disciples follow. Aaron's tending of the lamps with golden instruments reflects the constant need of the Lord's chastening hand in the lives of believers in order to maintain the light (Heb 12:5-11).

Day 7

DRAWING NEAR IN THE HOUSE – THE ALTAR OF INCENSE

Exodus 30:1-10, 34-38

The laver and the altar of incense were omitted from God's initial instructions for the making of the furniture for the tabernacle. Both have to do with priestly service and therefore the priesthood had to be instituted and consecrated before they could be introduced.

The altar of incense was "before the veil that is by the ark of the testimony, before the mercy seat that is over the testimony" (Exod 30:6). Although it was located outside the veil, it was closely associated with the Holy of Holies. When a priest offered incense on the altar he was as near to God as he could be. There would have been no mistaking a priest who had been there. The unique, perfectly balanced and pure fragrance would have permeated his person and garments. Its purpose was "to burn incense upon" (v.1) and fire was taken from the brazen altar to achieve this. The fire brought out the aroma of the incense, emphasising that there can be no true worship without sacrifice. On the Day of Atonement blood was placed on the horns of the altar to purify it. If Christ had not died, He would be unable to intercede for His people.

The incense was burnt morning and evening and was therefore "a perpetual incense before the Lord" (v.8). The beauties of Christ, portrayed in the incense, continually fill heaven with their fragrance. The crown (border) of gold (v.3) prevented the coals of fire and the incense from being displaced as the people journeyed. It is comforting to know that Christ's intercession for His people never fails. The altar had only two rings for the staves, which suggests that it may have been carried, and positioned in the Holy Place, diagonal-wise. If so, one of its horns would have pointed towards each part of Israel's camp, foreshadowing Christ's intercession on behalf of all His people.

David said, "Let my prayer be set forth before thee as incense" (Ps 141: 2). The altar of incense therefore witnesses to the privilege and importance of prayer. It is Christ who brings the prayers of the saints to God: "By him therefore let us offer the sacrifice of praise to God continually, that is, the fruit of our lips giving thanks to his name" (Heb 13:15). Peter reminds believers that they are "an holy priesthood, to offer up spiritual sacrifices, acceptable to God by Jesus Christ" (1 Pet 2:5). The blood on the horns of the altar illustrates that their prayers and praises ascend in virtue of His sacrifice and shed blood.

This altar may have been the smallest of the measured vessels, but it was the highest, speaking of the lofty position occupied by Christ as High Priest and the exalted ground believers tread in worship.

COLIN LACEY

Week 4

7 "GREAT" THINGS IN THE EPISTLE TO THE HEBREWS

Introduction

One of the themes of the Hebrews epistle is the excellence of the new covenant compared to the old. This is seen to be based on the greatness of both the person and work of our Lord and Saviour Jesus Christ. In view of this, it is not surprising that the word "great" should be a prominent word in this epistle. It occurs seven times, three of these directly relating to the person of our Lord and one directly to His work. The other three involve those who belong to Him.

He is seen as superior to everything in which the Jew boasted. If they had received the word of God, then He is the final revelation. If they had a covenant relationship with God, then He brought in a new covenant that far surpassed anything that they had known. If they knew something of approach to God and fellowship with God, then He has opened a way of access which is available to all at all times. It is little wonder then that the first great things spoken of in the epistle is "so great salvation". Here is a subject that will never be exhausted.

Israel had a high priest who entered symbolically into the presence of God. We have a great High Priest who has entered into heaven itself and invites us to draw near to the throne of grace. He is the answer to the "priest of the most high God" to whom Abram paid tithes (Gen 14:18-20). The greatness of Melchisedec is maintained by the silence of Scripture, while the greatness of the true Melchisedec is the subject of all Scripture.

If we are linked to such a Saviour, then we will find that there is a great fight to be endured with a great recompense in view if we are faithful. There is also a great witness to the certainty that it is all worthwhile, the more so because we look past those of earlier ages to consider the One who endured the cross, despising the shame.

The epistle ends with the assurance that we have a great Shepherd, who has triumphed over death, and who will now perfect His work in those who follow Him.

May we know the greatness of His power working in us each day.

Day 1

A GREAT SALVATION

Hebrews 1:1-3; 2:1-4

When we look into this important subject, we should look for some reasons why the salvation of God is so great. The fundamental reason is because the Saviour Himself is so great.

Hebrews 1 introduces the Son as the final and complete revelation of God to men. In contrast to a partial revelation extended over a long period of time, we now have a full revelation which has been given in the Person of the Son of God. John writes, "No man hath seen God at any time; the only begotten Son, which is in the bosom of the Father, he hath declared him" (John 1:18). Paul writes, "For it pleased the Father that in him should all fulness dwell" (Col 1:19). Our Saviour is not another prophet. He is the full revelation of God.

The work of the Son is next emphasised when we read, "when he had by himself purged our sins, sat down on the right hand of the Majesty on high" (Heb 1:3). Here we are brought to consider the work that He alone could complete. We can rejoice in the assurance that the work would be accomplished in the full power of Deity. 'Purged our sins' can be rendered 'made purification for sin'. This emphasises the full extent of the work. It is not simply that our sins have been purged, but rather the work is sufficient to deal with all sins. It is a complete work, with nothing to be added to it. This is clearly manifest in the fact that He "sat down on the right hand of the Majesty on high". This place was His eternally as the Son and morally in virtue of His perfect life. He now can claim that place in resurrection in all the value of His finished work. In this respect, He not only claims for Himself the place far above all, but He brings others to share it with Him (Eph 1:22-23).

The remainder of the first chapter gives another pointer to the greatness of our salvation as the contrast is made between the Son and angels. Angels are simply ministering spirits. They could bring physical deliverance to men. He is the Eternal Son. He alone could bring spiritual deliverance to us and deal with the question of sin completely. Even Michael "durst not bring against the devil) a railing accusation" (Jude 9), yet we have a Saviour who has destroyed "him that had the power of death" (Heb 2:14). Hebrews 2 begins by contrasting the message spoken by angels with the great salvation preached first by our Lord Jesus Himself.

He is great, His work is great and His victory is great, so the salvation He provides must be great indeed.

Day 2

A GREAT HIGH PRIEST

Hebrews 4:14 - 5:8

The second of the 'great' things we read of in the Hebrews epistle is our great High Priest. The earlier section has reminded us of the greatness of our Lord when compared with both angels and men, but now we come to consider the One who can rightly claim the highest office.

The purpose of God was always that the high priest should be the leader of the people, representing God to them in their presence as well as representing the people to God in His presence. Here we see how this is fulfilled in the One who is beyond comparison.

The description of our great High Priest given here is interesting. 'Jesus' reminds us of His humanity. He was Jesus of Nazareth. As to His humanity, He has already experienced every test of the natural life. He can fully sympathise with us because He has already been wherever He asks us to go. It is not simply that He sets us the example for us to follow, it is also that He faced the full weight of the circumstances of life and so He can sympathise and succour (Heb 2:18). These are explained in more detail when we come to the next chapter and we are brought to consider the "strong crying and tears" as the Son "learned obedience by the things which He suffered" (Heb 5:7-8). The one place where He could not sympathise is in the matter of sin. The phrase translated "yet without sin" is a statement that He could not be tempted by sin. It could be literally rendered 'apart from sin'. He has broken the power of sin, so John writes, "these things write I unto you, that ye sin not" (1 John 2:1). He could not sin and we are expected to live in a way that shows we are no longer its slaves.

Secondly, the title 'Son of God' reminds us of His deity. As such, He is not just representative of God but He is God Himself. On this basis, we are encouraged to hold fast. The next verses explain why this is true.

His place is on the throne of God and, because of this, the throne symbolised by the mercy seat (which only Israel's high priest could approach, and that but once a year) is no longer a threat of judgment and death but an assurance of acceptance and provision for every circumstance of life.

Why can we hold fast? Because our great High Priest has made provision for all that we could ever need. We need fear no circumstance because He ever liveth, His work will never end and therefore He is able to save to the uttermost (Heb 7:25).

Day 3

A GREAT MAN

Hebrews 7:1-10

Whilst the words "consider how great this man" were written concerning Melchisedec, they are clearly about the One who could say, "Before Abraham was, I am" (John 8:58). The verses in Hebrews 7 emphasise the way in which the statements of Scripture regarding Melchisedec are carefully written in order to emphasise the greatness of Him who is a priest forever after the order of Melchisedec.

The rule of Melchisedec is first emphasised. The fact that he is a king and a priest is itself unusual. The nearest to this in the history of Israel was Moses, who acted in a priestly capacity (Ps 99:6), and is spoken of as king in Jeshurun (Deut 33:5), although he never occupied either position in an official sense. Both titles, 'King of Righteousness' and 'King of Peace' are true of the Lord, although neither is used directly of Him. But Scripture shows that these titles belong to the Lord; "Behold, a king shall reign in righteousness" (Isa 32:1), and "His name shall be called … the Prince of Peace. Of the increase of his government and peace there shall be no end …" (Isa 9:6-7).

The silence of Scripture is used to emphasise the eternal Sonship of Christ. Verse 3 of this chapter is adequate on its own to answer any reasonable doubt regarding this truth. The wording is very clear. By the absence of detail in Scripture Melchisedec was "made like unto the Son of God". He is not the Son, but rather the Spirit of God saw fit to cause only those facts to be recorded that would allow him to be a type of Christ as the eternal Son of God, King and Priest.

The superiority of Melchisedec over Abraham is emphasised by the fact that Abraham paid tithes to him. Once again, the Spirit of God has left a record that shows the superiority of Christ to Abraham and, through this, to Levi also. The priest received the tithes but, when Abraham paid tithes, Levi was included in the action.

Greatness is seen in three further respects later in Hebrews 7:

1.   The Levitical priesthood could never bring about perfection. If this had been possible, there would have been no requirement for any alternative. The glorious assurance is that the Melchisedec priesthood has brought in perfection because it is not based on fallible men, but on the unfailing Son.

2.   Because the Son continues for ever, there is no changing of the priesthood. The Levites were subject to death, but our High Priest is never subject to death.

3.   Finally, there is the glorious assurance that, as a priest after the order

of Melchisedec, our Lord ministers in the value of the sacrifice that He has offered. In contrast to the daily repetitive offerings of the Levitical priest, He has offered one sacrifice which is sufficient to deal with every sin for all time.

Our High Priest is great because His work is perfect and His priesthood never changes.

Day 4

A GREAT FIGHT OF AFFLICTIONS

Hebrews 10:24-33

This subject reminds us of the difficulties in the pathway of the believer in this world. It may be that, in the goodness of our God, we ourselves have not been called to face the sufferings that these believers endured, but we must never lose sight of the fact that we are in a hostile scene. The enemy may, for the present, consider that his greatest gain will be achieved by leaving us alone, but we should realise that he is always ready to attack. There is no guarantee that the comfort that we enjoy today will continue in days to come. Paul warned Timothy, "all that will live godly in Christ Jesus shall suffer persecution" (2 Tim 3:12). This is a statement that leaves no option. It is the common lot of all believers to suffer. The persecution may take different forms, but the fact of its existence is still true.

As we read passages like this, there is a double challenge for us. The first must be to sympathise with those of our brethren and sisters in other parts of the world who are called to face such opposition. The second, and equally important, is that we must be ready to face similar opposition if it should come our way.

These believers not only willingly endured reproaches and afflictions, but they chose to stand with others who faced such trials. The first could not be avoided without an open denial of what they professed. The second was a choice that they made when they saw others who faced suffering and stood in need of encouragement. This should be a challenge to us. We encourage believers to avoid bringing the Name of our Lord into disrepute by association with people, places or practices that are not right for the saints of God. We should be equally careful to identify ourselves with others who suffer for Christ.

The writer of Hebrews is able to bear personal testimony to those who had compassion on him when he was imprisoned. The readers also could rejoice as their goods were taken as they realised that they had lasting treasure in heaven.

They could do this in the light of all that has gone before. We have been considering One who is the full revelation of God, a Saviour and a Priest, who excels angels and men and who accomplished a work that fulfils everything that was foreshadowed in the offerings of the Old Covenant. The believers were ready to suffer reproach and to identify with those who suffered in this way because they were identifying with their Lord. Are we ready to suffer with Christ now as much as we anticipate glory with Him?

Day 5

A *GREAT RECOMPENSE OF REWARD*

Hebrews 10:34 - 11:2

Here is God's perfect answer to the great trial of afflictions. If we are called to pass through great trials and tests, then we have the assurance that there is a reward at the end. While we do enjoy the blessings of the Lord in this life, we need to keep in mind that the Scriptures emphasise that the believer will always face difficulties. The consistent call of the Holy Spirit in the Word is how we can face the present in the assurance of a secure future.

Sufferings (Rom 8:17), afflictions (2 Cor 4:18) and persecutions (2 Tim 3:12) are watchwords for our pathway here. We can rejoice in the assurance that they draw us closer to our Lord, that they increase our enjoyment of His presence with us and draw us into deeper fellowship with Himself but, ultimately, it is not a pathway for the faint-hearted. In contrast, we have an absolute assurance for the future. Hebrews 11 will outline the way in which people of a past day, who knew far less than we do of our Lord and His ways, were prepared to venture all on the promises of God.

The first promise for us is that "yet a little while, and he that shall come will come, and will not tarry" (Heb 10:37). The Lord's coming should always be the overriding hope of every believer. We shall see our Lord. He is coming as He promised, to receive us to Himself (John 14: 3). On the day when we were saved, we entrusted our lives into His hand. Since that time, we have learned to know and love Him more as we have progressed on the pathway that He has marked out for us, but nothing will ever match the certainty that we shall meet Him, see Him and be like Him.

The next promise is that "the just shall live by faith" (Heb 10:38). This verse is quoted three times in the New Testament. On each occasion, the emphasis is on a different aspect. In Romans 1:17 it is the assurance that we have the security of a righteous standing in the sight of God. In Galatians 3:11 it is in the context of faith as the basis of justification and, as such, it lifts us above our failures to rest in the One who can never fail. In Hebrews 10:38, especially considering the examples of the next chapter, it assures us that there is clear evidence that all we need for life is available to us.

Does our faith claim the promises of God and make them realities that mould our lives?

Day 6

A GREAT CLOUD OF WITNESSES

Hebrews 11:32 - 12:3

The expression "so great a cloud of witnesses" is very closely linked with the last two subjects, the great fight of afflictions and the great recompense of reward. Between these earlier subjects and this one, the Holy Spirit has asked us to consider the testimony of men of God from the beginning of human history who lived by faith. The chapter ended with the comment that they were left to anticipate their reward because the Lord had decreed that they could not be made perfect without us (v.40).

There is probably an allusion here to the Greek Olympic Games where the competitors would all take part in their events, but the final crowning for each event was performed only at the end of the games. The early competitors would all be left to watch until the games ended. In this way, those of a past age stood both as a testimony to the power of God to triumph in those who relied on Him, and also as spectators of those like us who follow in their train.

In view of our calling we are encouraged to "lay aside every weight, and the sin which doth so easily beset us, and let us run with patience the race that is set before us". The allusion to the games continues in these expressions. The weights here are not sins, but hindrances which could be perfectly legitimate in the ordinary course of life. In the context, the sin of unbelief may be emphasised although every sin will rob us of strength for the race that we have been called to run. Patience has the idea of endurance against every obstacle, even what may appear to us to be deliberate and unfair tests.

The next verse gives to us the ultimate example for the race, our Lord Jesus Christ. It is good to know that the One who sits in judgment is the One who has already proved Himself the ultimate Victor. We are called to follow the example of One who saw the prize and suffered any amount of pain to achieve the goal. We will never suffer as He suffered. The pain and shame of the cross for Him went beyond the physical and mental sufferings that some have known, to the full weight of divine wrath poured out on Him, "made a curse" (Gal 3:13), "made to be sin" (2 Cor 5:21), "bearing our sins in His own body on the tree" (1 Pet 2:24). He not only "endured" (the same root as "patience" in Heb 12:1) but also "despised" the shame. It was counted for nothing in comparison to the joy that would result when not only He, but we too, will share His glory.

Is our eye on the prize that is set before us?

Day 7

A GREAT SHEPHERD OF THE SHEEP

Hebrews 13:10-21

This subject brings us to the conclusion of the letter. It is part of the writer's final expression of desire. He has brought before us the provision, the privileges and the challenges of the Christian life. In view of the exhortation to "go forth therefore unto him without the camp, bearing his reproach" (v.13), there may be a question as to how this will be accomplished. In this verse, four reasons are given why we may be confident.

The first reason is that "the God of peace" is in control. In the context here, the emphasis is on the fact that He is the author of the peace of mind that we can all enjoy when we rest in Him. Philippians 4 brings before us "the peace of God", enjoyed by those who avoid anxiety by "prayer and supplication with thanksgiving (vv.6-7), and the "God of peace" who is enjoyed by those who fill their thoughts with the good things detailed in verses 8 and 9.

The second reason is that His power has been declared by raising our Lord Jesus from the dead. Here is the ultimate declaration of His power to overthrow every enemy that stands against Him. This was the most common subject of the early preachers in the Acts. It is the vindication of the work of Christ (Rom 4:25), it is the assurance of our hope (1 Cor 15), it is the triumphant declaration of His victory over the host of darkness (Col 2:13-15). Here it is the assurance of the power available to us for our lives.

The third reason for confidence is the subject we are considering, "that great Shepherd of the sheep". Here is the certainty that there is One who is watching over us every step of the way. We may be confident because He has already revealed Himself as the One who lays down His life for the sheep (John 10:11) and knows His sheep (John 10:14). He proved Himself while here upon the earth as He kept all (except the son of perdition), even standing between the mob who came against Him and the eleven in the garden. We have considered Him as the One who understands the pathway that we take.

The final reason is "the blood of the everlasting covenant". Here is the certainty that every demand of God has been met. There is nothing left for us to do except to rest in His completed work. The result of this is that we can be perfected in every good work to fulfil His will in a way that is well-pleasing to Him.

What greater confidence could we need for our pathway here?

STEPHEN WHITMORE

Week 5

7 FEASTS OF THE LORD

Introduction

It was 3000 years ago that David, gazing into the night sky and observing the magnitude of stellar beauty, exclaimed "what is man that thou art mindful of him?" (Ps 8:4). The enormity of the expanse of the Milky Way left him breathless with awe as it impressed upon him the infinite wonder of God and the insignificance of man.

With his technical advances man believes that he is the master of his own destiny, and God is relegated to an irrelevance, but Leviticus 23 unfolds to us the eternal counsels of God being achieved against the backdrop of the changing scenes of man's history until they reach their glorious climax in an eternal rest.

As with many groups of seven in Scripture, these feasts divide into a set of four and three. The first four have a direct relevance to the Church, and the final three highlight God's future dealings with the nation of Israel. But they all begin with Passover. Were it not for this, the other 6 feasts would be meaningless, for in it we have God's eternal starting point. Passover, as we shall see, presents to us the death of Christ, and it is on the basis of what that death achieved that all of God's programme depends.

There are three different Hebrew words used to describe these feasts and the first of these occurs in verse 2 where, in the AV, it is translated "the feasts of the Lord". This word 'feasts' has the idea of a fixed appointment or set time. Neither Moses nor Israel were permitted to change the date nor details

10), and writing to the Romans he says, "Therefore we are buried with him by baptism into death, that like as Christ was raised by the glory of the Father, even so we also should walk in newness of life" (Rom 6:4).

As we think of the Lord's death today, let us show our gratitude by living wholesome lives. "Teach me, Lord, on earth to show **by my life** how much I owe".

Day 3

THE FEAST OF FIRSTFRUITS

Leviticus 23:9-14

Man's history is strewn with the unnecessary loss of human life, even though many such sacrifices have been made with the noblest of motives. However there is one sacrifice which would have eclipsed all others for its pointlessness, had death been the end. Never would any decease have been so tragic and so meaningless if that was all that happened. I refer to the death of our Lord Jesus Christ.

In 1 Corinthians 15 Paul spells out the consequences of a deceased Christ. He says that his preaching has no substance, our faith has no value, we would be unsaved, dead believers would be in hell and we would be of all men most pitiable if Christ were still in the grave. How wonderful therefore to reach the conclusion of that dark catalogue of potential consequences and read "But now is Christ risen from the dead, and become the firstfruits of them that slept" (v.20).

It is this great event, the resurrection of Christ, which is presented doctrinally in Corinthians, historically in the Gospels, and symbolically for us in the feast of firstfruits. That is why, unlike the other feasts, the Lord did not give instruction as to the date, but to the day it was to be kept: "And he shall wave the sheaf before the Lord, to be accepted for you: on the morrow after the sabbath the priest shall wave it" (v.11). The morrow after the sabbath brings us to the first day of the week, the day on which our Lord rose from the dead.

Verse 10 states that this feast could not be kept until the nation had arrived in Canaan, the land where all their hopes were set and to which they were moving. Therefore their future hope was associated with this feast. In the NT we discover that the same is true for us. Our hope, that to which we are moving, is all dependent upon and associated with the resurrection of the Lord Jesus. Says Peter, "Blessed be the God and Father of our Lord Jesus Christ, which according to his abundant mercy hath begotten us again unto a lively hope by the resurrection of Jesus Christ from the dead" (1 Pet 1:3).

The sheaf that the priest waved before the Lord is called firstfruits because it was the first sheaf of the harvest. Out in the fields were many more identical sheaves waiting to be brought in. And so it is for us. Says Paul "But every man in his own order: Christ the firstfruits; afterward they that are Christ's at his coming (1 Cor 15:23).

> "Death could not keep his prey, Jesus my Saviour
> He tore the bars away, Jesus my Lord!"

Day 4

THE FEAST OF PENTECOST

Leviticus 23:15-21

From the dawn of creation God kept a secret to Himself, a secret that He didn't even share with Abraham who was the friend of God nor with David who was a man after His own heart. In his letter to the Ephesians, Paul writes "Which from the beginning of the world hath been hid in God" (Eph 3:9) and just a few verses earlier he tells us what that secret was: "That the Gentiles should be fellowheirs, and of the same body, and partakers of his promise in Christ by the gospel" (Eph 3:6).

That divinely-guarded secret we now refer to as 'The Church', and the epistles to the Ephesians and Colossians unpack for us wonderful truth relative to it. But its beginning is recorded in Acts. What was acted out at this fourth feast annually by Israel, in ignorance, we now understand to be symbolic of the birthday of the Church. That is why we read in Acts 2:1, "And when the day of Pentecost was fully come…". The feast is never called Pentecost in the Old Testament: in Exodus 23:16 it is called the feast of harvest and in Deuteronomy 16:10 it is called the feast of weeks. Pentecost is a Greek word meaning 'fiftieth' and is based on the instruction in Leviticus 23:16 when the nation were told to "number fifty days".

In verses 16 and 17 we learn that there was to be a new meal offering of two loaves, each of which contained fine flour and leaven. How pregnant with meaning these statements are! This feast represents something totally new. For 2000 years God had dealt almost exclusively with one nation but, on that momentous Sunday recorded in Acts 2, God started something very different as Gentiles were brought in on an equal footing with the Jew. Maybe we cannot appreciate the magnitude of this today, but it was cataclysmic for those first century Jews.

Although there were two loaves, they formed one offering. As such these loaves represent the constituent elements of the church, that is, Jew and Gentile. Hence Paul writes, "For by one Spirit are we all baptized into one body, whether we be Jews or Gentiles" (1 Cor 12:13).

Finally, these loaves comprised fine flour and leaven, the fine flour typifying the moral excellence of Christ and the leaven typifying corruption. What these two ingredients symbolise is the truth of Christ in us (Col 1:27; Gal 2:20) and sin dwelling in us (Rom 7:16-18). However, please observe the important difference. Christ should be **living** in us, that is, His features should be actively manifested in us, whereas sin **dwells**, that is, it is present but it ought not to be active.

Day 5

THE FEAST OF TRUMPETS

Leviticus 23:23-25

This feast was to take place on the first day of the seventh month, a significant date for two reasons. Israel had two calendars, a religious calendar and a civil calendar, and the first day of the seventh month was the start of their civil new year. Secondly, the four previous feasts were all linked by time scales, but between the fourth feast and the feast of trumpets is a gap which cannot be accurately measured. This is because every few years the Jews added a month in that gap between the two feasts in order to synchronise their lunar year with the solar year.

These significant facts teach that now we are dealing with feasts that do not relate to the church, but to a new beginning for Israel. Hence this feast of trumpets is not symbolic of the rapture of the church but of the regathering of God's ancient people, Israel. In the epistle to the Romans Paul teaches that the Jews have been set aside by God for the present, but one day he is going to resume dealings with them (Rom 11:1, 12, 15). The final three feasts symbolise the ways in which God is going to deal with that nation, starting with the feast of trumpets.

In Numbers 10 Israel had to make two silver trumpets and we are told "And when they shall blow with them, all the assembly shall assemble themselves." (Num 10:3). So even in Old Testament times the blowing of trumpets was linked with the gathering of Israel together.

When we turn to the NT we find the symbolic relevance of this feast clearly presented to us: "And he shall send his angels with a great sound of a trumpet, and they shall gather together his elect from the four winds, from one end of heaven to the other" (Matt 24:31). For three and a half years prior to this event Israel will have passed through the darkest night in its sad history, previous persecutions being incomparable to the extent of her tribulation but, just when all seems to be hopeless, God intervenes.

In verse 24 we are told two things about this feast. It was a sabbath and it was a memorial. For centuries Israel has believed that in order to be right with God she must work, adhering to a ceremonial law and her self-effort. When this feast of trumpets finds its fulfilment she will appreciate that it is not by her works that she will be delivered, but by what God will do for her. Israel is to be passive, for it is a sabbath. It is also a memorial. Sadly, Israel has forgotten God but he has not forgotten them. "Nevertheless I will remember my covenant with thee in the days of thy youth …" (Ezek 16:60).

Day 6

THE DAY OF ATONEMENT

Leviticus 23:26-32

Leviticus 23 does not give the details of this important day, for they have already been recorded in chapter 16. We shall focus on what the day typifies rather than examine the details.

To appreciate the relevance of this day, we start by going back some 2000 years to the last time that Israel saw their Messiah. That was when He stood solitarily before Pilate, despised, rejected and with the voices of the people ringing out "His blood be on us, and on our children" (Matt 27:25). The following day He hung abandoned by them on a cross, and as the people stood around they reckoned Him to have been stricken, smitten of God and afflicted. As far as they were concerned, He was a blasphemer being judged by God.

Moving into the future, we find Israel passing through the darkest hour of her troubled history. Two-thirds of the nation are dead, the armies of the world are camped around her and, motivated by Satan, those armies are about to go for the nation's jugular. When all seems lost, the Son of Man appears from heaven in all His glory and then the Jews realise that the one coming as their Messiah and deliverer is the one they rejected and hung on a cross.

At last they recognise that "he was wounded for our transgressions, he was bruised for our iniquities" and in the words of Isaiah will say "Surely he hath borne our griefs, and carried our sorrows … all we like sheep have gone astray; we have turned everyone to his own way; and the Lord hath laid on him the iniquity of us all" (Isa 53:4-6). Then there will be awakened an unprecedented repentance and anguish (Lev 23:27, 29, 32) as the enormity of their guilt bursts upon their grief-stricken souls. The prophet Zechariah portrays that great day in Israel's experience: "And it shall come to pass in that day … they shall look upon me whom they have pierced, and they shall mourn for him, as one mourneth for his only son …" (Zech 12:9-10).

What the day of atonement presents symbolically will then be fulfilled "In that day there shall be a fountain opened … for sin and for uncleanness" (Zech 13:1). Describing this moment, Paul says "And so all Israel shall be saved; as it is written, There shall come out of Sion the deliverer, and shall turn away ungodliness from Jacob (Rom 11:26).

One point emphasised in Leviticus 23 is that on this day there was not to be any work done (vv.28, 30-32). Down through the centuries Israel has sought to achieve righteousness by works (Rom 9:31-32) but in that day she will realise "The chastisement of our peace was upon him; and with his stripes we are healed" (Isa 53:5). What Israel will comprehend in that day is something we have been led by grace to understand today.

> "Wounded for me, wounded for me,
> There on the cross he was wounded – **for me!**"

Day 7

THE FEAST OF TABERNACLES

Leviticus 23:33-43

This final feast derives its name from the fact that for the seven days of its duration Israel had to dwell in booths or tabernacles (v.42) To help us identify what the feast symbolises, let us summarise where we have reached in the typical teaching of Leviticus 23. Christ has died and risen, the church has been formed and removed, God has renewed dealings with Israel, gathering the nation from across the globe and bringing her to a point of national repentance. Her Messiah has returned to deliver her from all her enemies.

"Thou shalt observe the feast of tabernacles seven days, after that thou hast gathered in thy corn and thy wine" (Deut 16:13). The corn harvest represents those that are Christ's, for He has become the corn of wheat which has died and brought forth much fruit. But the wine harvest represents the time of God's wrath (Rev 14:19) culminating in the battle of Armageddon.

As a seven-day feast, Tabernacles represents an event that is protracted over a period of time, and it represents the 1000-year reign of Christ, normally called the millennium. As the seventh feast (seven symbolising completeness) Tabernacles brings to a climax all that the previous six feasts lead up to. That is why Paul describes the millennium as "the dispensation of the fullness of times" (Eph 1:10).

A characteristic of the millennium is rejoicing (Lev 23:40; Deut 16:14) and rightly so for it will be a time of unprecedented blessing for Israel, for the nations and for creation. Christ will be reigning, "he shall see of the travail of his soul and shall be satisfied" for "the earth shall be filled with the knowledge of the glory of the Lord, as the waters cover the sea" (Hab 2:14).

Although not part of this feast we would miss the whole point of Leviticus 23 if we did not observe that it ends where it begins, not with a feast but with a sabbath (vv.3, 39). However, the final Sabbath is different in that it is an eighth-day sabbath, representing a new beginning, a new rest. This sabbath closes the festival year and represents the Day of God – eternity.

Sin will not triumph, there will dawn an unending day of rest for God and His people, but where did it begin? At Passover, the death of Christ.

> Enduring the grief and the shame,
> And bearing our sins on the cross,
> O who would not boast of thy love,
> And count the world's glory but dross!

RICHARD COLLINGS

Week 6

7 'DOUBLE CALLS' IN SCRIPTURE

Job 33:14-17

Introduction

The fact that God has chosen on occasions to communicate directly with man is a remarkable thing. That He repeats His address should cause us to enquire as to the significance of the circumstances.

Principally, God speaks to make known His character and His will. In revealing this it naturally places upon man the responsibility to react positively. The pathway to blessing is not to resist the will of God but to yield to His prompting. The truth of this will be seen in the experiences of Moses, Samuel and Saul who, later, became the apostle Paul. A failure to recognise divine communication, or worse still, to show a haughty disregard for His commandments, results in a missed blessing or even God's correction.

In addressing Abraham and Jacob, God gave His blessing upon their actions. Surely there can be no greater comfort than to have the evident pleasure of our God expressed regarding the course we have followed. To be able to reflect as another could when he said "I being in the way, the Lord led me" (Gen 24:27) is truly rewarding.

When the Lord had cause to repeat Martha's name, it identified His priorities for her. This contrasted starkly with those matters which she had deemed important and which had become her pre-occupation. In busying ourselves it is all too easy for the service to become more important than the One we serve.

During the night that the Lord spoke Simon (Peter's) name with double

It is significant that the ready spirit demonstrated by Samuel finds a similar response from the Lord, for as the Psalmist points out, Samuel, along with Moses and Aaron, "called upon the Lord, and He answered them" (Ps 99:6).

Day 5

MARTHA, MARTHA

Luke 10:38-42

What a privilege for Martha that the Lord should take up her offer of hospitality. This privilege can still be enjoyed by those who would solicit His company (Rev 3:20).

Little wonder that she, in fellowship with her sister, set about delivering with energy and excitement the very best that she could muster. Her thrill of being able to minister to the Lord is almost tangible. There should be no less a sense of privilege when we are employed in ministering to the physical or spiritual welfare of the Lord's people today (Matt 10:40).

There is the danger in our eagerness to please, however, that we become judgmental of others who are not serving in the same way as we are. Mary, perhaps judging that the need had been met, took her leave to go and sit at the Lord's feet. This caused Martha to become agitated as she continued to busy herself in serving. No longer able to contain herself, she lobbied the Lord in a manner that betrayed her inner feelings. Sadly, her words record that she called into question that which was undeniable, namely the Lord's concern.

The Lord's measured response acknowledged both Martha's effort and sense of frustration, whilst at the same time diffusing a potentially explosive domestic situation. How often strife has resulted from our being more concerned about what others may or may not be doing rather than with the sincerity of our own service? When our eyes fix upon others and we are tempted to question "What shall this man do?" (John 21:21), we do well to remember the Lord's pointed retort, "What is that to thee?" (John 21:23).

The Lord discerned from Martha's outburst that she was of the opinion that Mary should be doing just as she was. There is surely no greater presumption than that which supposes we have the last word upon what the Lord deems acceptable service for others. The beauty of being employed in the Lord's service is that we each have the opportunity to provide that which can be appreciated by the One we serve, though diverse in its character. Our very own bodies teach us that diversity in function is necessary for the well being of the whole (1 Cor 12:12-27).

The Lord, in His positively gentle way, helped Martha to understand that He who "came, not to be ministered unto, but to minister" (Mark 10:45), is as pleased by our willingness to sit at His feet and receive His instruction as He is by our industry.

It is to Martha's lasting credit that some time later, on another occasion when the Lord enjoyed hospitality in Bethany, she had evidently learned the secret of contented service, for the Scripture simply relates that "Martha served" (John 12:2).

Day 6

PETER, PETER

Luke 22:31-34

It must have been a most dreadful experience, as Alfred Edersheim so eloquently puts it, "that night the fierce wind of hell was allowed to sweep unbroken over the Saviour, and even to expend its fury upon those that stood behind in His shelter". For all associated with Him it would prove to be life-affecting: for Simon Peter, especially so.

Not content with marshalling the forces of evil against the Lord, the Adversary demanded (for such is the force of the word 'desired') that His band of followers might also be thrown to the wind.

How significant a blow it would have been to the disciples if, on the night they lost their Lord, they were also to lose, as chaff in the gale, the one that they allowed to represent them as a group. Little wonder, therefore, that the Lord saw Peter as being of strategic importance, and singled him out for special prayer. In this context, we do well to "remember our leaders" (Heb 13: 7 Newberry margin) who occupy a position of crucial importance so far as the welfare of God's people is concerned. This makes them particularly attractive to the assault of the wicked one.

As an ill wind, Peter heard again the Lord speak of the evil one in connection with himself. Inevitably, he would recall his lowest moment when the Saviour was moved to rebuke him before his fellow disciples with the words "Get thee behind me Satan, thou art an offence unto me" (Matt 16:23). It would have been quickly noticed by Peter, however, that the tone of the Lord's voice was now altogether different. It was not now a stinging rebuke, but rather a sympathetic address from One who knew personally what it was to be the singular focus of the devil's assault. It is precious to realise that there is not an experience that we can be called upon to undergo that He has not known at first hand (Heb 2:18).

The prospect of failure would have been outrageous to Peter. However the Lord's use of "Simon", the name associated with the 'old man', should have alerted him to a dreadful possibility to which we are all prone (1 Cor 10:12). In only a few hours, standing alone in the crowd in the courtyard of the high priest's palace, the Lord's words would be far from his mind. Thankfully for Peter, he was still uppermost in the Lord's thoughts (Luke 22:61).

With deep gratitude for the Lord's intercession, Peter would undoubtedly reflect in later years upon the awful experiences of that haunting night, and take courage from the One who said 'I have prayed for thee'.

Day 7

SAUL, SAUL

Acts 9:1-8

Of all the lives affected by being repeatedly addressed by God, surely the life that saw the most radical transformation was Saul's. Never was there a Benjamite who lived out the prediction of Jacob more fully than Saul. The words might have been said of him directly, that he "shall ravin as a wolf" (Gen 49:27). Such was his ferocity in "persecuting the church" (Phil 3:6).

Yet it would be wrong to think that the Lord apprehended Saul, as he "made havoc of the church" (Acts 8:3), simply as a reaction to the chaos he was causing among His flock. The opposite appears to be the case, as the words spoken to him on the road to Damascus indicate. When He says to Saul "it is hard for thee to kick against the pricks" the Lord presents the picture of an animal objecting to being moved in a certain direction, despite being prodded. The statement suggests that here was a man who had been resisting divine persuasion for some time. Are we not all pleased that the Lord's perseverance exceeds our stubborn refusal?

What form the goading had taken we may never know. But what caused the goading to stop was not raging ever more furiously, but submissively yielding to its prompting. The animal that is moving in the way its master desires does not experience the sharp pain of the goad: it is only the wilful beast that requires redirection. How serene is the pathway of the one who hears and yields to the Lord's voice when He says "This is the way, walk ye in it" (Isa 30:21)

Whilst the encounter with the risen Lord had a transforming effect in Saul's life we should not think that he was any less radical thereafter. Rather, the zeal that characterised his former life was magnified in his new pursuit of a more worthy cause. He did not mellow in mediocrity. The one who could claim to be "more exceeding zealous of the traditions of my fathers" (Gal 1:14) had the moral right to exhort that "it is good to be zealously affected always in a good thing" (Gal 4:18). Such was the quality of his new life in Christ. Would that my spiritual energy outweighed the effort I put in to secular pursuits! Paul's constant motivation was, "that I may apprehend that for which also I am apprehended of Christ Jesus" (Phil 3:12).

How delightful at the end of a life of service to reflect and say "I have fought a good fight", not having resisted His will, and "I have finished my course", not having gone my own way (2 Tim 4:7). Of a truth, Paul certainly did "love his appearing" (Acts 26:16; 2 Tim 4:8).

JEREMY HOLIFIELD

Week 7

7 *"I AM"* TITLES OF THE LORD JESUS IN JOHN'S GOSPEL

Introduction

In using these remarkable titles of Himself in John's Gospel, the Lord Jesus is making a number of very important claims that only He could make. He affirms that He is able and ready to meet the needs of His people in every situation of life. Indeed, the use of the definite article repeatedly brings this lesson home to our hearts. As the Bread of Life (ch.6) He can satisfy the deepest longings of the heart. As the Light of the World (ch.8) He assures us that only He can guide and direct along the pathway of life as we seek to discover and do His will, whatever the cost. As the Door (ch.10) He claims that He is the only access to a life of security and blessing that preserves from danger and becomes increasingly fulfilling as we come to know and love Him better. The fact that He knows us intimately is a source of comfort to His people.

As the Resurrection and the Life (ch.11) He is uniquely qualified to quicken into spiritual life those who were dead in sin, and at the end of life's journey conduct us into the Father's presence. When we come to His wonderful words of assurance, "I am the way, the truth and the life" (ch.14) we discover that this is His great object in view. He wants us to enjoy His presence in this life and bring us into the Father's presence one day. The implication of these words is that those who reject Him and His word will inevitably drift through life, without direction, and will forfeit His blessing in a coming day.

By the time we arrive at chapter 15 we are in no doubt at all that He alone can save and satisfy. He is absolutely indispensable. He alone can satisfy, guide, protect, resurrect and present us to His Father one day. Who could question the validity of His own words "without me ye can do nothing"? We are linked inextricably with the True Vine with all the privileges and responsibilities which this involves.

He longs that we might be continually enriched as we draw ever closer to Him. He still invites His own, saying "… he who comes … believes (6: 35), follows (8:12), enters (10:9), hears (10:16) and abides, the same bringeth forth much fruit" (15:5).

Day 1

"I AM THE BREAD OF LIFE"

John 6:22-58

It had been an extremely tiring day for the Lord Jesus and His disciples. They must have been tired before it even started for a careful reading of Mark's account indicates that they were returning home after a period of intense activity. The Lord Himself was conscious how weary they were and this prompted His words of entreaty "come ye yourselves apart and rest awhile" (Mark 6:31). Those were days of incessant preaching and travelling but it is well to remember that the One who calls to service (Mark 1:17) is also the One who invites us to rest when necessary (Mark 6:31). He knows our limitations better than any other.

Now here are a company of workers, labouring in His service and they need to learn some vitally important lessons. They have watched with wonder as He meets the needs of the multitudes without the slightest difficulty (Mark 6:42). It only remains to be seen whether He can supply all they need as well! Each of the Gospel writers supplies us with important details which need to be considered if we are to understand His profound and remarkable claim recorded in John 6:35.

This remarkable teacher always chose His illustrations with great care. He knew that they had watched him take the loaves of a boy and offer thanks to God for them. They had themselves received the bread from His blessed hands, had gathered up the fragments of all that remained. With all this very fresh in their minds and with so little experience in His service they cannot possibly misunderstand His meaning. Some of the most important lessons in the Christian life have to be learned early and never forgotten. He says "I am the bread of life, he that cometh to me shall never hunger, and he that believeth on me shall never thirst" (6:35)

The statement can be considered as consisting of two parts. As the "true bread" He is in contrast to the manna provided for God's people in the desert. As the "bread of life" He is able to satisfy the spiritual hunger of all His followers. He wants us to feed on Him constantly and find all our satisfaction in Him. The twelve baskets that remained would remind us that there is more to satisfy our appetites, and we will never reach the stage of exhausting His blessed person. Would that we were always hungering and thirsting for Him!

Happy the believer who doesn't neglect the need for quality time feeding upon Him. We came to Him in all our need. We believed in Him and were saved. We must never forget that He alone can satisfy the deepest needs of our redeemed hearts.

Day 2

"I AM THE LIGHT OF THE WORLD"

John 1:9; 8:12; 9:1-12

This glorious Gospel opens by speaking of One who would shine in the deepest darkness. There would be one who would testify of Him (1:7) and the Lord Jesus Christ spoke in the highest possible terms of him. But John himself had no delusions of grandeur. Happy the believer who follows his example and can say from the heart, "He must increase but I must decrease" (3:30).

Those who have accomplished most for Him in this world have been like the "man sent from God, whose name was John" (1:6) who was "sent before him" (3:28). He was the Word (1:1) but, says John, "I am the voice" (1:23). He was the "light that shineth in the darkness" (1:5). John was not the "true light" but, for a short time, "he was a burning and a shining light" (5:35). Others said of him, "John did no miracle: but all things that John spake of this man were true" (10:41). There could be no higher commendation for the child of God in a world which rejected the true Light.

Now the Lord Jesus never promised His own an easy pathway down here. Those who walk in the light and follow Him have always been in the minority. At a strategic point in His public ministry there was a dividing of the ways amongst His followers and "from that time many of his disciples went back, and walked no more with him" (6:66). Those who would walk in the light as He is in the light will respond with the same conviction as Simon Peter: "Lord, to whom shall we go?" (6:68). He was the One who sought us and saved us when we walked in darkness. Indeed we were like the "man which was blind from his birth" (9:1). We were born in sin and shapen in iniquity. With that same simple trust of the man born blind we heard His voice, obeyed His command, and received our sight. Now to us who follow Him, and exclusively to His own, He makes a wonderful promise: "he that followeth me shall not walk in darkness, but shall have the light of life" (8:12).

What could be more wonderful for those who once walked in darkness? It seems then that there is a connection between these two statements in 8:12 and 9:5. The fact that a blind man, who had never been able to see, heard His voice and obeyed His instruction is hugely significant. He makes this staggering claim to men who are embarking upon the pathway of service for

Him. Not only would He have His own feed upon Him, He wants them to follow where He leads.

If we are to be effective amongst our neighbours, friends and family as this man was, then we must remember "the night cometh, when no man can work" (9:4).

Day 3

"I AM THE DOOR"

John 10:1-10

In this beautiful chapter of John's Gospel the Lord Jesus adopts two titles, calling Himself "the door" and "the good shepherd". He uses each title twice. "I say unto you, I am the door of the sheep, all that ever came before me are thieves and robbers; but the sheep did not hear them." These words imply that the door is **closed** to the Lord's enemies, protecting His sheep from the thieves who would steal them.

In verse 9 He adds to this glorious truth when He says "I am the door: by me if any man enter in, he shall be saved, and shall go in and out, and find pasture". These words indicate that the door is **open** to those who seek Him and find rest for their souls.

It is only after He has concluded His teaching about the door that He begins to speak of Himself as the Good Shepherd. There is nothing haphazard about the way these statements are recorded in John's Gospel. First He is the Door and then He is the Good Shepherd. This is the order in which people come to know the Good Shepherd. They must find Him as the Door before they can know Him as the Shepherd. Those wishing to join His flock must first draw near to Him for access.

Sadly some fail to see the importance of this principle. They drift about and have a casual acquaintance with His sheep, but they have never truly heard the voice of the Good Shepherd and are not truly saved. They may attend Sunday schools, Gospel meetings or other activities of a local assembly. They may become friendly with believers and participate in their outreach but they have never realised that no one is ever saved by drifting into His flock. As lost sheep and guilty sinners they must go direct to Christ who is the Door and He will welcome them in, forgive their sins and make them His own.

The church has always accomplished most when there has been a very clear distinction between the saved and unsaved, as was the case in the days of the early church when "of the rest durst no man join himself to them: but the people magnified them." (Acts 5:13).

Verse 10 is an important verse as it marks the transition from the Lord's teaching about the Door to that about the Good Shepherd. It is important to notice the two reasons which the Lord gives for His coming: (a) that they might have life and (b) have it more abundantly. As the Door He gives us life.

As the Good Shepherd He gives us **abundant** life. You cannot have abundant life until you have life itself. Life begins with Christ as the Door and goes on with Christ as the Good Shepherd.

Day 4

"I AM THE GOOD SHEPHERD"

John 10:10-30

Twice the Lord Jesus describes Himself as the Good Shepherd in these verses. "I am the good shepherd, the good shepherd giveth his life for the sheep" (v.11). He is therefore the Good Shepherd who **died**. "I am the good shepherd, and know my sheep, and am known of mine" (v.14). He is also the Good Shepherd who **lives**.

In verses 17-18 He develops the thought of His death as a laying down of His life. It was a deliberate and voluntary action. The conspiracy by the religious leaders, the betrayal by Judas, the rigged evidence and false accusations, the injustice of the verdicts, the weakness of Pilate, the disdain of Herod, the brutality of the soldiers, the journey to Calvary, the driving home of the nails and the raising of the cross – all this human activity suggests that men successfully plotted and achieved Christ's death. We must never lose sight, however, of the fact that His death was a laying down of His life with a view to His taking it up again on the third day.

In verses 14-15 the Lord likens the relationship between Himself and His own to that between His Father and Himself. The verb 'know', used four times in these verses, expresses knowledge arising from constant experience (W. E. Vine). The mutual understanding and appreciation existing between the Shepherd and His sheep is like that between the Father and the Son. Comparing the first clause of each verse, the Lord says "I know my own … as the Father knoweth me".

It does not surprise us to learn that His knowledge of His people is comparable to His Father's knowledge of Himself. But then we come to the second clause: "…my own know me … as I the Father"! Do we really know Him in this way? He asserts it, and certainly intends it. The personal knowledge of Christ should be the goal of every single believer. It was what Paul longed for, as a careful reading of Philippians 3:8-11 would indicate.

In verses 26-27 we notice that the Lord attributes these identifying qualities to those who have been eternally saved. They believe on Him, they hear His voice and they follow Him. Of such the Lord goes on to teach that they have three great blessings (vv.28-30):

a)   "… I give unto them eternal life" – This is a quality of life which involves the knowledge of God Himself.

b)   "… and they shall never perish" – Those who belong to Him are eternally safe and secure.

c)   "neither shall any man pluck them out of my Father's hand". The Lord Jesus unfailingly protects His sheep and neither men nor demons nor the devil himself can rob Him of them.

Day 5

"I AM THE RESURRECTION AND THE LIFE"

John 11:1-46

The home of His dear friends at Bethany was one of the few places on earth where the Lord Jesus Christ could always be assured of a warm welcome. Martha is to be commended for inviting the Lord Jesus Christ into her home (Luke 10:38). It was a decision which she never regretted and which affected her for the rest of her life. What could be more natural than to send for Him whose unfathomable love had so touched each member of this home (vv.3, 5, 36). What a comfort for our hearts to know that His love for His own will always exceed our weak, frail and changeable love for Him. Even the words for their estimation of His love (v.3) and the word used by John the evangelist to describe His love (v.5) are different in the Greek text.

His response to the memory of the sisters (v.4) was remarkable: "this sickness is not unto death, but for the glory of God". How this should encourage the heart of the dear believer whose sickness has cast a shadow upon their life and circumstances. Even when He chooses to delay His arrival there is always a reason (v.6). Some of our greatest blessings in the Christian life have been the result of His 'delays'! After all, He never arrived late during His brief sojourn down here. He always without fail arrived just at the right time. He is too wise and kind to cause His own to pass through suffering without a purpose. Nothing, not even the valley of the shadow of death, will separate us from His matchless love (Rom 8:38-39).

The Lord Jesus chose the moment carefully to make one of the most remarkable declarations that He had ever made. With great compassion He listened to the words of Martha, "Lord, if thou hadst been here, my brother had not died" (v.21). She was perfectly correct. Death could not have touched this home in the presence of the Author of life, the Creator and Sustainer of all things. Because of this the two malefactors died after He had offered up Himself to death. And so He makes this remarkable statement, "thy brother shall rise again in the resurrection at the last day ... I am the resurrection and the life: he that believeth in me, though he were dead, yet shall he live." (vv.23, 25).

What a revelation this was for Martha! His resurrection would be a guarantee that one day the dead in Christ would rise to meet Him in the air. Happy the believer who can see his or her sufferings from the divine perspective. How beautiful to notice that this compassionate Christ could sympathise with them in their grief. He loved Lazarus in his sufferings (v.3), during his life (v.5) and in his death (v.36), and we should never doubt His love for us.

Day 6

"*I AM THE WAY, THE TRUTH AND THE LIFE*"

John 13:36 - 14:8

In approaching this wonderful statement it is important to remember the context in which the Lord Jesus Christ makes this staggering assertion, "I am the way, the truth and the life; no man cometh to the Father but by me." He is answering the questions of some of His disciples. The same anxieties that plague God's people today caused His own some concern in those difficult days leading up to His crucifixion.

Simon Peter said unto him, "Lord, whither goest thou?" (John 13:36). He is followed by Thomas, "Lord we know not whither thou goest; and how can we know the way?" (14:5). The Lord's people can endure anything as long as they are in no doubt as to where He has gone and how they will be preserved until they arrive where He is, in the "Father's house".

In this title there is a magnificent resumé of some of His mightiest claims. Those who have learned to feed upon Him (6:35) are the same who want to follow Him (8:12). They are in no doubt that He is "the way" and for them it is enough to follow Him in the way. They have entered by "the door" (10:7, 9) and have found a place of perfect safety with the "good shepherd" who dies (10:11) and the good shepherd who lives (10:14). In happy fellowship with Him they have learned that He is "the truth" and they have come to trust Him implicitly. Indeed they are constantly listening for His voice for He knows them and they long to know Him better. For His own He is undoubtedly "the way and the truth". But there is more.

The one who can raise to life Lazarus who has been dead four days is "the resurrection and the life" (11:25). The one who cried "Lazarus come forth" (11: 43) was obeyed immediately. His voice was unmistakable. A careful reading of the Gospels leaves us in no doubt of His power and authority in heaven and on earth. How glorious to know and appreciate that He is undoubtedly "the way, the truth and the life". And He adds this glorious promise, "He that believeth in me, though he were dead, yet shall he live: and whosoever liveth and believeth in me shall never die" (11:25-26).

This is surely the truth that Paul urged the Thessalonians to hold on to in all of their sorrow and suffering as they were worried and anxious about these same truths. What can comfort the dear child of God today in all of his or her afflictions is to grasp and never lose sight of this truth. "For the Lord himself shall descend from heaven with a shout". Rest assured, dear believer, that that cry will be heard by all His own. He is indeed the Way, the Truth and the Life.

Day 7

"I AM THE TRUE VINE"

John 15:1-11

It was the night of the betrayal. The Lord and the disciples had been together in the upper room in Jerusalem. As they left that upper room and made their way through the darkened streets of Jerusalem, He began a new section of His teaching, saying "I am the true vine, and my Father is the husbandman".

It is remarkable that, having warned them that He would shortly be leaving them, He now teaches them how closely He will be linked with them in the days ahead. They are going to miss Him so much, but they are going to be linked with Him much more closely than ever before.

Twice in this passage the Lord refers to Himself as the Vine. In verse 1 He is the Vine in the Godward aspect, in relation to His Father. In verse 5 He is the Vine in the manward aspect, in relation to His disciples. A fruitless branch is a useless encumbrance on a vine. Its removal will divert nutriment into fruitful branches. If a Christian becomes unfruitful God may remove him from his sphere of fellowship and witness. The Father prunes every fruit-bearing branch so that it may bear more fruit. He will remove from our lives everything that hinders our fruitfulness.

Now it is vital that we understand what exactly constitutes a vine. It is undoubtedly the whole plant – roots, main stem, branches, leaves and fruit. It is all the vine. It follows therefore that when the Lord declares that He is the vine and we are the branches, He means that we are part of Him. He is not saying that He is one thing and that we are another. We are not to think of ourselves as separate from Him, additional to Him, serving Him with self-derived energy and effort. We have been made living extensions of Himself, offshoots from the main stem. As we abide in Him day by day, and He in us, fruit will appear and ripen as on the natural vine.

Each branch is valuable but none is indispensable. A branch can be severed without harm to the vine. The closing words of verse 5 are absolutely vital to grasp, "…apart from me ye can do nothing". If we lose touch with Christ, we become incapable of doing anything in His service. It is not that we limit or reduce our fruitfulness or effectiveness. It is rather that we can do nothing.

The Lord walked through life in unclouded fellowship with the Father, in the unhindered enjoyment of His love. His inner calm and joy in God were never disturbed save during the dreadful hours of His abandonment at Calvary. Such was His unfailing joy, and He desires to share it with us, that our joy may be full.

ANDREW RENSHAW

Week 8

7 *FEATURES OF THE FIRST* NEW TESTAMENT ASSEMBLY

Acts 2:1-4, 37-47

Introduction

It was one of the most dramatic days in human history, ranking with others as a 'day that changed the world'. The events of the Day of Pentecost were pictured in the Feast of Weeks (Lev 23:15-21) and predicted by Joel the prophet (Joel 2:28). Now the details were being recorded. The occasion remained vivid in Peter's memory, and he made reference to it when writing of "the Holy Ghost sent down from heaven" (1 Pet 1:12). So it features in picture and in prophecy, in history and in ministry.

The descent of the Spirit was demonstrated in a sound, a sound resembling "a rushing mighty wind", for the wind is an emblem of the Holy Spirit, (Ezek 37:9-14; John 3:8). His descent was demonstrated in a sight, "cloven tongues like as of fire", so appropriate for an occasion when tongues were used as a sign (v.4), and a voice was "lifted up" to convey the good news (v.14).

An inquisitive crowd gathered, and Peter preached the gospel in a way that was particularly relevant for his Jewish audience. His words were incisive, effecting repentance and, in the ultimate, bringing about the seven-fold response of verses 41-42.

These seven features give us early guidance for the functioning of a New Testament assembly. They are further expanded in the Acts and in the epistles but, undoubtedly, a foundation is laid in these verses, and a pattern is established that demands our attention. Christendom has discarded that pattern and has become a mixture of Judaism, Paganism, and Christianity. Among other things, the need for conversion has been ignored, the mode of baptism has been altered, and the breaking of bread has been misinterpreted, but the conduct of these converts does leave a model for subsequent generations. We must be diligent to adhere to that biblical prototype. The word of God never presents things in a haphazard way, so the order in which these seven things are mentioned must be significant. Salvation must always precede baptism, and these and other factors pave the way for participation in the breaking of bread. To tinker with the scriptural order is to depart from the divine ideal.

Day 1

"THEY ... GLADLY RECEIVED HIS WORD"

Acts 2:22-33

The word translated 'received' in today's topic is exclusive to Luke's writings. It really means that the hearers welcomed Peter's word, inasmuch as it was the truth of God. In so doing, they experienced conversion to Christ. In the context, this is the first step to the enjoyment of church fellowship. It is in contrast to what is practised in many denominations today, where membership is a mixture of saved and unsaved people. New Testament churches were composed entirely of believers, and so were called "churches of the saints" (1 Cor 14:33). The command "Be ye not unequally yoked together with unbelievers" (2 Cor 6:14) is as binding in an assembly setting as in other areas of life such as a marriage union, a business partnership, or recreational clubs.

Although Peter's 'word' was tailored for his Jewish audience, his style of presentation contains clear guidelines for today's preachers, guidelines that should be followed if we want to achieve the same results as Peter. Unfolding events gave him a launching pad for his message as in Acts 3:12-26, but on both occasions he was quick to turn the spotlight on the Lord Jesus. Allusions to current affairs or surrounding circumstances can be helpful in attracting interest, but we shouldn't loiter there: get to the point as soon as possible. Again, his message was well sprinkled with quotations from Scripture. These undergirded the facts he conveyed, another important lesson for today. Throughout his discourse the focus was firmly on the life, death, resurrection and exaltation of the Lord Jesus for, really, the gospel is all about Him. We dare not be deficient there. Further, there was opportunity for conversation with the audience, which gave rise to a call for repentance and the demand to distance themselves from those rejecting the Saviour. Nowadays we tend to neglect that aspect of things.

At a very practical level, on three occasions in his message (vv.14, 22, 29) Peter addressed the listeners as "Men of Judæa", "Men of Israel" or "Men and brethren", just as in Acts 13 Paul spoke to his audience on three occasions in a similar way. Preaching that never appeals to the congregation as 'friends', 'brethren', 'saints', 'beloved', or some other appropriate name tends to be cold. However, it can be overdone. Neither Peter nor Paul started every sentence like that but introduced it at a rate of almost once every minute!

Peter's word was received inasmuch as it was the word of God. That is the only instrument that can enlighten minds (Ps 119:130), engender faith (Rom 10:17), and effect regeneration (1 Pet 1:23). No wonder Paul said to Timothy, "Preach the word" (2 Tim 4:2).

Day 2

"THEY ... WERE BAPTISED"

Acts 2:41; Romans 6:1-11

On the Day of Pentecost the converts soon added the public act of baptism to their profession of faith. By baptism, they openly dissociated themselves from the crime of crucifying Israel's Messiah. There was uniqueness about that but, in the context, there are principles relating to baptism which are confirmed as we read on in the Acts of the Apostles.

Observe that receiving the word preceded baptism. Put plainly, only those who have been saved should be baptised. That fact is ignored in today's world but, in Scripture, the order is invariable. It is true that in the New Testament three households were baptised, but none of these cases gives license for baptising infants. We have no knowledge of the composition of Lydia's household except that there were "brethren" in it (Acts 16:40). Members of the jailer's household were old enough to believe for themselves (Acts 16:34). Those of Stephanas' household were sufficiently mature to addict themselves "to the ministry of the saints" (1 Cor 1:16, 16:15). In one situation where people had been baptised prior to their conversion, they were re-baptised after coming to Christ (Acts 19:1-5).

Note too that they were baptised immediately after conversion, as was the pattern right through Acts. The Ethiopian eunuch was baptised while still on his journey (8:36-39), and the jailer was baptised "the same hour of the night" (16:33). The longest recorded gap between salvation and baptism was in the case of Saul of Tarsus, a period of three days (9:9), and Ananias challenged him, "Why tarriest thou? Arise and be baptised"! (22:16).

In commissioning His apostles, the Lord Jesus commanded baptism (Matt 28:19), and by His authority Peter insisted that those who believed should be baptised (Acts 10:48). It is not necessary for salvation, but it is crucial if the new believer is to be obedient to his Lord's command. He did say, "If ye love me, keep my commandments" (John 14:15).

Clearly, the mode of baptism in New Testament times was by immersion in water. The word itself is really an anglicised Greek word meaning to dip. The fact that both Philip and the Ethiopian went down into the water for the baptism confirms the point (Acts 8:38-39), as does the spiritual significance of the ordinance. It symbolises a believer's union with Christ in His burial and resurrection (Rom 6:1-5). Sprinkling a few drops of water hardly satisfies the concept of a burial.

If you have never experienced baptism as a believer, ask yourself, "What doth hinder me to be baptised?" (Acts 8:36). If disobedience is the hindrance, that can be rectified at once.

Day 3

"THEY ... WERE ADDED"

Acts 2:41; Acts 9:26-30; Romans 16:1-2

Having been saved and baptised, three thousand converts were "added" to the existing company of believers. This brings us to consider the biblical pattern for reception to New Testament churches. Here, those who were added were newly converted, and we observed previously that only those who have been saved should form the membership of an assembly. The church of God at Corinth comprised "them that are sanctified in Christ Jesus, called to be saints" (1 Cor 1:2). That is why those who wish to be "added" to an assembly will be interviewed in a kindly way to tell their story of conversion. We have also noted that new believers were baptised, another necessity if the New Testament pattern is to be maintained. An unbaptised believer was never anticipated in the Scriptures, and would not qualify to be "added". It is also clear that those who were "added" were willing to subscribe wholeheartedly to the "apostles' doctrine". Apostolic teaching has now been enshrined in the New Testament, and defines the norms of Christian belief and behaviour. Again, deviation from that would disqualify a potential member. We conclude that those who should be "added" are baptised believers whose creed and conduct coincides with New Testament teaching.

As believers relocated, a letter of commendation facilitated their reception (2 Cor 3:1). For example, when Apollos moved to Corinth, he carried such a letter (Acts 18:27). Guidance for their content is found in Paul's commendation of Phebe (Rom 16:1-2). The Romans were assured of her salvation, for he calls her "our sister". There is a record of her service: she was a servant of the church, "a succourer of many". There was an appeal for her reception: "receive her in the Lord". When moving to a new area with a desire to be "added", difficulties and embarrassment can be avoided by maintaining this practice.

In abnormal circumstances, Paul arrived in Jerusalem without a letter (Acts 9:26). Barnabas was able to vouch for him, but not in a hurried encounter five minutes before the Lord's Supper! The apostles were contacted, and Barnabas provided the same information that a letter would have given: he assured them that Paul was saved, he had "seen the Lord in the way". He had been serving: "he had preached boldly at Damascus". So he was "added". Thus, in Bible times, people were added as new converts, or on the recommendation of other believers, usually by letter or, in unusual circumstances, by word of mouth.

The two words "were added" imply divine activity, but Paul's attempt "to join himself" (Acts 9:26) implies personal responsibility. Like him, every baptised believer in the Lord Jesus should have this deep desire to be linked to a New Testament assembly.

Day 4

"THE APOSTLES' DOCTRINE"

Acts 2:42; 2 Timothy 3:14-17; 2 Peter 1:19-21; 3:1-2

The early converts commenced their Christian lives with remarkable zeal, and sustained commendable consistency: "they continued stedfastly". Continuance is one of the great evidences of a real work of God in a man's soul. 'Stony-ground hearers' "endure but for a time": they have "no root in themselves" (Mark 4:17). Affliction and persecution finds them lacking, their profession a mere emotional response, rather than a genuine experience of repentance and faith. Help from God enabled Paul to "continue unto this day" (Acts 26:22). Continuance is the proof of reality!

The first of four things to which they devoted themselves was the apostles' teaching. At that stage a minimum of instruction had been given, most of it relating to the Lord Jesus but, with the passage of time, these apostles presented a whole raft of divine truth that the converts happily absorbed. Three of these apostles, with the addition of Paul and others, were inspired by the Holy Spirit to commit that truth to writing in what we now call the New Testament Scriptures. Like these early believers, we too have a responsibility to accept it in totality. Spiritual people will acknowledge that apostolic writings are "the commandments of the Lord" (1 Cor 14:37). The "apostles' doctrine" is the word of God.

The principles of the New Testament cover every area of our lives. There is instruction about personal holiness, family life, employment and assembly order. The doctrine of the New Testament also embraces a great range of topics. There is truth about the Lord Jesus, the unfolding of God's prophetic programme and the matter of the church and the churches, that is, the body of Christ and the churches of God. To emulate those who formed the first assembly at Jerusalem, we must subscribe to all that is revealed in these inspired writings. Adding to, or subtracting from, what is revealed places us in error, and leaves us unsuitable to form part of a New Testament assembly.

In contrast to the apostles' doctrine, there is what the Bible calls "doctrines of devils" (1 Tim 4:1). These emerged in "latter times", that is, subsequent to the apostolic age, and they became firmly entrenched in the thinking of apostate Christendom. Satan himself is the source of every doctrinal aberration. The genuine believer will be alert to that, and will continue to hold what is called "sound doctrine" (1 Tim 1:10), "good doctrine" (1 Tim 4:6), "the doctrine which is according to godliness" (1 Tim 6:3), and "the doctrine of God our Saviour" (Titus 2:10). Let us "continue stedfastly in the apostles' doctrine".

Day 5

"… *AND FELLOWSHIP*"

Acts 2:42-47; 4:32-37

The word 'fellowship' carries the basic meaning of 'sharing in common' (W. E. Vine). Obviously, the setting in which it appears must determine the scope of its meaning. For example, our living link with divine persons is described as fellowship "with the Father, and with his Son Jesus Christ" (1 John 1:3), and a genuine claim to have fellowship with Him can be made only by those who "walk in the light" (vv.6-7). Another kind of fellowship is the subject of Paul's thanks to the Philippians. There it is their "fellowship in the gospel", that is, their practical support of his missionary activities (Phil 1: 5). The reference to fellowship in Acts 2:42 must be different again. It is that union that exists between those who comprise a local church.

The membership of a New Testament assembly is not vague or fluid. There is a "within" and there is a "without" (1 Cor 5:12). In other words, at Corinth they knew exactly with whom they were in fellowship in that local testimony for God. Their meetings were open to the public, for an assembly is not a secret society, but "the whole church" stands in contrast to observers who merely attended (1 Cor 14:23). While the term 'assembly fellowship' is not a biblical expression, it is a biblical concept.

In Acts 2:42, the four items in which they "continued stedfastly" are in a significant order, in that the apostles' doctrine is mentioned before fellowship. Their fellowship was based on a common adherence to what the apostles taught, and two of the ways in which that fellowship was expressed were in the breaking of bread and prayers. Believers holding diverse doctrine could never be seen to be in fellowship with each other in any practical sense.

The fellowship that existed in the first assembly clearly involved their attendance at meetings for they were "together" (v.44), but it extended beyond the walls of any meeting place and was never confined to meeting times. The latter part of the chapter uses terms like "daily", and "from house to house", when describing the rapport between them. It did involve them in sharing their possessions but, at a spiritual level, there was unity in worship in that they were "praising God" (v.47). And there was solidarity in effective service, to the point that people were being saved "daily".

The warmth of the fellowship is encapsulated in the phrase "their own company" (4:23). To be gathered with kindred spirits proved to be a haven from the antagonism of the Jews. Be as keen to be present when the believers gather. Fellowship necessitates attendance. Fellowship involves affection.

Fellowship demands commitment. Fellowship requires your contribution. Continue steadfastly … in fellowship.

Day 6

"… IN BREAKING OF BREAD"

Acts 2:42; 1 Corinthians 11:23-34

Baptism and the Lord's Supper are the only two ordinances connected with New Testament assemblies. They have this in common, that both were instituted by the Lord Jesus in the Gospels, both were practised by the early believers in the Acts, and both were explained by the apostle Paul in the epistles. The similarities end there.

By way of contrast, baptism is once for all, and the breaking of bread repetitive: baptism is personal, and the Lord's Supper is collective, as indicated in the phrases "when ye come together in the church" and "when ye come together therefore into one place" (1 Cor 11:18, 20). Clearly, the breaking of bread is an assembly function. In Acts 2, the participants were baptised believers who continued in the apostles' doctrine and in fellowship. Undoubtedly there is a pattern there. There is no thought of any unbeliever partaking as some kind of 'means of grace'. No unbaptised believer participated, nor did any who held any doctrinal abnormalities.

Elsewhere in Acts there is guidance regarding the timing of the breaking of bread. Paul's journeys brought him to Troas and, despite his haste, he deliberately waited for almost a week to be present on "the first day of the week" when the assembly met to break bread (20:7). The word 'week' is plural, the suggestion being that it happened on every first day of the week.

To explain the breaking of bread, the Lord Jesus gave a special revelation to the apostle Paul (1 Cor 11:23-34). Paul had already alluded to the ordinance in the epistle, showing that our participation is an expression of our fellowship with each other (10:16-17), but now he quotes the Lord Jesus Himself to explain the symbolism behind the loaf and cup, His body and His blood. Eating the bread and drinking the cup is an act of remembrance (vv.24-25). Thus, a fundamental feature of the gathering is to remember Him. The hymns that are sung will focus on Him, and the prayers that are expressed will be in appreciation of Him.

Eating the bread and drinking the cup proclaims His death, and is done in anticipation of His coming (v.26). To whom do we show His death? The unbeliever and the unlearned can be present (14:24). Angels also survey the scene, one of the reasons that Paul advances for the covered heads of the sisters (11:10). So, to all interested parties, there is a proclamation of His death, a visual reminder of the work that He accomplished at the cross.

"This do" said the Saviour. With necessary moral fitness, the obedient believer will comply on every possible occasion (11:28).

Day 7

"… AND IN PRAYERS"

Acts 2:42; 1 Timothy 2:1-10

The early believers continued stedfastly in the prayers. Private prayer is crucial in every Christian life. When Paul was newly saved it was said of him. "Behold he prayeth" (Acts 9:11). At the end of his life he was equally earnest: "I have remembrance of thee in my prayers night and day" (2 Tim 1:3). Don't neglect it: "Men ought always to pray" (Luke 18:1).

In Acts 2:42 the reference is to collective prayer, the assembly prayer meeting. In modern times such gatherings are not so well attended as the breaking of bread, but for these new converts they carried equal status and were very often impromptu. When under threat, they prayed (Acts 4:23-31). When endorsing a new work, they prayed (6:6). When Peter was in danger, they prayed (12:5). When sending out the missionaries, they prayed (13:3). When feeling the pain of parting, they prayed (20:36, 21:5). The collective exercise of prayer was the spontaneous response in every circumstance.

Away from an emergency situation it is convenient to meet for prayer by arrangement, and the Scriptures regulate these gatherings (1 Tim 2:1-10). The basic theme of that epistle is behaviour in the house of God (3:15). Having dealt with personal matters in the first chapter, Paul introduces his subject in chapter 2 by using the phrase "first of all". This is clear evidence that the prayer meeting occupies a key position in assembly life. Is it such a priority with us? He explains how to pray, using a variety of words to show that prayer should be specific rather than general, intercessory rather than selfish, and appreciative rather than purely demanding. He tells us for whom to pray, and the scope is wide, "all men". In particular, he focuses on those in government, and the fact that stable conditions facilitate godly living and the spread of the gospel. Thereby God's desire for the salvation of men is brought to fruition. In light of all that, there is no need for public prayers to be repetitive and stereotyped: there is so much to pray for.

In addition, there is instruction about who should pray publicly. The men (males) (v.8), males who have "holy hands", for ungodliness will close God's ears to us (Ps 66:18). The mention of the males makes it clear that, as in other assembly gatherings, this principle is binding, "Let your women keep silence in the churches" (1 Cor 14:34). Sisters should be present, as in Acts 1:14, modestly dressed, and unostentatious in appearance (1 Tim 2:9-10), but their prayers will be as silent as Hannah's (1 Sam 1:13). Let us all be like these early believers and continue stedfastly in prayers.

JACK HAY

Week 9

7 *THINGS TO WHICH* "*YE ARE COME*"

Hebrews 12:22-24

Introduction

It is a glorious privilege the elect people of God enjoy today having been brought by His grace to a place and position even angels might envy!

Israel, when redeemed from Egypt's bondage, came to Mount Sinai with all its darkness, fear, and thunder, and learned the terrifying unapproachableness of God (Heb 12:18-21). Mount Sinai was for them a revelation of the dark mystery of God, the fearsome majesty of God, and the dreadful judgement of the God of thrice-called holiness. For Israel at Sinai it was all terror, fright, and alarm! Even mighty Moses, the servant of God, turned pale and cried, "I exceedingly fear and quake"! As someone has expressed it, "The law has its Sinai, but faith has its Zion", and that is where divine grace has brought us today. "Ye are come unto Mount Zion". Hallelujah!

Yes, God's elect today have not been brought to any earthly mount, no matter how awesome or holy that mount might have been! Neither have they been redeemed by the blood of a sacrificial lamb from the flocks of earth – but "richer blood that flowed from nobler veins" has redeemed them from a worse tyrant than ever Pharaoh was. Led by a Deliverer greater far than Moses, they have been brought to another mount, a heavenly mount! Being brought there they learn the secret of God's nearness, the joy of living with Him in the shadow of His presence – they discover the security of His everlasting arms, and what it means to be carried in His bosom.

In the following meditation we shall follow the seven glorious verities we

Christians have been brought to today. They were written originally by Paul to distinguish the sharp contrast between the superior things, or better things, of the Christian dispensation over those of the old Jewish religion. It was meant to encourage and inspire the Jewish believers to see they had gained far more under grace than they had left behind when under law! In these seven glorious truths Paul is lifting these besieged and persecuted saints high above their earthly Sinai under law, into the reality of a position they now occupy on the heights of that heavenly Zion under grace!

Day 1

"MOUNT SION ... THE HEAVENLY JERUSALEM"

Hebrews 12:22

"But ye are come unto mount Sion, and unto ... the heavenly Jerusalem". While it is true we have not yet arrived at this glorious location actually and physically, yet spiritually it is where we are assured faith has already brought us. This is where we belong – it is where our citizenship is recorded (Phil 3: 20) in that heavenly city established upon the everlasting hills of the Zion above. It is where we shall be at home for all of a glorious future eternity. Just as God finds His rest now in the finished work of His Son (John 17:4) so we find our rest where God finds His. God's 'rest' is in a Person, but it is also in the Place where that exalted Person has ascended to, the mount and the city of God. If Jehovah has chosen and desired the earthly Zion for His habitation (Ps 132:13), how much more the true and eternal Zion that is in heaven: "This is my rest forever: here will I dwell; for I have desired it" (Ps 132: 14). Now where God finds His rest is where we find ours in both the Person and the Place. What a breathtaking thought that is! Let us ring out a further 'Hallelujah' to the praise of His marvellous grace!

There is a further application of these verses which is most comforting. The seven 'verities' we are studying, and to which the passage assures us we have 'come', are certainly true of us now spiritually even though our eyes have never gazed upon their actual glory! However, our loved ones who have 'fallen asleep in Jesus' have most certainly come to these wonderful things, and experienced their reality! The writer has often meditated upon the rising journey of the spirit of the believer at the point of physical death until its arrival and entry into the city of God there on the heavenly mount! Carried by an angel band (Luke 16:22) the disembodied spirit of the just-released believer sees the soaring grandeur of mount Zion, and thrills at its first sight of the shining towers and dazzling splendour of the city itself. Then, entering through the gates, he is welcomed by a triumphant throng of exulting angels. Beyond them he is then received by the assembly of the firstborn among whom he finds he is already enrolled – his name recorded and well-known in that celestial City! Then to come to God as the mighty Vindicator of His people, and to the spirits of just men made perfect. Then to Jesus the mediator, and to the blood of sprinkling speaking better things than that of Abel.

This is the fascinating meditation we are now entering on by the help of God's Spirit.

Day 2

"AN INNUMERABLE COMPANY OF ANGELS"

Hebrews 12:22-23

On entering the shining city of God, the redeemed spirits of those believers newly released from their bodies, "which sleep in Jesus" back on earth, come to the first glorious inhabitants of that heavenly metropolis. They are described literally in the Greek text as 'myriads (ten thousands) of angels in festal gathering'. The AV "general assembly" (*paneguris*) meaning a festive and exultant assembly, is generally connected to the word "angels" and not the following clause "the church of the firstborn". What a sight to behold! A massed gathering of the heavenly host whose combined voices in thrilling harmony direct their praises to the high throne of God. They are undoubtedly praising God for His wisdom, love, and power, and celebrating His redemptive victory through Christ which has brought sinners of earth, cleansed and purified, safe home into this lovely city! And that is where we too have come spiritually as we pursue our earthly pilgrimage en-route home to that same heavenly Jerusalem. It is realities such as this that made Paul yearn for heaven, and comparing the two spheres in which the believer lives, "the heavenlies" and this present world, exclaim, "to die is gain" (Phil 1:21)! What a "gain" for our departed loved ones and fellow saints! Praise God!

Who are these lustrous inhabitants of that city above whose swelling chorus fills the vaults of heaven and echoes around the rainbow-circled throne? They are called "angels of God", literally 'messengers of God' (Matt 22:30), and are heavenly intelligences used in God's service as agents or messengers of His Divine will and protective care, particularly in God's work of redemption. One of their most exalted offices is to wait in the presence of the enthroned Divine Majesty and ceaselessly proclaim His holiness, glory, and eternity. This was the honour conferred on the rank of angel known as the "seraphim" in Isaiah 6, and the cherubim-like "living creatures" of Revelation 5:8.

They were created by God a distinct and heavenly order of spirit beings. Their numbers are vast but fixed. The prophet Daniel in his day (Dan 7:10) saw in vision the angel host surrounding the fiery throne, ministering to the Ancient of Days, and numbered them as "thousands of thousands … and ten thousand times ten thousand". In the final book of the Bible, the apostle John in vision saw the same judgement throne and precisely the same number of angels ascribing worthiness to the Lamb (Rev 5:11)! Thus they are deathless, and neither diminish nor multiply (Luke 20:36).

What a privilege is ours today to know these glorious creatures have been "sent forth" (present participle, 'being sent forth', stressing continuous angelic ministry) to serve us who are heirs of ultimate and final salvation, during this present church age (Heb 1:14), and with whom we shall live eternally in the golden city of God!

Day 3

"CHURCH OF THE FIRSTBORN"

Hebrews 12:23

Now we come to the most illustrious and privileged inhabitants of the heavenly Jerusalem, 'the church of the firstborn ones, whose names are permanently inscribed in heaven'. This is the body of the church, of which Christ is the risen Head, saved out of Jews and Gentiles throughout the two thousand year period of this present church dispensation, most of whom are already safe home in that glorious city!

The term 'firstborn' is used in Scripture as a title of dignity and rank not of time, and indicates the primacy of those thus described. Israel are given the title 'firstborn' in Exodus 4:22-23 when God called them out of Egypt, indicating their priority among the nations. Now here, in Hebrews 12, is a further instance of the apostle's assurance that Jewish believers had been brought into a far higher fellowship and dignity than ever they had under Moses and the old dispensation. Then, as members of the Jewish state, their title 'firstborn' gave them assurance that one day under their Messiah they would rule over the Gentile nations on earth. Now, as members of 'the church of the firstborn ones', they are elevated to a heavenly rank, and brought into union, not with an earthly leader, Moses, but with the 'firstborn of all creation' (Col 1:15; see Heb 1:6) from whom they derive their title and distinction. They rank now among the high nobility of the city of the living God, with their names indelibly enrolled as honoured citizens of that city! Hallelujah!

"…which are written in heaven". It is a thrilling thought that while we live out our lives here on earth in the very ordinary circumstances of life, like going to school and college, working in the office, or laying bricks on a building site where nobody thinks we are important in any way, there is a magnificent city above where our names are actually written down! Yes, your name, dear fellow-believer, is registered in shining letters in an actual book in the heavenly Jerusalem, indicating you are an honoured citizen of that exalted realm!

The Greeks had a custom in all their cities that the names of all citizens were inscribed on a tablet kept in a prominent place in one of the great buildings of the city. All those thus enrolled were entitled to live there and enjoy all the rights, protection, and privileges of citizenship. Our citizenship is thus eternally secured in that heavenly world! That is why the Lord told His disciples not to rejoice because they had miraculous powers granted them on earth, "but rather rejoice because your names are written in heaven" (Luke 10.20). Am I rejoicing in that fact today?

Day 4

"God the Judge of all"

Hebrews 12:23

Of the seven verities we are told we have "come unto", this is the most misunderstood and, for many, not easy to understand. Up to this point Paul has been lifting us higher and higher in revealing the heavenly privileges and glories we have arrived at as the redeemed people of Christ in this NT dispensation, in contrast to the earthly hopes of Israel in the OT. So we have been brought firstly to mount Zion and the heavenly Jerusalem; then we move higher to the glorious company of the angels; then higher still to the church of the firstborn.

Now, at the highest pinnacle of heavenly privilege, we are said to have come "to God, judge of all" (JND). In which case, we are to understand it as having come to God in the glory of His Being (there is no article in the Greek). It is His Person therefore that is indicated. The One who is Judge of all, to be feared and held in reverence for His consuming holiness (v.29), the awesomeness of His office, and who has power to consign to everlasting woe those who break His law, is the God to whom we have come, unafraid and with holy boldness!

Thus it becomes a word of utmost comfort and assurance for us today! The God who is Judge of all is not now judging us but rather justifying us! "Who shall lay any thing to the charge of God's elect? It is God that justifies." (Rom 8:33). And why is He now justifying us? Because "He spared not his own Son but delivered him up for us all" (Rom 8:32). Thus His wrath is appeased, and we may come, unafraid, to "God, Judge of all"!

Not so Moses who, when confronted by the fearful holiness of the Judge of all in dreadful power and unappeased wrath, said "I exceedingly fear and quake" (v.21)! He was exposed to the fury of the God whose law was violated by the very presence of sinful humanity as seen in Israel trembling at the foot of mount Sinai. There was no God-satisfying sacrifice offered for them as God, the Judge of all, came to them with His law. But how different for us who have come to Him, the living God, Judge of all, accepted in His beloved Son. How blessed and perfect therefore is our peace and acceptance. He who is Judge of all finds nothing to judge in us!

So today, beloved, let us rejoice in the great fact that we have everlasting life and will never come into judgment, but have passed from death unto life (John 5:24).

Day 5

"*THE SPIRITS OF JUST MEN MADE PERFECT*"

Hebrews 12:23

Who are these privileged and heavenly spirits who form another group to whom we have come? Four things are said of them by which we are able to identify them with accuracy: they are 'spirits'; the spirits of 'men'; they are 'justified' men; and, fourthly, they are 'perfected' men. Being 'men' they must have a history linked with earth, so were justified on earth, and their disembodied spirits are now perfected in that heavenly Jerusalem. They are seen as a group distinct from the church of the firstborn so are not church saints. They can only be, therefore, justified believers of the pre-Christian dispensation! They are the Old Testament saints who, like Abraham, were justified by faith during their earthly sojourn and, like Moses, had their names written in God's book (Exod 32:32-33) as being full citizens of that heavenly city that they all looked for, and now have arrived at (Heb 11:10,16).

These are the witnesses mentioned in Hebrews 11:39-40, Old Testament saints who bore a powerful and sacrificial witness for God during their day of suffering and trial on earth. It is said of them they could not be "made perfect" without us! That is, apart from the great event of 10:14, when Christ by His "one offering ... perfected for ever them that are sanctified", they could not realise the perfection procured by a finished work. This is because, "it is not possible that the blood of bulls and of goats should take away sins" (10:4) so, until the final, all-sufficient sacrifice was offered and then presented in person when Christ ascended to Paradise (Luke 23:43), they could not be made perfect!

Westcott puts it succinctly when he writes, "When the Son bore humanity to the throne of God – the Father – those who were in fellowship with Him were (in this sense) perfected, but not till then: see Hebrews 11:40". It is plain therefore that "being made perfect" does not embrace either the glory of the resurrection body or the final manifestation with Christ in glory when He returns to inaugurate His millennial kingdom! It refers to the all-important state of justification and acceptance with God on the ground of Christ's one, all-sufficient and perfect sacrifice.

What a thrilling insight this is, beloved, into the wonder of our fellowship, true now spiritually here on earth, but to be realised fully when we enter the pearly gates of that city on high! Not only to mingle with angels and church saints, but to enjoy fellowship with such Old Testament worthies as David, Joshua, Abraham, Elijah and great Moses. What must that heavenly Jerusalem be like! Even with a vivid imagination put into turbo-drive, we can hardly grasp the breathtaking thrill of what we have "come to" by rich grace and immense love. (A loud 'Hallelujah' here please)!

Day 6

"Jesus the Mediator of the New Covenant"

Hebrews 12:24

What a blessing that "Jesus" is in the heavenly Jerusalem, and we have come to Him there in the character of everything that lovely Name means. Of course He is supreme King of kings, and Creator and Upholder of all things, but He is there still bearing in His exalted majesty the meekness that characterised Him when incarnate among men on earth! He is still our beloved "Jesus"! What an encouragement! Our glorious Lord is unchanged, the same today in glory as He ever was on earth, still there bearing His Name of "Jesus".

"Jesus" is the name associated with his humanity, the name given Him at His birth (Matt 1:21). It is the name associated with His humiliation and death for sinners when suffering upon the cross (Matt 27:37), and the name of supremacy belonging to Him now in highest heaven; "God also hath highly exalted him, and given him a name which is above every name" (Phil 2:9). The Name so demeaned and despised by the Jewish leaders on earth is now exalted and revered in heaven.

That we are correct in emphasising the Person and the character of the Mediator to whom we have come, is seen in the title itself, "Jesus, the mediator of the new covenant". Please note, we have not come to the new covenant, marvellous and thrilling as it may be, but to Jesus the mediator of it! The emphasis is deliberate, for Paul wants to underline again the superiority of Jesus over Moses. The mediator of the old covenant was Moses, now dead, and his covenant is both ineffective and outdated. Jesus, who ever lives, is the mediator of "a better covenant which was established upon better promises" (Heb 8: 6), and is therefore a new covenant, new in time, that is, or fresh and recent. The Christians had received in this new covenant a possession and privilege the Jewish nation under Moses had never enjoyed!

It is His presence there in the heavenly Jerusalem in the character of mediator that preserves the ones come to Him, in perfect and eternal relationship with God. He will always be there, Jesus the mediator between God and redeemed men (1 Tim 2:5). For ever this mediator will bear in His body the marks of His sacrifice, and the new covenant, sealed and secured in His precious blood, will stand eternally as the unbreakable bond guaranteeing our presence in that blessed abode.

This covenant is the whole gospel story climaxing in His body given, and His blood outpoured. He will forever maintain the office of mediator, the One in whom God meets His people and blesses them, and in whom His people meet with Him and worship and serve Him, unto the ages of the ages.

Day 7

"THE BLOOD OF SPRINKLING ... "

Hebrews 12:24

"The blood of sprinkling" refers to the covenant-blood of Christ (Matt 26: 28), shed for sinners and speaking pardon to their consciences. It looked back to the blood Moses sprinkled on the book of the covenant and all the people at the inauguration and ratification of the old covenant (Exod 24:7; Heb 9:19-20). Not that the literal blood of Christ is to be found anywhere in heaven, or that we shall see it when there. Christ when He entered heaven is said to have done so 'by' or 'through' His own blood, and not *with* it! It was in virtue of the atoning efficacy of that blood He entered once for all into the holy place (Heb 9:12). So, the meaning is, we have come to the good of that blood sprinkling, and will stand forever in the value God puts upon it. The value God puts upon the blood of sacrifice depends upon the one who shed it and who consequently gives it value. That is why we get the contrast between the blood of goats and calves and Christ's own blood in Hebrews 9.12. The blood of animal sacrifices throughout the Old Testament was only a type anticipating the blood of the ultimate sacrifice that God's Son would offer when he shed His own blood.

It is called in this passage the blood of 'sprinkling'. What is the significance of 'sprinkling'? To 'sprinkle' is to personally apply the blood of Christ so that all its merits and benefits are received by the believer. While the ransom of Christ in His own blood was for 'all', only those who by faith personally apply or 'sprinkle' that sin-cleansing blood partake of its benefits.

Christ's blood is said to be 'speaking': it is living blood because in Scripture God relates blood to life! "For the life of the flesh is in the blood" (Lev 17:11), and when the blood is shed the life is given, and that outpoured blood has a wonderful message to convey! The blood of Christ 'speaketh' to divine justice that the sentence has been carried out in the death of the one mediator, "who gave himself a ransom for all" (1 Tim 2:5-6). Now justice is satisfied, and all for whom the ransom was paid may be justified and put forever beyond condemnation. What a voice this precious blood has and will have for all eternity!

It is 'speaking better things than that of Abel'. God reproved Cain concerning his brother's murder, "The voice of thy brother's blood crieth unto me from the ground" (Gen 5:10). Abel's blood was crying for strict justice and revenge, but Christ's blood is speaking better things than that. The blood of Christ proclaims a full atonement for sin, a perfect pardon, and eternal reconciliation for all who believe. Hallelujah!

MICHAEL BROWNE

Week 10

7 MIGHTY DEEDS OF SAMSON THE STRONG, WEAK MAN

Introduction

Samson is one of those delightful characters from the Old Testament whose life and exploits delighted us as children. Samson was the last of the Judges and these were sad days amongst the children of God.

In Judges 13:1 we read "the children of Israel did evil again in the sight of the Lord; and the Lord delivered them into the hand of the Philistines forty years". We do not read of them calling on Jehovah for deliverance and it seems a spirit of apathy had gripped the land. We live in last times, and we need to guard against the spirit of apathy laying hold on the people of God.

As for Samson we are told three things about him: first, his was a special birth; second, his was to be a special life; third, his was to be a special service. Sadly, he compromised his Nazarite character, and the would-be deliverer of his people died in captivity. His service was in his own home town, between Zorah and Eshtaol, and in his death he was buried there. We are all called of God to these three 'special' conditions, and must remember that we too can be both strong and weak. Where Samson began, there he finished his course. In spite of all his compromise and failure, he is named among the heroes of Hebrews 11.

His birth was special. Out of a barren womb, like other great men of Scripture, but none so great as He who came forth from the virgin's womb. As it was with Mary, so it is with this dear un-named woman that an angel brings her a glorious message of grace, love and truth. Oh the joy that must have filled this barren soul as life would spring forth from the dead! But her life would set the tone of his life of service. It is ever a challenge to godly parents to lead a life of example to their children for good. His un-named mother was an influence for good, in stark contrast to the two un-named women of the Philistines who would seek to ensnare the Nazarite in dubious relationships.

Day 1

SLAYING THE LION

Judges 14:1-7

At the commencement of his service for God, Samson moves on a pathway that is fraught with danger. He consciously takes himself down a dangerous road, enters into a dangerous relationship, and exposes himself to a very dangerous foe. If we deliberately court friendship with things that are contrary to God's word, we should not be surprised if they cause us to fall.

A Dangerous Road – "And he went down". On three occasions we read of Samson's downward path (Jud 14:1, 5, 7). But not only did he go down, his parents went down (14:5) and, eventually, his brethren went down from Judah to Etam (15:11). Our actions can have a dangerous effect on God's people. We may be strong and have the ability to resist certain things, but what of the weaker brother? Remember, we are "our brother's keeper."

Samson journeys to Timnath, 'the place of the vineyard'. As a Nazarite this was the very place where he ought not to be, for wine (figurative of all earthly joys) was forbidden him. He puts himself into the place of temptation, he is exposed to the forbidden fruits. This was not a place of separation but of earthly pleasures! We are called to live sanctified lives. Separated from earth's delights and defilements and to live unto Him the all-sufficient One! If we deliberately associate and court friendship with temptations, then our testimony may well end up marred.

A Dangerous Relationship – "I have seen". This reminds us of the error in the beginning. The Scripture says of Eve that "when she saw" (Gen 3:6) and so it is with Samson that the lust of the eyes, the lust of the flesh and the pride of life took control. His great weakness was his sensual appetite. This is the first of three Philistine women in his life. These relationships took him in a downward direction and ended in his humiliation and death. Notice how it began. He went down, he saw her, he talked with her and he became besotted. He ignored godly parental advice and the relationship ended disastrously. His desires outweighed the scriptural principle "be ye not unequally yoked" (2 Cor 6:14). This solemn message even today is still often sadly true.

A Dangerous Roar – "a young lion roared against him". It happened because he was in the wrong place, amidst the pleasures of earth, with the wrong person, a Philistine. The lion roared against him to instil fear (Amos 3:8). Man's worst foe comes out to destroy him at the very beginning of his service for God. Peter in his epistle reminds us of "Satan going about as a roaring lion seeking whom he may devour". However, the Spirit of the Lord came upon Samson and he rent the lion as a kid.

Consider the Master, for it was after John's declaration and Heaven's commendation that the lion roared against Him in the wilderness. The Lord defeated Satan with the Word of God. You and I need to abide in the Spirit of God and, by the power of God's word, "rend the lion" daily.

Day 2

REDEEMING THE RIDDLE

Judges 14:7-20

Again in this chapter we read that Samson "went down" to Timnath. Timnath can also be rendered 'the portion', but this is the world's portion and not God's. God would ever have his people enjoy the portion that He has prepared for them, yet how frequently we turn again and again to that which is not edifying or helpful. Paul will say that "all things are lawful for me, but all things are not expedient" (1 Cor 10:23).

We are called to travel the road of holiness and the pathway of truth but, for the second time, we see Samson walking where he ought not to have been. Even as he passes the spot where the "lion roared against him" he never thinks to retrace his steps as Abraham and Isaac had to do so many years earlier when they deviated into the land of Egypt.

As he journeys he is confronted by a strange sight. A honeycomb within the dead carcase of the lion. He eats of it and is refreshed. He gives of it to his parents and they likewise benefit, but to his ungodly companions it is a complete mystery. The world cannot comprehend the things of Christ. How can the eater yield forth meat? That is contrary to nature, but to you and me the death of the 'Strong Man' has brought sweetness to us. Little wonder they could not, and the world still cannot, comprehend the mystery of salvation.

Not only does he encounter a strange sight, he associates with strange companions. A Nazarite joined with Philistines! These are the children of Ham, a wandering nation who landed in Egypt, sojourned in the land, and travelled up the coast to the Promised Land without the experience of crossing the Red Sea, the Wilderness or the Jordan. They were like God's people but they were not God's people. They resort to subterfuge to gain advantage over the man of God. A God-given marriage is a joy to both parties, but that which springs of the unequal yoke oft-times leads to grave misunderstandings. The strong man who can rend the lion is unable to withstand the tears of a weeping woman. "A continual dropping in a very rainy day and a contentious woman are alike" (Prov 27:15) and as Delilah wore him down so he yielded his secret. Had this temptation required physical strength to endure, Samson would have been well able to cope. But only moral strength could have withstood

Delilah's guile, and it is her bittersweet words which beguile and entrap him.

Beware of the subtlety of the evil one! It was not the fiery darts which pulled Samson down, but the wiles of the devil. That which appears "all fair" on the outside may be dark and dangerous within, and she betrayed him to ungodly men.

Day 3

FOXES AND FIREBRANDS

Judges 15:1-8

It is most notable in this account of Samson's actions against the Philistines that we never read the expression "the Spirit of the Lord came upon him." On this occasion it may well be that Samson is moving in his own strength and zeal, although God is gracious to bless his actions. In our service for God we need to constantly examine ourselves to ensure that all we do is governed not by self-motivation, pride or walking after the flesh, but only by His will. God is sometimes gracious to bless our actions, in spite of our self-efforts, to accomplish his own purpose.

Samson once again goes down to Timnath. His purpose is to visit his wife, only to find that the world's standards of morality are vastly different from those of God. His wife has been given to another. He is immediately offered her sister as a substitute! The moral standard of our country today is at an extremely low ebb, and certainly does not consider divine principles. It cannot be emphasised too much that marriage is for life and that extra-marital relationships are wrong, as are intimate relationships outside the marriage bond, no matter how much the world condones such actions.

Samson had not only lost his wife, he had also lost his distinct identity in the eyes of the Philistines. In reply to the question as to who had fired their fields they said "Samson the son-in-law of the Timnite" (15:6). Once our testimony has been compromised before the world then our service for the Master will be curtailed. So Samson takes the fight back into the enemy's territory. First he attacks their produce, fields and vineyards, then their people with a great slaughter. However, the Philistines respond with fire for fire and burn his wife and father-in-law to death. The world is a harsh master and we must remember that, when we engage with them in spiritual warfare, our weapons are God's, "for the weapons of our warfare are not carnal, but mighty through God to the pulling down of strong holds" (2 Cor 10:4).

God can, and does, use unusual methods in His service to accomplish His results. But the objective of such actions is to demonstrate that it is of Him, and that man plays but a small part in the process. Consider the marked contrast between Samson and his 300 foxes, and Gideon and his 300 men. With Samson the foxes ran uncontrollably amongst the Philistines producing little glory for God, whilst with Gideon the cry was "the sword of the Lord, and of

Gideon" (Jud 7:20). God will bring blessing and victory, but he requires of us effort, commitment, diligence, prayer and total, absolute reliance on Him.

Day 4

TRAITORS AND TRIUMPH

Judges 15:8-20

After the slaughter of the Philistines, Samson departs from Timnath and dwells in the top of the rock Etam. Etam is not without significance for the name means 'the lair of the ravenous beasts'. He will certainly learn that lesson soon. His own brethren, the men of Judah, come up as ravenous beasts to betray him into the hands of the Philistines. We think of the Saviour, betrayed by his own brethren, crucified by gentile dogs, and who could say with the Psalmist, "many bulls have compassed me: strong bulls of Bashan have beset me round" (Ps 22:12).

The RV translates the end of verse 8 like this, "He dwelt in the cleft of the rock". Moses when he desired to see God's glory was placed in the "clift of a rock" (Exod 33:22) and enjoyed the goodness of God. May this be our desire, to dwell in the cleft of the rock and, like Moses and Samson, to enjoy safety, security, sanctuary and sustenance at His hands. Well might we take to heart the words of the hymn writer "Oh fly to the rock which is higher than I"!

But it is his brethren, the men of Judah, that come up against him to deliver him to the Philistines. Listen to their sad lament "the Philistines are rulers over us" (15:11). Jacob, in blessing Judah, said "Thy hand shall be in the neck of thine enemies" (Gen 49:8). Pre-occupied with themselves rather than with deliverance, they ask "what is this that thou hast done unto us?" (15:11). No longer can it be said of Judah "thou art he whom the brethren shall praise", and so Samson graciously submits himself to them to be delivered rather than afflict them. How low is their state, how far have they sunk in their appreciation of God's salvation! Yielding to their mortal foes it could be said of them that "where there is no vision, the people perish" (Prov 29:18).

In Genesis 37 it is Judah who says of Joseph "what profit is it if we slay our brother…? Come, and let us sell him…" (vv.26-27). So his brethren betrayed him who was to be called the Saviour of the world. We think of the Christ of God, betrayed, bruised, battered and put to death, but He submitted Himself to them as He said "this is your hour" (Luke 22:53). Yet a glorious triumph surpasses the anguish of the betrayal.

Doubtless the Philistines shouted with glee as they saw Samson bound by two new ropes and delivered into their hands. New ropes: these were man made, intertwined for added strength. They had never been used before and were specific for the task in hand. Just as Samson's brethren came prepared for the task, so they came in Gethsemane's garden. But men's preparations are foolish where God is at work. "I AM" he declares, and they fall back as dead men. Likewise Samson, liberated by God's power, takes a foolish thing, the jawbone of an ass, and slays a thousand men. It is not a powerful weapon, just an insignificant object, but just like a boy called David with his five stones we learn that little is much with God.

Day 5

THE GATES OF GAZA

Judges 16:1-3

After the slaughter of the Philistines, Samson dwelt at En-hakkore which means 'the well of him that cried'. God met his need and supplied sustenance so that he could say "this poor man cried and the Lord heard him, and saved him out of all his troubles" (Ps 34:6). However, we see again the downward trend in Samson's life. He does not continue to dwell on the rock but descends into the lower plain, to the town of Gaza. Remember Lot who saw the well watered plains of Sodom and Gomorrah, and think of the dreadful consequences that followed his departure to that place. However attractive it may appear on the surface, the Scriptures exhort us to "set your affection on things above, not on things on the earth" (Col 3:2).

Gaza means 'a stronghold', and Samson leaves the sanctity of the rock to enter such a place. The world is the stronghold of Satan and in Revelation 2, of the church at Pergamos, we are told that this is where Satan's seat is and where Satan dwelleth. Not only does Samson enter Satan's stronghold, he does so to enjoy the immoral pleasures that are on offer there. He visits the second un-named woman in his life whose purpose is to ensnare rather than encourage the Nazarite. Though un-named, her character is given: a harlot. That which panders to fleshly, earthly lusts is to the destruction of the soul. The wise man in Proverbs 23:27-28 warns of the danger of such an alliance. Joseph, when confronted with the unwarranted advances of Potiphar's wife, fled the scene.

Paul, as he writes to Timothy, warns "flee also youthful lusts" (2 Tim 2: 22). Remember, light has no fellowship with darkness. Being a child of God makes us different. Today many strive to be like the Philistines in order that we may be more attractive to them. Beloved, being a Christian makes us different, and it is only the power of Christ that attracts, not us!

The Philistines gather for the kill. Their enemy is trapped in the town. They compass him about, lie in wait and say "in the morning light we will kill him". But Samson arises after midnight and carries away the gates of the city, and their bars, those things which symbolise his entrapment. But note once again, the Spirit of the Lord is absent in this incident. Nevertheless, after this further mighty deed with divinely-given strength, Samson instinctively returns to Hebron, the place of fellowship, communion and association with divine promises and God

Beloved, think of the dark forces that gathered around the cross! Of their perceived entrapment of the Holy One as He is laid within the tomb with a stone across the door. Sealed in by the power and authority of Rome with a military force on guard. This mighty Man for God tears away the gates and bars of sin, death and hell to move to the heavenly Hebron to sit at God's right hand forever. Hallelujah what a Saviour!

Day 6

DELILAH AND HER DECEITFULNESS

Judges 16:4-17

"Love not the world, neither the things that are in the world" (1 John 2: 15). Samson once again embarks on an unholy relationship which ultimately will rob him of everything. He loves a woman of the Valley of Sorek whose name is Delilah. Delilah means 'languishing' or 'pining away'. She speaks of a beauty that is only skin deep and is transient and fading. Sadly, so many like Samson have not realised that this world passeth away and is only temporary. Cultivating friendship with the world places us outside of God's will and our spiritual lives will languish and pine away.

The ongoing weakness (and infatuation) of Samson has not escaped the eyes of the lords of the Philistines. Not now a full frontal attack, but by guile, subterfuge and corruption they say to Delilah "learn the secret of his strength." Ever and always the enemy will seek to learn the secret of our strength, and by whatever means deprive us of it to render us powerless in the Master's service.

Samson's association with Delilah ultimately takes him back to Gaza, this time as a helpless prisoner. Notice carefully the sorry sequence of events and the effects of Delilah's influence upon Samson.

She Promised Pleasure – she swore that she loved him yet all the while she was driven by ulterior motives. For a moment of pleasure "his soul was vexed unto death" and for this disillusioned man it was a bitterly learnt lesson, which brought forth death.

She Produced Compromise – daily she pressed him to reveal his secret. Little by little she wore him down as she edged closer to his true character knowing that, sooner or later, she would rob him of his strength. Finally, he revealed the inner source of his strength and he lost his distinctive character and separation. What did she do? She put him to sleep so that a heathen barber could shave his head and the Philistines trample his hair underfoot. In Numbers 7 the Nazarite shaves his own head and burns the hair on the altar to God.

She Produced Spiritual Barrenness – Samson said, "I will go out as before", but he failed to realise that he was powerless and robbed of his spiritual strength. He was out of touch with God and failed to realise that

God had departed. He lost his vision and he lost his liberty. This strong man, bound with brass fetters, grinds in the prison house. The chains of sin bind and produce tedious servitude in which there is no pleasure.

Day 7

TOPPLING THE TEMPLE

Judges 16:23-31

Poor Samson, deprived of his strength by an ungodly barber and robbed of his vision by the searing irons, he spends his days in the remorseless task of grinding corn in the prison house. But we see the hand of God in blessing upon His servant "Howbeit, the hair of his head began to grow again after he was shaved." With God "all things are possible" and the pathway of recovery is freely available unto all of His children. See their disdain for this mighty man of God. The hand of a little boy led him into the house of their god for their amusement! I think of the Christ of God "brought as a lamb to the slaughter, and as a sheep before her shearers is dumb, so he openeth not his mouth" (Isa 53:7). Oh the disdain and contempt of ungodly men for our blessed Saviour!

Consider three features of Samson in this his most glorious triumph:

His Recovery – "his hair began to grow". Sometimes we are guilty of forming hasty judgements of fellow believers when they wander from the pathway. But God is ever gracious, and recovery will be brought about when a spiritual awakening takes place in the soul and restoration is established. God ever works in His own mysterious way.

His Supplication – "Lord, remember me". Here in true repentance and confession the wanderer casts himself at the throne of grace. His plea is not for deliverance, or for the mighty deeds of his past to be taken into account, but that God will show his loving kindness unto him. Haven't we just to cast ourselves at His feet and ask for His favour?

His Request – "Lord, strengthen me". There is no request for his own personal safety. Only in and by God's enabling power can he achieve God's glory and be avenged. For God's purposes he will lay down his own life! Beloved, how much would we be prepared to sacrifice for God's glory?

Our Saviour and Samson both triumphed gloriously in their death. Both died among wicked ones. Both were taken by friends and buried in a special place, Christ in a new tomb, Samson between Zorah and Eshtaol. This mighty man finished his race where he began it. Let us also strive to do likewise.

JOHN HALL

Week 11

7 ITEMS OF "THE WHOLE ARMOUR OF GOD"

Romans 13:12-14; 2 Corinthians 6:1-10; Ephesians 6:10-18

Introduction

Two types of armour are mentioned in the New Testament. The first is 'hoplon', a light armour once used for the protection of active warriors. They needed to balance the weight of protective armour against the ability to move easily as they took the fight to the enemy. The Hoplite warriors of 450 BC took their name from this type of armour, and were renowned for their fighting prowess. Of the six references to 'hoplon' in the NT, only two are translated as 'armour' – "the armour of light" (Rom 13:12), and "the armour of righteousness" (2 Cor 6:7). Another translation of 'hoplon' occurs in John 18:3, and again in 2 Cor 10:4, where the word "weapons" is used. In Romans 6:13 we read, "Neither yield ye your members as instruments of unrighteousness unto sin: but yield yourselves unto God, as those that are alive from the dead, and your members as instruments of righteousness unto God". The two mentions of "instruments" in this verse are uses of the word 'hoplon'. These six references together convey the thought of equipment that affords protection to the wearer whilst enabling the fight to be carried to the foe. (In the first reference to "instruments" in Romans 6:13 we have the awful thought that the believer can negligently turn his equipment against the very things he should be defending, and afford defensive cover to sin. 'Friendly fire' is not a new thing, and still inflicts real casualties!).

The second type of armour in the NT is the 'panoplia', a word made up from the prefix 'pan' meaning 'whole', or 'every', and our first word for armour, 'hoplon'. Thus we get a word that means 'every protection', or 'whole defence'. This is the word used in Ephesians 6:13. The only other mention of 'panoplia' in the NT is in Luke 11:22 where the Lord Jesus speaks figuratively of the work He would accomplish in stripping away every defence of the devil's domain. The 'panoplia' enabled a warrior to stand against a foe superior in armament and numbers. The whole armour of God enables the believer to stand with confidence before the assault (Eph 6:11), remain standing during the assault (6:13) and afterward be found unharmed, still standing, and ready for the next assault (6:13).

Day 1

TRUTH

Ephesians 6:10-20

The expression 'gird up your loins' is akin to the more modern term 'roll up your sleeves'. Both expressions carry the thought of preparation for imminent action and the necessity, therefore, to fasten out of the way any encumbrance that would impede movement. Peter uses it of the mind (1 Pet 1:13) as he exhorts his readers to right thinking and holy living as an outcome of the grace of God in their lives.

Paul was in prison as he wrote the letter to the Ephesians (Eph 3:1; 4:1) and chained to a Roman soldier (6:20). Though his guard would not have been in full battledress, he would have been wearing his belt, breastplate and boots, for those three items of armour were the minimum essential daily dress of the Roman soldier.

A properly fitting belt was as important to the soldier then as it is to the soldier of today. It gave strength to the back and lower body during an arduous march, and ensured correct posture when carrying heavy loads. The belt was essential for walking and working. Perhaps, as he wrote, Paul also had the words of David in mind: "Lord, who shall abide in thy tabernacle? who shall dwell in thy holy hill? He that walketh uprightly, and worketh righteousness, and speaketh the truth in his heart" (Ps 15:1-2). For the Christian, walking, working and truth are intimately connected and form the 'foundation garment' of defence against the adversary.

As we wrestle (v.12), the belt of truth needs to be tight. The heavy Japanese Sumo wrestler constantly seeks a purchase on his opponent's belt so that he can bring him crashing down, but if we are "girt about with truth" the adversary can never gain a hold because he "is a liar, and the father of it" and "there is no truth in him" (John 8:44).

Verse 14 has the seventh reference to truth in the Ephesian letter (another group of seven to study!) and expositors are divided as to whether the reference here is to 'truth' as an attribute, or to 'the truth' as that body of doctrine otherwise called "the faith which was once delivered unto the saints"

(Jude v.3). Whilst both ideas can be applied, perhaps the former better fits the passage. Of the Lord Jesus in His millennial power and glory, we read "And righteousness shall be the girdle of his loins, and faithfulness the girdle of his reins" (Isa 11:5). Practical and integral honesty, truthfulness and faithfulness should mark we who belong to Christ in all aspects of our walking and working. The adversary could obtain no hold on the Saviour for He is the embodiment of truth, and his opportunity to gain a hold on us to bring us down will be denied if we have our "loins girt about with truth".

Day 2

RIGHTEOUSNESS

Ephesians 6:10-20

It has been said that a breastplate leaves the warrior's back unprotected. The idea owes more to the imagination of dear John Bunyan in 'Pilgrim's Progress' than to military history, and a breastplate that only affords protection from frontal assault would be both insecure and futile. Just as the loins are "girt about", so the upper body with all its vital organs is fully protected by the encompassing breastplate.

Defence of the heart is paramount. We are familiar with such expressions as 'strong-hearted', 'lion-hearted', 'weak-hearted' and 'faint-hearted'. Linked with these terms are the thoughts of courage and morale. Military history abounds with accounts of well-equipped soldiers fleeing from the battlefield, not because they *couldn't* stand, but because they *wouldn't* stand. There is a great need for us to be courageous and of good morale as we face the assaults of the evil one. The OT counterpart to the Ephesian epistle is the book of Joshua. Both deal with the people of God going in to actively possess and enjoy that which God has brought them into positionally. Let the word of God to his servant Joshua stir our blood and strengthen our hearts! He said to him, "As I was with Moses, so I will be with thee: I will not fail thee, nor forsake thee. Be strong and of a good courage … Only be thou strong and very courageous … Be strong and of a good courage; be not afraid, neither be thou dismayed: for the Lord thy God is with thee whithersoever thou goest" (Josh 1:5,6,7,9).

The breastplate of the believer is righteousness, and just as we saw with 'truth' that it can be both legal and practical, so it is with righteousness. Our breastplate is not made up of practical righteousness alone, for we should then be sorely exposed. Its strength and constitution is the positional righteousness we have in the sight of God through the efficacy of the blood of Christ and our standing in Him in virtue of His finished work at Calvary. Bless God! Such a breastplate is impregnable. Confidently we exclaim "Who shall lay anything to the charge of God's elect?" (Rom 8:33).

But practical righteousness is not to be ignored. Unconfessed sin and broken communion with God leaves the heart dreadfully exposed. The breastplate can only protect the heart from without, and for that it is perfect, part of the "armour of God". Loss of morale and failure of courage come from within, and the breastplate affords no protection from those things.

It must be desperately humiliating for a well-equipped soldier to flee from the battlefield because he has no stomach for the fight. Is it because he no longer believes in the cause? Practical righteousness matters, dear saints, and will make us bold to face the foe.

Day 3

THE GOSPEL OF PEACE

Ephesians 6:10-20

Once again we have an expression which can be legitimately interpreted in two distinct, but complementary, ways. The illustration here is of the Roman 'caliga', the on-duty boot (rather than the off-duty sandal) of the Roman soldier. The leather 'caliga' was similar to a sandal in that the toes were open, but it was heavier, studded and securely tied at the ankle. Its main quality was that it was a multi-terrain boot that would not slip. If the believer is to "stand" in the evil day, how secure the footing must be!

The question arises as to whether the phrase "preparation of the gospel of peace" means the activity of declaring the gospel or, alternatively, the grounding that the gospel of peace gives to the believer. As with the first two items of armour, the answer lies not in one thought to the exclusion of the other, but in seeing that two distinct lines of truth can be complementary to each other. The scholars tell us that it is not possible to state categorically the grammatical sense of this expression. It truly can mean either of the two thoughts stated. We therefore embrace both ideas and see once again that 'positional truth' and 'practical truth' are firmly wedded together. From the 'positional' angle, the gospel of peace provides the perfect non-slip footing that the Christian needs. The noun form of the word 'preparation' or 'readiness' is found in the Greek version of the OT Scriptures in Ezra 3:3, "And they set the altar upon his bases". When an angel spoke to Zechariah the prophet about "an house in the land of Shinar", he said "it shall be established, and set there upon her own base" (Zech 5:11). The sense of the expression "feet shod with the preparation of the gospel of peace" can therefore be 'feet firmly set upon the base of the gospel of peace'. And how blessedly true this is! Furthermore, the fact that our feet are "shod", that is, 'firmly bound' to this base means that the footwear and the base are one and the same. We do not just stand upon the base, but are firmly bound to the base. The Christian warfare is founded upon the gospel of peace! We cannot be moved, we cannot slip, because "being justified by faith, we have peace with God through our Lord Jesus Christ" (Rom 5:1).

The complementary, practical, viewpoint is that the Christian must be active in declaring the gospel of peace. Standing still for too long induces numbness and weariness. Those on sentry-duty know to constantly flex their feet in their boots, and the Scripture states "How beautiful are the feet of them that preach the gospel of peace, and bring glad tidings of good things" (Rom 10:15).

Day 4

FAITH

Ephesians 6:10-20

The first three items of the armour of God, the belt, the breastplate and the boots, were items worn by the Roman soldier whenever he was on duty. Whether in the safety of homeland barracks, or on active duty on the front line, these items were standard daily dress. As Paul expands the subject of the Christian's defence in the evil day, he looks at those pieces of armour which are put on once the alarm is raised and enemy action is a real possibility. At the first call to readiness, all the routine work in the camp ceases abruptly. The soldier tightens his belt, checks that his breastplate is secure and adjusts his boot straps. Moving to his designated position, he takes up his defensive shield. There would be other, smaller, shields in the armoury, but the one he takes is the 'scutum', made of laminated wood, linen and hide, bound with iron at top and bottom and specially designed to protect him from the incendiary arrows of the enemy. It is the shield often seen in pictures of the famous 'tortoise' formation adopted by legions when under fierce attack.

Paul, chained to his Roman guard, would doubtless have heard many accounts of combat experienced by soldiers who had served in all parts of the vast Roman empire. Some of their opponents would have been exceptionally brave, others equally as cruel, still more very clever in their tactics. As the guards perhaps tried to outdo each other with their war stories, the mind of the godly apostle would turn to the combat of the Christian, and he would translate scenes of deadly conflict on earth to similar scenes in the spiritual realm.

Of all the missiles used against them, the one the Romans feared most was the cruel fire-arrow. Arrows dipped in pitch, lit, and fired into the orderly ranks could cause terrible wounds. There was only one defence, and that was the shield.

So Paul, guided by the Spirit, exhorts the Ephesians, "Above all, taking the shield of faith, wherewith ye shall be able to quench all the fiery darts of the wicked (one)" (6:16). "Above all" does not mean that the shield is more important than any other piece of armour, but that it should be taken 'besides all of these'. It is indispensable when the enemy is near. As the fiery darts of doubt, temptation, personal unworthiness, knowledge of weakness and failure come flying towards us, all can be immediately extinguished by the shield of faith. Faith lays hold of the *promises* of God in times of doubt and fear, and faith lays hold on the *power* of God in times of temptation. Faith casts us upon our God who "is a shield unto them that put their trust in him" (Prov 30:5).

Day 5

SALVATION

Ephesians 6:10-20

As the tension mounts and an attack becomes imminent, the final items of armour must be worn. Again, well-acquainted with Roman military procedure, Paul is deliberate in his use of words. The exhortations "take unto you the whole armour of God" (v.13) and "Above all, taking the shield of faith" (v.16) both use the same Greek word for 'take' which means 'to lay hold on'. We are to positively 'lay hold on' the whole armour of God and the shield of faith, the word having the same force as in the verse "Then the soldiers, as it was commanded them, *took* Paul, and brought him by night to Antipatris" (Acts 23:31). But when he comes to describe the helmet of salvation and the sword of the Spirit, Paul employs a different word for 'take', one that means 'to receive'. It is used in the verse "Wherefore lay apart all filthiness and superfluity of naughtiness, and *receive* with meekness the engrafted word, which is able to save your souls" (James 1:21), and again, in Acts 7:59, "And they stoned Stephen, calling upon God, and saying, Lord Jesus, *receive* my spirit".

The defensive formation is in place, and some of the soldiers have not seen action before. Each is standing with his helmet and sword at his feet. Perhaps the dust cloud raised by the approaching enemy is clearly visible, and unproven soldiers lick dry lips and swallow hard. With that, the experienced, battle-hardened centurion stands in front of each of his men in turn and, bending down, lifts the helmet and places it upon the soldier's head. Again, he lifts the sword and puts it into the man's hand. All the while he gives words of encouragement that straighten the soldier's back, lift his shoulders, and convince him that under the leadership of this centurion the battle is as good as won.

All around the Christian, the battle rages for control of the mind. Rationalism, humanism, evolutionism and a host of other godless philosophies will be presented as fact, especially to younger believers whose experience of spiritual combat is very limited. Added to that, unhelpful disputation over so-called 'Calvinism' and 'Arminianism' undermine the faith of some by convincing them that what they cannot rationalise cannot, therefore, be true. Salvation involves the sovereign electing purpose of God and, equally, the full responsibility of man to be obedient to the gospel of His grace. The helmet of salvation in all its fulness, past, present and future, is divinely designed to protect the mind and confidence of the believer (see 1 Thess 5:8).

We must receive, as from the Lord's hands, the helmet of salvation, but remember that the helmet, like the breastplate, can only protect from external assault. We are responsible for what we feed our minds upon. "Whatsoever things are true … think on these things" (Phil 4:8).

Day 6

THE SWORD OF THE SPIRIT

Ephesians 6:10-20

So far the noise and dust of approaching battle have been distant, but drawing ever closer. The soldier, fully-equipped, is finding that the discipline, training and experience of his united formation are more than adequate to face the foe. The volleys of missiles, even the dreaded fire-arrows, have caused no harm, and he realises with growing confidence that they are aimed at the whole of his unit, not personally at him. But now, as the wicked horde comes closer, he can see individual faces, hear individual yells and, suddenly, there is direct eye-contact with a warrior in full cry who is coming at *him*. He stands fast, confident that his feet will not slip, lifts the shield of faith to absorb the incoming blows and, with the enemy upon him, jabs firmly and accurately with his short sword to bring the foe crashing to the earth at his feet. Turning swiftly, he thrusts his sword into another assailant and, suddenly, it is all over! The enemy, demoralised and repulsed, is in full retreat, and the soldier, tired but triumphant, is standing ready should they return. The ensuing conversations in the camp can be imagined. Says one, "My equipment was perfect to keep me safe when the enemy approached, but it was the sword that saved my life when it got personal".

The sword that the Christian must skilfully wield is "the sword of the Spirit, which is the word of God". This is the ultimate close-quarters defence, and nothing else will suffice. The Lord Jesus Himself, when faced by the devil in the wilderness, could have dealt with His foe in many different ways. However, He used nothing but "the sword of the Spirit, which is the word of God". "It is written … it is written … it is written" He replied, and "then the devil leaveth him" (Matt 4:4,7,10,11).

Dear fellow saints, we must stand foursquare on the word of God. We must read it, learn it, memorise it, understand it, meditate upon it for, without that defence, we are in the gravest danger when the fight comes directly to us. The attack can be sudden and deadly, and the use of the sword must be instinctive and accurate. No time then for concordances or favourite daily reading notes. The Spirit of God Himself will bring to our immediate recall the necessary Scriptures for the occasion, just as He will for troubled saints in a day to come. "But when they shall lead you, and deliver you up, take no thought beforehand what ye shall speak, neither do ye premeditate: but whatsoever shall be given you in that hour, that speak ye: for it is not ye that speak, but the Holy Ghost" (Mark 13:11).

Day 7

PRAYER

Ephesians 6:10-20

The urgent battlefield message "Send reinforcements, we are going to advance" which became corrupted to "Send three-and-fourpence, we're going to a dance" is an old chestnut. It does exemplify the need, however, for reliable, accurate communication once battle is joined.

Prayer is the vital seventh item in the armour of God for the Christian, the means of the believer's communication with heaven. Is it true that most of us pray some of the time, in some ways, with varying degrees of perseverance, for some of the saints? Is it even possible that some dear believer reading this book hardly prays at all? Listen to the words of Scripture: "Praying *all* the time with *all* prayer and supplication in the Spirit, and watching thereunto with *all* perseverance and supplication for *all* saints" (v.18). Is this not a huge challenge to us in the manner, consistency, earnestness and breadth of our prayer life?

The soldier needs the facility of immediate, reliable contact with his commander, not only to seek help for himself, but so that he might also call down help for comrades who are hard pressed and under attack. Perhaps ours is a rather selfish prayer life, one in which we speak of our own needs and those of immediate family, but rarely mentioning others who sorely need our help. So often we do not pray for others because we are not "watching thereunto". Is this one reason why so many assembly prayer meetings are cold, sterile occasions with no real sense of the Lord's presence? Perhaps in eternity we shall learn the extent to which we were prayed for when here on earth. How many prayed for your salvation? How many have wept for you before the Lord during your Christian life? Do you pray and weep for others?

Every one of us is the object, collectively and individually, of satanic assault. We must look out for each other, for sometimes we walk carelessly and complacently, deceived by a lull in the battle into thinking that the enemy has given up the fight. Do you see that believer whose attendance at the meetings has become sporadic? Have you been criticising them, or praying for them? That young brother who is being drawn into the orbit of a godless world, do you pray earnestly for him? The young sister who is responding to the courtship of an unsaved boy, is she the subject of your earnest, heartfelt supplication? Beloved saints, these things are real. They are today's issues, and the battlefield of Christian witness is strewn with injured, disoriented and frightened saints who desperately need help. "Continue in prayer, and watch in the same with thanksgiving" (Col 4:2).

PHIL COULSON

Week 12

7 ARROGANT QUESTIONS IN MALACHI

Introduction

Malachi is the last of the Old Testament prophets to speak, and whilst the exact date of writing is not known, it is after the rebuilding of the temple. The original temple, built by Solomon, had been destroyed when Nebuchadnezzar came from Babylon and took the southern kingdom of Judah into captivity. The date is therefore after the prophecies of Haggai and Zechariah for, in Haggai chapter 1, the temple was still in ruins. Both Haggai and Zechariah are precisely dated 520 BC.

What an encouragement it is to know that the Lord has His 'messenger' in every generation. Nothing is known about the man Malachi whose name simply means 'My messenger'. But what a message he had! Whilst the message was addressed to Israel (1:1), yet there is still a message for us today.

It is interesting to see that Malachi, 'the Lord's messenger', speaks of three other messengers in the book:

The Priests – they should have been messengers, but had failed (2:7).

John the Baptist – the one to prepare the way for "The Messenger" (3:1).

Jesus Christ – "the messenger of the covenant" (3:1). "He shall not fail".

When God speaks through His messenger there is a responsibility for the recipients to hear and obey. Sadly, when the Lord speaks to the returned exiles of the captivity, they will challenge what He says about them. Outwardly, they professed to serve God, love God, and worship God, but the Lord knew their true state and had to speak through Malachi, His messenger, unto them.

In seven of the challenges the Lord makes in the prophecy, the response is the same: "ye say, wherefore …? wherein …? what …?" Here was a people prepared to contradict what the Lord said, justify themselves in what they did, and ask for proof and evidence from the Lord for what He said about them.

How fittingly the prophecy closes, looking ahead to the second advent of Christ, when He returns to earth to set up His kingdom of universal reign. "And the loftiness of man shall be bowed down, and the haughtiness of men shall be made low: and the LORD alone shall be exalted in that day" (Isa 2: 17). In that day, what "The Messenger" says will be done. May we be helped now to hear and obey "The Messenger".

Day 1

THE LOVE OF GOD CHALLENGED

Malachi 1:1-5

"I have loved you, saith the LORD. Yet ye say, Wherein hast thou loved us? (1:2). This first of our seven statements is very delightful, in that the God who never changes, whose love never wanes, and whose faithfulness is unchangeable, reminds an indifferent, erring and changeable nation of that very fact. How faithful our God is! Just as Jeremiah wrote, we can each say "His compassions fail not. They are new every morning: great is thy faithfulness" (Lam 3:22-23).

The whole of the nation's history over the two millennia, starting with the call of Abraham (Genesis 12), right up to this point, had been characterised by 'highs' and 'lows'. There were times when they went on well with God, obeying, trusting, and loving Him: however there were also times of disobedience, doubt, and little love. One would wonder why God should want to love them when recalling such things as their unbelief in the wilderness, and their idolatry in the land. To such a people, however, God will say, as He had already said "The LORD did not set his love upon you, nor choose you, because ye were more in number than any people; for ye were the fewest of all people: But because the LORD loved you" (Deut 7:7-8).

The nation of Israel had been loved from the beginning, right from childhood: "When Israel was a child, then I loved him, and called my son out of Egypt' (Hos 11:1). How this should have touched the people now, all these years later. Sadly, the love of God is challenged by their response, "Wherein hast thou loved us?"

Perhaps the people were thinking of that barren, empty, wasted period of captivity in Babylon that had lasted for some seventy years, just a century and a half previous. God had never ceased to love them, in fact He took them through that experience because He loved them: "For whom the LORD loveth he correcteth; even as a father the son in whom he delighteth" (Prov

3:12). When the going is rough and steep for us, do we challenge the love of God, or do we recognise that "no chastening for the present seemeth to be joyous, but grievous: nevertheless afterward it yieldeth the peaceable fruit of righteousness unto them which are exercised thereby" (Heb 12:11).

What a privilege it is to be one of those who are loved of God in a very special way. It is true that the love of God is to the world, as John 3:16 reminds us. God now shows, however, that the one who is in fellowship with Him has all the blessings of God upon Him. Others will observe it, and acknowledge it. What a God is ours! What love He has shown!

Day 2

A RELATIONSHIP THAT DEMANDS RESPECT

Malachi 1:6; 2:1-9

"If then I be a father, where is mine honour? and if I be a master, where is my fear? saith the LORD of hosts unto you, O priests, that despise my name. And ye say, Wherein have we despised thy name?" (1:6).

We are here faced with a challenge. If God has so loved us, as He has; if God is our Father, as He is to those who are His children; if God is Sovereign, Lord and Master of us, as He should be – where is His honour? Where is His glory? Where is His fear? Where is His reverence?

This statement is addressed to the priests, who would have had the respect and honour from the people they served. What a sad position for them to be in as the recipients of reverence, and yet not to show due reverence to God whom they claimed to serve. The service the priests had, (they were the closest of all in the holy things) and the example they gave as leaders, would have impacted upon the whole nation. Each of us, whether we be servants or leaders, are all children of fathers, and by natural instinct show to them respect and submission. The Hebrew epistle exhorts us "furthermore we have had fathers of our flesh, which corrected us, and we gave them reverence: shall we not much rather be in subjection unto the Father of spirits, and live?" (Heb 12:9).

An appreciation of who God is, is vital to ensure that God has the respect and reverence that is due unto Him. The psalmist says, "God is greatly to be feared in the assembly of the saints, and to be had in reverence of all them that are about him" (Ps 89:7).

The prophet Isaiah speaks concerning the seraphim. As far as their speech is concerned, they cry in the presence of God "Holy, holy, holy, is the LORD of hosts: the whole earth is full of his glory" (Isa 6:3). As far as the deportment of the seraphim is concerned, they use four of their six wings to cover themselves in the presence of the Almighty (Isa 6:2).

The words that are said of Ruth as she entered into the presence of Boaz are delightful, and how pleasing to God it would be if we could follow her example: "she came softly" (Ruth 3:7). The Shunammite, so blessed by the servant of God, Elisha, "went in, and fell at his feet, and bowed herself to the ground" (2 Kings 4:37). May God so help us to have this same kind of submission, reverence, and respect as each of these women had, and may God help us not to get so 'over familiar' that we fail to give to God His rightful place. What a relationship we have to enjoy! Let us enjoy it, and still reverent and respectful be.

Day 3

THE LORD MUST HAVE THE BEST

Malachi 1:7-14

"Ye offer polluted bread upon mine altar; and ye say, Wherein have we polluted thee? In that ye say, The table of the LORD is contemptible" (1:7).

The priests whose duty it was to offer the sacrifices should have known the principles that God had laid out in the pentateuch regarding the requirements of the offerings brought for sacrifice (Lev 22:20-24; Deut 15:21, 17:1).

It is sad to think that those who should have known the requirements of a Holy God claimed not to know of their own failure, and be ready rather to justify themselves. God rightly sets high standards for His people to follow in their approach to Him, especially when it comes to worship, and only the best will do.

This principle is brought out by four questions that the Lord asks in verse 8. The answers should have been clear and obvious. It was evil to offer blind, lame and sick animals, and a governor on earth would not be presented with such. If he were, he would not accept such polluted things. The Lord is above the most notable of men: we should not therefore offer Him second best.

The Lord challenges the people further. He tells them that it would be better to bring nothing to the Lord, neither light the fire on the altar, because as long as their hands were bringing polluted things, the Lord would neither accept their sacrifice, nor be pleased with them. What a challenge for us as believers, all priests, that we are "an holy priesthood, to offer up spiritual sacrifices, acceptable to God by Jesus Christ" (1 Pet 2:5).

Scripture teaches us that there are times when things need to be put right with others, with ourselves, and with the Lord, before we are fit to function as "an holy priesthood". For example, "first be reconciled to thy brother, and then come and offer thy gift" (Matt 5:24). As to ourselves, prior to gathering for the 'breaking of bread', "let a man examine himself" (1 Cor 11:28).

If in Malachi's day there was little for God, verse 11 of our chapter looks forward to a day when the Lord will receive what is rightfully His. This worship will not be restricted to Israel, but will be from the whole world from the sunrise to sunset. The work of preaching the gospel of the grace of God in the entire world has brought saved sinners, as true worshippers (John 4:23).

There is, however, a future aspect when, in the thousand year reign of Christ, when Israel as a nation will be restored and brought back to their land, literal sacrifices will be brought again into the temple. "The Lord alone shall be exalted in that day" (Isa 2:11, 17), and worship will flow out from Jerusalem yet again.

Day 4

A LACK OF SPIRITUAL DISCERNMENT

Malachi 2:17 - 3:6

"Ye have wearied the LORD with your words. Yet ye say, Wherein have we wearied him? When ye say, Every one that doeth evil is good in the sight of the LORD, and he delighteth in them; or, Where is the God of judgement?" (2:17).

The coming of 'the messenger of the Lord' is the great antidote to the conditions of moral laxity in the earlier section, verses 10 to 16. There are two specific sins that God addresses through His messenger Malachi in the former portion. First, there was the sin of intermarrying with the idolatrous nations round them, something strictly forbidden by God (Deut 7:3-6); second, there was the sin of putting away their wives, which thing the Lord hates (2:16).

In the marriage state, God makes two into one (2:15), and Scripture teaches plainly "they twain shall be one flesh: so then they are no more twain, but one flesh. What therefore God hath joined together, let not man put asunder" (Mark 10:8-9). Two practical things to observe: only death breaks a marriage bond, and the Christian is only to marry "in the Lord" (1 Cor 7:39).

In days of spiritual blindness and indifference, like those when Malachi was speaking, the people had failed to remember the importance of these things, and had thus brought dishonour to the Lord. How solemn to remember how exposed we are to danger if we are away from the Lord. Our spiritual discernment is no longer sharp, but dull, and evil is seen as good. We may even think that God approves because He hasn't acted in judgement.

Peter, in his second epistle speaks of the scoffers who would, in effect, say the same words: "Where is the God of judgement?". Peter reminds them that the Lord will judge, just like He had in the past when he brought a flood on the world of the ungodly. So He will judge in the future, this time by fire. The fact that the judgement has not fallen yet is a demonstration that God "is longsuffering to us-ward, not willing that any should perish, but that all should come to repentance" (2 Pet 3:9).

Two messengers are presented in Malachi chapter 3: the first is John the Baptist, and the second is Christ. The first messenger was also foretold by Isaiah in Chapter 40:4. Both of these Scriptures tell of the work of John the Baptist in preparing the way for 'The Messenger', Christ Himself. John preached repentance, and expected to see evidence of repentance by changed lives.

The reference to the messenger "suddenly coming to his temple" is yet future. The descriptions given in verses 2 and 3 of what the messenger will do show that it is not His first coming for salvation in view, but rather His second coming when He will judge. May we now live so close to Him, that we rightly discern between what is right and wrong, and go in for that which pleases Him.

Day 5

BLESSINGS FOR THE REPENTANT

Malachi 2:10-16; 3:6-7

"Even from the days of your fathers ye are gone away from mine ordinances, and have not kept them. Return unto me, and I will return unto you, saith the LORD of hosts. But ye said, Wherein shall we return?" (3:7).

The heart of man from one generation to the next never changes. "The heart is deceitful above all things, and desperately wicked: who can know it?" (Jer 17:9). The Lord reminds the wayward people of Malachi's day that they were just like their forefathers. In fact, from the day they left Egypt, they had been a rebellious people (Deut 9:7-21). How true were the words of Moses to the Israelites before they went into the land of Canaan, "after my death ye will utterly corrupt yourselves, and turn aside from the way which I have commanded you" (Deut 31:29).

How comforting to know that the Lord has not, does not, and will not change. His holiness, righteousness, and justice will never be compromised, His promises will never fail, and His mercy, compassion, love and grace are ever stretched out to the returning sinner or saint.

Malachi, the messenger, has spoken, and will yet speak to the nation regarding things that were wrong and needed to be put right. What an encouragement to come back, knowing that when they returned and repented, the Lord would turn to them. Regrettably, the low spiritual and moral state of the nation was such that they were like the generation spoken of in Proverbs 30:12, "There is a generation that are pure in their own eyes, and yet is not washed from their filthiness". The generation of Malachi's day was not going to be the last generation like this either, for when our Lord was here there were the religious groups who thought they were righteous and had no need of repentance (Luke 15:7).

There is the blessing of forgiveness, cleansing, salvation, peace and so much more besides for the returning repentant sinner. Similarly, there are innumerable blessings for the returning saint. May God save us from saying "Wherein shall we return?" Both the unrepentant sinner and the erring saint are away from God and, therefore, until the Spirit of God does His own gracious work, there will not be a right appreciation of God. When we think rightly of God, then we think rightly about holiness, and rightly about sin. Our response then should be, "We must return".

In a world where sin is so rampant and no longer seen to be sinful in the eyes of the ungodly, it is easy for the believer to become complacent. The believer must always remember that, whilst in the world, he is not of the world. May the words of Jeremiah so challenge and exhort us, 'let us search and try our ways, and turn again to the LORD" (Lam 3:40).

WILL A MAN ROB GOD?

Malachi 3:8-12

"Will a man rob God? Yet ye have robbed me. But ye say, Wherein have we robbed thee? In tithes and offerings" (3:8).

The nation is now charged with robbing God on two counts: first, in material things, the tithe: second, in spiritual things, their offerings unto the Lord.

As far as the tribe of Levi was concerned, they had no inheritance in the land; the Lord was their inheritance (Num 18:20; Deut 18:2). The portion of the Levites was therefore the tithe from the rest of the tribes (Num 18:24). By their failure to offer the tithe, they had kept back from the Levites (the priestly tribe) what was due to them.

The book of the Acts records for us the early days of the New Testament assembly. How delightful it was when the Spirit of God at work brought souls to repentance and faith in Christ, and all shared what they had together (Acts 2:44, 4:32). If only we could recognise in a very materialistic day, that all that we have is God-given. As the psalmist appreciated, "for every beast of the forest is mine, and the cattle upon a thousand hills" (Ps 50:10). An important principle set before us here, is that how we deal with one another is actually how we deal with God. The Lord Jesus said "Inasmuch as ye have done it unto one of the least of these my brethren, ye have done it unto me" (Matt 25:40).

So what about our giving today? We have no instruction for believers relative to the giving of tithes, but we do have very practical instructions regarding the giving of material things in 1 Corinthians 16:2-3. Remember that "God loveth a cheerful giver" (2 Cor 9:7).

Turning to their offering of sacrifices, Malachi has already challenged the people because they brought torn, lame and sick animals (1:13). Now we learn that God had been robbed of that which was rightfully His – worship from His own. Worship is homage rendered to God by His own for who He is, and what He has done. Scripture teaches that worship is costly, involving preparation; it requires our time meditating in the word of God, and it will necessitate sacrifice. Is He not worth it? Of course He is, and worthy of far more besides.

All that turn back to the Lord would witness Him "open the windows of heaven, and pour out a blessing, that there shall not be room enough to receive it" (3:10). The next part of the prophecy is yet future, and points to the thousand year reign of Christ, when Israel will indeed be a "delightsome land". Believers will share in that administration "with Christ".

Day 7

LOATHSOME WORDS OR WHOLESOME WORDS?

Malachi 3:13 - 4:6

"Your words have been stout against me, saith the LORD. Yet ye say, What have we spoken so much against thee?" (3:13).

In this final challenge, the Lord exposes the error of their speech. In their departure from the things of God, not only had their walk been affected, but also their talk had become affected too.

The six things the Israelites said can be linked together in three groups of two. The first and last, the second and fifth, and the third and fourth. First they said, "It is vain to serve God". Last, they said, "they that tempt God are even delivered". Serving God was, to them, empty and worthless when they saw those around them being delivered who tempted God. In the second pair of statements they said "what profit is it that we have kept his ordinance", and "they that work wickedness are set up". Finally they said, "we have walked mournfully before the LORD of hosts", and "we call the proud happy". What's the point of being mournful, when those that boast in their pride are happy?

In each of these groups of statements, the Israelites may have been thinking of what they had been through in the seventy years of captivity in Babylon. Now they had returned, and they may have thought they were no better off. In fact, when they looked at the heathen around them, they felt worse off. The problem was, their return back to the land was not with the right state of mind and heart. Their service may have been right, but with the wrong motive. Their following of ordinances was right but, again, may not have been with the right motives. When our Lord was here on earth, he had to say to those of His day, "this people draweth nigh unto me with their mouth, and honoureth me with their lips; but their heart is far from me" (Matt 15:8).

In great contrast to this group, there was another group of a completely different kind, which feared the Lord. The psalmist says, "the fear of the LORD is the beginning of wisdom" (Ps 111:10). This faithful remnant would strengthen their faith, deepen their fellowship, and exhort and encourage each other by speaking often one to another concerning Him. Are our mouths and hearts full of wholesome words like these?

DAVID DALTON

Week 13

7 THINGS TO "CONSIDER" IN THE NEW TESTAMENT

Introduction

God would have us consider certain things in His word, for there are lessons which He wishes to teach us. As we reflect on the seven calls to 'consider' in the NT, we note that while the list is not exhaustive, it is very instructive. The first simple lesson we learn when considering the particular subjects brought before us by the Spirit of God is the importance of the practise of meditation. Surely the psalmist appreciated this, for how often he exhorts his readers by using the little word 'selah', that is, 'pause and consider'. It seems today that we are all living our lives in the fast lane with hardly time to draw breath. Ever increasing demands are being made upon what precious little time we have to spare. Let us move into the crawler lane, listen for the voice of God and learn what He wants us to know today.

Then, I note the variety of illustrations God uses in order to bring these subjects into relief. He will place before our heart's gaze creation, saintly men and the Lord Himself. These serve to edify (build us up), exhort (stir us up) and encourage (cheer us up). How wise is our God!

Although the word 'consider' is used in each of our references in the AV, five different words are employed in the original Greek text. The words are similar but have distinct shades of meaning which, when taken together, convey to us fully what God is asking us to do.

1. Take careful note of the lilies and thoroughly learn from them. This is no mere casual glance, but we are to think about what we are looking at.

2. The most used Greek word simply means to observe fully, that is, look from every angle, for each different view helps complete the picture. Whether we look at the ravens, the sufferings of the Lord Jesus, or the experiences of others.

3. Then we are asked to engage our mental faculty so that we can fully comprehend the truth of God. Sadly, many of us have become adept at merely feigning interest, whether we are reading or listening to the word of God, so it should not surprise us if we derive little benefit from our reading.

4. In relation to Melchisedec we are exhorted to be a spectator, thus ensuring that we do not miss any of the action.

5. Finally, we are to contemplate the sufferings of the Lord Jesus and estimate what those sufferings mean for us.

Let us take time today to consider those things that God says are worthy of our consideration.

Day 1

CONSIDER THE LILIES

Matthew 6:28

It would seem that when the Lord Jesus was here, men and women were concerned about what they wore and when their present clothes would have to be replaced. Many people in the world today would still be over-anxious about these things, yet many of us have enough and to spare and can discard clothes which we have hardly worn. Is there a lesson therefore in these verses for us? Certainly there is, for two characteristics mark the lily: its whiteness and its trumpet shape. The first would remind us of purity and innocence, and the second of praise. So the Lord shows how these lilies brought praise and glory to God. What a challenge to your heart and mine!

Let us think of the growth and beauty of the lilies. The lily neither toils nor spins, that is, either in the field or the home it has nothing to do but depend completely on God to clothe it. This simple lesson teaches us something of the care and compassion of our God. He truly is a faithful creator and is concerned about every aspect of His creation, for all was created by Him and for Him.

The Lord then contrasts the beauty of the lilies with the glory of Solomon who, despite his vast wealth and great wisdom, was not arrayed like them. This would teach us that there are beauties even in the simple things of life if we would take time to consider them. What beauty is seen in the life of a humble saint who simply depends on the Lord to supply his every need, and what glory is brought to God by that life.

We as believers are just like lilies, and ought to live so as to bring glory to our God. The Lord asks us to consider the lilies of the field, whereas Solomon in his Song reminds us that they also grow in the garden and in the valleys. Thus we are challenged as to the testimony we bear before the world and in the assembly, but what of the lily of the valley? Many a saint has passed through the valley, and the experience only served to make them more like their blessed Lord. The fragrance of their life impressed all who met them.

May we challenge our hearts for, if God so clothes the lilies that are only here for a short time, are we not assured that He will supply our need today and every day until the Lord comes to gather His lilies?

CONSIDER THE RAVENS

Luke 12:24

Today we will consider the ravens as the Lord so requested. There are three main passages in the Scriptures that call our attention to these birds. In Genesis 8 we learn what they feed on, in 1 Kings 17 we learn that they are used by God to feed others, and in Luke 12 we learn who feeds them.

Forty days after the ark rested on Mount Ararat, Noah sent forth a raven which went to and fro until the waters were dried up, happy to feed upon rotten, decaying flesh. But when the dove was sent forth, it found no place for the sole of its foot, and it returned to wait until new life appeared and God, in His goodness, provided food.

The challenge comes to you and me as to what we feed on. Sadly, some of God's people have scavenger minds which feed on the flesh, especially the sins and follies of others. Oh may God give us grace to feed on the person of the Lord Jesus Christ until His lovely features manifest themselves in our lives!

Elijah learned a different lesson, for even though God's people were disobedient, the ravens would respond to the command of God. They not only brought Elijah flesh, but bread as well. These birds were used by God to sustain His servant in his hour of need.

So many of God's people have problems today: "some are sick and some are sad and some have lost the love they had". Let us pray that we may be used by God to help someone on the pathway home to heaven.

In Job 38:41 God asks the question, "who provideth for the raven his food? when his young ones cry unto God …". It is lovely to think that because the young ravens know their God is a faithful creator who will meet their every need, they cry to Him. The Lord confirms this when He points out that the ravens do not work to provide food today, neither do they store up food against the winter, for they know that God will meet their need daily both in summer and winter. For whether the days are warm and balmy or cold and dark, God's goodness is unfailing.

The apostle Paul also appreciated this, for he wrote to the Philippian believers, "But my God shall supply all your need according to His riches in glory by Christ Jesus" (Phil 4:19). May our hearts be lifted up with the words of the old hymn:

> The raven He feedeth, then why should I fear,
>   To the heart of the Father His children are dear,
> So if the way darkens and clouds gather o'er,
>   I'll simply look upward and trust Him the more.

Day 3

CONSIDER WHAT I SAY

2 Timothy 2:7

In this second personal letter of Paul to his young friend Timothy, the apostle charges him in regard to the faith. Paul says, "consider what I say", not simply because he said it, but because what he spake with apostolic authority was the divinely inspired word of God. The authority of apostolic teaching was absolute. We therefore do well to take heed to this exhortation also. We should regularly and consistently read the word of God because the Lord Jesus Himself said, "man shall not live by bread alone, but by every word that proceedeth out of the mouth of God" (Matt 4:4).

Just as bread is essential to our physical well being, so God's word is essential to our spiritual well being. Job takes up a similar note when he says, "I have esteemed the words of his mouth more than my necessary food" (Job 23:12). It seems that Job could miss a meal, but not the word of God. I wonder how we fare in regard to this spiritual barometer? Most of us have three square meals a day, and perhaps snacks in between, yet it is possible to go from Sunday to Sunday without recourse to the Word. Surely 'seven days' without food makes 'one weak', so let us read and meditate on God's Word that our souls maybe satisfied.

But Paul's exhortation goes further and he emphasizes two particular issues in regard to the word of God. First, it has to be preserved, for he says "the same commit thou to faithful men" (2 Tim 2:2). We know that the Word is under Satanic attack from many quarters. It is therefore paramount that we defend it, for the Lord says, "Heaven and earth shall pass away, but my words shall not pass away" (Matt 24:35). So let us see to it that we preserve the Word without alteration or adulteration, for it is as unchanging as God Himself and needs neither updating nor modifying.

Second, the teaching of God's word has to be passed on to the generation following. So, parents, Sunday school teachers and youth leaders, make sure you are clearly focused as to your obligations before God. Other topics may interest your charges more, but they are of secondary importance. Elders I also exhort, being an elder myself, make sure the flock is being properly fed on the good wholesome food of the Word.

Paul goes on to say that to do this will take the endurance of the soldier, the energy of the athlete and the effort of the husbandman, but it will be worth the effort.

Day 4

CONSIDER THE APOSTLE AND HIGH PRIEST OF

OUR PROFESSION, CHRIST JESUS

Hebrews 3:1

In this call to 'consider', the Lord Jesus Christ is presented to us in a two-fold way – as Apostle and as High Priest. Both views are very precious. As the Apostle He has come from God to redeem us, and as the High Priest He has gone in to God to represent us. Moses was an apostle in the same way, one sent forth to redeem, and here he is contrasted with the Lord Jesus. The thought is that Moses was a faithful servant in relation to the tabernacle, God's house in the wilderness. He received instruction directly from God and saw to it that everything was done "according to the pattern showed to thee in the mount" (Heb 8:5). The outcome of his obedient service was that "the glory of the Lord filled the tabernacle" (Exod 40:34). But this man, the Lord Jesus, is counted worthy of more glory in that He was not only a faithful servant in the house, but also the obedient Son over His own house. What a contrast!

The faithfulness of the Lord is seen in His suffering when He came to earth from heaven, and also in that He is able to succour now that He has gone from earth back to heaven.

Let us consider His being sent into this world. He came with a commission from God. There was nothing attractive about the place to which He came for it was cursed by the fall. Neither was there anything attractive about the people, for they were dwellers in darkness and happy to stay in that condition. Nevertheless He came to do the will of Him that sent Him. He had very little to encourage Him while He was here for He was constantly scrutinized by men to see if they could find a flaw in His perfect character. They failed, but never gave up until at last they nailed Him to a tree just like a common criminal. To any of us, such treatment would have at best irritated us and, at worst, caused us to 'throw in the towel'. But Isaiah says of Him "He shall not fail nor be discouraged, till He hath set judgment in the earth: and the isles shall wait for his law" (Isa 42:4). The word 'discouraged' carries the thought 'to crack in pieces under pressure'. If He was anything less than God, that is exactly what would have happened, so intense was the pressure brought to bear upon Him. Yet even when forsaken by God He could say, "But thou art holy … but I am a worm" (Ps 22:3,6).

As we think of where He now is, we confess that the pathway He trod so faithfully has fitted Him for the work He now does, representing His people in their weakness before God. "For in that he himself hath suffered being tempted, he is able to succour them that are tempted" (Heb 2:18). We should give thanks today for the presence in heaven of a glorified man who is a faithful and merciful High Priest, one who can be "touched with the feeling of our infirmities" (Heb 4:15).

Day 5

CONSIDER HOW GREAT THIS MAN

Hebrews 7:4

The man mentioned in this verse is Melchisedec who first appears but briefly on the page of holy Scripture (Gen 14:18-20). The reason he is called 'great' is because his life is a lovely picture of the Lord Jesus Christ.

Melchisedec's greatness is seen in two ways; the greatness of his position and the greatness of his priesthood. In the first we have a beautiful picture of the Lord Jesus in all His millennial glory, for he is a King Priest. We note that he was King of righteousness then King of Salem (peace) (Heb 7:2). The order is important for it reveals that his kingdom was ruled in righteousness with no injustice, inequality, unfairness, prejudice or partiality. Peace was the result. How different from our world today!

Melchisedec was also priest of the most high God, for in him was conferred both religious and political power. He not only ruled his people righteously but he did so for the glory and honour of the only true God. Surely this would remind all our hearts of the millennial reign of our Lord Jesus, for God has decreed "Yet have I set my king upon my holy hill of Zion" (Ps 2:6).

We see one more point in this context, that there is no record of Melchisedec's birth or death, or his parents, for these have no relevance to his position. In this way he is made like unto the eternal, uncreated, Son of God.

The greatness of the Melchisedec priesthood is seen in his priesthood being untransferable. Here again he is but a picture of the Lord Jesus of whom it is said, "Thou art a priest for ever after the order of Melchisedec" (Heb 7:17). The Lord is the great High Priest who can neither die nor sin nor fail. How encouraging it is for us to know that we come to one who "ever liveth to make intercession…" (7:25).

We also note that every priest of old had to offer "first for his own sins, and then for the people's" (7:27), but how much better is our High Priest. He could not sin Himself, neither does He need to continually offer sacrifice for the sins of others. This He did once and for all when He offered Himself in all the sinlessness of His being.

Finally we thank God that our great High Priest has neither infirmity nor weakness, and is not marked by failure. "Let us therefore come boldly unto the throne of grace, that we may obtain mercy, and find grace to help in time of need" (Heb 4:16).

Day 6

CONSIDER ONE ANOTHER

Hebrews 10:24

To consider one another is one of three exhortations in this chapter. The writer has already exhorted his readers to draw near to God (v.22) and to keep the faith (v.23), but now he says, "consider one another". How timely and relevant these are, but we only concern ourselves with the last of them.

In a day of selfishness and self-centeredness how needful it is to be reminded of our responsibilities towards each other. We all have cares and worries that burden us, but let us take time today to think on other members of the family of God of which we are a part. Everyone has similar problems to our own, and what blessing can be enjoyed when we share one another's burdens.

Are there not times in all our lives when we wish the good Samaritan would come our way, binding up our wounds and lifting us up to help us along the way? There always seems to be plenty of priests and Levites who at best spare us a glance but then pass us by without so much as a word.

Perhaps a dear saint is struggling to keep their head above the water, and the Lord is giving us the opportunity to take this exhortation from the text book and put it into practical effect. If this is the case, how many of us will come through the test with flying colours?

But we not only have to think about others, good though that is, we must also provoke them unto love and good works. Sadly, most of us read our Bibles carelessly and therefore stop after the word 'provoke'. We have become experts at this in a negative sense. We can provoke ill feeling, anger, discouragement, discontentment and resentment, all of which only serve to cause strife and unrest where there ought to be harmony and peace.

The writer is thinking here of something more positive, and that is to provoke unto love and good works. True love is seldom made manifest in our world of hate and wickedness, but surely the one place where it should be seen is amongst the people of God. The Lord Himself says that our love one for another proves to the world that we are His disciples, and what a challenge that should be to all our hearts. Love must be displayed, so good works must accompany our profession of love, otherwise our profession is just empty words.

Can the world recognize that we serve the Lord Jesus Christ today by our obvious love for each other? Let us all consider others today.

Day 7

CONSIDER HIM

Hebrews 12:3

In this chapter the believer is seen as a runner in a long distance relay race. Others have passed the baton to us having run their race and we are left to take up the challenge. How we can complete our course is described in verse 1 where we have to discard anything that would be a hindrance to us. Also, we must not take any illegal short cuts which would mean disqualification. We must be marked by endurance and not be put off at the first hurdle or difficulty that comes our way. There have been many illustrious competitors who have run ever so well, and we are encouraged as we read about some of their exploits in the previous chapter. But the Spirit of God turns our attention to the greatest Competitor of all and focuses our attention on Him. Jesus, the captain and perfecter of our faith, is the one who ran the perfect race from start to finish. He never flagged for a moment, neither did He allow Himself to be distracted even momentarily. He knew full well the rigours and trials to be faced before He would breast the tape with that triumphant cry, "It is finished". What opposition He faced, and yet what joy filled His heart for He was doing the Father's will. His race has been run and the prize has been won, therefore He has taken His place at the right hand of God.

The great athletes of our day who run for their country in the Olympic Games study the form and technique of previous winners. From them they draw inspiration in the hope that they will reproduce their form and achievements in their own events. How often have we seen one of these athletes standing upon the winner's rostrum, the gold medal about the neck, tears glistening in their eyes, as the flag of their country is raised and their national anthem is played in honour of their achievement.

So the writer exhorts us to look away from everyone else and derive our inspiration from Jesus alone. We are to consider the dedication and determination that marked Him as He ran, and that enabled Him to say with complete confidence, "I have glorified thee on the earth: I have finished the work which thou gavest me to do" (John 17:4).

So let us run, for one day we will hear heaven's national anthem ring in our ears, "Unto him that loved us, and washed us from our sins in his own blood, and hath made us kings and priests unto God and his Father; to him be glory and dominion for ever and ever. Amen." (Rev 1:5-6).

IAN AFFLECK

Week 14

7 CREATION DAYS

Genesis 1:1-31; 2:1-3

Introduction

The Bible begins with a statement of fact: "In the beginning, God created the heavens and the earth" (Gen 1:1). There was a time in our world's history when this fact was accepted by men, but now they have become "fools" (Rom 1:22). Man's current theories about the commencement and development of life on earth are underpinned by moral, not scientific, reasons. No matter how impossible and irrational 'big bang' and 'evolution' theories are, sinners accept them to justify their lifestyle. (Rom 1:22-32)

Genesis chapter 1 reveals the God of creation and not the creation of God. Man seeks information about physics, chemistry, geology, astronomy, biology and anatomy. God hides His knowledge from us and instead reveals Himself in His work. Creation, rightly understood, will lead us to a deeper appreciation of God.

The plain account of the text is that God created the heavens and the earth, without pre-existing material, in a week of literal days. These days are marked off by the expression "the evening and the morning".

Creation was instantaneous – "And God said … and it was so". There is no allowance for the idea that God started the universe and then allowed it to evolve over millions of years.

The universe was created mature, with an appearance of age. When God created a tree, He did not plant a seed and wait over a period of years for it to grow and produce fruit. It was created a "fruit tree yielding fruit". The sun and moon were created to "give light upon the earth". Adam may have concluded that the sun had existed for millions of years, when in fact it was only two days older than himself!

When God surveyed His work, He saw "that it was good". Man is unable to produce such a work. His limitations lead him to believe he is observing a world that has evolved from primitive beginnings into something better. In fact, he is observing a creation that was perfect in its beginning and has been in decline since Adam introduced sin and death into the world.

"Thou art worthy, O Lord, to receive glory and honour and power: for thou hast created all things, and for thy pleasure they are and were created." (Rev 4:11).

Day 1

CREATION DAY ONE

Genesis 1:1-5

The opening verse of Genesis gives an overview of God's creative act. The Hebrew language is able to express singular, dual and plural terms. We can therefore understand that verse 1 teaches that God (plural) created the heavens (dual) and the earth (singular). Paul reveals that there is a third heaven (2 Cor 12:2). If only two heavens were created, then the third heaven must be the uncreated and eternal abode of God. It is from this eternal abode that God spoke our universe into existence.

The earth in its preliminary condition was "without form and void". The language describes a scene of waste and emptiness. Some have taught that this scene was the outcome of a war between God and Satan. The verse is simply teaching that the earth was shapeless and empty of inhabitants at its outset but within a week God would dramatically change this condition!

A further description of the earth is given in verse 2. There was "darkness upon the face of the deep". The psalmist provides further explanation, "Thou coveredst it with the deep as with a garment: the waters stood above the mountains" (Ps 104:6). The early earth was therefore covered by water and shrouded in darkness.

We are then introduced to the Spirit of God. He is found in the first and last chapters of our Bible. In Genesis 1, the Spirit of God is revealed as protector of the earth. He "moved" (lit. 'hovered') over its lifeless and undeveloped form. The Gnostics taught that the material world was evil and had no link with a good God. But we see that God has had a caring involvement with our world from the outset.

After the foundation of the earth was laid, God introduced light on day one. It is not stated that God created, made or formed the light. The divine command was "let there be light". Light already existed and was commanded on day one to illuminate the earth. Men assume that the source of light in our world is the sun, moon and stars. But these were not created until day four! Scripture clearly teaches that "God is light and in Him is no darkness at all" (1 John 1:5). From the uncreated third heaven, He "...commanded the light to shine out of the darkness..." (2 Cor 4:6).

So, Earth's life cycle has been defined since day one. Light and darkness, day and night have been the experience of its inhabitants ever since. But our God is working towards an eternal day when "...they need no candle, neither light of the sun; for the Lord God giveth them light..." (Rev 22:5).

Day 2

CREATION DAY TWO

Genesis 1:6-8; 2 Peter 3:4-7

Creation day two is perhaps the most difficult for us to understand. This is due to the limited information that God gives about His work on that day. God would rather have His people understand His love than know the details of how he formed the heavens (Deut 10:14-15).

Peter gives a helpful insight to this creation day. He distinguishes between the "world that then was" and the "heavens and earth which are now". We cannot use our understanding of the present world to interpret the first six chapters of our Bible. Our world is very different from the one inhabited by Adam. For example, God introduced seasonal changes into our world after the flood. We can therefore safely assume that Adam had no need of an overcoat, umbrella, sunhat, or snow shovel in the Garden of Eden!

What can be understood from the account of day two is that before plants, birds, animals or men could exist on earth, God had to provide an atmosphere that could sustain life. Paul's preaching at Athens stressed the basic fact that God "giveth to all life, and breath, and all things" (Acts 17:25). Ungodly and rebellious men have spent vast sums of money investigating whether life could exist on other planets. Our God merely spoke His desire for a firmament, and "it was so". Earth was made ready for the rich variety of life it has sustained until today.

The firmament that provided the atmosphere for life also acted as a division for the waters described as "the deep" on day one. The account of verse 7 provides us with the staggering image of God dividing the deep and physically moving part of the water from the surface of the earth into space!

How high in space the waters were positioned is not discussed. We could assume from our limited understanding that these waters acted as a barrier and protection to earth. Adam and Eve were naked in Eden and this water barrier may have been the means God used to moderate their climate and protect them from the harmful rays of the sun. It is useless to speculate further.

What we can be clear about is that when the events of day two were concluded, it is not recorded that "God saw that it was good". We are indebted again to Peter for an explanation of this omission. On day two, God had created the means of man's destruction, "...whereby the world that then was, being overflowed with water perished".

"... therefore have I uttered that I understand not; things too wonderful for me, which I knew not" (Job 42:3).

Day 3

CREATION DAY THREE

Genesis 1:9-13; Job 38:1-11

The creation is intended to give a clear message to men about two of the invisible attributes of God, namely, His eternal power and Godhead (Rom 1:20). The very least we can understand from the world around us is that the Creator must have awesome power at His disposal. That power was displayed in creation day two when an expanse of water was taken from the earth and moved into space. The third day was a further demonstration of divine power.

Although waters had been taken from the earth and moved above the firmament, the earth was still covered with water at the commencement of day three. God then commanded the dry land to appear. That is a simple statement in the word of God, but who can understand the forces involved in separating the dry land of earth and the waters of the sea? It is possible that the earth at this time was a large island. We can still see evidence of this in our world. Only a short distance of 55 miles separates Alaska and Siberia across the Bering Strait.

Having created a tripartite world of heaven, earth and sea that was capable of sustaining life, God moved to create vegetation. God made a distinction between the plants and the trees, for one has seed in itself and the other has seed in its fruit. On this third creation day we are introduced to the important principle that God has placed in our world limits and restrictions to the process of reproduction. The repetition of the phrase "after its kind" teaches us that while we can see variety within God's world, He has prevented the evolution of one species into another. The Lord taught the parable of a mustard seed that grew into a great tree to emphasis that the growth was Satanic in origin, for seeds are divinely restricted from becoming trees!

It is clear from Scripture that the third day is very important to the purpose of God. The greatest display of divine power since the creation of the world was when God raised His Son from the dead. The salvation of the believer, the future restoration of the nation of Israel and the introduction of the new heavens and earth are all based on the truth of resurrection associated with the third day. "…and that he rose again the third day according to the scriptures" (1 Cor 15:4).

Day 4

CREATION DAY FOUR

Genesis 1:14-19; 1 Corinthians 15:40-41

All current theories of the origin of the universe and the formation of planets and stars are in direct opposition to the clear and simple statements made about creation day four. The key to unlocking the mystery of the stellar heavens is to accept that the source of light in our world is a Person and not a planet. For there is a light that shines "above the brightness of the sun" and Paul learned its source is "Jesus whom thou persecutest" (Acts 26:12-15).

The proof of this was demonstrated on creation day three when plants and trees were created. It is not possible for vegetation to exist without light. But light had shone into our world from day one! The sun, moon and stars are therefore not required to give light, neither does the existence of our world depend upon their continued functioning. The Lord Jesus taught, "Immediately after the tribulation of those days shall the sun be darkened, and the moon shall not give her light and the stars shall fall from the heaven, and the powers of the heavens shall be shaken" (Matt 24:29).

The sun, moon and stars were "made" and "set" in the heavens for a specific purpose. Their light-bearing function is almost presented as incidental. God merely attached light to these heavenly luminaries, an action which David later described as the work of His fingers! (Ps 8:3).

Our modern world has moved far away from the object lesson being taught by the sun and moon. They were given not for light but for rule. The "greater light" of the sun and the "lesser light" of the moon control the lives of all creatures on earth. The length of a year and of a day on earth is determined by its relationship with the sun. The division of years into months is controlled by the moon. What God is teaching men through the sun and the moon is that earth will never be independent from the rule of heaven. Nebuchadnezzar, Ahab and Herod were just a few of the proud men on the page of Scripture who discovered this to be true.

The stars are introduced almost as incidental: "He made the stars also"! Many voyagers have used the stars to navigate their course. The stars shine in the darkness but their light is eclipsed by the rising sun. The believer is guided through the moral darkness of the world with a star shining in his heart, knowing that the sun will soon rise to bring righteousness and healing (cf. 2 Pet 1:19; Mal 4:2). "He telleth the number of the stars; He calleth them all by their names" (Ps 147:4).

Day 5

CREATION DAY FIVE

Genesis 1:20-23; Psalm 148

The days of creation can be studied as a sequence in which day one corresponds with day four, day two with day five and day three with day six.

On the first day, light was introduced into the world; on the fourth day it was attached to the light bearers. On the second day, the sea and the heavens were created; on the fifth day the fish and birds populated them. On the third day, the land with its plants and fruit was created; on the sixth day the animals and man were created who would feed on those things.

The waters brought forth both fish and birds on day four, whereas the earth brought forth the land creatures on day five. So God separated the creation of fish and birds from animals by their place and time of origin. Once again it is clearly stated that sea creatures and winged fowl were divinely restricted to reproduce only after their kind. Evolution from one species to another was impossible. It is also accurately stated that "fowl multiply in the earth", for although they fly in the heaven, they come to earth to build their nests.

It is also very important to recognise the different forms of life on earth. The plants and trees have *existence*, and the fish, birds and animals have *life*. But only man is "a living soul" (Gen 2:7). Peter emphasised this truth when he wrote about the "eight souls" saved in the ark (1 Pet 3:20). Noah had taken many living creatures into the ark but only eight people had a soul that was God-breathed and would live forever. Man's life is distinguished from the lower elements of creation by the fact that he alone is able to receive and respond to divine communication. "In Him was life; and the life was the light of men" (John 1:4).

In day five God revealed that He is interested in abundance, fruitfulness and multiplication for his creatures. The depths of the seas were given to the fish and sea creatures to explore and enjoy. The heights and expanse of the heaven were allocated to the birds. When the land creatures were made on day five, they were allowed to roam the breadth of the earth.

For the man in Christ, there is a new creation to be enjoyed (2 Cor 5:17). Paul reveals it as a vast four-dimensional creation, with "breadth, and length, and depth, and height" (Eph 3:18). God's great desire is that the believer enjoys abundance, fruitfulness and multiplication in this spiritual sphere.

"For with thee is the fountain of life: in thy light shall we see light" (Ps 36:9).

Day 6

CREATION DAY SIX

Genesis 1:24-31; Matthew 19:3-9

Creation day six was distinguished from the others through God describing His work as "very good". It was on this day that creation was crowned by the introduction of a man and a woman on the earth.

Before the man and woman were formed, living creatures, cattle and beasts were created. But while the man and woman shared the same creation day with the beasts, five times over it is emphasised that the living creatures could only reproduce after their kind. Once again, God placed restrictions and barriers in His creation to prevent the evolution of one species into another. Paul confirmed that, "all flesh is not the same flesh: but there is one kind of flesh of men, another flesh of beasts, another of fishes, and another of birds" (1 Cor 15:39).

Adam was also distinguished from all that had preceded him by the fact that he was "made" (v.26), "created" (v.27) and "formed" (2:7). God set him at the head of creation and made him in the divine "image" and "likeness". He would represent and express the invisible God to a visible creation. He was also given a limited but extensive dominion over the fish, the fowl and the cattle. God was showing at the very outset of the history of this world that He intended His creation to be ruled by a man.

Adam soon forfeited his right to this dominion but we understand that God's purpose was never dependent on the first man. There is today a man in heaven who is crowned with glory and honour, as a token to us that He will take up a dominion that far exceeds that given to Adam. The dominion of Christ is to be universal and will extend to "all things" (Heb 2:8-9).

At the conclusion of day six, God would describe His work as "very good". But at some point in this day, God said "it is not good that the man should be alone" (Gen 2:18). Adam recognised how perfectly Eve complemented him. In Eden, God presided over the first marriage ceremony and the two became one flesh.

Modern thinking would argue that men and women are only the product of parental and social influences. But the first man and woman in our world had no parents and no background history to their lives! It was God who created a male and a female and He still expects these differences to be preserved in outward appearance, behaviour and spheres of responsibility.

"Let thy hand be upon the man of thy right hand, upon the son of man whom thou madest strong for thyself" (Ps 80:17).

Day 7

CREATION DAY SEVEN

Genesis 2:1-4; Hebrews 4:1-11

It was a wise man who wrote, "I know that, whatsoever God doeth, it shall be forever: nothing can be put to it, nor anything taken from it: and God doeth it, that men should fear before him" (Eccl 3:14). Creation day seven reveals one of the fundamental principles in God's dealings with men. God will only rest upon a finished work.

How long God enjoyed His rest is not revealed in Scripture. We do not know how soon after his creation that Adam fell, but it is possible that God only enjoyed that first day of rest. The Lord Jesus revealed to the Jews who persecuted him for working on the sabbath day, "My Father worketh hitherto, and I work" (John 5:17). God had been unable to rest from the moment the first man Adam introduced sin and death into what had been a perfect creation.

But God's purpose is centred in Christ, the second man, who has cried from Golgotha's cross, "it is finished". God now rests in the finished work of His Son and He invites men to enter into that same rest. How simple is the way of salvation. Men must do what God has done, "for he that is entered into his rest, he also hath ceased from his own works, as God did from His" (Heb 4:10).

Each creation day was marked off by the expression, "the evening and the morning". God was therefore working from the darkness towards the light. But on the seventh day there was no mention of evening or morning. God's day of rest was free of darkness. The seventh day anticipates that eternal day when, "the city had no need of the sun, neither of the moon, to shine in it: for the glory of God did lighten it, and the Lamb is the light thereof" (Rev 21: 23).

When the poet William Shakespeare wrote, "all the world's a stage…" it is unlikely that he understood he was expressing exactly the truth taught by the apostle Paul in the epistle to the Ephesians. Thousands of years after the seven creation days, the apostle revealed the great truth of the mystery that had been hidden in God from the foundation of the world. The world was created "to the intent that now unto the principalities and powers in heavenly places might be known by the church the manifold wisdom of God" (Eph 3:9-11). The creation is merely a stage upon which God has introduced to an audience of angels His masterpiece, the church, the body of Christ!

"Unto him be glory in the church by Christ Jesus throughout all ages, world without end. Amen" (Eph 3:21).

ROBERT THOMSON

Week 15

7 "COMINGS" IN THE LETTERS TO THE THESSALONIANS

1 Thessalonians 1:1-10

Introduction

The words of the Lord Jesus are precious to those who love Him. His sayings are characterised by authority and certainty. They produce assurance, comfort, hope and devotion. We revel in the truth of them and are blessed by the doing of them. Among His many words, one particular promise has thus helped the Lord's people: "I will come again" (John 14:3).

This promise was not given to any of the holy prophets of old. It is not for Israel, the nation of special favour in that past age. Praise God, it is a truth which has been revealed for this dispensation of the church, and its teaching is found only in the New Testament. What an honour is ours to belong to this age when as the bride of Christ we are awaiting the soon return of Him who "loved the church, and gave himself for it" (Eph 5:25).

It is little wonder that this glorious truth, first revealed in the upper room, would loom large in the early epistles of our New Testament. The imminent return of the Lord Jesus for His people so thrilled the Thessalonian believers that they were waiting for Him (1:10). The word 'wait' literally means 'to abide up'. Their attention was fixed heavenward. They were eagerly anticipating the coming of "His Son from heaven" (1:10). So they kept on waiting for Him.

Seven times over in his two letters to the Thessalonians, Paul will use the word most closely identified with the Lord's return. It is the Greek word 'parousia', translated 'coming'. The sense of the word is not just to indicate the moment of arrival, but also the continuing presence of the one who comes. Thus, in these epistles, we are introduced to the rapture of the church, which happens at the moment of His coming. We are further taught concerning the judgement seat of Christ, in which we are viewed as continuing in His presence. Finally, we are still with Him, when He returns in glory. How sad that we also learn of a counterfeit 'parousia', but how comforting to know that the coming of Christ in glory will abolish the coming of the man of sin.

Day 1

JOY AT HIS COMING

1 Thessalonians 2:1-20

The final epistle penned by Paul was his second letter to Timothy, when he was only a short while away from being martyred for the cause of Christ. His last recorded words are tinged with pathos as he reveals the manner in which he had been forsaken, and no doubt harshly judged, by believers he had lived to help. However, he had in view a coming day when he would stand before "the Lord, the righteous judge" (2 Tim 4:8), and His assessment would stand in contrast to that of Paul's critics.

The same spirit of opposition and criticism can be seen in what is probably Paul's first recorded epistle, this letter to the Thessalonians. There were some who cast doubt on the motive and sincerity of Paul and his fellow preachers. So, in the second chapter, Paul defends the conduct of himself and his brethren, and says "our exhortation was not of deceit, nor of uncleanness, nor in guile" (v.3). He further asserts that "neither at any time used we … a cloak of covetousness" (v.5). Instead, their gentleness and irreproachable conduct was such that he appeals to the believers remembrance of how they had been "among you" (vv.7,10).

Furthermore, the results of the labours of Paul and his companions bore testimony to the genuineness and reality of their motive. He reminded them that having "received the word of God which ye heard of us" it was that "which effectually worketh also in you that believe" (v.13). The believers themselves were evidence of a work of God, wrought through the Lord's servants.

But Paul is not depending on the assessment of the Thessalonians. He has a higher motive than to meet with the approval of men. In relation to the gospel, he writes, "we speak; not as pleasing men, but God" (v.4). Further, in defending the purity of his motive, he adds "God is witness" (v.5). So at the end of this second chapter, Paul is looking ahead to the judgement seat of Christ. This is when every believer will be "in the presence of our Lord Jesus Christ at His coming" (v.19). Following the rapture of the church, we will be in His presence continually and there will be a review of our lives.

For the apostle, this anticipation brought hope, joy and the prospect of a crown of rejoicing (v.19). And this joy centred on the Thessalonians themselves. Their very presence at the judgement seat would be evidence of the fruit of his labours. No wonder he was satisfied to leave the assessment of his service to God. The criticism of men was unjust, but the Lord, the righteous judge, will ensure a just assessment and reward in that coming day of review.

Day 2

UNBLAMEABLE AT HIS COMING

1 Thessalonians 3:1-13

It is clear from the epistles of Paul that he had a burden to see those who were newly converted by faith, established in the faith. Thus Paul sent Timothy to the Thessalonians that he might "establish you" (v.2). He was desirous that the believers should be strengthened and supported in their faith. Afflictions would come, and it was important that they were helped so that "no man should be moved by these afflictions" (v.3).

Paul was not only concerned that they should be strengthened for the present but, in verses 12 and 13, he was anxious that they might be established with a view to the future. So he writes, "to the end he (the Lord) may stablish your hearts" (v.13). He is interested in their hearts, because he is now concerned with their love, as he was with their faith in the earlier part of the chapter.

Love is a misunderstood doctrine. Much that professes to be love is nothing but favouritism, partiality or an excuse for compromising with error. True love is an attribute of God and, as such, is righteous, impartial and unbiased. Indeed, as seen in God, love has its highest expression, and is exercised regardless of the worth or merit of its object. Calvary is the supreme example. Therefore love is selfless and sacrificial. It needs no reason for its exercise. It overcomes history, personality and prejudice. And it is most necessary in our relationships with one another. No wonder Paul wanted the Thessalonians "to increase and abound in love one toward another, and toward all" (v.12). Such an overflow of love would be a blessing to any assembly.

However, the importance of love is not restricted to the present. Indeed, it is essential that we are characterised by love now, because there is coming a day when we shall be "before God, even our Father" (v.13). If we have abounded in love, the fixed state of our heart which is the result will be manifested in His presence as being "unblameable in holiness" (v.13). The true nature of our love will be exposed in that day. Have we merely professed love, or practised love? John writes "My little children, let us not love in word, neither in tongue; but in deed and in truth" (1 John 3:18).

It is most interesting to observe that true love is manifested as holiness. How amazing to think that "at the coming of our Lord Jesus Christ with all His saints" (v.13), when He is revealed in all His glory and majesty, the holiness, which is the expression of our love, will also be publicly manifested. How important therefore, that our love abounds now so as to be "unblameable in holiness" then.

Day 3

RAPTURE AT HIS COMING

1 Thessalonians 4:13-18

The prospect of the Lord's return for His people, and His subsequent appearing in glory with the saints, was ever before the Thessalonian believers. They eagerly anticipated the imminent coming of the Lord. But they had a concern. What about those who had died? Would they miss out on being with Him at His glorious appearing? In what way would the Lord's coming affect them? Paul addresses these questions in verses 13-18 of this chapter.

It is one of the great prospects of the believer, that "When Christ, who is our life, shall appear, then shall ye also appear with him in glory" (Col 3: 4). Paul reassures the Thessalonians that death will not prevent any believer from participating in this glorious advent. He writes "them also which sleep in Jesus will God bring with him" (v.14). What is the guarantee that this will happen? In the same way that we believe in the death and resurrection of Jesus, "even so" (v.14) will those who sleep in Jesus share in the advent of Christ in glory. There is no doubt.

Why then will death not prevent the believer from sharing in the glorious advent of Christ? Paul points to "the coming of the Lord" (v.15), not here *with* His people, but *for* His people. In the upper room the Lord had promised "I will come again for you" (John 14:3), and this is when the promise is realised. At that moment of His coming, amazing events will take place that ensure every believer, asleep or alive, will share in the revelation of Christ in glory.

In the instant when "the Lord himself shall descend from heaven" (v.16), those who are "asleep" (v.15) shall not be preceded by those who are "alive and remain" (v.15). Instead "the dead in Christ shall rise first" (v.16). Far from being disadvantaged by death, they will have priority at His coming and rise first. From among the dead, out of land and sea, there will arise a great company of those who sleep in Jesus. His resurrection (v.14) is the guarantee that they will be raised. The living are caught up too. How blessed to think about that re-union in the clouds when "we which are alive and remain shall be caught up together with them" (v.17). But how blessedly higher is the prospect that "so shall we ever be with the Lord" (v.17).

The knowledge of this truth brings tremendous consolation to the Lord's people. Where there is real sorrow caused by the death of a saint, there is also a real hope. Death is likened to sleep from which there will be a glorious awakening. The Lord is coming for His own, asleep or alive. "Wherefore comfort one another with these words" (v.18).

Day 4

SANCTIFIED IN HIS COMING

1 Thessalonians 5:12-28

Sanctification and its related doctrine of holiness are themes which recur in this epistle. In them we learn that as believers we are set apart for God. This happened positionally the moment we were saved, and is the consequence of being in Christ. It is an unalterable fact, which is equally true of every believer.

However, as with all positional truth, there is a corresponding responsibility that devolves upon every believer. Thus Paul writes, "For this is the will of God, even your sanctification" (1 Thess 4:3). Here sanctification is viewed practically. As believers we are exhorted to live in moral purity. The reason given is "For God hath not called us unto uncleanness, but unto holiness" (1 Thess 4:7).

In this last chapter of the epistle, Paul desires that "the very God of peace sanctify you wholly" (v.23). This is sanctification permeating the personality. It therefore affects the whole being. Thus Paul continues, "I pray God your whole spirit and soul and body be preserved blameless" (v.23). It is interesting to observe the order in which Paul refers to the different aspects of our being. He begins with the spirit, which gives God-consciousness. He continues with the soul, which gives self-consciousness, and concludes with the body, in which the spirit and soul are housed. The world puts the body first, but we must learn the importance of giving priority to the spiritual.

The final accomplishment of our sanctification will be "unto (in) the coming of our Lord Jesus Christ" (v.23). At the moment of His coming, full and perfect sanctification will be realised in every one of His believing people. In that one glorious instant when He comes to the air to call us home, we will be morally perfect and gloriously sinless. The fact of this is assured, because "Faithful is he that calleth you, who also will do it" (v.24). Praise God we can anticipate this perfect sanctification with certainty. We are in no doubt that He called us. Equally, we can have no doubt that He will bring to completion the work, which He began in us. The knowledge of this truth should reassure the heart of each believer. We are in the hands of the faithful God, who cannot fail.

While our final and complete sanctification is assured, in the prayer of Paul there is a heartfelt desire that our lives here and now should be always moving towards that goal. It was his prayer in view of the coming of the Lord, that we should constantly keep before our vision the need to be "preserved blameless" (v.23).

By the keeping and preserving power of God, we can live in such a way that no accusing finger can be justifiably directed at us. In this we can be in measure now what we will be perfectly "in the coming of our Lord Jesus Christ"

Day 5

THE BRIGHTNESS OF HIS COMING

2 Thessalonians 1:6-10; 2:8

One of the many results of the grace of God in our lives is that we are "looking for that blessed hope, and the glorious appearing of the great God and our Saviour Jesus Christ" (Titus 2:13). We are of course looking for that moment when the Saviour comes for us, in which our bodies will be transformed and conformed to be "like unto his glorious body" (Phil 3:21). But such is the effect of the grace of God in our hearts, that we can look beyond that which will be glory for us, to look for that which will be glory for Him.

His first appearing, though marked by celestial movement and angelic announcement, went largely unnoticed. How different will be His second appearing, when "every eye shall see him, and they also which pierced him" (Rev 1:7). If the outside place was given to Him when He appeared the first time, at His second appearing the cry will be "Lift up your heads, O ye gates; Even lift them up, ye everlasting doors; And the King of Glory shall come in" (Ps 24:9). In Jerusalem, the place of His rejection, He will be received and recognised, and rightly acknowledged as "King of kings, and Lord of lords" (Rev 19: 16).

The truth of the appearing of Christ would be a tremendous encouragement to the Thessalonians. They were enduring "persecutions and tribulations" (2 Thess 1:4). But they will enjoy rest, because "the Lord Jesus shall be revealed from heaven" (1:7), and when He is thus revealed He will judge those who were troubling the saints. Not only so, these persecuted believers will be present "when He shall come to be glorified in His saints, and to be admired in all them that believe" (1:10). How amazing to think that we will be in that company through whom the Lord will be glorified and admired!

In the second chapter of this epistle, Paul writes of the man of sin and his coming. But how swift and decisive and complete will be his destruction. When the Lord comes in glory, this lawless man shall be consumed with the very breath of His mouth, and will be destroyed "with the brightness of His coming" (v.8). The visible brilliance and radiant majesty of the glory of Christ will not then be veiled. The last the world saw of Him was as He hung in shame and humiliation upon a tree. But in the day of His coming again to the earth there will be an outshining of His glory, and in that display of the majesty of His coming, the man of sin will be utterly abolished.

What a blessed hope this is, even the "appearing of the glory of our great God and Saviour Jesus Christ"! (Titus 2:13, JND).

Day 6

An Appeal Based on His Coming

2 Thessalonians 2:1-2

It is no surprise, considering the Thessalonians' occupation with the Lord's coming, that in his first letter to them Paul remembers their "patience of hope" (1:3). A further consequence of the Lord's coming was that "ye sorrow not, even as others which have no hope" (4:13). In the second Thessalonian epistle however, their hope is markedly absent. Having commended their faith, love and hope in the first epistle, he now only thanks God for their faith and love. What has happened?

False prophetic utterances, backed by erroneous teaching and a forged letter claiming Pauline authorship, had introduced false doctrine. It was taught that "the day of Christ (the Lord) is at hand (hath come)" (2:2). So they believed the seven-year period known as, and including, the Great Tribulation had come. No doubt much emphasis had been laid on the persecutions and tribulations they were enduring (2 Thess 1:4), and their experience was mixed with the error to convince the believers that this was not just tribulation, but the Tribulation.

The effect was disastrous. Once settled saints were now cast down from a secure and happy state. They were like a ship loosed from its moorings, buffeted by a storm. Once hopeful, they were now fearful. Such is the result of false doctrine.

In a day when many believers will defend the rights of those who teach and practice error more than they will defend the truth, let us be aware of the danger of error. We must not harbour sympathetic and accommodating feelings towards that which will destroy the enjoyment of spiritual life. Certainly Paul did not, and wrote "Let no man deceive you by any means" (2:3). These words are a necessary exhortation for today.

In the first epistle, Paul had already taught the Thessalonians that the coming of the Lord delivered them from enduring the wrath on earth which will be outpoured during the Tribulation. They were waiting for "Jesus, which delivered us from the wrath to come" (1:10). Thus he exhorts them to put on "for a helmet, the hope of salvation. For God hath not appointed us to wrath, but to obtain salvation by our Lord Jesus Christ" (5:8-9). The rapture takes us away from the sphere where the wrath of God will be poured out.

Now, in this second epistle, Paul beseeches them to "be not soon shaken in mind, or be troubled" (2:2), and the basis of his appeal is "by the coming of our Lord Jesus Christ" (2:1). The expectation of the believer is "our gathering together unto him" (2:1). We do not fear wrath to come. We are waiting for our Deliverer, and may this hope "comfort your hearts, and stablish you in every good word and work" (2:17).

Day 7

THE COUNTERFEIT COMING

2 Thessalonians 2:3-12

One of the many wiles of the devil has been to imitate that which is of God. Prophetically, a trinity of evil will imitate the Triune God. As well as Satan himself, there will be the anti-Christ and the false prophet. In this chapter we are introduced to the anti-Christ as the "man of sin" (v.3). He is dominated and controlled by sin. We learn further that he has a "coming", and of this Paul wrote, "whose coming is after the working of Satan" (v.9). He is not only controlled by sin, but is inspired by Satan, and his coming will be heralded and accompanied "with all power and signs and lying wonders" (v.9). The effect is deception, as his presence is "with all deceivableness of unrighteousness in them that perish" (v.10). Those who reject the gospel will be deceived by every unrighteous means available to this man.

The coming of the "man of sin" begins with revelation. The day of the Lord shall not come except the "man of sin be revealed" (v.3). Alongside a complete overthrow of the truth of God, he will suddenly and dramatically emerge onto the world stage. The church has been raptured. The Holy Spirit has been "taken out of the way" (v.7). The restraining influence is removed. There will be nothing to hold back his revelation, and in the confusion and uncertainty that follows the rapture, he will step forward as the man to solve the world's problems. Thus he signs a covenant with Israel (Dan 9:27), and restores peace and stability to a highly volatile hot-spot. His reputation soars.

Then comes his self-exaltation. After three and a half years he is no longer willing to co-exist with the religious system represented by Babylon, probably the climax of the Ecumenical Movement, and he "opposeth and exalteth himself above all that is called God, or that is worshipped" (v.4). Babylon is destroyed and he "as God sitteth in the temple of God, shewing himself that he is God" (v.4). Having abolished all other forms of worship, he assumes the place of God in the temple, and demands that worship be directed to himself. He is given authority to continue for forty-two months (Rev 13:5), during which time many will be "beheaded for the witness of Jesus, and for the word of God, and which had not worshipped the beast, neither his image" (Rev 20:4).

His coming ends in destruction. His days are numbered, and it is he "whom the Lord shall consume with the spirit of His mouth, and shall destroy with the brightness of His coming" (v.8). Praise God, the coming of Christ in glory shall bring to nought the counterfeit coming of the man of sin.

SINCLAIR BANKS

Week 16

7 DIVINE COMMUNICATIONS TO ABRAHAM

Genesis 12-13; Acts 7:1-8

Introduction

Of all the great men found in Genesis only Abraham is called the friend of God (see Isa 41:8; 2 Chron 20:7). Born in Ur of the Chaldees, and living there for over seventy years in a manner that is not revealed to us, he came to know God, a knowledge which changed his life in a remarkable way, and which caused a bright beam to shine right through the Scriptures.

After the Flood the Lord declared that he would not again destroy the world in this manner. Those who sought God were now to be called out of the world to follow Him. Abraham is the first recorded 'called out' pilgrim, leaving home, extended family, friends and all that was familiar to him and travelling to Canaan. To him was given the promise of that land as a home for his posterity, a promise that has shaped the course of history even up to this present day.

To him was also given the great privilege and responsibility of being the father of Israel according to the flesh (Rom 4:1), the nation to whom so much blessing was given (Rom 9:4) and from whom "Christ came, who is over all, God blessed forever" (Rom 9:5).

But more yet was bestowed on him. Not only was he the father of Israel, but also "the father of us all" (Rom 4:16), that is, the father of all believers. Although before him others had believed God, Abraham is the first of whom it is stated that he "believed God". This followed the promise that he would have a son (Gen 15:6). But the words that follow heighten the importance of the statement, that his belief was "counted … to him for righteousness". All who have believed have enjoyed the same blessing of having righteousness imputed or attributed to them because of their faith.

Friendships thrive on regular communication. When that ceases, friendship withers. The friend of God enjoyed communication with His God, and great lessons can be learned from looking at when God spoke and what God said. Today, communication from heaven may not be in the manner known to Abraham, but may we be encouraged that God has spoken and therefore desire to hear His voice.

Day 1

"THE GOD OF GLORY APPEARED"

Genesis 11:27 - 12:9; Acts 7:1-7

Ur of the Chaldees was doubtless a city of wealth, magnificence and idolatry. To the human eye it had all that man could desire to satisfy himself. Yet Abram was not satisfied and he came to know God in that godless society. The first divine communication to him of which we read was the call to leave all this behind and to travel into the unknown. The destination had been prepared by God, but when Abram was called it was simply to "a land that I will shew thee" (Gen 12:1). The land was identified, when he had reached there, as Canaan (Gen 12:7).

The first striking feature of this call was that, as Stephen tells us at his defence before the council, it came from "the God of glory" (Acts 7:2). In the midst of the magnificence surrounding him, Abram saw a glory that far exceeded anything that Ur could provide. In the light of such overwhelming glory, the glory of Ur became as nothing. So it is with all who turn to God; His attractiveness makes all else dim. The Thessalonians did not turn from idols to God, they turned to God from idols. The disciple John wrote, "we beheld his glory", so it is little wonder that they "left all" (Mark 10:28) to follow Him. So it was with Abram. Dissatisfied he may have been with Ur, but it took the glory of God to attract him away.

Note, second, that as has already been indicated, it was a call into the unknown. It was not that he was to travel alone, for the Lord would be present and show him the land, but as he left Ur behind his destination was not revealed. This also is true of all who heed the call to follow Him. It is a journey into the unknown, but it has the guarantee of His presence and His guidance. He also had God's promise of becoming a great nation, and of being blessed so that in him all the families of the earth would be blessed.

Today we have been called to follow Him in the pathway of life, not to Canaan, but to enjoy all the spiritual blessings in the heavenlies (Eph

1:3). Compare the glorious millennial kingdom and look now on the sad ruins of Ur; this gives some indication of what Abram left behind. So is it today. Those looking on may think, as they would do of Abram, that he was giving up the best for an uncertain future in reduced circumstances. Not so, he chose well as do those who follow the Master, knowing, as Peter did (1 Pet 5:10) that the glory will one day be revealed.

Day 2

RECOVERY FROM EGYPT

Genesis 12:10 - 13:18

Having reached Canaan, Abraham was faced with a famine. Rather than wait on the Lord he travelled to Egypt, the home of the great builders, warriors and administrators of that age. It is clear that Abraham recovered from the mistaken journey but, sad to say, there was left with Lot a love for things Egyptian. This is one of the dangers of failing in our obedience to Him. We may engage in activities and mix in company that is not helpful spiritually, from which we may be able to recover. Others who followed our example, however, may not be able to rid themselves of the desire for the things of the world into which we led them.

On their return to Canaan, a dispute arose between the herdsmen of Abraham and of Lot. It was expedient for the two groups to separate and Lot was given first choice. He "lifted up his eyes and beheld all the plain of Jordan, that it was … like the land of Egypt" (v.10). The matter was settled; by his actions he revealed where his heart lay, and down he went on a pathway that would lead ultimately to disaster. Sad it is to repeat that Abraham had given him a taste for that which would lead to the loss of his wife and of his testimony.

Abraham must have felt sadness at the departure of Lot as, since he had left Ur, Lot had always been with him. But the message from the Lord is one of encouragement. As Lot had lifted up his eyes (v.10) so now did Abraham at the command of the Lord. The time in Egypt and the loss of Lot had not changed the purpose of God. Northward, southward, eastward and westward, all that could be seen was still to be given to Abraham's seed. But there was more to be enjoyed than merely looking, he was to walk about the land and enjoy it.

The present enjoyment of that which is to be fully realised at a later time was not only the experience of Abraham; it ought to be our experience also. We have been blessed, not at a later date, but presently, with "all spiritual blessings in heavenly places in Christ" (Eph 1:3). Let us then "lift up our eyes" to appreciate them and "walk about" them to enjoy them. Little wonder that, at Hebron, Abraham built an altar.

Worship was his response and worship must be ours. Despite failure, all was still Abraham's and, despite failure, none of these heavenly blessings have been lost to us. May we respond by being men and women of the altar.

Day 3

THE PROMISE OF A SON

Genesis 15:1-21

The promise to Abram that he would have a son comes after the rescue of Lot from captivity following the defeat of Sodom (Gen 14: 13-16), and the intervention of Melchizedek, King of Salem (Gen 14: 17-24). It is, therefore, noteworthy that the Lord commenced with the words "Fear not". Why should he be in fear? It may be that he was afraid of retaliation from those he had smitten in rescuing his nephew. It may also be that the Adversary was suggesting that he had been overgenerous in allowing the king of Sodom to keep the spoils of war and that, as a result, he was the loser and had strengthened Sodom.

Both of these are addressed by the Lord in His opening greeting, "I am thy shield", guarding him against retaliation "and thy exceeding great reward", providing a reward that was far greater than anything he had allowed Sodom to take. Today the same suggestions are made to us, coming from the same source; fear for our physical well-being and fear to give to Him, lest we become impoverished. The promise of the Lord is, therefore, an encouragement that He is attentive to all the needs of those who scrve Him faithfully.

The reward Abram desired was that of a son, and it is good to see how directly he addresses this (vv.2-3). When speaking to God there is no arrogance, nor undue familiarity. There is also no withdrawn timidity. Abraham stated his desire unmistakeably, knowing that the Lord had already promised that his seed would possess the land. At this time, however, the son of his steward would become the heir, and that surely was not what the Lord had promised. If we honour the word of God and submit to it, we also can request that we see His promises kept. Some promises are conditional, such as in Philippians 4, where enjoying the peace of God is dependent on our praying (vv.6-7), and where the presence of the God of peace is dependent on us putting into practice the things that we have learned, and received and heard (v.9). The Lord delights in letting us see Him keep His promises when we bow to His will.

The remainder of the chapter with the revelation that Abram's seed would be "a stranger in a land that is not theirs" (v.13) points to their time in Egypt. Despite all that lay ahead, promises would be kept.

Here history is recorded before it took place, embracing times when His promise looked impossible to fulfil. But let us all take heart. When circumstances look bleak and His promises look far from fulfilment, remember that He is the creator of history and He is still on the throne.

Day 4

ABRAHAM'S JOY

Genesis 17:1-27

For years God had not spoken. The birth of Ishmael was the cause. Faith had faltered! Did it seem to Abram that the great days were over and that the voice of God, no longer a present reality, was only to be a memory? But God does not forget His promises and at last He speaks again. It may be that Abram now regretted his actions? Beyond this, however, it was time for the Lord to speak.

If we feel the coldness of a silent heaven, the loss of the warmth of fellowship once enjoyed with Him, let us look into our hearts and determine to put right the cause of this loss and be able to enjoy His presence and to hear Him speak to us from Scripture.

For the first time God uses the name "El Shaddai", the God who is 'all powerful and all sufficient'. Nothing and no one can stop the fulfilment of His purpose, neither Sarai's suggestion, Abram's failure, Ishmael's birth or the work of the Adversary. In the verses that follow note the repetition of the words "I will", "I have", "will I" etc. What He purposes He will make come to pass, and let us take heart in that. The great promises regarding our future blessing and glory will come to be honoured; He has declared it and no one can prevent it. We fail but "He faileth not" (Zech 3:5).

There are a number of strands to this message from the Lord. First, the new names given to Abram and Sarai. Abram (high father) becomes Abraham (father of a multitude) and Sarai (my princess) becomes Sarah (princess). The new names denote a new stage on the journey in keeping with the dignity of their calling.

Second, is the re-statement of the promise made previously (12: 2-3) but in an expanded form. Divine truth is revealed in such a way. It is not all imparted to us at one time but, like the dawning of the morning light, it comes gradually as we can bear it.

Third, is the giving of the covenant of circumcision which will mark Abram's descendents as being different from all others. Even today Christians must be different, not in the manner given to Israel, but by their conduct and manner of life.

Fourth, there is now specifically stated that the son will be born to Sarah. Abram responds with joy and his "mouth is filled with laughter"

(Ps 126:112). Surely, as we look at the great promises in the gospel, our hearts should be filled with joy. Let us heed the exhortation of Peter, "…yet believing, ye rejoice with joy unspeakable and full of glory" (1 Pet 1:8).

Day 5

"SHALL I HIDE FROM ABRAHAM
THAT THING WHICH I DO?"

Genesis 18:1-33

When the Lord speaks it is often in an unexpected way and at an unexpected time. Moses was shepherding his sheep (Exod 3:1-2) and Gideon was threshing wheat (Jud 6:11). These were days just like any other day with no prior notice of what was to take place, just as this day was for Abraham!

Three things are remarkable in this chapter. First, note the recognition of faith. In the heat of the day three men approach Abraham's tent. It has often been said that Abraham on this occasion entertained angels unawares, but that fails to observe the greeting which he uses. "My Lord" is what comes to his lips, 'Adonahay', a divine title. He recognised who it was gracing his tent with His presence and he responded in a fitting manner. Would we be able to recognise His voice should He speak to us today? It will not be as He did on this occasion, but through His word, or through circumstances, this could be the day when He speaks clearly. Would we hear and would we respond? Note the speed which marked him and observe that he, who was the master of the household, acted now as the servant, standing by his guests as they ate.

Second, observe the reassurance of faith. The promise which had been given to him previously (12:2,7; 13:15; 15:4; 17:7) is now restated. The laughter of Sarah as the promise of a son is mentioned is one of unbelief, but the answer of the Lord shows how the "impossible" can be done for there is nothing too hard for the Lord. When we face a situation which seems impossible, remember that, if it be His will, impossibilities are no barrier to Him. The same truth is found in Jeremiah 32:17. Sometimes our faith does falter, but let us remember His promises and rely on Him to keep them.

But we must not overlook the third issue as the future of Sodom is made known to Abraham. We see here the revelation to faith. God did not hide from Abraham, and does not hide from Christians, what He will do in the future. The judgment about to fall on that evil place was made known to Abraham and the judgment which will fall on this evil world and on all who have rejected the gospel has been made known to us in the word of God. In view of that, Abraham interceded for the righteous in Sodom.

Note Abraham's confidence in intercession. Let us respond to what we have learned by becoming men and women who pray, not only for the lost but, as with Abraham, for believers whose worldly life has damaged their testimony.

Day 6

"CAST OUT THIS BONDWOMAN AND HER SON"

Genesis 21:1-21

Ishmael was now fourteen years of age (see Gen 16:16 and Gen 21:5) and the promise of the Lord was honoured. Sarah gave birth to a son and Abraham named him "Isaac". What joy must have flooded the hearts of the parents as they thanked God that the "impossible" had taken place and Abraham was a father "in his old age" (v.2). But over the joy a cloud cast its shadow. Past sin and disobedience was the cause and Ishmael was the living reminder of it. What a warning to us all! May we so live that the sinful consequences of our actions do not darken future days.

In course of time the child was weaned and, at the celebration feast, Sarah saw Ishmael displaying his true character and openly laughing in mockery at the child. Abraham had laughed with joy (Gen 17:17); Sarah had laughed in unbelief (Gen 18:12); but now Ishmael displayed his contempt for the boy with his laughter. Do not dismiss this as a youngster's prank. Paul asserts clearly that this was an act of persecution (Gal 4:30). As a result Sarah demands that Ishmael be cast out, but this was a grievous demand to Abraham. Ishmael was his son and, as a father, he loved him. But the word of God confirms Sarah's demand and Abraham must bear the cost by acting to limit the damage of past sin in giving up Ishmael. Let us remember that sin comes with a price!

Note, however, that the great care God exercised over Hagar and Ishmael reveals again His compassionate heart. As they left, Abraham gave them a *bottle* of water, but God gave them a *well* of water from which the bottle could be replenished. When He gives He does so bountifully.

The lessons from this incident are used by Paul to counter the teaching in Galatia of those who asserted that salvation must be accompanied by keeping the law. These Judaisers claimed to be the true sons of Abraham, but Paul reminds them that Abraham had two sons. The argument in Galatians 4 has three strands to it. The first is that just as Ishmael had to give place to Isaac, so the law has given place to grace. The second is that as Ishmael was the son of a bondwoman, so the law brings into bondage those who seek to practice it (v.24). The last is that as Isaac was the son of a free woman, so grace brings true freedom (vv.25-26). Christians have something far better than the law. Grace has brought about our salvation and no work of ours can add to that.

Day 7

"Take now thy son"

Genesis 22:1-19

Years had passed since the birth of Isaac and Abraham may have expected that life would now continue in a quieter way. The promise of the Lord had been honoured and the question of the seed of Abraham had been dealt with. Now the future could be looked at with confidence. But, again, God spoke: "Take now thy son … and offer him for a burnt offering" (v.2). Abraham was asked to place Isaac on the altar and offer him as a sacrifice.

The first point to notice is that this call was unexpected. No prior notice was given to Abraham. Suddenly he is asked to bow to the will of God in doing that which appeared to be contrary to the promises he had received. It may be that God will speak and ask us to do the unexpected, not as asked of Abraham, but unexpected nevertheless.

The call was also unnatural. How could a father be expected to offer up his son? Could Abraham not simply assert that such as act was impossible? How many have been asked to do that which appeared to be beyond what is acceptable?

But the call was also unexplained. Why this demand should be made was not revealed to him, and it should be noted that he did not ask for an explanation. How often have believers been taken into circumstances which are painful, but for which no explanation is given?

The call was unique. Abraham did not have anyone to whom he could go for advice. No one else had been asked to travel this pathway and Abraham could have protested that he was being asked to do what no one else had ever done.

But Abraham obeyed without hesitation. Why was this? Hebrews 11:17-19 gives us the answer. When Isaac was promised he had faith that God could do the impossible. Now he weighed up all the issues involved in this new call. He carefully considered the promises that he had been given and, by faith, came to the considered conclusion that God could raise Isaac from the dead. This is echoed in his confident words "I and the lad will go yonder and worship, and come again" (v.5). He believed that even if he ascended the mount, built the altar, placed the wood on the altar and Isaac on the wood, plunged his knife into his son's bosom, burned the body to ashes and scattered the ashes to the four winds of heaven, then Abraham and Isaac would walk down from the mountain again together. Abraham had faith that no matter what he had been asked to do, God would honour His promise. May we hold on to all His promises. They will come to pass!

John Grant

Week 17

7 GENTILE CHURCHES TO WHICH EPISTLES WERE WRITTEN

Introduction

The apostle Paul had clear-cut convictions from the outset about knowing the will of God. He asked, "Lord, what wilt thou have me to do?" and, within days, through Ananias, he knew that he was a chosen vessel "to bear my name before the Gentiles, and kings and the children of Israel. For I will show him how great things he must suffer for my sake" (Acts 9:15). Probably Ananias was surprised at the mention of Gentiles, but from the start it was obvious that Paul was to be a pioneering traveller carrying the greatest message on earth, visiting towns and cities and countries never envisaged by the 'twelve'.

Why Paul? The answer immediately introduces us to the doctrine of God's sovereignty. God prepared the man long before he was even saved. Not only did Paul have a 'double-decker' brain and intellect, but he studied under the finest Jewish and Gentile philosophers.

Secondly, Paul was born and brought up in Tarsus, a Gentile city with a passing population of representatives from all over the then-known world. In order to communicate and debate this unique message Paul had to learn to be all things to all men.

In addition to his time in the university of life, he was going to be personally instructed in the school of God. We know from Galatians chapter 1 that he had time out in Arabia, as much as three years, in which God revealed to him exclusive truths which he was to communicate to early believers world wide. Amazingly, these were to be preserved to us two thousand years thereafter.

What about the places visited and the letters written? We can't help noticing that certain cities did not receive letters; Antioch, Athens, Berea and Troas for example. Those chosen by the Spirit of God were selected for a purpose, to educate and correct first-century saints, and to pass on information which would be relevant to believers in the twenty-first century.

In what order shall we deal with these Gentile assemblies? The order in which they were written, or in the order they were visited? Perhaps it would be wise to address them in the order in which they were placed in God's tome. I believe the order of the books in our Bible is as inspired as the words themselves. Thus we will start our journey where Paul finished his, at the centre of the Gentile world – Rome.

Day 1

ROME

Acts 19:21; 23:1-11; 28:11-16; Romans 1:1-15

Rome was the last of the true world powers. Although other dictators have tried to dominate, such as Napoleon, Stalin and Hitler, they have failed. Any person who had ambition wanted to visit the Gentile capital of Rome, the 'eternal city'. Paul was no exception. He especially wanted to visit it in his post-conversion days, and even indicated that he would have liked to have extended his travels to Spain also. We know Paul eventually arrived in Rome, but when he wrote the epistle, his ambition had not yet been realised. However, he was writing to believers there. Who then was instrumental in bringing the gospel to the city? Scripture doesn't reveal the identity of the messengers. Paul was always reluctant to build on another's foundation, thus indicating that it wasn't Peter who brought the good news initially. It was probably some of the strangers from Rome mentioned in Acts 2. No major figure in particular, just 'ordinary' saints gossiping the gospel. This is something we can all do.

The book of Acts can conveniently be divided into two parts, chapters 1-12, and 13-28. The first half is centred around the church at Jerusalem where Peter is the prominent figure. Paul features most in the second half, and the central church is Antioch. Extension of the gospel to Rome would have been in the second part of the book.

This is important to notice, because from Rome the great lie of Christendom eventually evolved. The union of church and state created a system which will one day be judged, and of course its *supposed* original head was Peter.

How significant therefore that Paul's subject is the true gospel. He wanted to "establish" the new converts (Rom 1:10) and, at the end of the epistle, he reminded them that it is Jesus Christ who has the "power to stablish you according to my gospel" (16:25). This true gospel centred around the effect of the cross of Christ, and this letter has become the greatest treatise on what the gospel really means and its subsequent practical implications in the life of the believer.

To have a church in Rome was a miracle in itself. To acknowledge Christ would immediately involve opposition and suffering. It challenged the very heart of the pagan system of Roman Emperor worship. How these early believers would have been thrilled to hear from the apostle. God in His wisdom rewarded them by seeing that Paul was able to obtain a 'free' journey and stay in Rome, albeit under house arrest for most of the time.

Under Emperor Nero, evidence of the holy Scriptures was ordered to be destroyed. How the believers would covet, hide and study every word that passed through their hands! What a challenge to us today in the west, where not only can we keep our Bibles, but our libraries are full of helps.

When the persecution eventually ceased in Rome, the new Emperor asked for a copy of the Scriptures, hardly believing that there were any left. Apparently, within days, a dozen copies were made available. God will always preserve His word, even after the heavens and the earth have passed away, so let us make a real effort to absorb its contents, and abide by its principles.

Day 2

CORINTH

Acts 18:1-18; 1 Corinthians 1:1-9

Paul visited Corinth during his second missionary journey, around 52 AD, and remained there for about eighteen months. It was a city renowned for its commerce, wealth and wisdom, together with its immorality and debauchery. Paul must have wondered, "Are we going to reach anyone in this city? Is it too corrupt for real blessing?" God told him beforehand "I have much people in this city" (Acts 18:10). That is why the sovereignty of God is such an incentive in our gospel endeavours.

If ever a city reflected the day in which we now live in the Western world, it was Corinth. Sin was the norm, and sinful pleasure regarded as the thing to be desired. During those eighteen months Paul saw an assembly established, but it wasn't long after his departure that the world crept into the lives and activities of the believers, leaving it in total disarray.

When the news came through, he had one of two alternatives. He could write off the assembly and disassociate himself from it or, on the other hand, attempt to address the problems and endeavour to lead it back to right paths. Thankfully he chose the latter. Paul may not have had an opportunity to visit the church personally again, but we know it was his dearest wish so to do. Some of the happenings at Corinth would not only have revolted us, but we would probably have cut the assembly off for its behaviour. Thank God for godly men who are willing to go to these types of gatherings with sensitivity and passion to help redress the situation.

The first and main question addressed was that of divisions caused by a party spirit. Amazingly enough, this is still one of the major factors that reduces assemblies to virtual inactivity and ineffectiveness. Unity within the bounds of the word of God is a must. Maintaining this unity, for the most part, is accepting each other as personalities and thinking of one another better than ourselves. This in return would help prevent us from indulging in sin, engaging in legal actions, asserting our rights and gifts and polluting the gatherings of the Lord's people with ungodly conduct. Rather, we should keep an eye on the Lord, preach and imitate Christ, and be willing, when problems arise, to be the first to try and help others who have fallen.

The outcome was seen in the second letter where, in response to Paul's criticism and godly anger, visible repentance was displayed. Remember the Bible is replete with the theme of forgiveness. When there is true repentance we should help and restore rather than maintain long memories. One of the most victorious passages in the whole of our Bible, 1 Corinthians 15, was written to a church that many would have given up as a lost cause.

Day 3

GALATIA

Acts 13; 14; Galatians 1:1-24

This is the one epistle addressed to a region rather than a town or city. The extent of the region in Asia Minor addressed by Paul is not certain. If it was a geographical Galatia it would denote the ancient ethnic kingdom of Galatia but, if addressed in its political sense, it would be the Roman province by that name. It matters not that scholars are divided on this issue. What is clear from the account in Acts chapters 13 and 14 is that Paul visited the southern part of Galatia which includes the cities of Antioch, Lystra, Iconium and Derbe.

The content of the epistle is clear, direct and easily understood. Paul was in a hurry to point out that the so-called 'new gospel' was no gospel at all. The people addressed were those who had been converted under Paul's preaching, but were in imminent danger from a message that deprived them of their Christian freedom by including Jewish customs, auspicious days and, probably, dietary laws. It was a 'gospel' where faith alone was not sufficient.

Paul reminded his readers that soon after his conversion he spent time alone with the risen Lord in Arabia (Gal 1:17). This probably was in Syria, over a period of three years. This is why Paul mentions that the gospel came not from men, but directly to him from God (1:11). Its substance did not come via a 'mother church' in Jerusalem, but from the living God speaking direct to the apostle. Paul was not influenced by any man, but by God Himself.

It is good that God, in His sovereignty, allowed the errors and false doctrines to be aired. We would otherwise never have had preserved to us such clear-cut arguments to contradict the errors manifestly seen in Christendom today.

Another lesson in the sovereignty of God is seen from Paul being detained, through sickness, from leaving the area (4:13). This meant that despite short-term suffering he had a longer time for preaching and teaching the gospel in its pure form. Often it is only in retrospect that we see God's dealings with us for good, even if initially it involves difficulty and trial.

The Galatian epistle is a helpful introduction to the Roman epistle which deals with the doctrine of the gospel in a more systematic form. It is one of those epistles that can easily be read in one sitting. Why not try it today?

Day 4

EPHESUS

Acts 18:19 - 19:10; Ephesians 1:1-6

I remember once listening to a speaker who said that the book of Joshua was "the Ephesians of the Old Testament". My immediate reaction was that this was one of those bland statements that evoke a lot of 'amens' but have no real substance. But maybe the speaker was right. Not only do both books express hope and victory, and promise a higher plane of experience and existence, but the cities themselves testify to the overcoming power of God.

Jericho stood as an impregnable fortress to be overcome before the children of Israel could enter their promised possession. Ephesus too was to be conquered before the gospel could progress. In this city resided one of the seven wonders of the then-known world, the temple of Diana. It was the seat of heathendom and idol worship. Surely this new message brought by a physically small and weak man could not possibly penetrate the walls of the enemy! However, the gospel not only reached Ephesus, but it broke down the walls and the idol Diana literally fell on her face!

Ephesus was a port in Asia Minor, home to approximately two hundred and fifty thousand people, and was the capital of the Roman province of Asia. Paul visited the city in his second missionary journey, in about 53 AD, but this first visit was fairly brief. Two years later, however, whilst on his third journey, he stayed for about two years, and saw a vast area evangelised. Some ten years on he was in Rome, writing to his fellow Christians in Ephesus. It was in Rome that he met with Onesimus, the runaway slave, and Tychicus, and took the opportunity to use them to despatch the three prison writings. These were the epistles to the Ephesians, Philippians, and Colossians, and in addition to these there was the personal letter to his friend Philemon. Paul exhibited the same feeling for the saints as did his Master before him. Remember Paul was on trial for his life, and yet the saints were paramount in his thoughts. The Lord was to enter a trial and sufferings untold, and yet he spent time in that last week before the cross in encouraging and instructing His own.

The Lord also promised the disciples a good future, and so did the apostle. He reminded the Ephesian believers that they could now enjoy a foretaste of things to come. Already they had spiritual blessings in the heavenlies, despite still being earthbound and persecuted. Ephesus had a love for its priestess Diana, but from the second letter to the Ephesians, in Revelation 2, we know that the early Ephesian believers had a genuine love and affection for their Saviour. Sadly, it was the loss of this first love that eventually brought down the assembly and caused the lampstand to be removed. No wonder Paul's first letter had exhortations to wives, husbands and children to exhibit that same sacrificial love to each other as Christ had for the church.

Day 5

PHILIPPI

Acts 16:6-40; Philippians 1:1-11

The only point of grief to the apostle in this epistle is that there was contention between two sisters, Euodias and Syntyche. If there was going to be any acrimony and clash of personalities, one would have thought it would have come from a brother, the Philippian jailer, and a sister named Lydia. On the one hand, a respected business lady and, on the other, a rough, crude, callous Roman soldier. It's amazing what the grace of God can do, especially in the lives of those the world fear and despise. These two early converts undoubtedly lived harmoniously, and the assembly itself brought so much joy to the apostle. The Philippians never forgot him, and ministered to him in prison in Rome where others failed in this duty. One can see the former jailer constantly reminding the saints of what it was like to be incarcerated under the Roman regime, and to make sure the man who had suffered so much at his hand now enjoyed some of the basic comforts of life.

The church at Philippi revealed how practical fellowship in difficult circumstances means so much. The Macedonian believers had little of this world's goods, but when they heard of Paul's situation in Rome they got together their love gifts and sent them by the hand of Epaphroditus. It was when he returned that they received the letter from Paul. This attitude of heart in the saints emphasises two important principles. First, rather than just pray for someone (and that of course is very important) make some contact, just to let them know that you are thinking of them. Second, the Lord is no man's debtor. Not only did they receive a letter of thanks but some of the choicest words ever spoken about the Lord Jesus were communicated to them. How we thank God time and again for those early verses in chapter 2, which set forth God's matchless Servant.

Despite Paul's imprisonment this letter is a note of triumph and joy. The theme of joy and rejoicing is mentioned more than eighteen times in the course of just four chapters. This re-echoes the sentiments of Paul and Silas in Acts 16 when, suffering from a severe scourging, they were thrown into a dark inner dungeon, shackled fast in the stocks in the dead of night, and yet sang praises unto God. There is no greater testimony to the Lord than when we rise above our circumstances and give Him glory.

It is so easy, in adverse conditions, to bemoan our lot and concentrate on the evil world round about us, but in this beautiful letter Paul asks us to look beyond the filth and adversity of the world and set our thoughts and hearts on those things that are pure, lovely and of good report. It was a good report from Philippi that elevated the heart and spirit of the apostle.

Day 6

COLOSSE

Colossians 1:1-29

There is no record that Paul ever visited Colosse. Maybe Philemon, or some other person visiting Ephesus, heard Paul speak, was saved and returned with the message (Acts 19:10). We know from the letter to Philemon that the church met in Philemon's house (Philem 1:2). Houses were the customary venues in early church history. One advantage of this was that there were no descriptions over the entrance, such as hall, chapel or church. "The disciples were called Christians…" (Acts 11:26). To be called a Christian set one apart, often inviting danger but exhibiting reality.

The main problem affecting the church in Colosse was, as Dr. Alexander Maclaren puts it, "A peculiar form of heresy singularly compounded by Jewish ritualism and oriental mysticism". This isn't surprising, because many of the early believers were Jews and philosophers. The early believers had to start afresh and live by a brand new truth. What a joy to see in recent days young converts, saved out of the world with no religious baggage, judging both doctrine and practise by the word of God alone! Like it or not, many local churches who profess to gather to the name of Christ alone have customs and procedures that do not correspond with NT principles, and are simply man-made rules and regulations. Remember too that the fear of man can bring a snare (Prov 29:25). Before introducing corrective teaching, Paul gave thanks for their faith, hope and love. He also made Christ his central theme, and wrote what has become one of the most-quoted passages in our Bibles concerning the deity and perfection of God's blessed Son (1:14-20).

As is usual in his epistles, Paul divides the letter into two parts. One deals with doctrine, and the other practise. He prays that the church be filled with spiritual knowledge and that they might walk worthily. We might try and walk worthily, but how many times do we pray for spiritual knowledge?

Slavery was still an important institution in Roman culture. Paul doesn't mention slave trading, but makes it perfectly clear to his friend Philemon that his former rebellious slave is now a brother beloved. If there is one theme that is emphasised in the personal letter to Philemon at Colosse, it is that in God's assembly there should be no social distinctions whatsoever.

Day 7

THESSALONICA

Acts 17:1-9; 1 Thessalonians 1:1-10

Thessalonica was the capital of one of the important districts of Macedonia and named after the wife of Cassander who built the city. Paul visited the city on his second missionary journey (Acts 17:1-9). The first epistle to the Thessalonian saints was written, probably in Corinth, following the return of Timothy from Macedonia.

Two great things that emerge from this epistle are how much can be accomplished in just three weeks stay, and how young babes in Christ could absorb such teaching. The believers were probably only six months old spiritually, but they were able to understand Paul's letter. What a contrast to those at Corinth who, after five years, had not grown at all and were still carnal (1 Cor 3:1-3). Lack of reading and studying of God's word is one evidence of carnality.

Paul had to flee from Thessalonica but, in his absence, the church grew. Many missionaries, ejected from certain countries, fear the worst, but on their return find spiritual prosperity. Remember that one may plant and another may water, but God alone in His sovereign power gives the increase.

These young believers were worried that although the joy of a changed life was theirs here and now, what about the future? They knew that salvation involved eternal life, but would they ever see their Christian friends again? What a thrill it must have been to hear of God's timetable for the future. The first epistle centres around the Lord's coming to the air, and they are given the great consoling words which have meant so much to so many believers that wait to see their loved ones again (4:13-18). Paul reminds them that, before their great entry into heaven, they will all be reunited so that together they will enter the Father's house and see the Saviour.

Sadly, their joy was overshadowed by false teachers who convinced them that their present suffering meant the day of the Lord, the Tribulation, had arrived (2 Thess 2:1-3). Paul therefore writes his second epistle to remind them that before the Lord descends to the earth there must first come a time of apostasy. Finally, Paul reminds them that the wonderful prospect of the Lord's coming should not cause them to just idly wait, but to continue walking orderly, and not be neglectful of the common responsibilities of Christians to live and witness for Christ.

BRIAN RUSSELL

Week 18

7 PROMISES IN PSALM 91 TO THE ONE WHO LOVES GOD

Introduction

Psalm 91, a Messianic psalm, the author of which is not named, is in two clear parts. In verses 1-13 the psalmist tells of his trust in God who is his shadow, his refuge, his fortress, his shield and buckler, and his habitation, showing how God has met his need as he has passed through the difficulties of life. Verses 14-16 are Jehovah's response to the man who knows what it is to live in close relationship with his God. It is in these last three verses that we have the sevenfold blessing of God revealed.

It is important to notice that these blessings are the province of the man who knows God. This is seen first of all in his use of divine titles: "the most High" (vv.1, 9); "the Almighty" (v.1); "the Lord" (vv.2, 9); and "my God" (v.2). Further evidence of this is given in his knowledge of the enabling, care and protection of the One who bears these titles. This knowledge is not merely academic, nor theoretical, and it is not just experiential. It is the knowledge of the man who knows what it is to dwell in the actual presence of Him who provides that enabling, that care, and that protection.

Similarly there is nothing casual about the love of the psalmist for God. This is a deliberate, conscious love. It is not mere emotionalism, but the deep-seated, heart-felt love of the man who knows the person whom he loves. It is the love of the man who knows the secret place, and who knows the most High as his habitation.

The opening phrase of v.14 gives the divine verdict on this love: "Because he (the psalmist) hath set his love upon me (God), therefore will I…". The God whom the writer knows in these different ways is the God who, in responding grace, will bring him into the practical experience of rich, complete, divine blessing.

How true of us. The more we get to know our God, the closer we are to Him, the greater our experience of divine blessing will be. Divine blessings are given abundantly, "God … giveth to all men liberally, and upbraideth not" (James 1:5), but those who will experience them most are those who are most in His presence.

Day 1

"THEREFORE WILL I DELIVER HIM"

Psalm 91:14

This is the first of the seven blessings set forth in verses 14-16, and relates very much to the verses which lead up to it. The psalmist has passed through difficult days. He has known the goodness of God, and has set his love upon Him. Now there is the future, and it is unknown. God in His grace gives the blessing of reassurance that, in whatever ordeals are to be faced, He will deliver his servant. The meaning is that He will keep him secure, and bring him to a place of safety.

Every believer knows, to a greater or lesser extent, what it is to go through times of trial, testing, and trouble. How reassuring to know that there is watching over us a God who says, "I will deliver him, I will bring him to a safe place".

When we pass through the waters He is with us (Isa 43:2); when the pathway is arduous we are strengthened and upheld by His right hand (Isa 41:10); when our foes multiply His right hand is still there to succour (Ps 138:7). Ultimately, if the Lord be not come, there is for each one of us the "valley of the shadow of death". We are not kept *from* it, but rather we are kept *through* it – "Thou art with me …" (Ps 23:4).

The writer of Psalm 91 knew deliverance from danger and deliverance through the trial. How different from the One who was delivered up for our offences. For Him there was none to save, there was none to help. The psalmist could say that "The Lord … hath not given me over unto death" (Ps 118:18), but God, we remember, "spared not his own Son, but delivered him up for us all" (Rom 8:32). Our Saviour knew what it was to be "a reproach of men, and despised of the people" (Ps 22:6). He suffered the scorn of His enemies and the piercing of hands and feet; He was the One who "became obedient unto death, even the death of the cross" (Phil 2:8). The result is that we now know what it is to have been delivered from bondage and the fear of death (Heb 2:15), from the power of darkness (Col 1:13), from this present evil world (Gal 1:4), and from the wrath to come (1 Thess 1:10).

Like the psalmist, we too have been delivered, and will yet be delivered when He who is our hope will bring us safely into His very presence. We can, therefore, echo the words of the apostle: "God … delivered us from so great a death, and doth deliver: in whom we trust that he will yet deliver us" (2 Cor 1:9-10).

Day 2

"I will set him on high"

Psalm 91:14

This promised blessing also comes with a specific reason – "because he hath known my name". The use of divine titles, as we have seen, indicates how well the psalmist knew his God. The names of individuals in Scripture were not given accidentally, or at the whim of parents; they had meaning and relevance to the person on whom they were bestowed. How much more does this apply to the titles of God.

In the preceding verses, the psalmist has shown that his knowledge of God is both personal and profound. His use of the various titles of God indicates that he not only had an appreciation of His position as the "most High", the One who "ruleth in the kingdom of men" (Dan 4:17,25,32), he also knew the power of "the Almighty" – El Shaddai; the permanence of "the Lord" – Jehovah; and the personal care of "my God" – Elohim. This knowledge was a recognition of the holy character and infinite worth of God, and is the province and privilege of those who dwell "in the secret place of the most High" (v.1), and who have made the Lord their habitation.

This is the one who will be set up on high. He will be in a place of exaltation, but also in a place of safety, for that is the sense of the phrase. Those whom God exalts are those whom He keeps.

Think of the position which is ours as those who have been redeemed by precious blood. Remember the privileges which are ours in Christ. Never lose sight of what we were and what we have become through sovereign grace. Are we not a kingdom of priests, a holy and royal priesthood? Have we not received the adoption of sons? Are we not accepted in the beloved? Truly, we have been set on high!

However, we must ever be conscious of the fact that our blessings derive from the person and work of the One who became low, who "though he was rich, yet for your sakes he became poor, that ye through his poverty might be rich" (2 Cor 8:9). He who was "brought … into the dust of death" (Ps 22:15) knew what it was to "sink in deep mire, where there is no standing" (Ps 69:2), and could say, "I am a worm, and no man" (Ps 22:6).

With thoughts like these, it is fitting that we should take heed of the injunction of the apostle: "Humble yourselves therefore under the mighty hand of God, that he may exalt you in due time: Casting all your care upon him; for he careth for you" (1 Pet 5.6-7).

Day 3

"I WILL ANSWER HIM"

Psalm 91:15

Countless people know what it is to call upon God. The repentant sinner, in deep conviction, will echo the words of the publican and cry, "God be merciful to me a sinner" (Luke 18:13). That such a cry is heard in heaven is one of the wonders of divine grace, and is a continual testimony to the efficacy of the work of Christ on the cross.

The redeemed saint will call upon God for strength, guidance, and help in every aspect of daily life and witness for his Lord. This ought to be our constant habit, for without that strength which is made perfect in weakness, without the leading and guiding of the Holy Spirit, and without that help which can only come from the Lord, we will achieve nothing, we are in real danger of going astray, and we will be powerless in our service for the Master.

Many of God's dear people know what it is to call upon the Lord in times of distress, doubt, and trouble, seeking from Him solace, assurance, and succour. They know from personal, often bitter, experience that "the salvation of the righteous is of the Lord: he is their strength in the time of trouble" (Ps 37:39).

What is common to all of these situations is the promise which is given here to the psalmist: "He shall call upon me, and I will answer him". It is a source of constant marvel to us, and a reason for thankfulness and worship, that we have a God who answers us when we call upon Him, and whose ear is not heavy that it cannot hear (Isa 59:1).

What is even more amazing is that our God not only responds to our cries, but knows our needs even before we ask Him (Matt 6:8). He "is able to do exceeding abundantly above all that we ask or think" (Eph 3:20). What faithfulness, what care, what dependability, what reassurance, what encouragement!

While these things are so precious to us, our minds necessarily turn to the One who called, and for whom there was no such answer. How can we ever comprehend those deep sufferings on the cross which caused the Saviour to cry, "My God, my God, why hast thou forsaken me?" (Matt 27.46)? The second verse of Psalm 22 is so poignant and full of meaning, reflecting something of the experience of Christ: "O my God, I cry in the daytime, but thou hearest not". And the following verse gives us the awesome reason: "But thou art holy, O thou that inhabitest the praises of Israel".

Let us ever remember what He experienced so that we might fully rest upon this promise: "He shall call upon me, and I will answer him".

Day 4

"I WILL BE WITH HIM"

Psalm 91:15

The second of the three promises in verse 15 flows naturally from the first. It is one thing to answer a call, it is quite another matter to come alongside the one who is calling and be with him in his trouble. Our God promises to those who call upon Him, to those who are in trouble, both His answer and His presence.

Isaiah brought to Israel the reason for, and the result of, this promise. God said to His people then, "Fear not: for I have redeemed thee, I have called thee by thy name; thou art mine. When thou passest through the waters, I will be with thee … when thou walkest through the fire, thou shalt not be burned …" (43:1-2). They were God's people, His own possession, and He would never abandon them.

As we have seen in connection with the first promise, we are not told here that we will be exempt from trouble, nor are we told that we will necessarily be delivered from it. We are, however, given the greater promise that there is One who will be with us in the trouble. Daniel's three friends knew that presence in the midst of what otherwise would have been certain death. Looking into the furnace, Nebuchadnezzar had to exclaim that he could see "four men loose, walking in the midst of the fire, and they have no hurt; and the form of the fourth is like the Son of God (Dan 3:25). How perceptive! The One whom Shadrach, Meshach, and Abednego served so faithfully was Himself true to His promise and was with them in the furnace.

We, too, are redeemed; we, too, have been called by God. We are His, having been bought with a price (1 Cor 6:20; 7:23). We can lay claim to the promise that when we pass through the waters of tribulation and distress He is with us. How great a comfort to know that what the Lord said to His disciples, He also says to us: "Lo, I am with you alway" (Matt 28:20).

Again, our thoughts turn to Christ. He who cried to the One who had promised never to fail nor forsake His servant (Josh 1:5), He who cried to the One who will never forsake His own (Heb 13:5), is prefigured in Psalm 22:11, for when trouble was near there was none to help Him. He was forsaken by those closest to Him, and even by God Himself (Matt 26:56; 27:46). The aloneness of the Cross must have been a searing experience for the Lord.

May each of us be able to grasp hold of this promise in times of adversity and trouble, for it is "the Lord thy God, he it is that doth go with thee; he will not fail thee, nor forsake thee" (Deut 31:6).

Day 5

"I WILL DELIVER HIM, AND HONOUR HIM"

Psalm 91:15

The first point we need to notice in this promise is that the word "deliver" used here is a different word from that in v.14. There it incorporated the idea of bringing into a safe place; here it can have the meaning of equipping for battle or conflict. In this context we immediately think of the battle armour of the believer as set forth in Ephesians 6.10-18.

Notice that the armour in Ephesians is already available to us; it is our responsibility to put it on and use it. Notice, too, that there is equipment which is for defence and that which is for attack. There are times when we need to defend ourselves against the assaults of the world, the flesh, and the devil.

We must not restrict ourselves, however, to that which is purely defensive. We must advance, and whether it be in our own spiritual development, or in the spread of the gospel, we are not to stand still but to make progress, to grow, and to "abound more and more" in the things of the Lord (1 Thess 4:1).

It is significant that in Ephesians 6 Paul writes twice of "the whole armour of God" (vv.11, 13). He wants to remind the Ephesian believers of the fact that He who says, "I will deliver…", will also provide all that is required for that deliverance. We need to recognise that our strength is "in the Lord, and in the power of his might" (v.10), and that prayer is a vital element of our armoury (v.18).

The second part of the promise is "honour", and this word has in it the idea of weight, riches, glory. While we revel in the fact that for the believer there is future glory, there is also present responsibility. To His people Israel, God said that it would be "them that honour me I will honour" (1 Sam 2:30).

The Lord Jesus Himself echoed this when He said, "If any man serve me, him will my Father honour" (John 12:26). God's honour is not bestowed lightly, and we must remind ourselves that these promises were made to a man who lived close to God.

For the believer there is the prospect of an exceeding and eternal weight of glory (2 Cor 4:17), a body like unto His body of glory (Phil 3:21, JND) and, for shepherds, a crown of glory (1 Pet 5:4). For the Lord there was on earth no honour or glory from men. From them He received rejection, opposition, hatred, violence, reviling and, ultimately, the death of the cross. All this that we might share in the glory and honour which are rightly His!

Day 6

"With long life will I satisfy him"

Psalm 91:16

In Old Testament times, obedience to God was rewarded by prosperity and longevity. In Exodus 20:12, "days … long upon the land" was the promise to those who honoured father and mother. To those who kept God's statutes and commandments, the promise was that they would prolong "thy days upon the earth" (Deut 4:40). The finding of wisdom would bring length of days as well as riches and honour (Prov 3:13, 16).

In this present dispensation this is clearly not the case. What then are we to make of this promise? The answer lies in the use of the word "satisfy". A life which is "full of days" need not necessarily be satisfying, as many have discovered. A life which is lived in the presence of God will always be satisfying, no matter how long or short it is.

For the believer today, satisfaction is not found in the material and temporal world, but in those things which are spiritual and eternal. "We look not at the things which are seen, but at the things which are not seen: for the things which are seen are temporal; but the things which are not seen are eternal" (2 Cor 4:18). To spend a life in pursuit of so-called worldly satisfaction can lead to nothing but emptiness and disillusionment and, sadly, this can even be true of the Christian who is no longer "Looking unto Jesus" (Heb 12:2). A life lived close to God, following the Saviour, being led by the Spirit, will always be a life which is pleasing to the Saviour and satisfying to the saint. What God promises to those who dwell in His habitation (Ps 91:9), in the sanctuary, is a quality of life which surpasses anything earth can offer.

Again we can turn our minds to One who did not know actual "long life" for "he was cut off out of the land of the living: for the transgression of my people was he stricken" (Isa 53:8). It is because of this that we have the promise and privilege of a satisfying, satisfied life.

In Psalm 16, David triumphantly states that in the presence of God there is fullness of joy, and that there are pleasures for evermore at His right hand (v.11). For the believer the full satisfaction of joy and pleasure will not come until we are in the presence of our Lord, but surely there is a measure in which we can enter into the good of these things while here on earth. Both Paul (Gal 5:22) and Peter (1 Pet 1:8) bring before us the joy experienced by the believer in this life. How much greater that satisfaction, that joy will be in a day to come!

Day 7

"I WILL ... SHEW HIM MY SALVATION"

Psalm 91:16

This is the climax of the promises and of the psalm. It is the ultimate result of dwelling in "the secret place of the most High", of knowing God in the personal, intimate way described by the psalmist.

Israel knew the salvation of God from their hard bondage in Egypt, but we have known deliverance from a much greater bondage than theirs ever was. The bondage of sin, the thraldom of Satan, held us in an inflexible grasp, and would still do had it not been for the grace of God towards us in bringing us into salvation.

That salvation is secure. The work has been done – "Christ died for our sins" (1 Cor 15:3); the foundation of God is unchanging and sure – "The Lord knoweth them that are his" (2 Tim 2:19); and we have the witness of the Spirit in our hearts – "The Spirit itself beareth witness with our spirit, that we are the children of God" (Rom 8:16). Neither the world, the flesh, nor the devil can break that threefold cord, for nothing "shall be able to separate us from the love of God, which is in Christ Jesus our Lord" (Rom 8:39). We rest with absolute assurance on the finished work of the Saviour.

We have been told often that salvation can be viewed in three aspects. We have been saved from the *penalty* of sin – that took place on the day of our conversion. We are saved from the *power* of sin – that is our daily resource as we wrestle against the promptings of the "old man". We will yet be saved from the *presence* of sin when we are in the presence of Him who is sinless, and who purchased our salvation at such a great cost. How our hearts should overflow with thanksgivings, praise, and worship as we consider Him who is the captain of our salvation, and the author of eternal salvation (Heb 2:10; 5:9).

Just as salvation is unshakeable, so are all the promises of God, being "in him ... yea, and in him Amen, unto the glory of God by us" (2 Cor 1:20). We stand in relationship to One who is "the mediator of a better covenant, which was established upon better promises" (Heb 8:6), and the promises given to us are "exceeding great and precious" (2 Pet 1:4).

In conclusion, therefore, let us remind ourselves that these promises are based on the work of our blessed Lord, are infinite in their scope, and are given to us in grace. In response, let us also remember that they are most appreciated by those who know their God, live daily close to Him, and know His habitation as theirs.

IAIN WILKIE

Week 19

7 MOUNTAIN SCENES IN MATTHEW'S GOSPEL

Joshua 14:6-15

Introduction

Matthew wrote his Gospel mainly for Jews, proving Jesus fulfils the OT prophecies of the Messiah, and foreshadows His future second advent of kingdom glory. All Scripture is for us, if not about us, and there is much doctrinal and devotional truth for believers today in Matthew's Gospel. The following articles major on the devotional aspects.

Mountains figure a great deal in the Bible; they are pivotal in its history. Great men and dramatic events are associated with them: Noah offered burnt offerings on Ararat; Abraham offered up Isaac on Moriah; Moses received the law on Sinai; Caleb claimed his inheritance on Hebron; David ruled from Zion; Elijah destroyed the prophets of Baal on Carmel. These are places of divine elevation and revelation where we breathe a rarefied atmosphere and enjoy heavenly breezes.

Caleb's vision of Hebron never dimmed. The divine promise was never forgotten, so he claimed Hebron – "give me this mountain" (Josh 14:12). It was a bold claim of faith, but God is always ready to give "every good gift and every perfect gift" (James 1:17).

To obtain it, Caleb scaled the heights, dispossessed the foe and enjoyed the fruitfulness of his inheritance. Are we bold enough to say 'give me' in order to possess our possessions? We must "get me to the mountain of myrrh" in the heavenly places, seeking things above, combating our foes, to enjoy fellowship, fragrance and fruitfulness.

> "Lord lift me up and let me stand
> By faith on heaven's tableland;
> A higher plane than I have found,
> Lord, plant my feet on higher ground".

Seven mountain scenes are described by Matthew; 'Mount' Calvary is not included as it is not so described. We will climb these mountains in company with the Saviour, sample the views and share by faith the memorable experiences of the disciples. May our meditations bring us to higher ground, far above the "restless world that wars below"!

Every mountain has a corresponding valley. The word 'mountain' is used symbolically for problems, but faith can move mountains (Matt 17:20; 21:21). What an encouragement in the midst of mountainous difficulties! One day all the world's intractable problems will be solved, "every valley shall be exalted, and every mountain and hill shall be made low" (Isa 40:4). Lord how long? Hasten Thy coming!

THE MOUNT OF TEMPTATION

Matthew 4:1-11

The temptation (to test or prove) of the Lord Jesus took place immediately after His baptism; "then was Jesus led … to be tempted …" (Matt 4:1). It was the devil's challenge to the declaration of the Sonship of Christ – note the repeated "if thou be the Son of God". He approaches the Lord subtly as the tempter (v.3), the devil (v.5), and Satan (v.10), and attacks first the body, then the spirit and the soul – the whole person. It is the same strategy as in Eden, namely the principles of "the lust of the flesh, and the lust of the eyes, and the pride of life" (1 John 2:16). The Lord is holy, and cannot respond to evil suggestions. They did cause Him inward pain, however, "He suffered being tempted" (Heb 2:18).

There are at least five reasons for the temptations:

1. **To prove His Person** – materials are often tested to prove their reliability and validity. Similarly Christ was tempted that it might be publicly evident that He is Holy and He is God who "cannot lie" and "cannot be tempted with evil".

2. **To prevail where Adam failed** – Eden and the wilderness are in stark contrast. Adam had every advantage, Christ had none. But what Adam lost, Christ in manhood has regained, and far more, for God and mankind.

3. **To prepare for Priesthood** – "He was in all points tempted as we are, apart from (the question of) sin" in order to be able to succour those who are tempted. Sympathy for those in affliction does not depend on the experience of sin, but on the experience of similar circumstances.

4. **To provide an Example** – in His temptation the Lord exposes the tactics of Satan, and exemplifies the way to resist and repel him, by the intelligent use of the word of God.

5. **To proclaim His Authority** – "get thee hence, Satan" and "the devil leaveth him" demonstrate our Saviour's superiority. What a comfort this is to know! This temptation (vv.8-9) was the most subtle as it included all the elements of passion, pride and power endemic in human nature. It took place on an "exceeding high mountain" where the Lord was shown and offered "all the kingdoms of the world and the glory of them" if He would worship the devil. To accept would avoid the Cross with all its suffering. Unhesitatingly the Lord quotes the Scripture, "Thou shalt worship the Lord thy God, and him only shalt thou serve".

Christ in manhood will one day receive the kingdoms and the glory from His Father. "Ask of me and I will give the nations for thine inheritance and the uttermost parts of the earth for thy possession" (Ps 2:8). "The kingdoms of this world are become the kingdoms of our Lord, and of his Christ; and he shall reign for ever and ever" (Rev 11:15). Hallelujah!

Day 2

THE MOUNT OF INSTRUCTION

Matthew 5:1-16

The 'Sermon on the Mount' is a proclamation of the King's manifesto and mandates for His kingdom. It is a reflection of the character of the King Himself. It is not a way of salvation, for the Lord is addressing disciples. The teaching is relevant for all believers as it contains abiding moral and spiritual values. Moses received the precepts of the law; Christ reveals the principles of grace. Sinai is rather negative and outward; the Sermon is positive and inward. The teaching is upward about God, inward about us, outward about the world, onward about heaven; "never man spake like this man"! His message is unique and unequalled.

Character and Conduct (ch.5) – The Sermon begins with 'blessed' and ends with a 'bang' ("great was the fall of it", 7:27). Thus the Lord firstly attracts the people's attention and finally attacks their conscience. He is the master Preacher. 'Blessed' means to be supremely happy, enjoying a sense of divine favour. These beatitudes (beautiful attitudes) in verses 3-9 reveal the secret of a happy life based on holiness, and extol the virtues of humility, meekness, righteousness, mercy, purity and peacemaking. Those who practice and preach them are promised their due reward both now and in heaven. Such characteristics develop experience, endurance and influence (vv.10-16), and act as salt and light in society. Salt preserves, flavours, thaws and heals. Do we have a corresponding moral affect on people around us? Light attracts, reflects and directs. Do we attract by our lifestyle, reflect Christ and direct souls to our Saviour?

Communion and Confidence (ch.6) – The private life of unbelievers may not be considered important, but the private life of the saint is of the utmost importance. Here the Lord touches on the secret life before the Father: "thy Father, which seeth" (v.18); "your heavenly Father knoweth" (v.32). How searching! He deals with the matter of giving (manward), praying (Godward) and fasting (selfward), and insists on their diligent exercise before the Father. These are the marks of sincerity and truth. Then the Lord warns of materialism instead of "laying up treasure in heaven". He knows our needs and will provide "according to his riches in glory".

Challenge and Choice (ch.7) – The Lord brings His hearers to the crossroads of life (vv.13-29). He throws out the challenge and presents the choice. There are two roads, the broad or narrow; two trees, corrupt or good; two houses, on the rock or on the sand. Which road are we treading? What fruit are we bearing? What character are we building? So the sermon ends, searching our hearts. The challenge and choice demand a change.

Day 3

THE MOUNT OF INTERCESSION

Matthew 14:15-33

Alone in Prayer (vv.22-23). The Saviour was seeking communion with His Father and the Lord therefore "constrained the disciples to get into a ship and go before him to the other side, while he sent the multitudes away". Crowd control is not easy, but the Lord arranges everything according to His purpose. It is a mark of His dignity and authority. Then "He went up into a mountain to pray and he was there alone". All night He prayed, interceding, among other matters, for the disciples who were now in the midst of a storm. This is a precious picture of Christ as our High Priest, ever living "to make intercession for us". How often are we alone with God?

Amidst the Storm (v.24). Distance and darkness separated the disciples from the Master and they were in grave danger, "tossed with waves for the wind was contrary". But "He saw them toiling" (Mark 6:48). If only we were conscious of such watchfulness in times of trouble. He is nearer than we think! The disciples felt abandoned, yet they should have remembered that the Lord thrust them into the storm. "He constrained them". They were to "go before Him". He was coming, and to the "other side" they would arrive! It was all part of His purpose; "the dark threads are as needful, in the Weaver's skilful hand, as the threads of gold and silver in the pattern He has planned".

Astride the Waves (vv.25-27). It was the darkest hour and the delay had become unbearable. Then the Lord "went unto them walking on the sea". Yet the disciples thought it was a spirit and were filled with dread. Immediately the familiar voice was heard above the sound of many waters, "be of good cheer, it is I (I am), be not afraid". One can only imagine the relief and peace that flooded into their hearts.

No circumstance is beyond His control. The disciples looked, then listened. Do we look for the Master and listen for His voice in the midst of a storm?

> "Still He looks with tender eye,
>   Still He to His own draws nigh,
> Still He has beneath His feet,
>   Waters that around us beat".

Adoring the Saviour (vv.28-33). Peter overcame his fear and stepped out on to the water, but his faith was inadequate and, beginning to sink, he uttered a short and simple prayer, 'Lord, save me". That cry drew forth the mighty hand of Christ to deliver him. Back in the ship the wind ceased and, worshipping Him, they said "Thou art the Son of God". The experience, though frightening, was well worthwhile.

Day 4

THE MOUNT OF COMPASSION

Matthew 15:29-39

The Context. This is the scene of the feeding of 4000, besides women and children, on a mountain side. The more familiar feeding of 5000 is recorded in all four Gospels, but this event is mentioned only by Matthew and Mark. The two miracles are often referred to as the double-miracle, and thus the critics and cynics aver them to be the same. It is clear, however, that they occurred on separate occasions. The times, people, circumstances and locations are all different. Indeed, Jesus Himself refers to them both in Matthew 16:9-10 as separate events. So why are there two similar miracles? John Heading comments "there could have been more; two are recorded, since two is the number of effective witness".

The Crowds. The Lord was thronged by multitudes of people, some drawn by need, others by curiosity. The power and personality of the Saviour drew people to Him in droves, bringing with them the sick and the disabled, the young and the old. Many came from far (Mark 8:3) to see and hear Him. They were an eager and expectant crowd, and Jesus "went up into a mountain and sat down" ready as ever to receive them and speak to them. Let us pray that such an interest might be kindled today, and the voice of the Lord be heard by the unbelieving multitudes!

The Cures. After the teaching, there was healing. Teaching always had priority. The Lord is concerned for the body as well as the soul, and one blessed day we shall be perfect in both. There were all sorts of disabilities represented, but nothing was beyond the power of the Saviour. The text simply says "He healed them". What lovely compassion! He manifested "the powers of the world to come", in which kingdom there will be no disabilities at all. The people were ecstatic, and "wondered, when they saw the dumb to speak, the maimed to be whole, the lame to walk, and the blind to see: and they glorified the God of Israel" (Matt 15:31).

The Compassion. Unlike the feeding of the 5000, Jesus Himself initiates this miracle. "I have compassion on the multitude, because they have been with me three days". Their provisions had run out, their bodies were tired and the Lord was concerned "lest they faint in the way". How marvellous that the Lord of Glory should show such compassion and consideration, but it is just like Him! May we emulate Him more? He then multiplied the loaves and fishes to feed that vast crowd "and they did all eat and were filled". Seven baskets full remained: there was no want, but there was also no waste!

Day 5

THE MOUNT OF TRANSFIGURATION

Matthew 17:1-9

Setting of the Verses. In the previous chapter is Peter's memorable confession of Christ as the Messiah and Son of God (16:16), and the first mention of the crucifixion (and resurrection) by the Lord, followed by the stringent claims of discipleship. Although Peter acknowledged the person of Christ, he failed to understand the passion of Christ; he and the disciples were left confused and bewildered. However they were soon to be reassured on the holy mount.

Scene of the Vision. Only Peter, James and John were selected to accompany the Lord. They had been with Him to witness the raising of Jairus' daughter, and they would see the agony of Gethsemane. Observe in v.1, "Jesus bringeth them" – their direction; "up into a high mountain" – elevation; "apart" – separation. Do we fulfil these conditions to obtain a glimpse of His glory?

Sign of Victory. The transfiguration was confirmation of the person and work of the Saviour, and of the glory that would follow. It was a sign that victory was assured, notwithstanding death and suffering, for Christ would triumph and the kingdom glory be revealed. The transfiguration was a foretaste and foregleam of that glory. These three disciples later suffered for their Lord by martyrdom and exile, but what an encouragement this experience was in later days! (2 Pet 1:16-18).

Sight of the Vision. The dramatic changes in the appearance of the Lord are celestial (sun and light) in Matthew, terrestrial (snow and earth) in Mark 9 and spiritual (prayer and altered countenance) in Luke 9, appropriate to their different presentations of Christ. Matthew says "His face did shine as the sun and his raiment as light", suggesting sovereignty and purity, twin themes of Matthew's Gospel (cf. Gen 1:16; 2 Sam 23:3-4; Mal 4:2). The Saviour was enveloped in a blaze of glory, not reflected or conferred, but intrinsic and inherent; "Who being the brightness of his glory" (Heb 1:3)

Sound of a Voice. Suddenly Moses and Elijah, representatives of the law and the prophets, appear in glory. What plain evidence of heaven, and life after death! We also "shall appear with him in glory" (Col 3:4). They talk about His decease (exodus), verifying His earlier pronouncements and assuring the disciples that His death would be no accident, but an accomplishment. Peter's comment "let us make three tabernacles" was interrupted by "a bright cloud" (the shekinah?) and a voice which said "this is my beloved Son in whom I am well pleased", affirming the truth of Peter's confession. The disciples fell on their faces and when they "lifted up their eyes they saw no man save Jesus only". May we be inspired by the coming glory!

Day 6

THE MOUNT OF PREDICTION

Matthew 24:1-31

The Period Foretold. The lead-in to this prophecy is "your house is left unto you desolate … ye shall not see me henceforth, till ye shall say, Blessed is he that cometh in the name of the Lord" (23:38-39). These statements mark the rejection of Christ at His first advent, and His reception by Israel at His second advent. This discourse, as Jesus sat on Mount Olivet, concerns matters between these two events. The 'glory' departed from the sanctuary in Ezekiel 11:23, so the 'glory' in the person of Christ now departs; "Jesus went out and departed from the temple" (24:1). The prophecies are distinctly Jewish: the church and the rapture were mysteries to be revealed later.

The Pattern of Events. This extends to 24:31 after which parables and illustrations of the end times are introduced through to chapter 25. The destruction of the temple by the Romans in AD 70 is predicted in verse 2, and the answer to the disciples' question "what shall be the sign of thy coming?" is then dealt with. Deception religiously; distress nationally (wars); disasters naturally; depravity socially; "all these are the beginning of sorrows" (vv.4-8). These things intensify in the first half of Daniel's 70th week after the rapture of the church. Persecution, hatred and hostility will be such that "the love of many shall wax cold" (vv.9-14). In the mercy of God, multitudes will be saved in this period (Rev 7:4-17). Worse conditions come in the second half of Daniel's 70th week, the time of Jacob's trouble (Jer 30:7). The "abomination of desolation" set up in the temple will commence a time of unparalleled suffering, and unprecedented religious deception marked by counterfeit signs and wonders, the great tribulation (v.21).

The Prospect of His Coming. The revelation of Christ will be universal, public and dramatic (vv.27-31). The whole sky will suddenly shine with lightning, followed by the darkening of the sun and moon, and the falling of heavenly bodies. Then "every eye shall see him" as He comes in power and glory (Rev 1:7). The nations will be judged, Israel will repent, and the millennial reign begin. Final victory and vindication for the valiant Son of God at last!

The Purpose Intended. Prophecy is not given to satisfy curiosity, it has a higher purpose. "See that ye be not troubled" (v.6); the gracious Saviour does not want us to fear. "Whoso readeth, let him understand" (v.15): He wants us to know His purpose. The injunctions "take heed", "believe it not" and "behold I have told you" (vv.4, 23, 25, 26); He wants us to be prepared and to live in the light of coming events.

Day 7

THE MOUNT OF COMMISSION

Matthew 28:16-20

The Place. The Lord's ministry commenced in Galilee of the Gentiles (4:15-16) and it ends there. Jerusalem had formally and finally rejected Him; Galilee was full of many Gentiles so, anticipating their blessing, He turns to them. Thus He said to His disciples "after I am risen I will go before you into Galilee". The Good Shepherd was gathering His scattered sheep to meet with them again. After the resurrection the angel said "He goeth before you into Galilee". The risen Saviour Himself repeated that (28:7, 10). Thus "the eleven went away into Galilee into a mountain as Jesus had appointed them". This meeting was crucial to the launch of the gospel and may be where they met "above 500 brethren at once" (1 Cor 15:6).

The Person. "When they saw him, they worshipped him" prostrating themselves before His majesty. Do we thus worship? Eight times in this Gospel Christ is worshipped. Yet "some doubted". This hardly refers to the eleven who were now confirmed believers, but others were present who found it hard to believe their eyes. But soon such doubts would vanish. This is natural enough, and lends credence to the story. May our occasional doubts be dispelled? Resurrection is more difficult *not* to believe in view of the facts and the many witnesses.

The Power. "All power (authority) is given unto me". What a proclamation of victory! The erstwhile victim is now the victor. All His enemies vanquished, the risen conqueror reigns supreme. Praise His Name! Authority in good hands is the right use of power. All power was His before the cross but now, as "the firstborn from the dead", He exercises authority over the new creation.

The Programme. The fourfold commission "go, disciple, baptise, teach" has a universal application, "all nations". This is the responsibility of every believer, not only the preachers. We have a solemn duty to evangelise in our family, community, school, college, business or wherever. What contribution are we making?

> "Shall I go and empty handed?
> Shall I meet my Saviour so?
> Not one soul with which to greet Him
> Shall I empty handed go?"

The Promise. "Lo I am with you all the days, even unto the end of the age". How precious! This is more than a promise, it is a fact. Matthew, by the Spirit begins with "Emmanuel", God with us, and he ends "I am with you".

RAY DAWES

Week 20

7 FEATURES OF THE MAN OF GOD IN 2 TIMOTHY 2

Introduction

In presenting to Timothy seven figures of the man of God, Paul has in mind that continuance in the things of the Lord can never be taken for granted. He has just been speaking of the departure, possibly from the faith, certainly from Paul himself, of Phygellus and Hermogenes (2 Tim 1:15), believers of whom we know little but whose defection doubtless caused much grief to the apostle. In contrast, the heart of Paul had been much comforted by the selfless devotion of Onesiphorus. This dear brother had actively sought out the apostle (1:17) and ministered to his practical needs regardless of the fact that Paul was chained to a Roman guard.

Paul knows that his earthly course is almost over, and others must pick up the baton and run with it. Understandably, he fears for them. He recalls all the hazards, privations and trials that he has endured for the Lord, and counts them but "light affliction" against the backdrop of eternity (2 Cor 4:17). But how will the next generation fare? Will they show the same determination, commitment and devotion to the work of the Lord?

Is an older saint reading this passage and feeling very much as the apostle did? You are thinking of the sacrifices you have made, your lifetime commitment to the local assembly in good times and bad and, perhaps, you are despondent because you cannot see the same features of tenacity and commitment in a rising generation. Fear not, beloved brother, dear sister. Assembly testimony will not collapse if you and your peers are taken home to glory before the Lord comes. Remember, each assembly belongs to the Lord and is infinitely precious to Him. He will have men and women in place to continue the work for His glory, but He expects participation from you and from them.

Very kindly, let me ask what you are doing to prepare others to continue the work? Do you simply bemoan the loss of a faithful generation, or are you actively investing prayer and encouragement in the rising generation? Each of these seven figures will instruct Timothy as to his responsibility, but the fact they are written at all proves that the aged Paul was facing up to his.

Day 1

THE DEVOTION AND RESPONSIBILITY OF A CHILD

2 Timothy 2:1-2

The tender description of Timothy as Paul's "son" eloquently declares the place the younger man had in the heart of the apostle. It is widely supposed, on good scriptural grounds, that Paul had led Timothy to Christ, completing the chain whose first links had been Timothy's godly mother and grandmother (1 Cor 4:15; 2 Tim 1:5). The word "son" should more accurately be translated 'child', better emphasising both the responsibility of care that Paul felt for him, and also the responsibility that Timothy bore to pay good heed to Paul's counsel and instruction. It is a joy to every father to know that his children share the same values and interests that are precious to him, and the apostle John expressed the same thought concerning those who had been brought to faith in Christ through his ministry: "I have no greater joy than to hear that my children walk in truth" (3 John 1:4).

Fathers, what impressions are we making on our children? Will their foremost memory of us be that we loved the Lord, revered His word, delighted in His people and put the local assembly at the centre of our lives? Are we training our children for earthly success at the expense of heavenly reward? May God grant us the great wisdom we need to see that our children grow up "strong in the grace that is in Christ Jesus" (v.1).

It has often been pointed out that, in verse 2, Paul has in mind four generations of godly men. As he thinks of the preservation of all that had been revealed to him, "that which is perfect" (1 Cor 13:10), he is not looking only at Timothy but also at a further two generations beyond. Paul, as he writes, is around sixty years of age, and Timothy about forty years old. The younger man has been consistently and systematically taught by the older over many years of fellowship together. All that Paul had taught had been verified by witnesses, and Timothy could have the utmost confidence in the veracity of all that had been committed to him. He was now the repository of a body of truth that must be faithfully, accurately and fully passed on to the next generation of faithful men. They, in turn, would bear the grave responsibility of diligently transmitting to the generation after them the things that Timothy had passed to themselves. What a privilege! What a responsibility!

Let us see to it, in the fear of God, that we discharge fully our responsibility to pass on the truth of the word of God to those coming behind. Leaving a legacy of dogma, mantra and tradition will neither bring reward to us nor help to those who have to continue the work when we have gone. Only "the same" will suffice.

Day 2

THE DUTY AND RIGOURS OF A COMBATANT

2 Timothy 2:3-4

Every kind father will do his best to shelter his children from the rigours of life but, eventually, they have to face the icy blast of life and its trials for themselves. Referring back to his exhortation to Timothy to "be strong in the grace that is in Christ Jesus" (v.1), Paul explains why that strength will be vital. Timothy will have to learn to endure affliction and trouble in his service for the Lord, and his attitude toward such suffering must be that of the soldier on active duty. The word translated "endure hardness" in verse 3 is used four times in the NT, and three of those references are in the second letter to Timothy (2:3; 2:9; 4:5). The fourth reference is, "Is any among you *afflicted*? let him pray" (James 5:13).

A good soldier is one who puts duty first, recognising that others are counting on him. He knows that his duties are often going to demand uncomfortable conditions, irregular hours, interrupted sleep and missed meals. Separation from family and loved ones will be frequent, and safe return uncertain. The burden of the conditions he must endure is often increased by the knowledge of loved ones having to cope with illness or troubles at home, but he must focus his mind on the work that duty demands. He has to shut off his mind to all the affairs of civilian life, however pressing and legitimate they may be, for the duration of his tour of duty. He has to "war a good warfare" (1 Tim 1:18), not only for his own survival but, above all, that he may please the commanding officer who, by enlisting him, placed his confidence in him.

The work of the Lord is suffering today because so many believers refuse to move out of their 'comfort-zone'. Shortly before writing this article, the author met a dear sister in Sri Lanka who, every Lord's Day, undertakes an eleven-hour round trip beginning at 4am so that she can remember the Lord with the assembly in Colombo. How often our prayer meetings are poorly attended because the saints are too tired to come, or have not had time for their meal after work. Should we really come hungry or unrested? Most definitely yes! For the most part we live in the lap of luxury, yet we will not make the smallest sacrifice of our comforts in order "that (we) may please him who hath chosen (us) to be a soldier". Shame on us if we will neglect the assembly gatherings because we think we may have a cold coming on, or an undeveloped headache may be lurking! Where is our sense of duty, of commitment, of readiness to endure a little hardship out of love for the one who unreservedly gave Himself for us at Calvary?

Day 3

THE DISCIPLINE AND RULES OF A COMPETITOR

2 Timothy 2:5

Today's verse contains the only two mentions in Scripture of the verb which, translated "strive" in the AV, fully means 'to compete as an athlete'. Indeed, the Greek word is the one from which our English word 'athlete' is derived. Thus Paul directs Timothy's attention to a different kind of discipline from that of the soldier. The soldier endures hardness and rigour because of his sense of duty, but athletes will go to amazing lengths of self-denial simply because they want to excel. The sport that began as a simple pastime has become deadly serious. Early keenness revealed an aptitude that, once trained, became an ability to excel. With that increasing interest in the sport came a growing belief that the athlete could become the world's best and, after that was realised, nothing else mattered. Do remember, dear younger Christian, that this growing dedication of the athlete is only a picture of what an earnest believer should be. Enjoy your sports at school or college, but be very careful. Aptitude leads to ability, and ability to prowess. Then comes excellence and the goal to be the best, and Christian lives have been wasted in the pursuit of sporting fame and success.

Which of us has not admired the dedication of the athlete who has Olympic glory in view? For years before that all-important race, the athlete has risen early, paid strict attention to diet and trained relentlessly. While friends relaxed and engaged in idle pursuits, the athlete pounded out the long, lonely miles, enduring the pain and the blisters for the sake of winning the prize. The application of these things to the Christian race is very clear, but we must not miss Paul's main point.

All the dreaming, training, pain and dedication will amount to nothing if the athlete does not strive according to the rules. The modern world of sport is awash with performance-enhancing drugs, and the burning desire to win has made cheats of many. Paul does not have deliberate cheating in mind here, however, but rather the thought that ignorance of the rules will lead to disqualification as surely as foul play. If the victor's crown is to be won, it must be won fairly and in accordance with all the rules of the game.

The sense of loss for the disqualified athlete, after years of training, must be devastating. Some high-profile athletes have been stripped of titles because they failed drug tests, and they have pleaded passionately, and probably honestly, that they had unknowingly ingested the forbidden substance.

Ultimately, though, the disqualification stands, because carelessness in diet, ignorance of the rules and lax discipline are no excuse. Inattention can cause the loss of the prize just as surely as will blatant cheating. We must ever remember, "Yet is he not crowned, except he strive lawfully".

Day 4

THE DEDICATION AND REAPING OF A CULTIVATOR

2 Timothy 2:6

Paul now turns to the picture of the husbandman, or farmer, to illustrate another important aspect of the disciplined life that Timothy must follow as a man of God. He has in mind the consistent, lonely, unseen, wearying labour of the cultivator. This is the man whose produce is sought, and taken for granted, by all, but very few who benefit from his toil will ever know the extent of the effort he has put in. Not for him the medals of the soldier in combat, nor the adulation of the crowd for an athlete who has breasted the tape. He has to think in the long term, season by season, with patience an essential virtue. His labour is hard and relentless, and so often the harvest is heart-breakingly poor. Yet, year by year, he ploughs, sows, cultivates and patiently waits, always in hope of the harvest. Perhaps a suitable paraphrase of our verse would be 'The husbandman must labour before he can be partaker of the harvest'.

What is the reward? Is it earthly or heavenly? Whilst some measure of reward on earth might be seen, we must remember that dutiful, brave soldiers may not win every fight; disciplined athletes, striving lawfully for the crown, may not win every race; dedicated, hard-working husbandmen can work to the point of exhaustion and still see some harvests fail. And what of you, dear saint? Have your many years of devoted service in the gospel, Sunday school work, shepherding of the assembly seen more disappointments than trophies? If earthly reward and observable results are the end of such self-denial, life would simply be an ordeal.

Lift your eyes from the disappointments of time, and fix them on the day when you will stand before the Lord who has watched with tender eye all your labours down here. "And then shall every man have praise of God" (1 Cor 4:5). As befits any teacher of the Word, Paul had first exemplified in his own service those things which he was now enjoining upon Timothy. He had proved himself to be dutiful as a soldier, "I have fought a good fight"; disciplined as an athlete, "I have finished my course"; dedicated as an husbandman, "I have kept the faith" (2 Tim 4:7).

Praise God there is a time of reward in prospect for the believer, the Judgement Seat of Christ. It is there that faithfulness, diligence and steadfastness for love of the Saviour will be openly shown and rewarded. Paul lived in the good of that, for he said "Henceforth there is laid up for me a crown of righteousness, which the Lord, the righteous judge, shall give me at that day: and not to me only, but unto all them also that love his appearing" (2 Tim 4:8).

Day 5

THE DILIGENCE AND REWARD OF A CRAFTSMAN

2 Timothy 2:15-18

Although these verses refer particularly to the need for Timothy to be diligent in "rightly dividing the word of truth" as a teacher, we should not restrict the meaning to that alone. Once again the emphasis is upon striving, and the word "study" carries the meaning 'be diligent' or 'strive diligently'. The object of the diligent striving is that the believer, whatever his or her particular avenue of service for the Lord, might be able to 'present themselves unto God, approved'. This approval means 'to be put to the test with a view to being approved by the examiner'. The whole picture, then, is of Christians as artisans, showing absolute diligence in craftsmanship so that, when the time comes for that workmanship to be examined by the divine eye, it will meet the divine standard.

As Paul writes to Timothy at Ephesus, perhaps he has in mind the great number of people in that city who earned their living by producing statuettes of Venus. He had vivid memories of the events in Acts 19, and the anger of the idolatrous, greedy craftsmen who created such an uproar in the city. Paul knew that amongst that throng there had been some true craftsmen but, also, others who simply mass-produced junk.

One of the tricks used by careless sculptors of the marble statuettes was to disguise the blemishes and mistakes in their work with wax of a similar colour. A wise buyer, looking for quality of workmanship, would have the statuette carried out from the workshop and placed in the sunlight for a while. The bright rays of the sun would soon expose any wax that had been used and, on the basis of this test, the craftsman would either stand approved or condemned. This was what Paul had in mind when he wrote to the Philippians, "that ye may approve things that are excellent; that ye may be sincere and without offence till the day of Christ" (Phil 1:10). The word "sincere" literally means 'tested by sunlight'.

Shoddy workmanship is associated today with the scourge of 'cowboy tradesmen' who use the cheapest of materials and plenty of filler to hide their total lack of intention to do a good job. If they are exposed they are shameless, moving on to their next botched job without a flicker of conscience. Men who displayed such an attitude to spiritual things were Hymenaus and Philetus. It would seem that Hymenaus had earlier been exposed and disciplined (1 Tim 1:20), but was still shamelessly peddling his false doctrine.

Beloved, let us show all diligence in every part of our service for the Lord. We want our craftsmanship to be worthy of Him, and fully approved by the divine Examiner.

Day 6

THE DISTINCTIVENESS AND READINESS OF A CHANNEL

2 Timothy 2:19-21

To be overly concerned with the house in these verses is to miss the point. It is not a reference to the great house of Christendom, but simply the use of a great house as a figure. Within a great house there is a variety of vessels, differing in design, material and purpose. Also, it would be a mistake if "the vessels of gold and of silver" were simply equated with "some to honour", and those "of wood and of earth" linked with "some to dishonour". The relative honour of each vessel lies not in its constitution, but in the master's purpose for it.

The sovereignty of the master in choosing a vessel of one design and material over another must be recognised. It would not be in keeping with his dignity if he drank wine from an earthen cup at his dinner table, so gold or silver would be the material of his choice. Such a vessel would hold a position of relative honour, admired by his guests and indicative of his wealth and status. Down in the quiet gloom of the cellar, however, the wine lies in a wooden cask, and might be decanted into an earthen amphora before being transferred again into a silver carafe before it is served. Each vessel, and each material, is exactly suited to its task, and whilst the perceived honour of each differs, none is more important than another, and none is redundant. A golden water pot might say something about a master's wealth, but it would be useless for the task. The heat-conducting gold would soon render the cool well-water lukewarm and most unpleasant to drink. The master has his vessels in particular places in the house, and they are suited for specific tasks by virtue of their design and make-up.

The essential requirement is that every vessel is "sanctified, and meet for the master's use, and prepared unto every good work". Each must, therefore, be in good repair and, above all, clean. The context would show that Paul has doctrinal purity in mind rather than moral fitness, equally essential though that is. The "profane babblings" of verse 16 will only ever "increase unto more ungodliness", a sharp contrast with being "prepared unto every good work". The teaching of those committed to error "will eat as doth a canker", spreading like a disease, a sharp contrast with being "sanctified, and meet for the master's use".

Only knowledge of, and submission to, the word of God will keep the believer at a state of readiness for the Master to use, howsoever and whenever it might please Him.

Day 7

THE DIGNITY AND RESPECT OF A COUNSELLOR

2 Timothy 2:24-26

In speaking finally of "the servant of the Lord", Paul shows what all his teaching has been leading to since he called Timothy "my son" (v.1). His desire is that his 'child' might, by following all the godly advice, admonition and counsel of his father in the faith, mature into a "servant of the Lord". The 'child' is literal, and "the servant of the Lord" is literal. The five figures in between show how the former becomes the latter. To the end that the truth might be faithfully passed on from one generation to another (v.2), Timothy must not simply be able to teach that which is right, he must also be able to refute that which is wrong. To state the truth is good, but to explain it is better. To be able, in addition, to show why erroneous doctrine is false, is best. This is the required standard of the servant of the Lord, the same ability that the overseer must possess, "holding fast the faithful word as he hath been taught, that he may be able by sound doctrine both to exhort and to convince the gainsayer" (Titus 1:9).

In teaching, explaining and defending the truth, however, Timothy must be careful to display godly character. As he faces up to "those that oppose themselves" (v.25), he must never let his stand for what is right degenerate into a fleshly determination to win the argument. This pitfall has ruined many an assembly and many a personal standing before the saints. The word of God is never to be used as some kind of punchbag between the flailing fists of carnal men. It is the word of God, and should be held in reverence and godly fear. "The servant of the Lord must not strive" but with kind forbearance and quiet humility expose error for what it is by skilfully teaching the truth.

The desired goal is not to win the argument but to win over those who oppose. They should be so persuaded of the truth of Scripture that, under the good hand of God, they repent of their erroneous stand and acknowledge the truth. In so doing, "they may recover themselves" (lit, 'recover their senses') and intelligently remove themselves "out of the snare of the devil" in which they had become captive. That snare is the same as he set in the Garden of Eden, the snare of doubt, distortion and denial of the word of God. Brought back to his senses by faithful teaching and the grace of God, the repentant opposer of the truth can extricate himself from the devil's snare and return to the will of God. There are countless such believers ensnared in the false doctrines of Christendom today. May God graciously raise up true, diligent servants of the Lord to rescue them and return them to the will of God.

PHIL COULSON

Week 21

7 UNITING BLESSINGS IN EPHESIANS 4:4-6

Introduction

"There is one body, and one Spirit, even as ye are called in one hope of your calling; one Lord, one faith, one baptism, one God and Father of all, who is above all, and through all, and in you all."

In our text (to be read daily this week) there are seven mentions of the word 'one'. Three refer to the Godhead and four refer to believers in the church. Altogether these blessings are shared by Christians everywhere and unite us as one. To understand the verses properly we need to view them in their setting.

In Ephesians the apostle Paul teaches great truths about God's purposes for Christ and the church. Then he applies these doctrines practically to daily Christian living. The thought of walking, that is, our public testimony, is prominent (2:10; 4:1,17; 5:2,8,15). What we believe should affect how we behave.

Paul's focus is the church comprising every believer of this age of grace, not individual local churches. Several word pictures show that the church is the *body* of Christ (1:22-23; 4:15-16; 5:23). All of the members are "fitly joined together", functioning together under Christ's headship. The church is seen as a *bride* (5:30-32). In marriage two become "one flesh" and are bound together in love. The church is also like a *building* (2:19-22). All of its component parts are "fitly framed together" giving strength and stability.

Our text is found in a section emphasizing the unity in the body, (4:1-16).

Believers should seek "to keep the unity of the Spirit" (vv.1-3), as described in the list of seven 'ones' (vv.4-6). Different gifts have been given to promote the blessing of all (vv.7-11). The ultimate purpose is to bring us all to "the unity of the faith" and likeness to Christ Himself (vv.12-13). The final verses remind us that Christ is the Head of the church and the various members are bound together in harmony and strength (vv.14-16). Appropriately, love is prominent throughout: "forbearing one another in love" (v.2); "speaking the truth in love" (v.15); "edifying … in love" (v.16).

The lesson for us is clear: love, unity and strength go together. What characterises the church as a whole should also characterise every local assembly, and ought to characterise every believer in personal living.

Day 1

"*ONE BODY*"

Ephesians 4:4-6

The church which is the body of Christ began on the day of Pentecost (Acts 2). Down through the centuries it has grown as more and more people have trusted in Christ for salvation. It will be completed only at the Rapture when the Lord returns to the air and calls His people home. The church is largely invisible: many of its members are already in heaven, some are on earth and it is possible that others have not yet been born. No believer can ever be separated or excommunicated from the body. Each is eternally secure.

The Scriptures teach that Christians should meet in local churches. These are identifiable groups of believers who gather together to His Name and who hold divine truth in common. They represent God upon earth. No one group can claim to be the body but each group should reflect the spiritual character of that body. Sadly, not every believer is associated with such a local assembly. It is sadder still when a person who is in fellowship has to be disciplined and put out of the local company because of sin.

The picture of the body would remind us that:

1. The members are controlled by the Head. God has given this headship to His Son (Eph 1:22; Col 1:18). Every believer needs to show this in practice by being obedient to Christ and His word. Has He not loved the church and given Himself for it?

2. We have different functions. There are many roles for the different members to fulfil. In the local assembly we worship and honour God, we encourage and build up one another, and we pray for and witness to an unbelieving world. All of these functions are motivated by love (1 Cor 12-13).

3. We have different gifts. God supplies a gift to every believer enabling each to fulfil his or her role (Eph 4:7-8, 11-12; 1 Cor 12:4-7, 28-31). Some are public gifts but many are not. Are you using the gift God has given you?

4. We work together. This is a vital requirement for a healthy body. The members need to cooperate rather than compete or conflict with one another. What would happen if the eye saw the food the body needed, the hand lifted it up, but the mouth refused to eat it? The result would be starvation!

5. We are all important. The unity of the body is maintained by the diversity of its members. Each of us is precious to God and vital for the welfare of the whole (1 Cor 12:18-27).

Maintaining spiritual unity amongst believers requires effort and diligence. That is why Paul exhorts us to "endeavour" to keep it (Eph 4:3).

"ONE SPIRIT"

Ephesians 4:4-6

The Holy Spirit is a divine Person and in a special sense we are living in the age of the Spirit. In the Old Testament God was *for* His people, acting always in love, and sometimes in judgment, for their ultimate blessing. With the coming of God's Son, Emmanuel, into the world we see God *with* His people. With the Saviour's return to heaven and the descent of the Spirit we now understand that God, the Holy Spirit, dwells *in* His people in this age of grace. Every believer is part of the one body through the baptism of the Holy Spirit (1 Cor 12:13). He indwells each one (John 14:16-17).

The Holy Spirit's ministry is taught in every chapter of Ephesians (1:13; 2: 18,22; 3:5,16; 4:3-4,30; 5:9,18; 6:17-18). If we confine ourselves to the letter we will learn some truths found nowhere else in Scripture. These concern the blessings and responsibilities that all believers share.

1. The seal (Eph 1:13). The indwelling Holy Spirit is God's seal of ownership on those who have trusted Christ. The moment we believe, God says in effect, "You are mine"! This sealing secures us eternally for God and can never be undone. It holds good "unto the day of redemption" when Christ returns for His own (Eph 4:30).

2. The earnest (Eph 1:14). The Holy Spirit is our guarantee of the blessings to come. His presence within us is one of the first blessings of our inheritance. In Christ we are immeasurably rich (Eph 1:3). Truly, every one of us is a spiritual billionaire!

3. Power (Eph 3:16,20). The promise given to the disciples was "ye shall receive power after that the Holy Ghost is come upon you" (Acts 1:8). By His power our faith can grow and our lives and witness can really count for Christ.

4. Fruit (Eph 5:9). If we are determined to let the Spirit control us, not only will our witness yield results (others will be saved) but also our lives will become more and more like our Lord's. His goodness, righteousness and truth will be seen in us.

5. Grieving the Spirit (Eph 4:30-32). We grieve the Spirit whenever we disregard His leading and guiding according to God's Word. A bitter, critical and unforgiving attitude will hinder His work in our lives and rob us of power.

6. Being filled with the Spirit (Eph 5:18). This is a divine command and can take place again and again. Each time I consciously empty myself of sin and selfish desire, the Spirit can fill me more and use me more. When the Spirit fills and controls our lives, we will be mighty for God. We also will be a thankful and joyful people (Eph 5:19-20).

Day 3

"ONE HOPE"

Ephesians 4:4-6

Hope is common to every believer, although some may enter into the good of it more than others. Certainly, before we trusted Christ, we were without God and without hope in the world (Eph 2:12). We were at a distance from Him and bound for destruction.

In Christ everything has changed. Our *past* has been forgiven (Eph 1:7), our *present* is enriched (Eph 1:3) and, with such a sure and certain hope, our *future* is secure. Twice over in Ephesians, hope is linked with calling (1:18; 4:4). God has a hope for us ("the hope of his calling") and He has given us hope in Him ("hope of your calling").

God's Hope (Eph 1:18). Behind God's divine call is divine purpose. The letter to the Ephesians is full of teaching about God's will. Paul was so in touch with God that his two prayers in the epistle were simply reflections of that divine will (1:17-23; 3:16-21). The clues to finding the references to God's purposes are the little word 'that' and the phrase 'according to'. Only a few of the references will be quoted. You can search for the others and discover that God has wonderful purposes for His own good pleasure, for Christ and for the church.

Some of the reasons why He has called us and chosen us in Him are: "that we should be holy and without blame before him in love" (1:4); "that we should be to the praise of his glory" (1:12); "that in the ages to come he might shew the exceeding riches of his grace in his kindness toward us" (2:7). What is clear is that God's hope for us, at least in terms of developing Christian character, is not just a future hope but one that can be worked out in the present. We should be cooperating fully with Him now.

Our Hope (Eph 4:4). We might well ask, "What exactly is our hope?" Is it hope of heaven, or is it hope of Christ's return? Is it hope of freedom from sin and suffering, or is it hope of an inheritance and reward? Is it hope of being reunited with loved ones who have died, or is it the hope of seeing our Saviour, being like Him and with Him for ever? There is no good reason to rule out any of these. We can enjoy them all. The Christian hope that believers share has all of these elements but perhaps we could summarise them best in one word, "Christ"!

The conclusion of the matter is this: God's hope and purposes for us, and our hope in Him, will surely be fulfilled. Face today with confidence. He keeps His word!

Day 4

"ONE LORD"

Ephesians 4:4-6

The lordship of Jesus Christ, the Son of God, is prominent in the writings of the apostle Paul. This was one of the first truths revealed to him when he met the Saviour on the Damascus road. Saul of Tarsus, as he was then, had two questions. The first related to Christ's *identity*: "Who art thou, Lord?" He learned that the glorious Lord was the same man called Jesus whose followers he had been persecuting. Then he had another vital question that related to Christ's *authority*: "Lord, what wilt thou have me to do?" Paul's desire was to serve the Lord and be obedient to His will. This would remain the defining characteristic of the rest of his life as he sought to spend and be spent for his Master. Related to Paul's submission to Christ's authority was his confidence in Christ's *ability*. His Lord was in full control of every happening in his life (2 Tim 1:12).

Christ is Lord of His creation and also Lord of His church. These two aspects of Christ's lordship will be fully manifested in a coming day. In our text the focus is on His lordship in the church. In Ephesians we have already seen that he is Head of His church (Eph 1:22; 4:15; 5:23). In the local church too, headship and lordship are closely bound together (1 Cor 11).

Think for a moment of the significance of the eloquent symbols in the local assembly:

1. A pool. I identify with the Lord who died and rose again.
2. A head covering. I submit to the Lord who is now on high.
3. A loaf and a cup. I remember the Lord until He comes back again.

The first includes *a backward look*. Believer's baptism is a public confession of faith in Christ and proclaims His victory over death and the grave. The second implies *an upward look*. A sister's covered head and a brother's uncovered head testify that the Lord is supreme and that His glory alone should be seen. Finally, the Lord's Supper is *a forward look* to His soon return, for it is only "till he come".

The truth of the lordship of Christ has personal and practical lessons for us all. Because of who Christ is, He has the right to direct our lives and have us do what He desires. We learn this slowly. We are so self-centred that often there is tension and conflict in our souls.

Is there someone or something that has displaced the Lord in your affections? Is there an area of your life that He does not control? Are you holding on to a secret sin? Acknowledge His lordship today, and allow Him to be Lord of all.

Day 5

"ONE FAITH"

Ephesians 4:4-6

The word 'faith' can mean different things in the Scriptures. For example, it is used to describe the initial act of believing that brings salvation, "For by grace are ye saved through faith" (Eph 2:8). Then again, it can mean the principle by which the Christian life continues and is practised day by day, "For we walk by faith, not by sight" (2 Cor 5:7). Another use of the word refers to the common body of gospel truth that Christians share (Phil 1:27; Col 1:23). It is this shared knowledge that Paul is referring to in our text.

Although Christians differ over many things, there are fundamental truths concerning Christ and His work that remain as foundation stones of our faith. They must not be moved or taken away. John Newton put it like this:

> "What think you of Christ? Is the test
>   To try both your state and your scheme;
> You cannot be right in the rest,
>   Unless you think rightly of Him".

Let us think of just a few of these foundation truths concerning Christ:

His absolute deity. The Lord Jesus is the eternal Son of God, the Creator and Sustainer of all things. Four great 'chapter ones' speak of His glories (John 1; Col 1; Heb 1; Rev 1). In becoming man He did not cease to be God but He voluntarily limited Himself to the form of a servant (Phil 2:7). John wrote his Gospel so that we might believe that "Jesus is the Christ, the Son of God; and that believing ye might have life through His name" (John 20:31).

His perfect humanity. One cannot call oneself a Christian if one denies that Christ came in human form (1 John 4:3). Errors concerning His humanity sprung up in the first century and still circulate today. He was a true man (resting, John 4:6; sleeping, Matt 8:24; hungering, Matt 21:18; thirsting, John 19:28; weeping, John 11:35; agonizing, Luke 22:44). He was sinless (Heb 4:15) and perfect (Mark 1:11; Luke 23:41). Indeed, He could not sin (John 14:30). None other could be our Saviour.

The total sufficiency of His work. On the basis of His death at Calvary the Saviour accomplished a work that satisfied a holy God (Phil 2:9), provided salvation for a lost world (1 John 4:14), and defeated a relentless foe (Heb 2:14).

In a future day the mighty Conqueror will redeem a fallen creation (Rom 8:22-23) and be manifested as the King of kings and Lord of lords (Rev 19:16).

The vital necessity of His salvation. There is salvation in Christ alone (Acts 4:12). It is not Christ plus works, law, baptism, the church or anything else. Make sure He is your Saviour and you are resting in Him alone.

Day 6

"ONE BAPTISM"

Ephesians 4:4-6

There are two baptisms relevant to all believers. One is the baptism in the Holy Spirit when the church was formed on the day of Pentecost. The other is the symbolic act when a believer is immersed in water as a public testimony to faith in Christ. It is more likely that, in Ephesians, Paul has in mind the first of these as relating to the church which is His body.

The historical event that took place on the day of Pentecost (Acts 2) will never be repeated. The Lord had foretold that the Spirit could not come until He had departed to His Father (John 16:7). Fifty days after His resurrection (or ten days after His ascension) the Holy Spirit descended as the Lord had promised (Acts 1:5) and the church was born.

Four simple questions concerning Pentecost yield four important answers:

Who was the baptiser? In water baptism one believer baptises another but at Pentecost the risen Christ was the baptiser. He had told His disciples that the Spirit could not come until He went away. Each of the gospel writers quotes the words of John the Baptist concerning the Messiah, "He shall baptise you with the Holy Ghost" (Matt 3:11; Mark 1:8; Luke 3:16; John 1:33). The baptism with fire that John also mentioned looks forward to a coming day of judgment. It does not refer to the "cloven tongues like as of fire" in Acts 2:3.

Who was baptised? The church which is Christ's body was baptised. This is viewed as an entity that includes every believer. By that one baptism all believers are constituted members of the church which is His body.

What was the medium of baptism? The baptism did not take place in water but in the Spirit. Paul explained it thus, "by (Gr. 'in') one Spirit are we all baptised into one body … and have been all made to drink into one Spirit" (1 Cor 12:13). It is the Spirit who now indwells, enlightens and empowers that body and every believer who is part of it. It is true to say that we are in the Spirit, as it is also true to say that the Holy Spirit is in us.

What is the significance of that baptism? You might say, "I was not present on the day of Pentecost. How can that event affect me?" The same could be asked of the great events that took place upon the cross and in the tomb. You know that your salvation and justification rests upon what Christ accomplished at Calvary so long ago. In the same way your inclusion in the church which is His body rests upon what He did at Pentecost.

Day 7

"One God and Father of all"

Ephesians 4:4-6

There are great truths in the word of God that we cannot fully understand but must simply believe. This causes us to wonder and, when we wonder, we worship. Who can comprehend the greatness of our God? All we can do is bow our knees and lift our hearts heavenward in thankfulness and adoration.

The Bible teaches that God is one. At the same time we learn that there are three 'Persons' in the Godhead: Father, Son and Holy Spirit. We must accept both truths. The divine Persons work together in perfect harmony and are equal in power and glory. Ephesians is full of references to the 'Trinity', as this truth has come to be called. Sometimes one verse is enough to show this: "For through Him (the Son) we have access by one Spirit unto the Father" (2:18).

In our text we learn of His pre-eminence – "above all"; His power – "through all"; His presence – "in you all". He is immortal, invisible and unchanging. He is omnipotent, omniscient and omnipresent. He is holy, righteous and just. He is light, truth and wisdom. He is good and gracious, loving and merciful. He is true and faithful. He is our God! He is also the Father of His children. He lovingly cares for us and chastens us, for we need both. He never tires of us drawing near in all our weakness and crying out to Him, "Abba, Father"!

And so we come to the last of this sevenfold unity. Unity is a spiritual condition of mind and heart that all of us have to learn. Endeavouring to maintain unity is often misjudged to be a wishy-washy exercise in compromising the truth. In fact, unity rests foursquare on the truth and fulfils it.

Many of us are people of strong convictions. We need to be, for we live in perilous days when some are departing from the truth of God. Although we cannot associate with such departure, we should have a real and genuine love for every true believer everywhere. In our local situation we should be those who promote unity and peace according to the word of God. This is what the Saviour commended and Paul instructed (Matt 5:9; Eph 4:3).

If we find ourselves slipping into the habit of criticising other believers and assemblies, we should draw back. We are on dangerous ground and assisting the enemy. Satan's master plan is to seek to divide and dismember the body of Christ. Thank God, he will fail. Rather, let us share and enjoy these seven wonderful divine blessings of the church. In the local assembly let us give of our very best and be those who seek to build, bind and beautify the people of God.

Clark Logan

Week 22

7 SIGNS OF NEW LIFE SEEN IN NAAMAN THE SYRIAN

2 Kings 5:1-19; Luke 4:27

Introduction

When the Lord went back to His home town of Nazareth and spoke in the synagogue, they "wondered at the gracious words which proceeded out of his mouth" (Luke 4:22). Their amazement soon turned to anger when He selected Naaman to illustrate the grace of God to a Gentile. That wonderful day in Naaman's life was the day he experienced not just a physical cleansing from leprosy, but a spiritual change as he came to worship the true God. In his cleansing we see a picture that we can apply to those who turn from sin and put their faith in the Lord Jesus.

His religion consisted of elaborate ceremony, but he learned that God very rarely uses the spectacular and impressive. Naaman needed humbling, and it all began with the recommendation of Elisha by his wife's maid who was a foreigner, a servant and a woman. Elisha wouldn't even speak to him and he was given something undramatic to do. So it was, when we were saved, all pride was removed and we humbly confessed sin. Naaman discovered that money could not achieve his healing and there was only one way in which he could be delivered. The only thing we contributed to our redemption was our sin, and we came through the one who is "the way" by simple faith.

Paul describes our salvation in 2 Corinthians 5:17: "If any man be in Christ, he is a new creature: old things are passed away, behold all things are become new". We are not a piece of patched-up humanity but a new creation with a completely new set of values and a desire to please the one who gave us new life. We see a radical change in Naaman whose whole life had been transformed. In Philippians 3:3 Paul summed up the whole Christian life: We "worship God" – that's Godward; "rejoice (or 'boast') in Christ Jesus" – manward; "and have no confidence in the flesh" – inward. Similarly, *upwardly* Naaman worshipped the true God (v.17), *outwardly* he was not ashamed to speak of his Lord (v.15) and *inwardly* he had become acutely aware of his sin – "Lord, pardon thy servant". The transformation in his life was seen in seven specific ways, and we will look at each in turn.

Day 1

CONVERSION TRANSFORMS OUR BEHAVIOUR

2 Kings 5:15

The first sign of life is quickly seen in Naaman's behaviour. When we are first converted we may find it very difficult to put into words what has happened to us. However, the very way we live our lives shows clearly that we belong to the Lord. Indeed, whenever a profession of conversion is not accompanied by holiness of life, it must be understood that the person concerned is not yet a Christian.

We are in no doubt that a change took place in Naaman's life, and this is quickly seen in how he behaves towards Elisha. Naaman had expected Elisha to come out and heal his leprosy in a spectacular manner and took offence when this didn't happen (5:11). Now there is a marked difference as he stands before Elisha in humility. All pride has gone. Like the leper in Luke 17:17-18 he returns "to give glory to God" and honours Elisha as God's servant. All his aggression has vanished and he treats Elisha with respect. Conversion changes the way we treat people. We will no longer be aggressive, but will value them as God's creation and will show love towards them. Before conversion a man loves things and uses people; after conversion, he loves people and uses things.

We are also told that, as Naaman stood before Elisha, he stood with "all his company" (v.15). He was not afraid to admit he had been wrong before his own servants. We should never be ashamed to stand before others and say we have behaved wrongly, as such an admission can have a profound effect on a watching world.

The truth of the Scripture "God resisteth the proud, but giveth grace unto the humble" (James 4:6) is seen in the way that Elisha now treats Naaman. His change of behaviour makes Naaman teachable and useable, and an example of how to help new converts is given to us. Firstly, Elisha is happy to meet him, while before he had been unavailable for the best of reasons. We need to be continually available to help God's people. Secondly, Elisha lets Naaman speak first and does not seek to put words into his mouth, but waits to hear his confession. Someone who is truly converted will not need undue pressure from us, but will soon provide clear evidence of a changed life.

There has been a total change of priorities in Naaman's life. Previously he had thought that the king of Israel could bring great blessings into his life. But he now realized that those who are truly influential are those who have influence with God. Let us endeavour to choose our friends carefully (see James 4:4).

Day 2

CONVERSION TRANSFORMS OUR

RELATIONSHIP WITH GOD

2 Kings 5:15

We are now left without any doubt that Naaman had not only been cleansed of his leprosy but he was also a sinner transformed by the grace of God. He now makes a public, clear and outspoken confession that Jehovah alone is God, which he is able to do because he has experienced the power of God in his life. Although our lives will show that we are saved, we must not underestimate the importance of making a spoken confession of our faith in the Lord Jesus. This is emphasised by Paul in Romans 10:9.

Both in Romans 10 and here, the confession is based upon knowledge. In Romans 10 we know that the Lord was raised from the dead, and in Naaman's experience there is a clear statement as to the uniqueness of God. Our faith is based firmly on the knowledge of facts and Paul underlines this in 1 Timothy 2:4, "who will have all men to be saved, and to come unto the knowledge of the truth". Salvation is inseparably linked with "the knowledge of the truth". As believers, we do not only testify to the truth that salvation is alone found in the Lord Jesus, but we also live in accordance with the truth of God as revealed in the word of truth. We see this in Naaman's life as he concentrates, not on his cleansing from leprosy, but on what he has come to know about God. There is a clear distinction between verse 11 and verse 15. In verse 11 he says "I thought", while in verse 15 he says "I know". He no longer relies on his own reasoning but, in coming to know God, he can speak with certainty and assurance. His confession contains two elements. In acknowledging the God of Israel to be the only God, he positively affirms the uniqueness of God. At the same time he draws the conclusion that the gods who he previously believed in did not exist. We live in a world where many gods are believed in and, although we must not be offensive, we must not be afraid of upsetting others by claiming that there is only one God. Elisha would have been overjoyed to hear this confession, just as Elijah was to hear the confession of the woman of Zarephath in 1 Kings 17:24, "Now by this I know that thou art a man of God, and that the word of the Lord in thy mouth is truth". She had seen God at work in the raising of her son, producing in her a new relationship with God which was the same experience as that of Naaman.

Day 3

CONVERSION TRANSFORMS OUR GIVING

2 Kings 5:15

Naaman had just confessed that he believes there is only one God, and this leads immediately to a desire to give. Our consumer society is summed up by the words of the prodigal son "give me". But here is a sign of conversion: Naaman wants to give a "blessing" or 'a present'. Harrington Lees wrote "The most sensitive part of civilised man is his pocket, and one of the fiercest fights a preacher has to wage is when his preaching touches the pocket of his hearers".

That fight was won in the heart of Naaman, and the proof is seen in that he urged Elisha to take the gift. This is not just a mere carrying out of a duty, but Naaman has an overwhelming desire to give because he has been given so much. Later on, when Gehazi lied to Naaman and told him that Elisha had changed his mind and would now accept a gift (vv.22-23), Naaman offers him two talents rather than one. Gratitude is one of the surest signs that God is at work, and we see that generosity marks him out: he had been turned into a giver.

Why is giving so important for the believer today? Giving cannot be separated from the gospel. The gospel, in fact, is giving. It is the centre of John 3:16 "for God so loved the world that he *gave* his only begotten Son". Thus there are many scriptural examples of conversion affecting the pocket.

When Zacchaeus experienced salvation, he gave half of his goods to the poor and made fourfold restitution to those he had robbed (Luke 19: 8). As soon as the Philippian gaoler was saved, his attitude to Paul and Silas was wonderfully changed and he "washed their stripes", "brought them into his house" and "set meat before them" (Acts 16:33-34). Naaman, Zacchaeus and the gaoler all lived out the truth of 2 Corinthians 9:7, "Every man according as he purposeth in his heart, so let him give, not grudgingly, or of necessity: for God loveth a cheerful giver".

God not only expects us to give our money in furthering His work but He also expects us to give of our time in serving Him. Naaman took what may have been a thirty mile trip from the river Jordan to the house of Elisha, when he could have gone straight back to Syria. Why? Because he now valued the man of God and wished to spend time with him discussing the things of God. Let us take time to be with the children of God, for in doing so God will be glorified and we will be blessed.

Day 4

CONVERSION TRANSFORMS OUR OBEDIENCE

2 Kings 5:16-17

Although Naaman had offered a gift, Elisha refused to accept it. In refusing a gift Elisha taught Naaman important lessons:

1. God's blessings cannot be deserved or bought. In pagan religion, blessings were received only if payment was made. Elisha taught Naaman that the God of Israel could not be bought with gold or silver.

2. God's servants cannot be bought. Elisha showed that his motive was to serve God honestly and that he was not serving for "filthy lucre" (1 Tim 3:8). Paul leads by example in Acts 20:33, "I have coveted no man's silver, or gold, or apparel".

3. God was the power behind the miracle. If Elisha had accepted the gift, Naaman could have thought that it was through Elisha's power that he had been cleansed. Elisha did not want to confuse Naaman. He was careful not to diminish the glory due to God. It is so easy to proudly think that we have achieved success in service, but we must learn the reality of the Lord's words, "for without me ye can do nothing" (John 15:5).

Although Naaman had enthusiastically offered a gift in verse 15, he had to learn that it was not the occasion for making a gift. He eventually complies and shows practical obedience to the Lord's servant. Indeed, he seems to have learned his lesson so thoroughly that instead of making a gift, he now asks for a gift! One crucial sign of life is seen in a ready obedience to God's word and this is a recurring theme throughout the word of God. We are not to wait to be 'convicted' about issues. If God has commanded something, do it.

Obedience is essential because:

1. It is the purpose of our redemption by God. Peter says we are "elect ... unto obedience" (1 Pet 1:2), and this stresses that God's purpose in election is that we are marked by obedience.

2. It is the proof of our devotion to God. The Lord Jesus said "If ye love me, keep my commandments" (John 14:15). We cannot avoid this truth. If we do not obey the Lord, then we do not love Him. The moment we disobey His will, we show that our love is not what it should be.

3. It is the pathway to know God. "If any man will do his will, he shall know of the doctrine, whether it be of God, or whether I speak of myself" (John 7:17). Obedience to God's will, as revealed in God's word, will lead to a greater appreciation of our Lord. The Lord Jesus gives us the greatest example because, to Him, obedience was both a delight (John 4:34) and absolute (Phil 2:8).

Day 5

CONVERSION TRANSFORMS OUR WORSHIP

2 Kings 5:17

Before his conversion Naaman worshipped false gods, but now his worship is transformed and he will only offer burnt offerings and sacrifices to the Lord in an outpouring of true worship. True worship is:

1. An evidence of conversion. God had worked in his life and now he expresses thanksgiving to God. God is delighted when those who were once unthankful now show that they are saved by praising Him.

2. Experienced after conversion. An unbeliever cannot worship because he does not know God. In Naaman's case there was no thought of worship until he came to know the true God, and then it was at the forefront of his mind.

3. Exclusive in character. Naaman did not add the God of Israel to the list of gods he already worshipped, but he realized that worship of the true God had to be exclusively directed to Him. The words of the Lord in Matthew 4:10 are appropriate, "Thou shalt worship the Lord thy God, and him only shalt thou serve". To worship God also means that He is able to take first place in all that we do. Our service is only acceptable to God if it stems from an attitude of worship and appreciation of Him. If we want to serve the Lord, not out of drudgery, but out of a full heart, we must never neglect our times of fellowship with God.

4. Exercised consistently with confession. Naaman confessed "I know that there is no God in all the earth but in Israel" (v.15) and now showed that he believed what he said by worshipping the only true God. A sign of a true believer is one whose confession is backed up by his actions, and we can expect to look for fruit in the lives of a new convert – "by their fruits ye shall know them" (Matt 7:20). Elisha would have been encouraged as he saw Naaman's actions. Elisha refused to take a gift because his message that cleansing cannot be achieved by any merit of Naaman's would have become confused. Elisha's consistency was rewarded as the new convert also acted consistently.

We have a wonderful opportunity to influence new believers by living consistent godly lives before them, and what joy we will have if they follow our example (1 Thess 2:19-20). Naaman makes an emphatic commitment to true worship when he says "thy servant will henceforth ...". Nothing will deter him from worshipping, even though he knows it will not be easy. Let us redeem the time and spend time in meditation so that, in particular, we may come to the Lord's supper with full and prepared hearts.

Day 6

CONVERSION TRANSFORMS

OUR VIEW OF OTHERS

2 Kings 5:17

Naaman's next action appears rather peculiar. He asks for two mules' burden of earth. Some would say that Naaman wished to use the earth because he thought that the God of Israel could only be worshipped on Israelite soil. This is incorrect because, in verse 15, Naaman has strongly confessed that "there is no God in all the earth but in Israel". There is no doubt that the God he now worships and serves is a universal God.

He took the earth back home because he had a message for his own family and his own people, and by use of a vivid illustration he wanted them to come to believe in the God he now believed in. They believed that the God of Israel was simply a national god who did not belong on Syrian soil. As the soil was emptied out before the watching Syrians he would be saying that just as Israel's soil was now on foreign territory, so Israel's God was not just restricted to Israel.

As soon as Naaman has been converted he shows a concern for others and concentrates on how he is going to witness to his people. He may be in danger of losing his job but he will not turn his back on God. Instead, he plans to confess his faith in the true God.

It must be stressed to new converts that they must take a stand for God immediately so that there is no doubt as to who we belong to. This very action of collecting earth is also a witness to his servants that a dramatic change had taken place.

In v.12 he had shown great contempt for Israel's rivers and yet, just in a short period of time, he now proposed taking Israel's humble earth to Damascus, which showed that his whole perspective had changed. New converts show the reality of their new birth by their changed appreciation of the world around them, and this will be evidenced by their being "not conformed to this world" but being "transformed by the renewing of your mind" (Rom 12:2).

Naaman may have had a further purpose for the earth, and planned to build an altar in accordance with Exodus 20:24. This would be a witness to the Syrians that he had no desire to worship their gods but, amidst idolatry, he would establish an altar to the true God.

Our task today is to maintain witness to the true God in the midst of heathen darkness. It may well have been that joining him in worship was the little maid who started it all by bearing a faithful witness.

Day 7

CONVERSION TRANSFORMS OUR EMPLOYMENT

2 Kings 5:18-19

Naaman's new-found faith is evidenced in his concern for how he will behave when he returns to his official duties as captain of the host of the king of Syria. These duties involved escorting the king on his visits to the temple of Rimmon (a title of the storm god Hadad). Naaman was now clear in his belief that the God of Israel was the only true God and that Rimmon was nothing, but tells Elisha what he intends to do when he accompanies the king to the temple.

Verse 18 may be rendered, "when my master goeth into the house of Rimmon to bow down there and he leaneth on my hand and I bow down … when he boweth down". Thus the only reason that Naaman would bow down was that his master leant on his arm when he bowed down. Although Naaman would necessarily have to bow physically with him, he would remain loyal to the only true God.

Sadly, many new converts have been stumbled by the unwise comments of believers, but Elisha wisely confines himself to the simple comment "Go in peace". This may merely imply his acceptance of Naaman's actions, as he acknowledges that his heart would be right, or Elisha may have known that Naaman would be saved from any position of compromise by being excused from his duties and, therefore, Elisha did not need to comment. Alternatively, Elisha knew that conviction would work its way and, when faced with the reality of going into the temple of Rimmon, Naaman would make a stand against idolatry.

We do not know what Naaman eventually did, but we do know that he was a man who was prepared to let God work in every part of his life. Similarly, how we behave in our employment is crucial in living for God. God would not have all of us to give up secular employment, but our aim should be to glorify God. "Whatsoever ye do, do it heartily as to the Lord, and not unto men … for ye serve the Lord Christ" (Col 3:23-24). If our aim is to continually serve the Lord, then we will be honest in our work and God will be glorified.

Naaman's sensitivity is beautifully displayed in that he says "In this thing the Lord pardon thy servant". He is aware that whenever he would go into the temple he was in danger of displeasing God and would set his mind constantly on his God. A similar sensitivity is vital for the believer in that we are only one slip away from ruining our testimony. We need to live out the truth of Psalm 16:8, "I have set the Lord always before me".

NEIL OSBORNE

Week 23

7 BLESSINGS FOR THE BELIEVER IN PSALM 23

Introduction

The rich language of this psalm has brought joy and comfort to countless numbers over the centuries. It flows from the pen of a man who had a deep experience of the Lord. David was a shepherd from his youth and showed skill and bravery in maintaining the wellbeing of his flock. It was that character that equipped him to be the shepherd king of Israel when God took him "from following the ewes to feed Jacob his people and Israel his inheritance; so he led them according to the integrity of his heart and guided them by the skilfulness of his hands" (Ps 78:70-72).

David knew the Lord as the "Shepherd of Israel", (Gen 49:24, Pss 80:1; 100:3), but much more intimately as "My Shepherd". That assurance gave rise to the feeling of satisfaction delineated in his outflow of appreciation for the Lord's provision, as firstly he speaks about Him (vv.1-3), and then directly to Him (vv.4-5). How blessed for we who are believers in our Lord Jesus Christ, to know that this one with the illustrious title JEHOVAH ROHI (v.1), is not only the Shepherd of Israel, but of each individual child of God!

Our Lord Jesus, when on earth, "saw the multitudes, and was moved with compassion … because they were as sheep having no shepherd" (Matt 9:36). It was a reflection on Israel's blindness that their Shepherd was in their very midst longing to satisfy and care for them, yet they failed to recognise Him. Our NT beautifully describes Him as the Good Shepherd (John 10:11) the Great Shepherd (Heb 13:20) and the Chief Shepherd who will yet come for His own (1 Pet 5:4).

It was He who, when we were lost in the wilderness of sin, went out at such cost to Himself to find us and to bring us home (Luke 15). Peter writes, "ye were as sheep going astray, but are now returned to the shepherd and bishop of your souls" (1 Pet 2:25).

We will consider the verses of this lovely psalm step by step to see what the Lord has done for the believer. May we join the ranks of those who have found strength and comfort, in life and death, from the knowledge that the Lord has promised his presence at every step of our earthly life.

Day 1

THE EFFECT OF THE SHEPHERD'S PLENITUDE

Psalm 23:1; John 10:7-18

The Lord is my shepherd, therefore I shall not want! This expression of unquestioning confidence is possible because David knows that he is under the shepherd's care and every need will be catered for. A link is often made between this psalm and the preceding Psalm 22 where the sufferings of Christ are vividly set forth, and a NT commentary from Romans 8:32 is applied as follows: "He that spared not his own Son but delivered him up for us all" is the subject of Psalm 22. "How shall he not also with him freely give us all things" sums up Psalm 23.

The remainder of Psalm 23 details those areas of life where the Lord graciously undertakes the cause of his people, whether it is for refreshment, guidance, or companionship in the darkest of valleys. David's relationship with the Lord will not immunise him against life's many difficulties. As a youth he knew the bitterness of being under-valued and misunderstood in his own family circle. He knew loneliness and privation as he fled from Saul, and later the defection of his own son Absalom. But throughout, he prized his relationship with the Lord, and indeed was honoured by the Lord as "a man after his own heart" (1 Sam 13:14).

He had also learned from experience that a shepherd must not only provide for, but also protect, his flock. He knew the hazards of marauding predators such as lions and bears, (1 Sam 17:34-36). The Lord as shepherd would stand between him and the adversary; therefore he will not lack protection.

If the psalmist could rest contentedly in that knowledge, how much more should we who belong to this present age of grace. Our God cares for sparrows, even taking account of their fall (Luke 12:6). He feeds the fowls of the air, and graces the lilies of the field with beauty (Matt 6:26-30).

Those who trust the Lord for salvation are "blessed with every spiritual blessing … in Christ" (Eph 1:3). It is only reasonable therefore that those who trust him with spiritual and eternal matters, also trust him for lesser material things, relating to time. Elsewhere another psalmist writes, "The Lord will give grace and glory: no good thing will he withhold from them that walk uprightly" (Ps 84:11).

You and I who know the Lord belong to a most privileged company. We live in a godless world that is dark morally and spiritually, a world that is aimless as to direction and fast heading for judgement. The Lord has saved us from that condition and, having brought us to Himself, has made ample provision for us in every circumstance.

Day 2

THE ENVIRONMENT OF THE SHEPHERD'S PEACE

Psalm 23:2; Mark 6:34-44

"He maketh me to lie down in green pastures; he leadeth me beside the still waters" – pastures of tender grass and waters of perfect quietness! These words convey the idea of tranquil rest and satisfaction. This is not compulsive driving, but the gentle influence of one who deals tenderly with his own, ever seeking their good. Here we find an answer to a question posed in the Song of Songs, "Tell me, O thou whom my soul loveth, where thou feedest, where thou makest thy flock to rest at noon" (Song 1:7).

The idea is beautifully illustrated by another expert shepherd, Jacob, on the day he met Esau when returning from Padan Aram. "…the children are tender, the flocks and herds with young are with me: and if men should overdrive them one day, all the flock will die … I will lead on softly, according as the cattle that goeth before me and the children be able to endure …" (Gen 33: 13-14). It is also more perfectly expressed in words relating to our Lord, "He shall feed his flock like a shepherd: he shall gather the lambs with his arm, and carry them in his bosom, and shall gently lead those that are with young" (Isa 40:11).

David is clearly enjoying the presence and provision of the Lord, as also we should be as we feed and refresh ourselves from his word. We recall that Psalm 22 brings our thoughts to Calvary, where the sword of Jehovah awoke against His shepherd … the man that was his fellow! Everything was so different there! Instead of green pastures and quiet waters, we hear the Saviour's cry, "I thirst", and the sound of a quaking earth and rending rocks as he suffered to bring us to God (Matt 27:51). Well might we sing, "The storm that bowed thy blessed head is hushed for ever now, and rest divine is ours instead; whilst glory crowns thy brow". Now that dark experience is past, and the Shepherd leads His people out, going before them, and they follow because they know His voice as they go in and out and find pasture (John 10:4-9).

The Lord ever seeks the best for His people, and supplies abundantly. One day a multitude of 5,000 men followed the Lord Jesus out to a *desert* place and, whilst the disciples would have sent them away empty, the Lord fully satisfied them with five loaves and two fishes (Mark 6:34-44). The evangelist Mark makes the remarkable statement that the Lord commanded all of them to sit down on the *green grass*!

We live in a world of turmoil, where even believers are under pressure from external circumstances, and many are stressed to the limit. To us, as to the disciples of old He would say. "Come ye yourselves apart … and rest awhile" (Mark 6:31). Our Shepherd leads gently, softly, into an environment of which the world knows nothing.

Day 3

THE ENRICHMENT OF THE SHEPHERD'S PATHWAY

Psalm 23:3; Isaiah 40:1-15

Life's circumstances are such that the most spiritual of the Lord's people have days of disappointment, discouragement and even depression. These conditions may adversely affect our relationship with the Lord, sometimes even resulting in a back-slidden state. We thank God for the tender restoring ministry of the Shepherd who knows about our flagging spirits, and is ever at hand to meet our need.

The Lord taught his people in the wilderness, "I am the Lord (JEHOVAH ROPHIKA) that healeth thee" (Exod 15:26). Elijah also knew something of this when, under a juniper tree in the wilderness of Beer-sheba, he prayed that his life might be taken away (1 Kings 19:4). The psalmist had similar experiences. It was in such a day of distress that "David encouraged himself in the Lord" (1 Sam 30:6). We may be sure that this was not an isolated experience for David, but that he often resorted to the solace of the Lord's presence, as this verse makes clear.

Recall, too, the Saviour's words on one of Peter's dark days, "I have prayed for thee … and when thou art converted (restored JND) strengthen thy brethren (Luke 22:32). The result was that Peter himself became a shepherd of God's flock under the authority of the Chief Shepherd (See John 21:15-17; 1 Pet 5:1-4).

The word 'restoreth' suggests the idea of recovery or renewal. The verb is often translated 'return'. In v.2 David is drinking from the Shepherd's inexhaustible stream (cf. John 4:13-14; 7:37-39), and that reservoir of grace is available to every believer today just as it always has been. There he has the refreshing that he so much needs, but yet he knows that within him there is the tendency to wander.

"He leadeth me in the paths of righteousness". This is the second mention in the psalm of leading (see v.2), but the two words in the Hebrew text are not exactly the same. In v.2 the word seems to have a gentler tone, whereas here it may, if necessary, involve some discipline (see Strong's Concordance). We may not always recognise that the Shepherd knows what is best for us. After all, in unconverted days "we turned every one to his own way" (Isa 53:6). Now, however, we are under His ownership, bought by Him at infinite cost, and He conducts us in right paths for our good, and for His glory. Our Shepherd can never lead us other than in paths of righteousness, for the integrity and honour of His holy person is at stake, hence, "for his name's sake". May we be given grace to acknowledge His Lordship and to follow where He leads.

Day 4

THE EXPERIENCE OF THE SHEPHERD'S PRESENCE

Psalm 23:4; 1 Peter 1:3-12; 2:21-25

This verse introduces us to some of the darkest foreboding areas of life's pilgrimage. It may relate not only to death itself as a stark reality, but also to those times when the way ahead seems difficult and dangerous, and our trust in the Shepherd is severely tested. The extremity of the test is found in the words "even though I walk", but the psalmist's confidence is that he will come through the valley, gloomy though the experience might be. We know that at Calvary our Shepherd has passed through a valley darker than we shall ever know, and He went that way alone! He will never take us where He cannot walk with us.

From a spiritual standpoint, this world for the believer is similar to the "shadow of death" (Isa 9:2; Luke 1:79). However, the Lord Jesus came to shed the light of His presence upon men and women and to deliver them from that condition. It is good to remember that a shadow always pre-supposes light, for the light casts the shadow. We may be sure therefore that the gloom is temporary, and the Shepherd will lead us out of it into the light.

We need to observe several things here! First, that now the psalmist changes from speaking about the Shepherd, to speaking directly to Him. Second, the emphasis is not on the valley experience, so much as on the fact that he has companionship in that experience. Third, because his companion is the Shepherd Himself, he need fear no evil. Adversity, affliction, calamity might come our way, and such things are not lightly regarded, but as and when they come, He is there to support and comfort and to bring us through.

The young Hebrews in the fiery furnace experienced this (Dan 3), as did the disciples in the storm (John 6:17-20). When the Lord commissioned those early evangelists it was with His promise, "Lo, I am with you alway, even unto the end of the world" (Matt 28:20). Saints in various circumstances down the years have clung for comfort to that word, "I will never leave thee, nor forsake thee" (Heb 13:5).

The rod is the instrument of government and rule. It is always good to acknowledge the Shepherd's Lordship! He has the power to smite the enemy, and will do so in defence of those who are precious to His heart. We may lean upon the staff for support and strength, but here it is "his rod and his staff"! Together they provide assurance and confidence to the psalmist as he sees them in the hand of the Shepherd whose chief interest is our wellbeing.

Day 5

THE ENJOYMENT OF THE SHEPHERD'S PROVISION

Psalm 23:5; Psalm 100:1-5

A well prepared table is always a pleasing sight, not only because it contains the essentials to satisfy hunger, but also because it often indicates the desire of whoever has spread the table to enjoy the company and conversation of others as they sit around it. The table is the place of fellowship as well as food.

The table is first mentioned in Scripture when God instructed Moses about the table of shewbread in the tabernacle (Exod 25:23). The twelve loaves on it represented Israel's tribes before God in relationship with him. On a less happy occasion, the Israelites asked in unbelief, "Can God furnish (prepare) a table in the wilderness? ...can he give bread also? can he provide flesh for his people?" (Ps 78:19-20). Yet, in spite of their hardened hearts, God gave them "of the corn of heaven. Man did eat angels' food: he sent them meat to the full" (Ps 78:24-25). That table was prepared in a great and terrible wilderness, where there were fiery serpents and scorpions (Deut 8:15), when God in grace miraculously met their every need. Elijah too was revived at such a table (1 Kings 19:5).

The spiritual condition of the psalmist is so different! He lives in the enjoyment of the Shepherd's care and, at this table, he is satisfied, contemplating the full provision made for him although all around may be hostile.

It was with the same tender compassion and shepherd care that the Lord Jesus, when on earth, spread a table in a desert place, and from the most meagre resources fully satisfied 5,000 men beside women and children; and again when he fed the 4,000 (Matt 14:21; 15:38).

We too are passing through the wilderness of this world. We also may feel the hostility of surrounding enemies, such as the world, the flesh and the devil, but we too are able to enjoy the congenial atmosphere of a table as we sit in the Lord's presence and enjoy fellowship with Him. It is the Lord's Table, distinct from the Lord's Supper (1 Cor 10:21). He would have us spend time there, feeding on Christ, and so maintaining spiritual health and vigour. The natural man knows nothing of the secret satisfaction that such a place affords and, sadly, even some believers are apt to forget the value of this place of fellowship.

We observe that David, having freely enjoyed the provision of the Lord, showed the kindness of the Lord to others. Mephibosheth, lame and disfigured by a fall, was brought from the outside place into David's presence to eat at his table as one of the king's sons (2 Sam 9). An appreciation of the Lord's Table should have a practical effect in our showing kindness to others.

Day 6

THE ESSENCE OF THE SHEPHERD'S PROFUSION

Psalm 23:5; Psalm 84:1-12

"Thou anointest my head with oil; my cup runneth over". Some expositors see in these words the picture of a banquet at which a special guest is being entertained: a prepared table, an anointed head and an overflowing cup. It all conveys the idea of fullness and abundance, reminding us of the words of the bride, "He brought me to the banqueting house, and his banner over me was love" (Song 2: 4). Yet at the same time there is a lovely and natural charm in viewing the whole psalm as a pastoral scene and looking at this verse in that way (cf. *What the Bible Teaches – Psalms – J. Flanigan*).

The idea of anointing is familiar to readers of the Old Testament, and the Hebrew word most often used suggests the anointing as a symbol of being set apart for God in a special way. The first such anointing was of a pillar at Bethel (Gen 31:13) but, usually, priests, prophets and kings were anointed in this way, including David himself when anointed by Samuel (1 Sam 16:12).

The Hebrew word used here, however, is different. It is used only a few times and elsewhere suggests 'making fat or enriching'. David is thinking of the abundance of blessing conferred on him by the Lord, and sees it as the crown of his privileges.

Oil in Scripture typifies the ministry of the Holy Spirit in the Lord's people, as our NT confirms. John tells his readers, "Ye have an unction (anointing) from the Holy One ... and that which ye have received abideth in you" (1 John 2:20-27).

The anointed head, especially when the oil was mingled with perfume, could not but be noticed, and the child of God has a dignity that marks him out as different from the world. It enables him to live on a higher plane in the enjoyment of the spiritual heritage which is his by grace.

The overflowing cup speaks of the psalmist's joy here. We are not specifically told what the cup contained, but the psalmist speaks of it as 'my cup'. So it is a portion from the Shepherd's hand which he has made his own! The Scriptures speak of the cup of salvation (Ps 116: 13); of consolation (Jer 16:7); and of blessing (1 Cor 10:16), all of which are precious to the believer.

We must not forget, however, the cup connected with our Lord's sufferings. He was the Shepherd who was smitten (Matt 26:39; John 18:11). It was because He drained that cup completely that we are able to enjoy the blessings of the heavenly places, knowing that the Great Shepherd, risen from the dead, has made our position secure and caters for every aspect of our wellbeing.

Day 7

THE PSALMIST'S EVERLASTING PROSPECT

Psalm 23:6; John 14:1-14

The final verse of the psalm takes its character from what has gone before, and the epilogue of confident assurance is based on David's experience of the Lord in the past. Reflecting on the constant care of the Shepherd for him, like Samuel he sets up an 'Ebenezer' – "hitherto hath the Lord helped us" (1 Sam 7:12). He feels safe in the knowledge that the same Lord who has so richly taken care of the past will not leave him now, but will continue his loving-kindness right to the end of the pilgrimage.

In their absolute sense, goodness and mercy belong to the Lord, and these are the twin attributes that will ensure all that is beneficial for the whole of our earthly sojourn. They will closely pursue the believer at all times and in all circumstances. We cannot see the way ahead, but he can, and he knows what is best for us. Job said, "He knoweth the way that I take; when he hath tried me I shall come forth as gold" (Job 23:10).

Hitherto, David has spoken of the Shepherd being with him, leading, feeding, refreshing, guiding, protecting and accompanying him even in the valley of the shadow of death. Now, however, his thoughts turn to his being with the Shepherd beyond the ravages of present conditions, to dwell with Him for ever in a place where evil can never encroach.

David always seems to have had a deep love for the house of the Lord. (Pss 26:8; 27:4). It was this that put it into his heart to build the temple (1 Kings 8: 17-18), although the work was to be done by his son Solomon. It is of course the presence of the Lord that constitutes the house of the Lord, and the place would be nothing without the Person. The fugitive Jacob was to learn this as he slept on the stone pillow at Luz (Gen 28:16-17). So what David delights in here is the confidence that the fellowship with the Lord which he now enjoys, will be known in a richer, fuller sense when he is in His presence for ever.

It is difficult for us as believers in this age of grace to read these words without connecting them with the words of our Lord Jesus to anxious, troubled disciples, "In my Father's house are many mansions … I go to prepare a place for you and … I will come again, and receive you unto myself" (John 14.2-3). Our Shepherd's heart will only be fully satisfied, as will ours be also, when, after the chequered experience of the wilderness years, He brings us to that place of unending bliss.

ALEX WISEMAN

Week 24

7 FEATURES OF STEPHEN

Introduction

As is so often the case when there is blessing among the people of God, problems arise, sometimes from without and sometimes from within. So "when the number of the disciples was multiplied, there arose a murmuring" from within (Acts 6:1) and, at the end of chapter 5, there was opposition from without. It was good that they could find "seven men of honest report, full of the Holy Ghost and wisdom" to help the saints (6:3).

The first one named is "Stephen, a man full of faith and of the Holy Ghost" (6:5); "full of faith and power" (v.8); full of wisdom and fervour (v.10). In chapter 7 he is full of the Word and, at the end, his vision is full of the Lord Jesus.

Stephen is such a commendable servant, and if ever the early church needed one, it was just then. For some reason, known only to God, this man is removed and disappears as quickly as he appears on the pages of Scripture. It is always good to encourage our hearts in the Lord and note that though God removes His servant, His work continues. His ways are past finding out. In Antioch we find those believers who had been "scattered abroad upon the persecution that arose about Stephen" (11:19), and the very man responsible for Stephen's death is teaching them. God is sovereign and over all; only He can do a work like this. Well might we trust Him. As for God's servant Stephen, he comes and goes in just about two chapters of our Bible, but what a remarkable example and testimony he has left. He was a man who was suddenly and unexpectedly taken before the council, but was able to turn to the Scriptures and fervently and eloquently present Christ in over fifty verses of chapter 7. Saul (Paul) probably never forgot this discourse, and no doubt Stephen's words left deep impressions on his soul. Years later, Paul would begin his own defence in exactly the same way, "Men, brethren and fathers". He went on to say that "when the blood of thy martyr Stephen was shed, I also was standing by, and consenting unto his death" (22:20). What a testimony, example and witness Stephen was for God.

Day 1

A MAN FULL OF FAITH

Acts 6:1-8; 7:2-8

It seems appropriate that this man who was full of faith, and lived by faith, was occupied with one of the great heroes of faith in our Old Testament, Abraham. In Acts 7, as he stands before the council to give his defence, Stephen starts with "the God of glory who appeared unto our father Abraham" and, as he brings this great man of faith before them, it would no doubt have strengthened his own faith. What a stimulus and strength it is to be able to resort to the Scriptures in times of need, both for ourselves and others. The very countenance of Stephen was altered: "his face was as the face of an angel" as he started to pour out his soul and expound the Scriptures (6:15).

He spoke of God's calling Abraham out in covenant relationship with Himself and Abraham's commitment and response to God's call. We remember the writer to the Hebrews takes up the same strain and reminds us that Abraham, "when he was called to go out into a place which he should after receive for an inheritance, obeyed; and he went out …" (Heb 11:8). By faith he left, and by faith he lived (v.9). He sojourned in the land of promise and by faith "he looked for a city which hath foundations, whose builder and maker is God" (v.10). He believed God when he did not know where he was going, or why, or how. Faith is all about believing God, whether we think of the faith that saves as we look back and rejoice in salvation, or faith that keeps us presently seeking to live for Him and trusting Him in all the circumstances of life. It is faith that enables us to look with certainty to that coming day when we shall be caught away to be forever with the Lord (1 Thess 4:17). "Faith brings into our present all the power of God's future, and feeds upon God's promises as a present reality" (C.H.Macintosh).

Stephen was one who sought to keep the faith, and was prepared to live and die for what he knew to be of God. As we read through the gospels, whether we think of companies or individuals, where there is little or no faith there is little or no blessing. But when "He saw their faith" there was blessing and peace, gladness, joy and rejoicing, even in the storms of life. It is good to remember that when the storm is such that our faith fails, He is faithful. We remember how "he arose, and rebuked the wind, and said unto the sea, Peace, be still. And the wind ceased, and there was a great calm" (Mark 4:39). Is this not how Stephen died, rejoicing in the Lord Jesus, and with forgiveness in his heart for others? "He fell asleep", a man full of faith, at peace in the midst of the storm.

Day 2

A MAN FULL OF THE HOLY SPIRIT

Acts 6:1-8; 7:9-15

If the first eight verses of Acts 7 are mainly about Abraham, the great man of faith, then the next eight are mainly about Joseph, of whom Pharaoh says "Can we find such a one as this is, a man in whom the Spirit of God is?" (Gen 41:38). We find that Stephen, a man full of the Holy Spirit, has been occupied with the Joseph of our Old Testament, a wonderful type of our Lord Jesus Christ. There can be no doubt that the person who is full of the Spirit will be spending time in the word of God, praying, contemplating and allowing the Spirit of God to do His work in their soul. It is the Spirit's work to reveal to us the truth of God and the Person of Christ, to enlighten our minds and to illuminate the page of holy Scripture to feed our souls.

The Lord Jesus told His disciples that, after His ascension, there would be the coming of the Holy Spirit (the Comforter) who would not only be with them but in them. The believer is, therefore, indwelt by a divine Person, the Holy Spirit of God. We cannot have more of Him, but He could have more of us. Paul says "Quench not the Spirit" (1 Thess 5:19). As Wuest puts it, "Stop stifling and suppressing the Spirit". Again, "Grieve not the holy Spirit of God" (Eph 4:30). The Spirit's work is to guide us into all truth, to show us things to come. The Lord Jesus said "He shall testify of me" (John 15:26); "He shall glorify me: for he shall receive of mine, and shall shew it unto you" (16:14); "He will reprove the world of sin" (16:8).

What a privileged people we are compared to this great man Joseph, and yet what a remarkable life he lived for God. In the midst of rejection, suffering, temptation and testing, followed by promotion, power, fame and authority, he trusted God and acknowledged the hand of God in all the circumstances of his life. His brothers never really could identify or understand his heart or his words, "Come near to me, I pray you" (Gen 45:4): "Ye thought evil against me; but God meant it unto good … Now therefore fear ye not: I will nourish you … and he comforted them, and spake kindly unto them" (50:20-21).

Stephen, a man full of the Holy Spirit, in his dying words for his persecutors, could say "Lord, lay not this sin to their charge" (Acts 7:60), and we remember a far greater than Joseph or Stephen, our beloved Lord

Jesus Christ, who said those lovely words, "Father, forgive them…" (Luke 23:34). Oh, that we might know something of the controlling power of the indwelling Spirit to enable us to live for God in this world.

Day 3

A MAN FULL OF GRACE

Acts 6:1-8; 7:17-44

If ever a man needed grace, it was probably in the circumstances that surrounded Stephen in Acts 6 with murmuring among the people of God. It is so easy to cut people off and make matters worse, but he had an understanding, gracious spirit and way with him. Once again Stephen's acquaintance in meditation with some of the great men of the Old Testament will help him now. He thinks of Moses, and tells us that even at his birth he was "exceeding fair" in the sight of God. Stephen's words concerning Moses bring before us the wonderful, gracious attitude of this man who was so sorely provoked on many occasions by his own people. Yet we remember that he failed in what was perhaps his strongest virtue, his meekness, when he called the people of God rebels. Some of the saddest words in the Old Testament are to be found in Psalm 106, where we read "they angered him also at the waters of strife, so that it went ill with Moses for their sakes: because they provoked his spirit, so that he spake unadvisedly with his lips" (Ps 106:32-33). Moses never entered the land because of this failure, though he was a man who would have given his life for the people of God; one who was so meek and gracious and had such influence with God.

Stephen seems quite happy to serve tables and to minister to others as he moves among the people of God, and why not? He was only following in the footsteps of his Master, the One who said "I am among you as he that serveth" (Luke 22:27), the One who "laid aside his garments; and took a towel, and girded himself" (John 13:4). Paul, writing to the Corinthians could say, "Ye know the grace of our Lord Jesus Christ, that, though he was rich, yet for your sakes he became poor, that ye through his poverty might be rich" (2 Cor 8:9). The Lord Jesus was "full of grace and truth" (John 1:14). May God give us all grace to serve one another in love and, in doing so, to serve Him. We know that we are all the recipients and beneficiaries of divine grace, for "where sin abounded, grace did much more abound" (Rom 5:20) and, "for there is no difference: for all have sinned, and come short of the glory of God; being justified freely by his grace through the redemption that is in Christ Jesus" (Rom 3:22-24).

We might well say with the psalmist "Come and hear, all ye that fear God, and I will declare what he hath done for my soul" (Ps 66:16). "Let us have grace, whereby we may serve God acceptably with reverence and godly fear" (Heb 12:28).

If Moses was exceeding fair at his birth, Stephen's face depicted something of the lovely spirit of grace as they "saw his face as it had been the face of an angel" (Acts 6:15). "Let the beauty of Jesus be seen in me, all His wondrous compassion and purity".

Day 4

A MAN FULL OF POWER

Acts 6:1-8

On the face of it, men must have looked on Stephen and seen him as one who had no power to do anything against the opposition which had risen up against him. But we know that God's power and strength is seen in his attitude, bowing to the divine will of God. God's power had been seen in the great wonders and miracles which Stephen did among the people, but now he was going to be taken home to heaven and one of those responsible for his death will continue the work. No one could have known how God was moving behind the scenes to bring about His purposes. "How unsearchable are his judgments, and his ways past finding out!" (Rom 11:33). We remember that "precious in the sight of the Lord is the death of his saints" (Ps 116:15) and "blessed are the dead which die in the Lord" (Rev 14:13).

It would not be long before Saul of Tarsus, who was giving consent to Stephen's death, making havoc of the church and breathing out threatenings and slaughter against the disciples, would be prostrate in the dust, confessing Jesus of Nazareth as Lord. It is only God's power that can bring about such changes in a person's life, and it is only His power in us that can keep us and enable us to live for Him, whatever the circumstances, even to, in Stephen's case, giving his life.

It must have been a great encouragement to Stephen as he remembered the power of God displayed in the days of Moses, how he brought the people of God "out, after that he had shewed wonders and signs in the land of Egypt, and in the Red sea, and in the wilderness forty years" (Acts 7:36). This man Stephen, who was full of power, must have wondered with Moses at that great sight at Sinai, how the bush burned and was not consumed. Well might we tremble and take our shoes from off our feet when beholding an even greater sight. We think of the One who came down to deliver; we remember the fire of God's wrath. We draw near in spirit to Calvary and wonder and rejoice that a holy God has been satisfied. The One who brought the people of God out of Egypt is the same One who led His disciples out "as far as to Bethany, and he lifted up his hands, and blessed them" (Luke 24:50).

We have no power in ourselves but rejoice in One who, in resurrection, could say, "All power is given unto me" (Matt 28:18). We might well "be strong in the Lord, and the power of his might" (Eph 6:10), and seek with Paul to "know him, and the power of his resurrection" (Phil 3:10)

Day 5

A MAN FULL OF WISDOM

Acts 6:1-10

As the religious leaders listened to Stephen, "they were not able to resist the wisdom and the spirit by which he spake" (Acts 6:10). This was Stephen putting into practise what the Lord Jesus had taught concerning witness for Himself in future days of persecution: "But before all these, they shall lay their hands on you, and persecute you, delivering you up to the synagogues, and into prisons, being brought before kings and rulers for my name's sake. And it shall turn to you for a testimony. Settle it therefore in your hearts, not to meditate before what ye shall answer: For I will give you a mouth and wisdom, which all your adversaries shall not be able to gainsay nor resist" (Luke 21:12-15). Stephen had no time to prepare beforehand what he would say but, in a moment of time, he looked to heaven for present help in time of need. What a wonderful combination we have here of the product of the servant's meditation on things that had been food for his soul, and the gracious, immediate power of the Lord to recall it all, so that it comes forth with wisdom, power and fervour from his lips. No wonder they were unable to resist the wisdom and the spirit by which he spake! God's word in God's power had such an effect not only on them, but also on His servant whose very countenance was such that they "saw his face as it had been the face of an angel" (Acts 6:15).

In the beginning of chapter 6, Stephen needed wisdom as he moved among the saints seeking to restore unity and joy instead of division and murmuring. We remember that James tells us that "the wisdom that is from above is first pure, then peaceable, gentle and easy to be intreated" (James 3:17) and there is no room for envy and strife in our hearts. "Who is a wise man and endued with knowledge among you?" (3:13). "If any of you lack wisdom, let him ask of God, that giveth to all men liberally, and upbraideth not; and it shall be given him" (1:5). Job asks the question "Where shall wisdom be found? … It cannot be gotten for gold, neither shall silver be weighed for the price thereof … the price of wisdom is above rubies … Whence then cometh wisdom?" (Job 28:12, 15, 18, 20). "The fear of the Lord is the beginning of wisdom" (Ps 111:10). The wisdom of man is foolishness with God, and true wisdom only comes down from above.

We thank God for One who came down and manifested the wisdom and power of God as a man in this world. Luke says of Him, "Jesus increased in wisdom and stature, and in favour with God and man" (Luke 2:52). "In whom are hid all the treasures of wisdom and knowledge" (Col 2:3) Paul

wrote, and his prayer for the Colossians was that they "might be filled with the knowledge of his will in all wisdom and spiritual understanding" (1:9). To the Roman believers Paul wrote, "O the depths of the riches both of the wisdom and knowledge of God!" (Rom 11:33). May we, like Stephen, make known something of "the manifold wisdom of God" (Eph 3:10).

Day 6

A MAN FULL OF FERVOUR

Acts 6:1-10; 7:51-60

The fervent spirit that characterised Stephen had a tremendous effect on all who heard him. His passion and zeal in what he believed and rejoiced in brought about this glowing countenance which must have inspired and strengthened many of the multitude of those who believed and were part of the church. Now, confronted with opposition from unbelievers, he turns to the Scriptures which seem to be part of his very being. Eloquently and fervently the words flow from his lips. His purpose was not to justify himself but rather to present Christ as the Just One, of whom he says "ye have been now the betrayers and murderers" (Acts 7:52). The result was "they were cut to the heart" (v.54) and, whilst it resulted in them stoning Stephen, who knows what was accomplished for God and for eternity? We do know that a young man, Saul, never forgot what he heard and what he saw, and one cannot help but think that he was not the only one to be brought into blessing.

Enthusiasm is infectious, and we have every reason to be enthusiastic in what we believe. What a privileged people we are, indwelt by the Spirit of God and having the inspired word of God which we know is living, powerful and will never pass away. We are able to feed our souls daily in His word, the Spirit of God teaching us, taking of the things of Christ and revealing them to us. Why is it that so often we are poverty-stricken? Why is it that we can enthuse about so much that is just temporal and yet miss out on what is spiritual and eternal? Let us pray that we might be in the enjoyment of all that there is in Christ and, like Stephen, be able to share it with others. He could have sung from the heart "I'm not ashamed to own my Lord or to defend His cause".

Apollos, in Acts 18, was not only instructed in the way of the Lord but he was fervent in the Spirit, that is, *fervent in preaching*. Paul exhorts the Roman believers to be *fervent in practice*, serving the Lord (Rom 12:11). Epaphras, in Colossians 4, was *fervent in prayer*, "labouring fervently for you in prayer" (v.12), and James reminds us that "the effectual fervent prayer of a righteous man availeth much" (James 5:16).

As we consider our Lord Jesus, the One in whom God found all His delight and pleasure, our countenance, like Stephen's, should reflect something of the beauties and glories of Christ. We too should be characterised by enthusiasm, zeal and godly fervour.

Day 7

A MAN WHOSE VISION WAS FULL OF CHRIST

Acts 7:51-60

Some of the best known words in our Bible were so meaningful and true for Stephen at his death. "Yea, though I walk through the valley of the shadow of death, I will fear no evil: for thou art with me" (Ps 23:4). What wonderful words are these which he now speaks as, full of the Spirit, he fixes his eyes on heaven, sees the glory of God and cries, "Behold, I see the heavens opened, and the Son of Man standing on the right hand of God" (Acts 7:56).

When he had said these words they cried out and, stopping their ears, ran upon him, cast him out and stoned him. We rejoice today that those heavens are still open and the Son of Man, our blessed Lord and Saviour, is still at God's right hand. There, as our intercessor, our great High Priest, is One who understands, cares and comforts and who will soon come to take us to be forever with Himself. Perhaps the greatest experience Stephen ever had in his life was at his death. Certainly the greatest experience of all was when "he fell asleep" and knew what it was to be with Christ. Paul, one of those responsible for Stephen's death, tells us after much suffering of his own that he longed to depart to be with Christ, which he says is "far better".

Perhaps the stones were incidental to Stephen now he had seen the risen Saviour standing, waiting to receive his spirit as he prayed "Lord Jesus, receive my spirit". Kneeling down before his Lord, he prays for his persecutors, "Lord, lay not this sin to their charge. And when he had said this, he fell asleep" (v.60). What a lovely expression this is, describing as it does the death of the believer.

It was good that devout men carried Stephen to his burial and made great lamentation over him. How they must have loved him, and what a miss he must have been, but we "sorrow not, even as others which have no hope".

Stephen has come and gone so quickly on the pages of Scripture, a man so full, fervent and faithful. Years after, Paul starts his defence in exactly the same way as Stephen did, and says "When the blood of thy martyr Stephen was shed, I also was standing by and consenting unto his death" (22:20). Thank God, through wondrous grace they are now both with their Lord, and we anticipate a day when with them, we shall be with Christ in glory.

HAROLD HATT

Week 25

7 MENTIONS OF CHRIST AS HEAD OF THE CHURCH

Introduction

Most of us understand the term, 'the Head'. If we were at school we would use it to describe the most senior person in the school. In large businesses it is used to describe the 'chief executive' or 'chairman' of the organization. If we say someone is 'heading up' something we would usually understand that this means they are leading and directing, and are ultimately responsible for the way things are done.

The word of God speaks on a number of occasions about the Lord Jesus Christ as 'the Head'. Three references are found in Ephesians, three in Colossians and one in 1 Corinthians.

1 Corinthians 11 defines the order that God has designed for the blessing of mankind. This order is recovered in the gatherings of the church. In Ephesians the fact of Christ as head of the church is related to the work of Calvary, the resurrection and the glory that the Lord received on his ascension. The second reference in Ephesians stresses the dependence that the body (the church) has on the head for growth, and the third reference reminds us that the head is the one who preserves and cares for the body.

When we read through Colossians, we find that we are being taught the credentials of the head. Firstly, the wonder of the one who is the head of the church strikes you as you read the accolades that are attributed to Him. The next reference teaches us that Christ is the head of every type of authority. The final reference in Colossians is there to teach us that the Lord is the means of the unity of the church. Man-made unity does not work; the church is united as one body because Christ is the head.

It is our delight to be linked to such a wonderful Saviour. He is not the failing head of a church appointed by failing men, but He is the Christ, the Son of the living God. We need Him, we worship Him, and there is no church without Him. As you read this week's studies, may you grow in your appreciation of the one who is our Head.

Day 1

CHRIST THE HEAD – HIS AUTHORITY DEFINED

1 Corinthians 11:1-16

The teaching about Christ as 'head' is brought to the attention of the believers in Paul's first letter to the Corinthians. The order that God intended for the world was lost at 'the fall'. The church has the opportunity to restore this for God. It can, however, only truly be seen in the meetings of the church (11:4-10). Later in the same passage, Paul deals with any opposition that there might be to this teaching by stating "if any man seem to be contentious, we have no such custom, neither the churches of God" (v.16).

Paul's desire that the believers should be aware of this truth is highlighted when he stresses "I would have you know" (v.3). This tells us how important the truth is to God, and the benefit that it is to the believers when they understand it. The world has made it a focus to undermine this truth in every way possible. Equality of the sexes has been promoted on the basis that anything else makes the female inferior, weak and suppressed. The word of God paints a much different picture.

The structure God designed is as follows; "the head of every man is Christ; and the head of the woman is the man; and the head of Christ is God" (v.3). These are not stepping stones to the top, or levels of importance, but the orderly way in which God has arranged things for our good.

It is obvious that the Lord Jesus Christ is not inferior to God. He is the Son of the living God and is described by Isaiah as "Wonderful, Counsellor, The mighty God, The everlasting Father, The Prince of Peace (Isa 9:6). Luke records that he will be called "the Son of the Highest" (Luke 1:32). In fact all references in the Scriptures will only reveal that the Lord Jesus Christ is equal with the eternal God. The fact that 1 Cor 11 states that "the head of Christ is God" cannot infer that Christ is inferior to God. The statement means that He has taken the position in God's order of bringing all of God's purposes to fulfilment, and of bringing everything under God the Father's control. This is so that God (Father, Son and Holy Spirit) may be all in all.

So it follows that the fact of man being the head of the women is not one of superiority and inferiority, but it is part of the structure and order that God has put in place for the good of mankind and for the fulfilment of the overall purposes of God.

Day 2

CHRIST THE HEAD – HIS ABSOLUTE PREEMINENCE

Ephesians 1:1-23

Reading the letter to the Ephesians, one never ceases to be amazed at the unbelievable truths that we are presented with. In chapter one we wallow in the wonder of being accepted with God, of being forgiven, of unlimited divine wisdom being available to the believer, of learning about the good pleasure of God's purposes and of discovering that God is in control of everything.

More exciting and thrilling truths keep overwhelming us with the majesty of the divine dealings of our God. In addition to this, we discover that we have an integral part in the things that he is doing.

Then we are confronted with God's purpose for our lives, the identifying mark of the Holy Spirit upon our lives and the rich future that is ours with Christ. Paul goes on to tell his readers that he is praying for them. In his prayer Paul asks God to open the spiritual eyes of his audience so that they will experience the knowledge of God. One of the things he prays about is that we would know "the exceeding greatness of his power to us-ward who believe". This power, Paul tells us, is the same power that God used when he raised his Son from the dead.

Paul does not stop at the resurrection, he reminds us that the power of God took Christ not only from death to life but from earth to heaven, and seated Him at the right of God exalting Him to his rightful place. The final stage of this account of His powerful return to glory tells us that the Lord has had all things put under His feet. This means everything is under His authority. At the highest level to which the Lord is exalted, He is described as "head over all things to the church, which is his body".

The descriptive terms 'head' and 'body' use the analogy of the human body and a human head. One without the other is incomplete. The body cannot function without the head. The head is incomplete without the body. In human terms the head is the means by which the body has the ability to function. Without the direction of the head the systems that we have in our bodies could not function, yet without the body the head is incomplete.

Despite the fact that we cannot understand why God has arranged it so, the last verse of Ephesians 1 teaches us that the same is true in the church's relationship with Christ. The Scripture states that Christ is incomplete without the church and yet He is the one who fills all in all. What a wonderful truth and what a wonderful Saviour!

Day 3

CHRIST THE HEAD – SUSTAINER OF THE CHURCH

Ephesians 4:1-16

In Eph 1:22-23 we discovered that Christ is "head over all things to the church, which is his body". This truth explains why Christ cares and provides for the church.

The church is that company of all believers who have ever lived since the commencement of the church on the Day of Pentecost, until the Lord returns to take those who are "in Christ" to heaven, at the event that we have come to know as 'the rapture'. The term we are looking at today teaches us that Christ as the head of the church has done everything possible to ensure the church grows.

A lot of the truth in this letter is about the Lord Jesus' relationship to the church. The emphasis is on the fact that the church is a body and that, as people grow from infancy to adulthood, so the church commenced on the day of Pentecost in its infancy and is growing until, one day, it will be a full grown adult (Eph 4:13).

When we think about our physical growth, we are aware that we need food, exercise, rest and a safe and secure environment to grow into mature and well-adjusted adults. The quality of the food is important: periods of activity and exercise are essential, as well periods of rest. A safe and secure environment will make it easier to develop properly.

The responsibility for all these things in the natural realm is normally entrusted to our parents. The parallel for the church is stated in Ephesians 4 where the Lord Jesus provides everything that is needed for the growth of the church.

The Lord Jesus as 'head' has given gifts to the church so that we are well fed. That should result in our growth and development (Eph 4:11). The gifts in this passage are the men God has given to equip God's people to serve Him so that the 'body of Christ' will grow. The church as it grows is growing up into (unto) Christ (Eph 4:15). This means that the Lord Jesus Christ is the reason why the church is growing and He is the object and purpose of its growth.

Just as we in our physical growth develop the features of a mature man or woman, so the church as it grows is becoming more and more like the Lord Jesus (the perfect man – Eph 4:13). This should be true of every believer individually but, even where it is not true of every believer, it will be true when in the future the church is complete and we, at the rapture, shall be changed into His likeness (2 Cor 3:18; Phil 3:21).

Day 4

CHRIST THE HEAD – SAVIOUR OF THE CHURCH

Ephesians 5:22-33

In the passage we are now considering we see the evidence of the love that the Lord Jesus has for the church. The Lord is not 'head' as an office bearer, but as the one who has the deepest interests and good of the church in His heart.

As you read Eph 5 you will find that the picture of the marriage of a man with a woman is used to focus our minds on the relationship that the church has with Christ. In its truest sense the relationship of Christ with the church is the true picture of a perfect relationship; our marriages should be a reflection of this.

The husband is the head of the wife even as Christ is the head of the church. 'Even as' means in the same way as Christ is the head of the church. What way is that? It is explained by the next statement, as Christ is the saviour of the body. The word 'Saviour' firstly means simply what we understand it to mean, that is, He died for us. In Acts 20:28 we learn that the church of God was purchased "with his own blood". The Lord has saved us: the one who is the head of the church is also the saviour of the church. It was his blood that purchased our salvation.

The second meaning that can be given to the word 'Saviour' is that of 'one who preserves and protects'. This is the current work of the 'head' of the church. We are being preserved and kept by the Lord. Our role as members of the body of Christ is to be obedient to the Lord who loves us, saved us and preserves us.

In the passage, the future outcome of the way the Lord deals with the church is highlighted. The passage says that the Lord gave Himself to "sanctify and cleanse" the church. That is, to set it apart specially for Himself and to cleanse it from impurity. Another outcome given is to "present it to himself a glorious church". The Lord wants the church all for Himself and to reflect His glory, and this will be realised in that future day.

Additionally, the passage stresses that "Christ also loved the church" and that He nourishes and cherishes the church. That is, He feeds and provides care and comfort for the church. These lessons, when applied in a Christian marriage, will be a preservative.

At the end of this section Paul finishes by reminding us that we are members of Christ's body and that as a result we will know His constant care.

Day 5

CHRIST THE HEAD – HE HAS THE FIRST PLACE

Colossians 1:1-20

Today we begin to look at another New Testament letter where the Lord Jesus is described three times as 'the head'. It is clear that the truth about the Lord Jesus as 'head of the church' is an important one, especially where a local church is involved. In the New Testament, every local church is an independent unit, responsible alone to God for the way its affairs are managed. In each local church there should be elders (appointed by the Holy Spirit and recognised by the members of the local church – Acts 20:28; 1 Thess 5:12-13; Heb 13:7, 17). These elders answer to God for how they care for the people of God. They are described as shepherds (caring, feeding and protecting God's people), overseers (those that watch over God's people) and elders (men of maturity). While local churches should have fellowship with each other, they are answerable to God alone. This group of men in each local church answer to the Chief Shepherd, the Lord Jesus (1 Pet 5:4).

In the verses we are considering today, the Chief Shepherd is called "the head of the body, the church" (v.18). The letter to the church in Colosse has many similarities to the Ephesian letter we have looked at already. The emphasis in Colossians is on the fact that Christ is the head of the church. The Holy Spirit gives much emphasis in the letter to proving why the Lord Jesus is uniquely fitted to be the head of the church.

The Lord Jesus is described as the redeemer (v.14), and the revealer (v.15) because He is "the image of the invisible God", that is, God manifest in the flesh. Then we find the Lord Jesus described as "the firstborn of every creature". This reminds us of the fact that He ranks above every created being (not as one who was Himself created, but as the one who created all things for Himself). The Lord is then described as the one who existed before everything and who maintains everything.

To this impressive list of credentials the Holy Spirit adds, "And he is the head of the body, the church" (v.18) and then, almost without drawing breath, the list of accolades to the Saviour continues. He is the beginning of everything, but specifically in relation to the church. He is the foundation on which the church stands (1 Cor 3:11; Eph 2:20). The Lord is the firstborn from the dead; not just the first to be raised eternally, but the one who has the highest position assigned to Him. In

all things He must have the first place. Is that the place that we give to Him in our lives?

Day 6

CHRIST THE HEAD – PRINCIPALITIES AND POWERS

Colossians 2:1-10

It is a wise thing to be clear in your thinking about the Lord Jesus. The men who had come to Colosse were determined to undervalue the Lord Jesus Christ. They taught, among other things, that the Lord Jesus was just an angel who had come down to earth and that He certainly was not God. Some taught that the Lord Jesus had become 'Messiah' or God at His baptism and that He was only endued with divine power for the three year period of His public ministry.

Paul writes (guided by the Holy Spirit) and makes it very clear that the Lord Jesus is the living God, full stop. No question, no argument. We have seen the evidence provided in chapter 1 to support this. In chapter 2 we are confronted with the fact that presently the "fulness of the Godhead" dwells in the Lord Jesus. In other words, this is still the case long after He returned to heaven. When we add the evidence of chapter 1 to this truth stated in chapter 2, it can be clearly seen that the Lord Jesus is eternally God.

To counteract the false teaching that had come to Colosse, the Lord Jesus is announced to be "head of all principality and power" (v.10). In chapter 1 it has been made clear that everything was created for Him (v.16). It does not matter the level or sphere of authority, it was all created by Him and for Him. The Lord Jesus is "head of all principality and power". He is superior to, and in command of, every form of power and authority.

Often when the term 'principality and power' is used it relates to authority generally, good or bad, earthly or heavenly, but when the expression is used in Col 2:15 it relates solely to evil powers.

Three things (among many others) happened at Calvary: first, the Lord Jesus answered the demands of God in respect of His holiness (Rom 3:26); second, the Lord Jesus made salvation available to fallen humanity (Rom 3:26); third, the Lord Jesus dealt with the devil and the fallen angels (Heb 2:14; Rev 12:9).

At Calvary the Lord Jesus dealt with the issues of sin and death and, in doing so, annulled Satan of his power. The full impact of this will be seen in a future day. The Lord Jesus robbed the forces of evil of their power and triumphed over them in doing so. Just as we wait for the day when we shall know salvation in all aspects of our lives, the day is coming when the Lord will put into action the sentence that was passed at Calvary. He is "head of all principality and power".

Day 7

CHRIST THE HEAD – HE IS TO BE HONOURED

Colossians 2:11-23

This is the last day of our studies about Christ, the Head. Has it made a difference to you as you have learned or rediscovered something of the wonders of this truth about the Saviour? Did it make you bow in worship as you realised the way God has so carefully organised things? Was your reaction one of joy and gratitude when you realised that God has included you in all of His purposes because of your links with the Lord Jesus? Our reaction should have been all of these things at the very least.

In the verses preceding the one we are concentrating on today (v.19), the writer has been warning his readers of the dangers of false teaching about the Lord. They are being warned that if they do not continue to give the Lord Jesus the prime place of importance in their lives, or to seek His guidance, then they will fall foul of the false teaching that was confronting them. By undermining the truth concerning the Saviour they were in fact not giving Him his rightful place. What about us? Could it be said of us, "not holding the Head" (v.19)? Would the way we live leave onlookers to conclude that we do not really honour the Lord Jesus? It is a major challenge!

In Colosse there were men who thought (falsely) that they were the 'last word' when it came to what they knew. Imagine their wonder when they discovered that the Lord Jesus has no limit to His wisdom and knowledge (Col 2:3). The wisdom and knowledge of the Lord Jesus is of incalculable value; they are described as "treasures" (v.3) and do not all lie on the surface. When valuable discoveries are made they are normally the result of great searching and hard work. The more the Christian gets to know the Lord Jesus the more they find treasures that are hidden in Him.

The false teachers in Colosse were promoting false worship. They promoted the worship of angels and had promoted themselves through a type of humility that was not God-honouring (it was a form of self-inflicted physical punishment, Col 2:23) and they were dabbling in the things of the spirit world, a most dangerous practise. The result of all this false teaching was that they had demoted the Lord Jesus and were not honouring Him as "the Head". The Lord alone can unite the church, and He is the means of its continued growth and good health. We need to be aware of the beliefs we hold about the Lord Jesus, as wrong teaching can seriously damage our spiritual health.

STEPHEN BAKER

Week 26

7 REFERENCES TO
"CHRIST … AFTER MELCHISEDEC"

Introduction

Who would have thought that a better man than Abraham was his contemporary and lived in the same land? Yet, while many chapters are devoted to Abraham and his experiences, four verses of history and one of prophesy are all that Old Testament Scripture has to say about this great man Melchisedec. He was no more than a man but, when we consider that the Holy Spirit describes him as better than Abraham, we must give due consideration to him.

Genesis 14:17-20 tell us his name, that he was king of Salem, that he brought forth bread and wine for Abram, that he was priest of the Most High God, that he blessed Abram and God and that he received tithes of Abram. The timely circumstances are also recorded for us in the surrounding verses. These things, together with the fact that his ancestry and descendants, his birth and death are unrecorded, are expounded by the writer to the Hebrews in chapter 7. His highest commendation is that he was "made like unto the Son of God" (Heb 7:3).

His name means King of Righteousness and his title King of Peace. Surely righteousness and peace kissed each other in him, but in a far deeper sense in our Lord Jesus Christ (Ps 85:10).

While no mention is made in Hebrews of the bread and wine Melchisedec provided, the fact that he met Abram returning from the slaughter of the kings is stated. The defeat of these kings of Shinar (Babylon), Ellasar (Greece?),

Elam (Persia?) and of nations, denotes Abram's victory over *the world*. However, he has still the king of Sodom to face, and he is strengthened for this encounter with *the flesh* by what Melchisedec provided. This first mention of bread and wine in the Scriptures reminds us of the Lord's provision for us so that, with our hearts constantly reminded of Him, we are strengthened for our encounters with the enemies of our souls.

The second OT reference, Psalm 110:4, is universally recognized as Messianic. It tells us that Melchisedec was the human head of a priestly order, and that significant fact is the basis of the seven references in Scripture to the order of our Lord's High Priesthood. This will repay our consideration in our readings throughout the week.

Day 1

"HE THAT IS CALLED OF GOD"

Psalm 2:1-9; Psalm 110:1-7; Hebrews 5:1-6

The early verses of Hebrews 5 deal with the *function* and *fitness* of the high priest in Israel. Verse 4 highlights for us the most important fact that the high priest must be called of God. Korah, and later Uzziah, would have intruded, but Aaron was invited (called) by God to become high priest.

It is only in verse 5 that Christ is introduced in the chapter as similar to Aaron. He is so different in relation to the matter of personal sin but He, like Aaron, did not glorify Himself to become High Priest. Aaron and his sons were designated by name to minister in the priest's office (Exod 28:1). In like manner, Christ is designated as Son of God in the reference to Psalm 2:7. Hebrews 4:14 refers to Him as "Jesus the Son of God" in the only reference in our Bibles to **"a great high priest"**.

It should be noted that His Sonship is by divine decree in the eternal past – "the Lord hath said" – but to be declared in the future from the psalmist's viewpoint – "I will declare the decree" (Ps 2:7). Such a declaration was undoubtedly made at Jordan, and on the mount of transfiguration, but Romans 1:4 refers to the declaration of His Sonship by the resurrection of dead ones. Even if this includes His raising of others, there is no doubt that His own resurrection is particularly alluded to. The three NT references to Psalm 2 are all in contexts which refer to Christ as risen and glorified.

He is then designated as priest in the quotation from Psalm 110. His priesthood is not related to the eternal past but to the eternal future, and is not after the Aaronic but the Melchisedec order. God's call of Christ as priest has been pronounced as clearly as that of Aaron and His functions for us are vastly superior.

So far as *sacrifice* is concerned, He made a once for all offering for our sins (He had none of His own) and it is by Him that we offer the sacrifice of praise to God (Heb 13:15).

His *sympathy* is not conditioned by personal infirmity, but by perfect humanity. Chapter 4:15 intimates that He cannot but be touched with the feeling of our infirmities because He was in all points tried as we are, sin apart. Matthew Poole suggests that He had all the *sense* of human infirmity but none of the *sin*.

We can therefore trust Him to carry out for us every function that Aaron, ideally, should have performed for Israel.

Day 2

"CALLED ('SALUTED') OF GOD"

Hebrews 5:7-10

If the earlier verses of Hebrews 5 deal with the *example* of Aaron as called by divine invitation to become high priest, verses 7-9 deal with the unique *experience* of Christ as a man.

John 1 records consecutive days at the beginning of the Lord's public ministry, and chapter 12 tells of His coming to Bethany six days before the Passover. This was again followed by five consecutive days (the tenth to the fourteenth days of the first month) in which He moved in Jerusalem. This period culminated in Gethsemane, Gabbatha and Golgotha. No doubt prayers and supplications marked the Lord Jesus throughout the days of His flesh, but the description by the Hebrew writer of "strong crying and tears" (v.7) most fittingly portrays Gethsemane. His prayer was not to be saved *from* death, but *out of* death, and His subsequent resurrection demonstrates that this prayer was heard and answered.

For the second time in the epistle He is now referred to as being made "perfect". There is no suggestion that there was ever imperfection in Him: the expression means He has become, by means of human experience, perfectly fitted for His God-given office. His sufferings fitted Him as the captain of salvation (2:10) and, here, His supplications gave perfect suitability to be "the author of eternal salvation unto all them that obey him" (5:9).

Eternal salvation is guaranteed to us, not because of our ability to keep it, but by His ability to keep us. His intercessions on our behalf are vital in this regard.

With this in view He is "called of God an high priest after the order of Melchisedec" (v.10). The word for God's call in verse 10 is different from that used in verse 4. It is the only time it is used in Scripture, and has been variously translated 'saluted', 'greeted' or 'named'. The idea may be illustrated from 1 Chronicles 11:20, where it is said of Abishai that he "had a name among the three". Abishai was given public acknowledgement for his leadership in a way similar to the various orders in the honours system in Great Britain.

God has given to Jesus a name that is above every name (Phil 2:9). Perhaps this name is 'Lord Jesus Christ', the exact sequence of the words in Greek that are rendered "Jesus Christ is Lord" (Phil 2:11). In Hebrews 5:10 the name or title is "high priest after the order of Melchisedec".

We could describe this verse as Christ's investiture as High Priest. God Himself desires that all should know that He is uniquely addressed as such because of the perfect fitness acquired in the days of His flesh. We therefore ought to honour Him and to appreciate the prevailing virtue of His prayers and supplications on our behalf.

Day 3

OUR PRECURSOR IS OUR PRIEST

Hebrews 5:11 - 6:20

The writer to the Hebrews would have loved to expound the Melchisedec priesthood of our Lord at the close of chapter 5, but their spiritual state necessitated the long parenthesis from 5:11 to the end of chapter 6.

It is sad to read of saints becoming such as have need of milk (5:12) and requiring to be warned of the danger of apostasy in the early verses of chapter 6. We are, however, glad to read "But, beloved, we are persuaded better things of you, and things that accompany salvation, though we thus speak" (6:9). The closing verses of the chapter then bring us very beautifully to the third reference to our Lord as our High Priest after the order of Melchisedec.

Verses 17-18 tell of **a double assurance** that we have in God's *purpose* (counsel) and His *promise* (oath). He condescends not only to reveal what He has purposed for us, but also to confirm it by His oath. The latter part of verse 18 then shows we have **a double advantage**, whereby our past is dealt with in Christ as our refuge and our future is secure with the hope set before us. Verse 19 describes this hope as **a double anchor** of the soul. We know that an anchor must not only be strong but must also take hold in a secure location. So this hope is both sure in itself, without any possibility of failing, and it is steadfast in its foundation within the veil.

Verse 20 finally gives **a double ascription** of titles to our Lord. He is our Precursor and our Priest. These titles give us a wonderful prospect, and we can depend on His support throughout our present sojourn. As our forerunner He is already within the veil and we can be absolutely certain that our final destiny is there.

1 Corinthians 15:20 and 23 tell us that Christ is the firstfruits in resurrection, the guarantee of a full harvest consisting of all those who are His at His coming. Resurrection will result in the change to be like our Lord (v.51) with bodies of glory like His (Phil 3:21). We will then be translated to be for ever with Him where He is (1 Thess 4:17). What a blessed prospect is ours!

We are, however, still living in a hostile world. This may perhaps be only for a short time, for His coming could be today. But centuries have rolled on since the letter to the Hebrews was written, and His High Priestly ministry has supported every saint in every generation, enabling them to continue for Him in the light of His coming.

Day 4

A CHANGED ORDER OF PRIESTHOOD

Hebrews 7:1-12

Chapter 7 of Hebrews begins with a comprehensive summary of the **information** we have about Melchisedec as recorded in Genesis 14. The facts that he was king of Salem and priest of the most high God are recorded first because of their importance, followed by the record of his meeting with Abram.

Inferences are then drawn that Melchisedec's name signified that he was "King of righteousness", and his position was that of "King of peace. He also had no recorded parentage, beginning of days or end of life, with the conclusion that he was thus "made like unto the Son of God". From this it is clear that Melchisedec is not the Son of God but, as king and priest, prefigures the Lord Himself. Zechariah says He "shall sit and rule upon his throne; and he shall be a priest upon his throne" (Zech 6:13), while His pre-existence and triumph over death are truths which are dear to the hearts of His people.

There follows, in verses 4-10, the **interpretation** of the relationship that Abraham and, therefore, Levi and the Aaronic priesthood, had to Melchisedec. Two facts are highlighted, namely the giving of tithes by Abraham and the blessing he received from Melchisedec. From the first we are asked to consider the greatness of Melchisedec and, from the second, we are told of his undoubted superiority. The whole thrust of these verses is to show the precedence in time, and the superiority in character, of the Melchisedec order of priesthood. The rest of the chapter gives **instruction** in relation to Christ and has the remaining four references to His Melchisedec priesthood.

The first of these deals with the change in order of priesthood that was necessary because the Levitical system could not bring God's people into a perfect relationship with Him. The law, by which Aaron and his sons officiated as priests, demanded a fresh offering on each occasion an Israelite sought to approach God.

Another priest of a different kind must therefore rise in all the dignity of His own greatness. He will not be called (a third Greek word translated 'called', and meaning 'spoken about' or 'referred to') as after the Aaronic order. In fact the law will require to be changed to accommodate this change of priestly order.

It should be noted that the law is not changed before its claims have been fully met. The Lord Jesus in His life, death and resurrection magnified the law and made it honourable (Isa 42:21).

Because of this, our relationship with God through Christ is indeed perfect, and we can approach Him through Christ our High Priest at all times on the basis of His finished work.

Day 5

THE SIMILITUDE OF MELCHISEDEC

Hebrews 7:12-17

When Melchisedec met Abram, Levi was yet in the loins of his father (v.10). The nation was in embryo when the meeting took place. Genesis 15 then tells of 400 years which would pass before the giving of the law. A priest after the order of Melchisedec need not therefore be of the tribe of Levi. The law, however, when it was enacted, not only restricted the priesthood to the tribe of Levi but, still further, to Aaron and his sons. This law must therefore be changed so that another priest, of a different character and a different tribe, should arise.

Two things are said to be evident; firstly "that our Lord sprang out of Juda" (v.14) and, secondly and even more evidently, that this priest should be "after the similitude of Melchisedec" (v.15).

The Pharisees said "Out of Galilee ariseth no prophet" (John 7:52). The chief priests said, "Write not, The King of the Jews" (John 19:21). Here the Hebrew writer says that Moses said nothing about priesthood in relation to the tribe of Judah. The law and its exponents deny the Lord all His offices. We do know that Uzziah the king was smitten with leprosy for presuming to go "into the temple of the Lord to burn incense upon the altar of incense" (2 Chron 26:16). Infringement of the law of Moses concerning the priesthood carried very severe penalties. Even a Levite, Uzzah, who put his hand out to steady the ark of the covenant lost his life (2 Sam 6:6-7). The law must therefore be changed so that the Melchisedec priesthood of our Lord might be legally recognised.

Now it is said that the priesthood of our Lord is "after the similitude of Melchisedec". The only other time the word translated 'similitude' is used in the NT is again in Hebrews, "we have not an high priest which cannot be touched with the feeling of our infirmities; but was in all points tempted **like as** we are, yet without sin" (4:15). What grace on the part of our Lord to allow Himself to be like us in temptation as a man down here (though we are assured that there was nothing in Him to respond to such temptation) and then to have His priesthood described as like that of Melchisedec. Regarding Melchisedec we have, however, observed in verse 3 that he was "made like unto the Son of God". (What an honour this gives to a man who functioned as priest of the most high God).

So we conclude that our Lord's likeness to Melchisedec is because of his likeness to the Lord.

Day 6

"*THE POWER OF AN ENDLESS LIFE*"

Hebrews 7:15-25

In reading the Old Testament we are impressed by the number of priests who played an important part in the history of Israel. Ezra records seventeen names in his own genealogy, some illustrious and others unknown (Ezra 7). We know that this list does not include Eli in Samuel's day, or Jehoiada who was so influential with King Joash, but it manifests the truth that "they were not suffered to continue by reason of death" (Heb 7:23).

By contrast, our High Priest "is made ... after the power of an endless life" (Heb 7:16) while the next verse gives the scriptural basis for this by referring, for the third time in the chapter, to the words of Psalm 110:4. The emphasis here is on the words "for ever", stressing the unchangeable nature of His priesthood.

As believers in our Lord Jesus Christ we have been blessed with eternal life and are assured that this life fits us for the presence of God for eternity. We share this life in common with every believer. It is, however, supported by the "endless life" of our great High Priest. His life is indissoluble, or indestructible, and has unlimited power available for the support of His own.

The law is said to be "weak through the flesh" (Rom 8:3), bringing out the fact that no mere man had the inherent power to fulfil its demands. Here in Hebrews the law in relation to the priesthood is said to be both weak and unprofitable (7:18) and that it made nothing perfect (v.19). The answer both to our sin and to our perfect acceptance is in the Son of God as our Saviour and as our great High Priest. The law is therefore abolished in order to bring in "a better hope ... by the which we draw nigh unto God" (v.19). This better hope is not the enhancement of our attitude of expectation, but the ground of our hope becoming manifest. In essence, the Lord Jesus as our great High Priest is the one by whom we draw nigh to God and, since His priesthood is indissoluble, we can be assured of constant access to God.

In addition to the personal approach, through Him, enjoyed by His people, "He ever liveth to make intercession for them" (v.25) and, through this, "he is able also to save them to the uttermost". While it is true that the worst sinner can be saved from his sin, the sense of this verse is that our salvation covers the uttermost of our need as those who come to God, and the uttermost of time till we are at home in His presence.

Day 7

THE OATH OF HIS PRIESTHOOD

Hebrews 7:18 - 8:1

The final reference to the Melchisedec priesthood of our Lord is found in Hebrews 7:21. The Aaronic priesthood was instituted without an oath but, concerning the Melchisedec priesthood, emphasis is placed on God's oath in Psalm 110:4.

The first scriptural reference to an oath by God is in Genesis 22:16-18. It tells of His promise to Abraham that his seed should be as the stars of the heaven and as the sand of the sea. John Gill, in his commentary on Hebrews 6:13, says "Swearing is ascribed to a divine person after the manner of men, and in condescension to them; and God is never introduced swearing, but in matters of moment and of great importance". That Abraham's spiritual seed is included within the sworn promise of God is significant.

The further reference in Psalm 110:4 regarding the Melchisedec priesthood of our Lord has implications for Israel in the future as well as for the church of the present dispensation. At the end of the psalm the anti-Christ is dealt with, and Messiah triumphantly enters His millennial kingdom. In Hebrews 7:22 we are told "By so much was Jesus made a surety of a better testament (or, 'covenant')" and while the new covenant is with the house of Israel, we in the present day enter into its blessings. When the Lord Jesus instituted the Lord's supper He said, "This cup is the new covenant in my blood", and each Lord's Day we bring this afresh to our remembrance.

Moreover, the high priest of the new covenant is **our** High Priest according to Hebrews 7:26; 8:1. Such a High Priest became us (Matthew Poole says, "was convenient, congruous, suitable, useful, and necessary for us") and the features highlighted fit Him perfectly to represent us at "the right hand of the throne of the Majesty in the heavens".

We can do no better than conclude our studies by looking at the features of Christ, a High Priest after the order of Melchisedec, in Hebrews 7:26: **He is holy**: not here the usual word for 'holy' meaning 'separate', but describing that which is in harmony with the divine constitution of the moral universe. This describes what Christ is in relation to God. **He is harmless**: there is no evil in Him which would have an adverse effect on others. **He is undefiled**: in Himself there is no trace of pollution. **He is separate from sinners**: the previous features manifest the moral distance that there is between Himself and men. **He is made higher than the heavens**: yea, seated at God's own right hand. **He is ours**! "We have such an high priest" (Heb 8:1).

ERNIE NELSON

Week 27

7 CAUSES OF SUFFERING IN PETER'S FIRST EPISTLE

Introduction

Scripture is replete with examples of the principle that suffering precedes glory. The instance that is probably best known to us is the occasion when the Lord Jesus Himself drew near to the two disciples on the road to Emmaus, and said to them "O fools, and slow of heart to believe all that the prophets have spoken: ought not Christ to have suffered these things, and to enter into his glory? And beginning at Moses and all the prophets, he expounded unto them in all the scriptures the things concerning himself" (Luke 24:25-27). The things expounded by the Saviour that day would surely have unfolded a long history of faithful men who had suffered much for their faith before being vindicated by God. In those Old Testament examples, as well as from prophetic Scriptures directly speaking of Himself, the Lord would have shown the necessity of His sufferings preceding His glory.

The essential link between suffering and glory was not understood by Peter for a long time. Revelation that Jesus was the Christ of God had been given to him by the "Father which is in heaven" (Matt 16:16-17), but he and his fellows disciples still had much to learn about divine purpose. "From that time forth began Jesus to shew unto his disciples, how that he must go unto Jerusalem, and suffer many things of the elders and chief priests and scribes, and be killed, and be raised again the third day. Then Peter took him, and began to rebuke him, saying, Be it far from thee, Lord: this shall not be unto thee. But he turned, and said unto Peter, Get thee behind me, Satan: thou art an offence unto me: for thou savourest not the things that be of God, but those that be of men" (Matt 16:21-23).

This severe rebuke to one who had so recently been blessed might make us think that Peter was harshly treated by the Lord. But no, that could never be the case. The Lord knew the source of Peter's well-meaning but ignorant words. He had heard such an overture before – in the wilderness when He was being tested of the devil. "Again, the devil taketh him up into an exceeding high mountain, and sheweth him all the kingdoms of the world, and the glory of them; and saith unto him, All these things will I give thee, if thou wilt fall down and worship me. Then saith Jesus unto him, Get thee hence, Satan ..." (Matt 4:8-10). What the devil was offering was glory without the suffering, and the Saviour answered His adversary from the word of God.

Many years later, a much wiser Peter lifted his pen to write to saints who were suffering. In his epistles he speaks in equal measure of suffering and glory and, with the Lord's help, we will look at some of the things he wrote under the inspiration of the Spirit of God.

Day 1

SUFFERING WRONGFULLY

1 Peter 2:11-25; 2 Samuel 16:1-4; 19:24-30; Psalm 101:5-6

We have an in-built tendency to excuse ourselves when faced with any accusation, true or false, a tendency that we inherited from our first parents Adam (who blamed Eve for his transgression) and Eve (who blamed the serpent for her failure). Pride will always make us try and deflect an accusation, often by pointing out some real or imagined fault on the part of the accuser. But when we are falsely accused, and the false accusation has serious effects, the bitterness, pain and desire for revenge can be very real indeed. How should a believer react in such a case?

Peter, wise and experienced now, points us to Christ. He explains that if we suffer patiently because of our faults, there is no glory in that. The suffering is the outcome of our own folly and failure. But if we "endure grief, suffering wrongfully" (1 Pet 2:19) because of our conscience toward God, and we bear that suffering with patience, then God is honoured and we are blessed.

Think of Mephibosheth, the son of Jonathan, to whom David had shown the kindness of God (2 Sam 9:1-13). He had a lovely spirit, like that of his father, and he loved David for the undeserved favour and kindness that had spared him from the sword and made him to "eat continually at the king's table". But David's goodness did not lie well in the heart of Ziba, Saul's servant, and he evidently bore deep resentment that none of his fifteen sons had been so favoured. Jealousy is very cruel and, when David was forced to flee Jerusalem because of Absalom's revolt, Ziba saw an opportunity to get even with Mephibosheth. The fact that they were both the undeserving recipients of royal grace escaped Ziba, and his jealousy of Mephibosheth made him hate him.

As David passed the summit of Olivet, Ziba met him with a supply of food and wine. When David asked about Mephibosheth, he was told that he had stayed in Jerusalem in the hope that David would be overthrown and the house of Saul would be re-established with Mephibosheth upon the throne. What a desperate lie! What evil character assassination! David believed what he had been told, and gave all Mephibosheth's property to Ziba (16:1-4). Only after the death of Absalom, and David's return to Jerusalem, was the truth revealed. It was immediately evident from the appearance of Mephibosheth that he had been in deep distress about David. To his sorrow had been added the pain and loss of Ziba's slander, yet he bore no malice. When David said that Mephibosheth's land should be divided between him and his accuser, he said "Yea, let him take all, forasmuch as my lord the king is come again in peace unto his own house" (19:30). What a godly response from one who had suffered wrongfully!

Brethren, it is a very serious matter to slander another. The devil is "the accuser of our brethren" (Rev 12:10), and dare we do his work for him? And you, dear saints, who are suffering wrongfully, be like the Saviour who "committed himself to him that judgeth righteously" (1 Pet 2:23).

Day 2

SUFFERING FOR RIGHTEOUSNESS' SAKE

1 Peter 3:8-16; Matthew 14:1-12; Mark 6:14-29

What price faithfulness to God and His word? It is one thing to sit in the comfort of an armchair and lay down the law about this, that and the other thing, but how ready are we to stand boldly and with lion-like courage for the things of God? Does faithfulness turn to compromise when we feel the heat of opposition? Is faithfulness put to one side when family members or close friends are involved in an issue? What does it mean to suffer "for righteousness' sake"? John the Baptist knew, and his faithfulness cost him his life.

We would have thought it faithful and very courageous of John to have gone in once unto King Herod to tell him that it was not lawful for him to have his brother Philip's wife. But Mark's account makes it clear (in the original language) that John kept on repeating the charge, something that we would probably judge to be going too far. John certainly proved the truth of the angelic message concerning himself before his birth, "For he shall be great in the sight of the Lord … and he shall go before him in the spirit and power of Elias, to turn the hearts of the fathers to the children, and the disobedient to the wisdom of the just; to make ready a people prepared for the Lord" (Luke 1:15, 17). Elijah went once and again unto Ahab and his dreadful wife Jezebel, knowing that his was a lone voice as he spoke out for God. The words of Ahab have echoed down through the centuries, and are still to be heard today, as faithful men of God stand fearlessly for the truth of God: "Art thou he that troubleth Israel?"

(1 Kings 18:17). Is it not the case that men who stand for the truth in local assemblies are often branded as troublemakers? Now, brethren, we must not confuse strong will with faithfulness, neither is an arrogant assertion of being correct a faithful stand for God. The kind of faithfulness displayed by John and Elijah was costly indeed. It was a faithfulness that drove these men to their knees and to their God, a faithfulness that caused John to experience fear and doubt in prison (Matt 11:3) and Elijah to wish himself dead under the juniper tree (1 Kings 19:4). Let us not dare to desecrate the memory of truly faithful men by claiming that a carnal display of unyieldingness, however technically accurate, is faithfulness and an example of suffering "for righteousness' sake".

It should be a very rare thing to "suffer for righteousness' sake" in a local assembly, but the probability of it occurring in gospel outreach is increasing rapidly. The appeasement of the Islamic movement, and threatened restrictions of liberty in preaching, could soon place great demands upon our courage and faithfulness. What an encouragement to know that "the eyes of the Lord are over the righteous" (1 Pet 3:12) and we need not be "afraid of their terror, neither be troubled" (3:14). It may well be the will of God that we should so suffer. If so, it will only be for the purifying of our faith and for His glory.

SUFFERING FOR WELL DOING

1 Peter 3:17; Numbers 13:16 - 14:10

It would be nice to think that those who are in the enjoyment of spiritual things would be admired by others aspiring to the same. Alas, such is not the case for, where spiritual growth is being stunted by carnality and the flesh, resentment and even enmity will arise in the heart towards those who are in the good of divine things. It has often been remarked that occupation with Christ will produce likeness to Christ, and He was the One who exemplified suffering for well doing. Those who exhibit, by grace and the indwelling power of the Holy Spirit, features of Christ in their lives will inevitably suffer in the same way. The holy life of the Lord Jesus was a constant rebuke to those whose boast was in the law but whose hearts were far from its spirit. We have only to recall the Jews' criticism of the Saviour when He healed people on the sabbath, to see the reaction of disobedient hearts to the witness of a holy life.

Suffering for well doing is illustrated in the experience of Joshua and Caleb, the two faithful spies whose report of the promised land was so positive. The divine assessment of the land was that it was "a good land, a land of brooks of water, of fountains and depths that spring out of valleys and hills; a land of wheat, and barley, and vines, and fig trees, and pomegranates; a land of oil olive and honey; a land wherein thou shalt eat bread without scarceness, thou shalt not lack anything in it; a land whose stones are iron, and out of whose

hills thou mayest dig brass. When thou hast eaten and art full, then thou shalt bless the Lord thy God for the good land which he hath given thee" (Deut 8:7-10). Such was God's estimation of the land for His people. What would their estimation be? That is what the spies were sent to determine.

The report that carried the day was an evil report: "The land, through which we have gone to search it, is a land that eateth up the inhabitants thereof; and all the people that we saw in it are men of a great stature. And there we saw the giants … and we were in our own sight as grasshoppers, and so we were in their sight" (Num 13:32-33). The contrary report of Joshua and Caleb only brought them into the danger of being stoned to death by the people.

Did Joshua and Caleb suffer for well doing? Very much so. For each day the spies had spent in the land, the children of Israel must spend one year in the wilderness (Num 14:34), and Joshua and Caleb would share the forty years of wandering. We never read of a complaining word, even from Caleb who was an old man by the time he gained Hebron as his inheritance. These men truly knew what it was to "suffer for well doing, than for evil doing".

Day 4

SUFFERING AS A BUSYBODY

1 Peter 4:12-16; Numbers 12:1-15

The word used by the Spirit of God for "busybody" in 1 Peter 4:15 is unique to this verse. The meaning of the word, however, is very similar to that used by Paul to the Thessalonians, "For we hear that there are some which walk among you disorderly, working not at all, but are busybodies" (2 Thess 3:11) and to Timothy, "And withal they learn to be idle, wandering about from house to house; and not only idle, but tattlers also and busybodies, speaking things which they ought not" (1 Tim 5:13). A look at the context of these two latter verses will show that, in the Thessalonian reference, men are in view and, to Timothy, Paul is speaking about women. The conclusion is therefore clear, that both men and women can become busybodies. The busybody is the person who is forever meddling in the affairs of another, always having something to say about this one or that. The person who knows how to discipline everyone else's children while leaving their own to run riot is a busybody. The one who repeats, with no concern about verification, some titbit of gossip is a busybody. The person who neglects their own responsibilities in the assembly but has plenty to say about that of others is a busybody. Such people, perhaps to our surprise and shame, are listed by Peter with murderers, thieves and evildoers (1 Pet 4:15).

Miriam, the sister of Moses and Aaron, was a busybody, and she suffered because of it. On the face of it she and Aaron spake against Moses on account of his marriage to an Ethiopian woman, a matter that was no business of theirs and certainly not contrary to the law, for such marriage, at that time, was not forbidden. The question of his marriage was not the real issue they had against Moses, but rather the second point they made: "And they said, Hath the Lord indeed spoken only by Moses? hath he not spoken also by us?" (Num 12:2). Here were the high priest of Israel and his sister, a prophetess (Exod 15:20), daring to meddle in the divine order that had set Moses as the leader of the nation. Discontent with their own dignified duties, they realised they could not assault Moses' position so they attacked him on a personal basis. Fellow-leaders and fellow-family members! How despicable the flesh can be!

Let us note, with godly fear, five very important words from this passage of Scripture: "And the Lord heard it" (12:2). Should we repeat them, beloved saints of God? "And the Lord heard it". All our busybody tales, whispers, rumours and half-truths about our fellow saints; the Lord hears them. "Speak not evil one of another, brethren" (James 4:11).

God judged Miriam the busybody, and she became leprous. Why was Aaron not judged in the same way? Interestingly, the verb in Numbers 12:1 is in the feminine singular, indicating that Miriam was the instigator of the trouble. Also, in mercy, God would not deprive the people of their high priest through uncleanness. But we are left in no doubt as to how God views busybodies.

Day 5

SUFFERING AS A CHRISTIAN

1 Peter 4:12-19; Acts 5:12-42; 7:51-60

What is it that can turn shame into song and disgrace into glory? Peter tells us from his own experience – it is suffering as a Christian. How devastated we would feel, and what damage would be done to the local testimony, if for crime we were reviled by the authorities and imprisoned. But Peter, who once spoiled his testimony through fear of man, became the bold preacher of the early chapters of the book of the Acts, and his faithfulness to Christ soon brought him, and his brother in the Lord, John, to the notice of the Christ-hating authorities. The two men were commanded "not to speak at all nor teach in the name of Jesus. But Peter and John answered and said unto them, Whether it be right in the sight of God to hearken unto you more than unto God, judge ye. For we cannot but speak the things which we have seen and heard" (Acts 4:18-20). As soon as they were released "they went to their own company, and reported all that the chief priests and elders had said unto them" (4:23) and then – they prayed! And what a prayer meeting that was! Saints united in common cause and with a real sense of their dependence on God. Their prayer was brief, scriptural and powerful. They did not ask for the threat to be removed but that, in the trial that was under divine control, the Lord would "grant unto thy servants, that with all boldness they may speak thy word" (4:29). That prayer was immediately and wonderfully answered, "And with great power gave the apostles witness of the resurrection of the Lord Jesus: and great grace was upon them all" (4:33).

We wonder how soon it might be, if the Lord remains away, that we will have to learn to pray like that. Liberty that we have taken for granted, and perhaps used so little, for the preaching of the gospel, may soon be curtailed. What reaction will there be among us to saints who are arraigned in court, mocked in the press and jailed for preaching the Word? Will we stand with them? To do so will be to suffer as a Christian, something that a great many of our brethren and sisters in other lands already know a good deal about.

Did Peter and John back off, content that they had made their stand? Was the counsel of their brethren not to provoke the authorities? Very soon they are in prison, and boldly testifying to their captors "We ought to obey God rather than men" (5:29). "They departed from the presence of the council, rejoicing that they were counted worthy to suffer shame for his name" (5:41).

Soon afterwards, our beloved brother Stephen, surrounded by a fierce mob who were stoning him, "kneeled down, and cried with a loud voice, Lord, lay not this sin to their charge. And when he had said this, he fell asleep" (7:60). Are you – am I – ready to suffer as a Christian?

Day 6

SUFFERING ACCORDING TO GOD'S WILL

1 Peter 4:12-19; Genesis 45:1-15

"Let them that suffer according to the will of God commit the keeping of their souls to him in well doing, as unto a faithful Creator" (1 Pet 4:19). This verse is not speaking of what we often call the permissive will of God, but of His sovereign, elective purpose. Would God ever intend that any of His dear children should suffer? Yes, Job was one of them and Joseph was another.

Careful reading of Genesis 45 will show just how much Joseph was aware that his long history of suffering prior to his days of glory was controlled and directed by the God of heaven. After he had privately revealed his identity to his brethren, Joseph told them, "Now therefore be not grieved, nor angry with yourselves, that ye sold me hither: for God did send me before you to preserve life" (Gen 45:5). He continues, "God sent me" (v.7); "So now it was not you that sent me hither, but God" (v.8); "Go up to my father, and say unto him … God hath made me lord of all Egypt" (v.9).

God would never ordain suffering for one of His children except He had a specific purpose in view and also gave to that child unique grace to recognise His will and to submit to it. His ways are "past finding out", and Job said "Behold, he taketh away, who can hinder him? who will say unto him, What doest thou?" (Job 9:10, 12). Sometimes the cause of suffering in a believer's life is clearly self-induced or because of external factors. At other times it is necessary simply to bow and acknowledge the sovereignty of God. Jairus could not have known that his faith in a time of great suffering was going to be the means of an unknown woman coming into blessing (Luke 8:41-55)!

Day 7

SUFFERING FOR SINS

1 Peter 3:18, 22

Whatever the cause of suffering in a believer's life, the source of strength to glorify God in it all is to lay hold on the Lord Jesus Christ. To be linked by faith with Christ is to be linked with suffering, "For even hereunto were ye called: because Christ also suffered for us, leaving us an example, that ye should follow his steps … who, when he was reviled, reviled not again; when he suffered, he threatened not; but committed himself to him that judgeth righteously: who his own self bare our sins in his own body on the tree …" (1 Pet 2:21-24).

The divine bestowal of grace to meet a particular trial has been witnessed in the lives of many believers. God glorifies Himself in the testimony of His saints, and we must remember that it is not every saint that God can trust with a trial. How important it is that we "consider him that endured such contradiction of sinners against himself, lest ye be wearied and faint in your minds" (Heb 12:3). We would not be long in considering the sufferings of the Saviour before our own trials were brought back into perspective. Think of His suffering, and of the glory that has followed: "For Christ also hath once suffered for sins" – not once upon a time, but once for all – so that propitiation might be made and that God might move out in grace, at no expense to His righteousness, to meet the need of sinners. "The just for the unjust" – our sinless Substitute – "that he might bring us to God" – the wonderful truth of reconciliation – "being put to death in the flesh" – the awful horrors of crucifixion – "but quickened by the Spirit" – praise God for the victorious resurrection of our Lord Jesus Christ! "Who is gone into heaven" – His bodily ascension – "and is on the right hand of God" – O the blessedness of His intercession! – "angels and authorities and powers being made subject unto him" – the glorification of the blessed Man of Calvary!

> Bearing shame and scoffing rude,
>   In my place condemned He stood;
> Sealed my pardon with His blood:
>   Hallelujah! What a Saviour!
>
> "Lifted up" was He to die,
>   "It is finished" was His cry;
> Now in heaven, exalted high:
>   Hallelujah! What a Saviour!"

PHIL COULSON

Week 28

7 STATEMENTS CONCERNING THE LORD IN HEBREWS 1:1-4

Introduction

It is helpful to see that the seven statements of truth concerning the Lord Jesus in Hebrews 1:1-4 have one important purpose in view. They show Christ's perfect fitness to be the final Revealer of God to men. The author of this epistle is writing to Jewish readers, as will be seen from the reference to the Jewish fathers in verse 1 and the numerous references in the epistle to Jewish customs and religion. The readers of this epistle were well versed in Jewish tradition and history, and many of them were slow to give up what to them was long-standing national heritage. The great task of the writer, therefore, is to establish in their hearts and minds the superiority of Christ and His sacrifice over the priests and ritualistic sacrifices of the Levitical economy. The background and possible objections of his readers demand that the author's proofs must be convincing, and his arguments irrefutable. Notice how some of the descriptions in these opening seven statements of truth are developed and explained further in the chapter. The Son is linked with verse 5. The Heir is linked with verses 6-9. The Agent in creation is linked with verses 10-12. The Enthroned Messiah is linked with verses 13-14.

The long sentence (vv.1-4) with which the chapter opens is like entering a beautiful temple, each clause being like a row of stately pillars supporting the roof. The temple front is a very imposing sight, causing one to approach with the mind filled with awe and a fitting spirit of reverence. This should be true of us as we look at these seven wonderful statements. Christ is seen supreme in His relationship with history. He is the end of all history, for He is the Heir. He is the beginning of all history, for He has made the ages. He is before all history, for He is the brightness of God's glory. He is throughout all history, for He is the upholder of all things.

Day 1

THE SON

Hebrews 1:1-4

It is significant that the descriptions concerning the Lord Jesus in this great passage begin with His Sonship. This title clearly sets forth the eternal deity of the Saviour. It is instructive to see in the early chapters of this epistle that the superiority of the Lord Jesus is based on His Sonship. A contrast is made, with important references to the Lord being the Son of God. If He is greater than the prophets, it is because God has finally spoken in the Son. If He is greater than angels, then they are but created beings. He is the uncreated Son of God (v.6). If He is greater than Moses then, while he was a servant in the house, the Lord Jesus is the Son over the house (3:6). If He is greater than Aaron who had to die like all mortals, then He is Jesus the Son of God who ever liveth, perfectly fitted in His sympathy and sufficiency to be our great High Priest (4:14). The Hebrews needed to grasp the fundamental truth that their Messiah was the Son of God.

The final and full revelation of God by the Son is contrasted with the imperfect and fragmentary character of the old dispensation. The contrast is twofold. The methods of the revelation, and the agents of the revelation, in the past dispensation prior to Christ's coming, were imperfect compared to the revelation of God brought in through, and in, the Son. The methods were various and the messengers were many but, in the Son, God has spoken completely and revealed Himself in one uniform way.

The prophets lived in different periods and spoke of the coming Messiah-Saviour (see Acts 3:21,24). Contrasted with the Son, the prophets were sinful men, speaking in different manners in dreams, visions and symbols. They were men who did not always understand their message and, like John the Baptist, were only signposts pointing on to the Lord Jesus. The stress in Hebrews 1 is that now there is only one agent of revelation instead of the many prophets. The One who stands in the relationship of Son to God has brought to man a revelation which is perfect in its character and, therefore, complete in its contents. This truth indicates that the Son must be the last Speaker, and the only Speaker, of the new era.

The aim of the writer in stating the fact of the inferiority of the earlier revelation, was that the Hebrew Christians might not cling to it believing it was final. As believers let us thank God for this revelation and be in the good of it.

Day 2

THE HEIR

Hebrews 1:1-4

In the eternal counsels of God, Christ is the destined heir of every existing thing in the universe. Though He does not possess all things now, He will yet do so. While it is true that the inheritance belongs to Him by right because He is the Son co-equal with God, yet He has earned the right to possess all things because of His incarnation, His life and the redemption wrought in His death.

It is interesting to notice four ways in which we see the heirship of Christ:

1. He is Heir to the throne of David. The Lord Jesus will sit upon the throne of His father David. He is the Son of David (Matt 1:1) and, as such, He will inherit the throne. The millennial throne, as seen in Hebrews 1:8, is His.

2. He is Heir to the land of Israel. As well as being the Son of David, the Lord Jesus is also the Son of Abraham (Luke 3:34), and the promises made to Abraham will be fulfilled.

3. He is Heir to the Nations. God has said to the Messiah, "Ask of me, and I shall give thee the heathen (nations) for thine inheritance" (Ps 2:8). We can contrast this with the prayer of the Lord Jesus, "I pray not for the world" (John 17:9). The Lord Jesus is not making request for Israel or the nations, but for His own. When the Lord returns to the earth, all in Psalm 2 will be fulfilled and the Lord will then put forth His claim for the nations. All nations will be under His dominion.

4. He is Heir to the World. The Lord's title to the earth is acknowledged in Psalm 24:1, "The earth is the Lord's, and the fulness thereof". The devil and man dispute this statement, but the psalm goes on to show that the earth belongs to the Lord Jesus by right of His creatorial ability (v.2), moral purity (vv.3-5), glorious victory (vv.7-9), and eternal deity – He is "Jehovah of hosts".

How wonderful that as believers we are heirs of God and joint heirs with Christ (Rom 8:16)! We shall share with Him all that the Father will give Him in the coming day. What a stupendous thought is this; that on the cross, that which was mine – my sins – He took. But, blessed contrast! – all that is His is mine to enjoy in measure now, in the time when we shall reign with Him, and forever!

As associated with Christ "all things" are ours (1 Cor 3:22). On the cross He became poor and was deprived of all things that we might possess all things. Blessed Saviour!

Day 3

THE CREATOR

Hebrews 1:1-4

One reason why the Lord Jesus is mentioned here as Creator is to show that God really appointed Christ as Heir before the world was made. The phrase "the worlds", or "the ages", is parallel with "all things" in the previous statement, denoting the whole of creation. The Lord Jesus was before all worlds. His glory then reaches forward and backward, for He is Heir of things to come and the Maker of the ages. Here is another proof in this passage of the deity of Christ, for the divine work of creation in all its aspects is ascribed to Him. Eight times in the NT the Lord Jesus is mentioned as the creator of the world. The statement of John 1:3 shows the truth of the Lord's creatorial ability, "Without him was not anything made that was made". Christ is the great originator of creation. He is not part of creation. These words show the utter impossibility of the Lord being no more than a created being. If not even the slightest thing was created without Him, it is clear He cannot be a creature. If creation could not do without Him neither can the believer – "Without me ye can do nothing", said the Saviour (John 15:5).

Today, science and men try to eliminate the Person of Christ, but the believer by faith accepts the teaching of the word of God. It must be remembered that Christ is here being contrasted with the prophets. As the Creator He is greater than the prophets. They are creatures, but He is the Creator. They owe their very being and existence to Him.

What an incredible thought it is, that He who by His power brought into being the physical universe, was the same who hung in shame upon the cross! The unfolding of the glories of Christ in the opening section of Hebrews 1 presents Him as the great Sin-Purger. It is a deep descent from worlds to wounds, from planets to pains and from making of stars to the receiving of scars. Opposites are happily wedded in Christ; His might and His meekness, His sovereignty and His suffering, His glory and His grace.

> He made the forest whence had sprung,
>   The tree on which His body hung.
> He died upon a cross of wood,
>   Yet made the hill on which it stood.
>
> The sky that darkened o'er His head
>   By Him above the earth was spread,

The sun that hid from Him its face
By His decree was poised in space.

How wonderful that the Son who is the Creator is also our Saviour, Friend, Provider and Helper. He will never fail us!

Day 4

"*THE BRIGHTNESS OF HIS GLORY, AND THE*

EXPRESS IMAGE OF HIS PERSON"

Hebrews 1:1-4

This Scripture would greatly increase the believer's understanding of Christ's glorious Person by giving Him, in His pre-existent state, the name of "the effulgence of his glory" (v.3 RV). This word 'effulgence' is found only here. It is a timeless term and contains in it an allusion to the sun and its radiance. How beautiful! We may note that the radiance of the sun is as old as the sun itself and, without it, the sun would not be the sun. So the Lord Jesus is co-eternal with the Father. The Son is the outshining of the divine glory, expressing in Himself the majesty of the divine Being. In the Hebrew writer's praise of the Son, he is still moving in the high sphere of the Son's eternal relations. He has not yet touched the earth. We do not believe that the "effulgence of his glory" and the "express image of his substance" refers only to what the Lord was as incarnate. We can dismiss this view with confidence, for the participle clause, "Who being," points to what the Saviour is in His essential nature, regardless of time.

The Lord is also the 'exact impression' or 'representation' of God. The word only occurs here and means 'character'. W E Vine says, "The word character was either a stamping instrument or the image stamped. The image stamped is the exact impression of the stamping instrument. 'Hupostasis' came to denote essence, substance, and the inner nature. Christ is the very representation of the Divine nature". The essential nature of God is seen as putting its unique stamp upon the Person of Christ, so that the Son bears the exact impress of the divine nature and character. What a lofty and wonderful description we have here of the Person of Christ! It makes so clear that the Lord Jesus possesses all the attributes of deity. He is not a fragment of the divine, but all the fulness of deity perfectly, physically, permanently and personally dwells in Him.

It has been rightly said that a Saviour who is not quite God is like a bridge broken at the further end. The statement concerning Christ here should leave no doubt in the mind of the believer that Christ is God. If this is true, and thank God it is, then it should have a profound effect upon our lives, causing us to serve Him with joy, considering no sacrifice to be too great to make for Him.

> The brightness of Thy glory and
>   Thine express image too.
> Was He Who brought Thy powerful hand
>   And loving heart to view.

Day 5

THE UPHOLDER

Hebrews 1:1-4

The One who is the Creator also maintains, by the power of His own word, the whole of the universe. Men may speak of the various parts of the universe as being controlled by the laws of nature, but these laws are Christ's laws. The laws of nature are under His control. As the Creator, the Lord is not only independent of His creation, but creation is dependent upon Him. The picture is not that the Lord is an Atlas, holding up upon His shoulders the great burden of the universe, neither is it only the thought of ruling and guiding, but rather that He sustains the world in maintaining its coherence and carrying on its development. To Him belong the functions of providence. Paul states a similar truth when he writes that by Christ "all things consist" or "hold together" (Col 1:17). If He were to withdraw His sustaining power, the universe would be in complete chaos. He who is creation's light and reason is also its co-ordinator. This work is going on all the time, and has done so without a break or blunder through the ages. It is a work unseen, vital, unknown by men, but too often forgotten even by the believer. This great truth concerning Christ's almightiness emphasises again His essential deity.

This activity of Christ within creation bears very much on His fitness to be the full and final Revealer of God. The One who fulfils the functions of providence is the One who can reveal providence, who can tell us what the course of nature and history means, and what is the great purpose running through the ages. It is Christ alone who interprets all these and gives the secret to fallen man of the ultimate divine purpose in creation. Without Christ nothing really would make sense. What men have tried to understand, Christ reveals. Christ has come and been in His creation. It is true He was perfect man, and by His lovely humility, gentleness and patience revealed God, yet because this is written to Hebrews they needed to see that He who was to them the despised Nazarene, was the all-powerful Son of God. What does the fact that Christ is the upholder of all things mean for the believer today? Well, creation hangs together wonderfully, and under the Son's perfect control all its movements fulfil His will. The same ought to be true of the believer's life under Christ's control. Is this the case with us?

Day 6

THE SIN-PURGER

Hebrews 1:1-4

"When he had by himself purged our sins". The statement indicates the efficacy of the sacrifice of Christ to deal with sins effectively. It is good to see that the same Lord who is powerful in His sustaining of the creation is equally powerful in cleansing His people from their sins. The cleansing of sin is a prerogative of God alone, so that once again we see Christ's deity implied and presupposed. This is the only time in this wonderful opening paragraph that the writer touches the earth. It would be easy to wonder whether such a supreme Being spoken of here could ever have visited this world and been in time conditions, but the amazing fact is HE HAS! This work of purification did not take place in heaven, but on earth, for purification implies blood shedding, and blood shedding implies death, and death, of course, demands a life on earth. Three precious thoughts at least are suggested here for the hearts of every believer to ponder on and rejoice in:

This divine work of the purification of sins was **a personal work**, for it was not something that the Lord Jesus caused to be done by some other agent. He did it unaided on the cross. Alone He endured the darkness, alone He experienced the forsaking, alone He had placed upon Him our sins, and alone He was judged for them and triumphed in paying the price that no mere man could pay.

It was **a priestly work**, for in the thought of making purification of sins is already presented the work of Christ as High Priest, which subject figures so prominently in the doctrine of the epistle. True, officially our Lord did not commence His High Priestly ministry until He entered heaven, but the words used by the Holy Spirit here suggest a picture of the high priest's work. On the Day of Atonement, for example, Aaron used means of propitiation (two goats) outside of himself in order to secure cleansing of the people's sins for one more year, but the Saviour used nothing external to Himself in effecting purification for sins.

It was **a permanent work**. It will never need to be repeated. The truth of the once-for-all sacrifice of Christ is also a very vital theme touched on in this epistle (cf. 9:27). It insists on the eternal character of the work of Christ on the cross. What a contrast with the Jewish sacrifices of the imperfect old economy. With these offerings for sin there was repetition, weariness and monotony, and their most fatal defect was that they were sacrifices "which can never take away sins". How hopeless we would be if the Scripture stopped there. Praise God, it continues with this heart-thrilling statement, the basis of heaven's eternal song, "But this man, after he had offered one sacrifice for sins for ever, sat down on the right hand of God" (Heb 10:11-12)!

Day 7

"SAT DOWN ON THE RIGHT HAND

OF THE MAJESTY ON HIGH"

Hebrews 1:1-4

What a glorious conclusion to the description of Christ's great Person! Having seen His completed sacrificial work on the cross we now have His enthronement in heaven. The Lord Jesus has so effectively dealt with our sins in His death that He now has gone on high without them. The dark depths of suffering and humiliation that were His are now blessedly rewarded by God in taking Him to the heights of heaven. The description of Christ's enthronement is really a proof of the ability of the One who undertook the work of the purging of sins. This fact is the token of His finished work. The Hebrews needed to know that He who was Jesus of Nazareth, despised and rejected, was exalted by God to sit on His right hand. The right hand of the heavenly throne speaks of the place of power and administration. Sat down in such a position, the Lord Jesus administers all things for His people. He is there for us, to dispense blessing, mercy and grace (4:16) and to represent the cause of His people before God. Pathahiah in the days of Nehemiah "was at the king's hand in all matters concerning the people" (Neh 11:24). Our Lord Jesus is the true Pathahiah, and at God's right hand He will never fail His people.

It is most interesting to find in the epistle to the Hebrews a fourfold description of the Lord's enthronement. Each is a little differently worded according to the context in which it is set, and each highlights a particular aspect of the Person of Christ. In this verse the Lord is seen as the Sin-Purger. It is **the throne of His efficacious work** that is in view, in contrast to OT prophets and angels who could never have achieved such a work. In 8:1 it is **the throne of His everlasting priesthood**. There He is seen in contrast to the Levitical priests who never sat down. In 10:12 it is **the throne of His exalted manhood** and the contrast in this reference is with OT sacrifices which could never take away sins. Finally, in 12:2, it is **the throne of His encouraging example** and we are bidden to look to Him who once suffered here, lest we be despondent in our minds. The contrast there is with the men of faith in chapter 11; they never carried faith to perfection as He did.

> He fills the throne – the throne above
> He fills it without wrong;
> The object of His Father's love,
> The theme of angels' song.

JOHN STUBBS

Week 29

7 MENTIONS OF "THIS MAN" IN LUKE'S GOSPEL

Introduction

"This man" – why did those that used this language in relation to our Lord Jesus describe Him thus? It is sad to discover that, apart from the last mention of these two words in the gospel by the malefactor in chapter 23, this description was used either in derision or indifference. His own people's estimation of Him was that He was a man, and only a man; "thou being a man, makest thyself God" (John 10:33). We view Him differently, as the apostle Paul states, "God was manifest in the flesh" (1 Tim 3:16)

It is fitting that Luke, possibly the only gentile writer of our New Testament, should record these sayings for us, as the thrust of his gospel is to reveal the Lord Jesus as the Son of man. He will record unique details in respect of the perfect humanity of the Saviour. In chapter 2 he relates the circumstances at His birth, the visit of the shepherds, at eight days the circumcision, the presentation of Him to the Lord at the temple when Simeon took Him up in his arms, and that Anna "spake of him". We have there the only glimpse of Him as a boy of twelve, with the first recorded words He spoke. In chapter 3, His human genealogy is recorded, beginning with "began to be about thirty years of age". We are keenly aware of His interest in humanity in this gospel as we see Him frequently as guest in various homes. His sympathy is revealed in chapter 7 when He draws nigh to the gate of the city of Nain to heal the broken heart of the woman and restore her son to life. Luke is careful to record she was a widow, and this was her only son. The question by the lawyer in chapter 10 "who is my neighbour" will record from the lips of the Saviour, in what we call 'the parable of the good Samaritan', a beautiful picture of One who, while He journeyed, came to where we were. This gospel will not close without the proof of this being experienced by the two on the road to Emmaus; "Jesus himself drew near" (Luke 24:15).

As we consider "this man" let us comfort our hearts that His interest in us today is still the same.

Day 1

"THIS MAN, IF HE WERE A PROPHET ... "

Luke 7:36-50

This is one of at least seven instances where Luke records the Lord Jesus responding to an invitation to dine. It is clear from the narrative that Simon had not extended his invitation out of love and affection to the Lord; there was no water (v.44), no kiss (v.45), no anointing (v.46). Little did Simon realise that as he "spake within himself" (v.39) as to whether or not this man was a prophet, that he would quickly discover that the thoughts and intents of his heart were already known.

The lesson for us is easy to find. It is good to desire the presence of Christ in the home, but the purity of our motive is essential. May it always be like the home at Bethany where we feel the Lord was warmly welcomed. To return to the events that caused Simon such consternation, the entry of the woman "which was a sinner" (v.37).

There is frequent mention of sinners in this gospel. Of the 42 NT mentions, sixteen are recorded in Luke's Gospel. Earlier in this chapter the Lord reveals that the people saw Him as "a friend of publicans and sinners" (v.34). Thankfully we are glad He was, otherwise we would have been left without hope in this world.

This account of the woman and her worship is one of the many instances in the gospels where no name is given and, strikingly, where no words are spoken. The common saying "actions speak louder than words" is evident here. There is a lovely progression: she knew where He was (v.37), she procured the ointment and, despite no doubt the scathing looks of Simon and others, she allowed the inner feelings of her heart to be publicly demonstrated in her outward actions. The perfect tense used in verse 48 "thy sins are forgiven" indicates that, prior to this, she had exercised faith in Christ, and her act of devotion here was flowing from that experience.

It would be a noble exercise today, if opportunity arose, to be able to demonstrate our love to the Lord, as He is still the object of ridicule and hatred. The example used by the Lord of the two debtors reveals the true state of the heart of Simon, especially when we hear his grudging reply to the Lord's question "I suppose that he to whom he forgave most" (v.43). It is good

to remember that, despite what we were, we have been "frankly forgiven" (v.42). The narrative closes with the guests' scepticism about the Lord being able to forgive sins, but prior to that we take note of the value the Lord places on the devotion of this woman, "she loved much" (v.47). May our love for Him be deepened.

Day 2

"THIS MAN RECEIVETH SINNERS"

Luke 15:1-2

The opening verses in this chapter define the two kinds of audience that confronted the Lord Jesus; those that came "to hear him" and those that "murmured". The last verse in the previous chapter, "He that hath ears to hear, let him hear" drew a response from the publicans and sinners, and they were anxious to hear Him. In the first verse of that same chapter, when the Lord was in the house of a chief Pharisee to eat bread, "they watched him", revealing that their purpose was to criticise. The same division in humanity is still with us.

In Luke 5:32 He is *calling* sinners; in 7:34 He is *befriending* sinners; and here, in v.2, He is *receiving* sinners. We can see from the teaching of the three parables that the Lord spoke in the previous chapter, that it revealed the true condition of the heart of the Pharisees then, and is the attitude of many today. In v.7 there are those that seek to portray their own seeming merit and importance; in v.12 those that live selfishly showing seeming acts of kindness and seeking recompense for good deeds done to others – a 'good works philosophy'; in verses 16-24 those that place no value on the free and gracious invitation to the "great supper" provided at such cost.

The following parable, in three sections and unique to Luke, is principally in response to the statement by the Pharisees and Scribes "this man receiveth sinners", but there are precious truths there for the believer as well. We can see the interest and labour of divine persons to recover the lost:

The sheep was an object of pity by the shepherd, which caused him to "go after that which was lost, until he find it" (v.4). This is a lovely picture of the Lord Jesus who made a great downward journey to find us, as beautifully described by the apostle Paul, "being found in fashion as a man, he humbled himself, and became obedient unto death, even the death of the cross" (Phil 2:8).

The silver was an object of value, and light was required and diligent search made until it was found. This pictures the work of the Holy Spirit in the world today.

The son was an object of love, despite his insensitivity to his father. This pictures the love of the Father towards us – "the Father sent the Son to be the Saviour of the world" (1 John 4:14).

Joy and rejoicing are the sequel to each narrative. Which category do we find ourselves in today? Are we rejoicing at having been found, or are we like the sheep – lost in danger; like the silver – lost in the dark; or like the son – lost at a distance?

Day 3

"WE WILL NOT HAVE THIS MAN TO REIGN OVER US"

Luke 19:11-27

The Lord tells the parable of "a certain nobleman" immediately after the meeting with Zacchaeus in Jericho, when Zacchaeus "received him joyfully" (v.6) and the crowd then murmured that the Lord had again "gone to be guest with a man that is a sinner" (v.7). In some of the parables the Lord is concealing truth from the hearers which He later revealed to His disciples, but here we are not only given the reason for the parable (v.11) but it would be clear to the audience that murmured that they were the citizens referred to who "will not have this man to reign over us".

We must note the grace displayed by the Lord that, despite the curse upon Jericho in the days of Joshua (Josh 6:26), He will enter and pass through on this His final journey towards Jerusalem, in order to bring sight to the blind beggar and salvation to Zacchaeus.

It is clear from v.11 that the people believed in a coming kingdom, but their concept of how it would be established and who would reign over it were far removed from the divine plan. To accept that this lowly man from Nazareth, mingling with publicans and sinners, could be their Messiah was beyond their comprehension. Verse 14 sums up their feelings, "his citizens hated him". The psalmist had written long before He came, "they that hate me without a cause are more than the hairs of mine head (Ps 69:4).

In a few days this burning hatred will reach a crescendo when the Lord arrives at Jerusalem. He reveals He is going into a far country and will return (v.12). We know He has gone back to heaven, and the next event in the divine calendar is the return to the air for His own (1 Thess 4:17) but, beyond this event, it will be a glorious day of vindication when He returns to the earth to set up His kingdom and to be received as the rightful king of Israel.

Meanwhile, the parable reveals that we are expected to "occupy till I come" (v.13). There are ten servants, ten being the number of responsibility, and they are all given the same amount to trade with pending the nobleman's return. On his return the first two servants had traded successfully, but one had done nothing with what had been entrusted to him.

In a world where the attitude still is "we will not have this man to

reign over us" it would be fitting for us to own our allegiance to Him, and serve in the light of the day of review. Will it be "gold, silver, precious stones" or "wood, hay, stubble"? (1 Cor 3:12).

Day 4

"I FIND NO FAULT IN THIS MAN"

Luke 23:1-5

The final journey from Jericho was over, and the Lord Jesus arrived at Jerusalem, by way of Bethphage and Bethany, and went to the Mount of Olives. The final scrutiny of Jehovah's perfect servant was about to begin. He sent two of His disciples to bring the colt, in fulfilment of the prophecy of Zechariah (Zech 9:9), and rode into Jerusalem, surrounded by the multitude of disciples who began to "rejoice and praise God" (Luke 19:37). The scrutiny began with the Pharisees saying, "Master, rebuke thy disciples" (19:39). This is not the King they were looking for. He truly was "just and having salvation; lowly, and riding upon an ass". We note His tears as He drew near to the city, as He alone knew the calamities that would come upon them in the not too distant future. After He again cleansed the temple, and taught daily in the outer court, the chief priests and the scribes scrutinised Him and "sought to destroy him" (19:47).

In chapter 20 they continued to scrutinise Him, asking "by what authority doest thou these things" (v.2); "is it lawful to give tribute unto Caesar" (v.22) and, having failed to find a flaw in Him, "they durst not ask him any question at all" (v.40).

In chapter 22 we find, sadly, that the scrutiny of the Saviour by Judas, for three and a half years, results in Judas taking steps to betray Him. The last Passover is kept by the Lord Jesus, followed by the institution of the supper with the eleven disciples. He crosses the brook to enter Gethsemane with them, where He will eventually withdraw "a stone's cast" (v.41) and "sweat as it were great drops of blood" (v.44) as He contemplates the supreme sacrifice He is about to make.

We come to the final scrutiny by His own people. Taken and bound like a common criminal, He is led to the house of the high priest where the first marks of man's cruelty were inflicted upon Him. The trial is brief, as the sentence was formed in their wicked hearts beforehand. After a lonely night, the silent sufferer is hurriedly taken in the early morning to face the scrutiny of Pilate. We find in our verses that the charge against Him has changed. He is now accused of "perverting the nation, and forbidding to give tribute to Caesar" (23:2). This, in their thinking, was calculated to have more weight before Pilate. After a short period of questioning, Pilate's conclusion is what multitudes have since gladly confessed; "I find no fault in this man". It is so refreshing, when the day's events have perhaps highlighted our faults and failings, to consider this lovely man "who, when he was reviled, reviled not again; when he suffered, he threatened not" (1 Pet 2:23).

Day 5

"*I … HAVE FOUND NO FAULT IN THIS MAN*"

Luke 23:13-15

From the records of Luke and John it appears that on three occasions Pilate confronts the Jews and affirms his conviction that he found no fault in this man. His declarations of the Lord's innocence were made during his initial examination (Luke 23:4; John 18:38); after the Lord Jesus is brought back from Herod (Luke 23:14) and again after the scourging (John 19:4). Pilate knew "that for envy they had delivered him" (Matt 27: 18) and that it seemed, from the response he had received when he first stated he found no fault in the Lord Jesus (v.5), that it was highly unlikely they would drop the charges against Him.

Therefore, when Pilate discovered that the Lord Jesus "belonged to Herod's jurisdiction" (v.7) he cunningly decided to send Him to Herod to rid himself of this troublesome business. This Herod was the son of Herod the Great who "slew all the children that were in Bethlehem, and in all the coasts thereof, from two years old and under" (Matt 2:16). All the cruel traits of his father had already been manifested in his life, as he was responsible for the beheading of John the Baptist (Matt 14:10). It would be obvious, then, that the Lord Jesus would not be treated with kindness or consideration by this evil man. Herod's gladness to see the Lord was not out of genuine interest, but merely to satisfy his curiosity or even, perhaps, to confirm that this was not John the Baptist "risen from the dead" as he had previously thought (Matt 14:2). Despite the questions and the accusations of the chief priests and scribes, the Lord Jesus remains silent. Truly the words of the prophet Isaiah were being fulfilled "he was despised, and we esteemed him not" (Isa 53:3). The true character of Herod is now exposed; with his men of war they "set him at naught" (v.11) – literally counted Him as nothing, valueless and of no interest to them. Their abuse expressed, they send Him back to Pilate. All that these events had accomplished was to create a friendship between these two men based on their rejection of Christ.

Pilate now has to reconvene the court and announce his verdict on this dual enquiry, "I have found no fault in this man". The Jews are incensed by this verdict, and will not listen to the reasoning of Pilate or bow to his authority. They will settle for no less than crucifixion. Peter will later sum up their attitude; they "denied him in the presence of Pilate, when he was

determined to let him go" (Acts 3:13). Whether by those that loved Him, or the myriads that hated Him, there is only one of whom it can be said, there is "no fault in this man" – our Lord Jesus Christ.

Day 6

"AWAY WITH THIS MAN"

Luke 23:15-25

Pilate, having appealed to the multitude on the grounds of both his and Herod's examination of the Lord Jesus, concluding that "nothing worthy of death is done unto him" (v.15), now attempts to pacify them by stating he will "chastise him and release him" (v.16). This has no effect on them, but rather increases the intensity of their demands that He must not be freed under any circumstances. We are then introduced to the strange custom of releasing a prisoner of the people's choice at the time of the feast (Passover). We have no indication why or when this custom was introduced, but it would appear it was calculated to be a means of the Roman authorities showing favour to the Jews at a time when there was the likelihood of tumult with so many of them visiting Jerusalem for the Passover. Possibly Pilate thought if he offered them the release of the prisoner Barabbas, who had committed such heinous crimes, they would accede to the release of Jesus. Matthew describes Barabbas as "a notable prisoner" (Matt 27:16); Mark and Luke record the crimes he was guilty of – sedition and murder.

In recent times Israel has negotiated with nations opposed to them for the release of prisoners, but have always insisted that no one would be released by them "with blood on their hands". Yet this is exactly what they demanded at the trial of the Lord Jesus. Barabbas was a Jew and, most likely, would soon have faced the death penalty by crucifixion. This further attempt by Pilate to secure the release of the Lord Jesus also fails due to the chief priests and elders persuading the multitude to ask for the release of Barabbas (Matt 27: 20). Despite further remonstration with them the voice of the mob prevails, and Barabbas is set free. Luke lays the blame squarely where it belongs, "whom they had desired" (23.25). Matthew records the fateful words that have followed their history from then until now, "His blood be on us, and on our children" (Matt 27:25). Whilst we understand the blood-guiltiness on Israel's part, it is also true that, beyond these touching scenes, He was "delivered by the determinate counsel and foreknowledge of God" (Acts 2: 23). We are faced with the same choice in our lifetime – Christ or Barabbas. In Barabbas is pictured the wayward rebellious nature that refuses the claims of God upon us, the root cause being sin, while on the other hand there is the offer of a full and free pardon and cleansing through the precious blood of the Lord Jesus shed for us at Calvary. Have you made the right choice? "Choose you this day whom ye will serve" (Josh 24:15).

Day 7

"*This man hath done nothing amiss*"

Luke 23:39-43

Luke, the writer who takes careful note of humanity in the varied circumstances of life, is the only one to record the details of the conversion of the dying malefactor. We dwell a little on the events leading up to this. Despite having been so cruelly treated by His captors, and having endured the terrible scourging, the Lord turns to address the tearful women that followed Him; "weep not for me, but weep for yourselves, and for your children" (23:28).

There are two words, frequently used when we proclaim the message of salvation, that are only mentioned once each in our Bible; Luke has one of them – "Calvary" (v.33). The other word is "Eternity" (Isa 57:15). Our hope for eternity is based upon the mighty work done by the Lord Jesus at Calvary.

Long before the Lord Jesus came, Isaiah had prophesied He would be "numbered with the transgressors", would "bare the sin of many", and make "intercession for the transgressors" (Isa 53:12). Of the seven sayings of the Lord Jesus on the cross, Luke will record three in this chapter, (vv.34, 43, 46). The first cry, "Father, forgive them", could be identified with the intercession Isaiah spoke of. It is a precious thought that, though numbered with them, He makes intercession for them. Perhaps the malefactor who came in to blessing was first moved by hearing these words of the Lord Jesus, and began to think that there might be forgiveness for him. Matthew records that, initially, both malefactors joined with the mocking throng that stood around the cross, (Matt 27:44), but when his fellow criminal said "If thou be Christ, save thyself and us" (Luke 23:39) it drew a quick response from him. The basic truths of the gospel thus unfold: "dost thou not fear God" – a reverential fear of God; "we receive the due reward of our deeds" – a frank acknowledgement of guilt; "this man hath done nothing amiss" – a full acceptance of the sinlessness of the Saviour; "Lord, remember me" – a confession of Jesus as Lord.

The knowledge of this malefactor is surprising. How had he learned about a future kingdom and the possibility of him being a subject in it? His life is soon to end but, later, as the soldiers come to break his legs to hasten death, he has the absolute assurance that he will be immediately ushered into the presence of Christ in paradise. He had no opportunity to show in life the evidence of the change at the 'eleventh hour', but we gladly acquiesce with his majestic statement concerning our Lord Jesus – "this man hath done nothing amiss".

Robert Miller

Week 30

7 PORTRAITS OF CHRIST IN HEBREWS 13

Introduction

Hebrews chapter 13 is the crown gracing the brow of this inspired letter and glitters with the glory and pre-eminence of Christ. There is a seven-fold presentation of our lovely Lord in this chapter which we shall follow in our continued meditations on the 'sevens' of Scripture.

The whole epistle sustains one dominant theme from first to last – the supremacy of Christ! From chapter one where we see Him in the character of Son greater than the prophets of old, and in whom God has spoken His final word, through to chapter thirteen where the divine story comes to its thrilling climax, Christ is supreme. Apart from Christ God has nothing more to say. Having exhausted His vocabulary in Christ God has no further revelation for mankind. The whole message is Christ! Christ in His glorious person, Christ in His priestly ministry, and Christ in His perfected sacrifice. As to His person He is greater than the angels (chapter 1); as to His priestly ministry He is greater than Aaron (chapter 5); and as to His perfect and completed sacrifice we see Him as the enthroned Sin-purger (chapter 1) sat down on the right hand of the Majesty on high!

The reason for the Christ-exalting theme of the epistle is to establish the superiority of Christ's comprehensive ministry over that of Judaism founded upon the Mosaic code. It is again an encouragement for Paul's readers to go on to Christian maturity, and to realise the "better" things they now possess in Christ. Nine times over they are told of these "better" things. Christ is better than the angels (1:4); they have a better hope (7:19); a better covenant and promises (8:6); better sacrifices (9:23); a better substance (10:34); a better country (11:16); a better resurrection (11:35); and Christ's blood speaks better things than that of Abel (12:24). All these better things are because of their union with the true Messiah, Jesus Christ. Now the epistle ends with this 7-fold presentation of their majestic Messiah in chapter 13. He is seen to be:

1. The Omnipresent Christ – v.5
2. The Helping Christ – v.6
3. The Unchanging Christ – v.8
4. The Suffering Christ – v.12
5. The Rejected Christ – v.13
6. The Mediatorial Christ – v.15
7. The Shepherding Christ – v.20

Day 1

THE OMNIPRESENT CHRIST

Hebrews 13:5

Here in chapter thirteen is the practical application of the doctrinal 'meat' Paul has given in the early chapters of this great epistle. The complaint levelled against the Hebrew Christians had been, "For when … ye ought to be teachers, ye have need that one teach you again which be the first principles of the oracles of God; and are become such as have need of milk, and not of strong meat" (5:12). That "strong meat" has now been delivered in those doctrines enshrined in the Hebrew letter – the pre-eminence of Christ, His absolute deity, His Melchisedec priesthood and superior covenant. He has given them the doctrines of the believer's security, the place and privilege of their worship, the value of faith, and the place of divine discipline in their lives. Now he concludes in chapter thirteen with this practical application of the doctrines just expounded.

The person of Christ towers over this section in the seven verses mentioned above, the first of which speaks of His 'omnipresence', "He hath said, I will never leave thee, nor forsake thee". We are to understand this statement not only as a precious promise that we shall never be deserted by Him no matter what the place or circumstances may be, but also of His certain and abiding presence with us to intimately know what those circumstances are! Consequently we may apply this promise of His constant presence to the six directives for a God-pleasing life just given from verses 1 to 5.

The Lord's presence is with us: remembering this let us at all times maintain that love of the brethren which is the characteristic attitude of one believer to another (v.1). We are His, He shed His blood for us, so let us love each other as He does. Fraternal love is then exemplified in showing

hospitality to strangers for which there is a special blessing – in so doing both Abraham and Lot entertained angels unawares (v.2). The Lord is there: then let us have a compassionate concern for those beloved believers imprisoned and mistreated for His name's sake (v.3; cf. Matt 25:35-36). The Lord is nigh: He is watching, let us show respect for marriage and sexual responsibility, and not profane what God has rendered holy. Those who do so by either heterosexual or homosexual defilement will not escape God's judgment (v.4). The Lord who possessed neither property nor even a penny (Luke 20: 24) is with us: let love of money therefore not be a dominant influence in our lives. This call to contentment is based on the promise of the Lord's unfailing presence (v.5). Our omnipresent Lord is with us: there is no need therefore to put our trust in wealth when we can trust absolutely in the One who promises "I will never leave thee, nor forsake thee".

Day 2

THE HELPING CHRIST

Hebrews 13:6

The believers "help" is fundamentally spiritual and derives immediately and triumphantly from the exalted Lord. "So that we may boldly say, The Lord is my helper".

We must pick up here the thought of the previous verse (Let your life be free from love of money and be content with what you have) and the immediately following assurance that no matter what inadequacy the believer may feel, his lack is more than balanced by the assured presence, and therefore help, of His risen and all-sufficient Lord. He has Christ, and having Him is to be in touch with the infallible source of everything he could require in the particular situation of his need. All our help is therefore spiritual and will lead to a life unimpeded by the love of money and dependence upon it. To have funds is permissible for the believer to maintain a God-honouring life before the ungodly, "That ye may walk honestly toward them that are without, and that ye may have lack of nothing" (1 Thess 4:12), but not to make it the main prop of our lives. The world system around us makes money its focus and trust, and has therefore a purely materialistic outlook for security and wellbeing. The world has no real, loving God to look to and trust in – no supernatural and spiritual dimension in its reckoning, and so rests its hope upon gold and silver and gross material things. But that is not to be the case with the believer. He has a living Lord to trust who understands perfectly his frailty and shares his fears and who is a very present help in trouble. Which is why the constant exhortation of the word of God is to turn us to Him as our Helper. We see this beautifully illustrated in Paul's charge to Timothy, "Charge them that are rich in this world, that they be not highminded [always the danger when material wealth is in our possession], nor trust in uncertain riches, but in the living

God, who giveth us richly all things to enjoy" (1 Tim 6:17).

Who is it who is our "helper"? It is the One whose power and glories have been presented all through this wonderful epistle. The same Lord who made the worlds and upholds all things by the word of His power, the very One who went to the cross and purged our sins in that triumphant act of reconciling love and who now is seated on the right hand of the Majesty on high, is the wondrous Helper who undertakes my little need in my insignificant circumstances down here in this world! Yes, He cares for me, and is truly my Helper.

Day 3

THE UNCHANGING CHRIST

Hebrews 13:8

These Hebrew believers were challenged to "remember" or cherish in memory their past assembly elders, the God-appointed guides and leaders of their local churches (v.7), but only to highlight the comforting truth that while these human leaders have passed on, they still have the supreme Leader with them, "Jesus Christ the same yesterday, and today, and for ever" (v.8).

In three verses (7, 17, 24), Paul shows that the work of a true spiritual elder consists in teaching the word of God and providing an example of faith whereby they, like Stephen and James before them, had sealed their testimony with their death. They were to be remembered in their death (v.7), obeyed and submitted to in their lives (v.17), and always respected and honoured in the discharge of their local ministry (v.24). Now these faithful men had passed on and had left a fragrant memory and faithful testimony behind them, but there was still One who remained, the Apostle and High Priest of their profession – Jesus Christ the same yesterday, and today, and forever! What a comfort this would have been to those dear saints who felt, like the disciples in John 13:36-37, bereft and orphaned at the loss of their beloved spiritual guides. Jesus Christ, unchanged and unchanging was still there!

His was the only Name remaining for comfort and the continuation of their present testimony. The names of the departed leaders are not mentioned – they were known but had passed into memory. It was Jesus Christ who was now to occupy their thoughts and be the focus of their faith. He had comforted His disciples and assuaged their fears in the past when walking with them during His earthly ministry. As He had been in the past, so He was still in their needy present, unchanged and unchanging, like the mighty rocks of the ocean.

In His immutability, the unchanging One, He is marked out as essentially divine, equal with Jehovah who cried, "I am the LORD, I change not" (Mal 3:6). Yes, Jesus the Messiah is wholly and unreservedly God. He had a "yesterday" when He was in the form of God and considered it no robbery to the high dignity of the Father to be equal with God (Phil 2:6). In that eternal "yesterday" He obeyed the counsel of the Father and became incarnate as a

man in time so that he could sacrifice Himself as the sinner's Substitute, and endure the death of the Cross. In His "today" He is the resurrected Son of God, risen and crowned at God's right hand, the loving and sympathetic interceding High Priest of all His people, awaiting the day when He will return to take His Bride and rule the nations of earth in peace and equity. Then "forever" He will establish His everlasting kingdom and bring His chosen saints as co-heirs into that glorious endless reign. Hallelujah!

Day 4

THE SUFFERING CHRIST

Hebrews 13:12

"Wherefore Jesus also, that he might sanctify the people with his own blood, suffered without the gate". This verse is an application of the typical truth introduced with the phrase "we have an altar" in verse 10, alluding to the altar of Israel and the ritual of the offering of the bullock and goat of the sin-offering on the Day of Atonement (Lev 16). The blood of such offerings was brought into the holiest by the high priest and sprinkled on the mercy seat, and their bodies burned outside the camp, the priests being forbidden to eat the flesh of such sin offerings. This Old Testament ritual is then applied to the sacrifice and sufferings of our Lord Jesus Christ. This shows it was always intended to be a type of Christ's death for sinners when He suffered crucifixion outside the gate of Jerusalem to sanctify His repentant and believing people with His own blood. It is a mistake to identify the "altar" of verse 10 with either the person of Christ or His cross as many do.

It is this writer's view that when Paul says, "We have an altar", he is referring to "we Jews" and the Temple altar used in Jerusalem for the ritual of the Day of Atonement. It cannot be Christ for He is not a present altar but a past Victim-Sacrifice, and is never anywhere else alluded to as an "altar"! The immediate application to Christ as the anti-typical sin-offering in verse 12 is then fully applicable and has real force. He suffered without the gate that by His blood He might sanctify His believing people. The Old Testament type was the 'shadow'; Christ in the historical reality of His sacrifice at Calvary becomes the 'substance'.

As the ultimate sin-offering what depths of unparalleled sufferings He endured. "Is it nothing to you, all ye that pass by? behold, and see if there be any sorrow like unto my sorrow, which is done unto me, wherewith the Lord hath afflicted me in the day of his fierce anger" (Lam 1:12). It was the "fierce anger" of a holy, holy, holy God that "laid on him the iniquity of us all" when He made "his soul an offering for sin" (Isa 53:6, 10). How His sensitive holy soul was made to suffer when He, the One who knew no sin, was made "sin" for us!

With unshod feet, bowed knee, and trembling soul, we meditate today on what awesome depression of spirit could wring from His tortured lips the horrified cry, "I am afflicted and ready to die … while I suffer thy terrors I am distracted. Thy fierce wrath goeth over me; thy terrors have cut me off … Lover and friend hast thou put far from me, and mine acquaintance into darkness" (Ps 88:15-18).

Surely the response of our grateful hearts must be, "Thank you, Lord, for saving my soul"!

Day 5

THE REJECTED CHRIST

Hebrews 13:13

"Let us go forth therefore unto him without the camp, bearing his reproach". They took our glorious Lord, refused His Messianic claims and wilfully denied His miraculous signs. They mocked Him, scourged Him, spat on Him, smote Him, hurled the foulest abuse in His face – and in a final act of blasphemous reproach thrust Him outside the gates of the very city where He as God had long chosen to put His Name there! For He "loveth the gates of Zion more than all the dwellings of Jacob" (Ps 87:2). What must He have been thinking when they shut fast those city gates, cruelly telling Him by so doing that His presence there was a desecration, and He had no place within its sacred precincts! "We will not have this man to reign over us"! O Jerusalem, Jerusalem, what have you done to your suffering King? We weep a thousand tears as our spirits try to grasp the enormity of their sin and folly! In later years John explained this terrible phenomenon when he wrote, "He was in the world, and the world was made by him, and the world knew him not. He came unto his own (creation, things), and his own (people, nation) received him not" (John 1:10-11).

And so they put Him in the outside place, just as the sin-offering in Exodus and Leviticus was put in the outside place. The inescapable conclusion is then drawn in Hebrews 13:13. Since Jesus was given the outside place of rejection and reproach by the discredited leadership of an obsolete religious system, then that is the place His (Jewish) followers should occupy too. How can they remain any longer in a religious system that gave their Lord and Saviour the outside place? Surely that would be a betrayal of, and a disloyalty to, Him in His rejection! Therefore the irrefutable logic of the argument calls them to "go forth therefore unto him without the camp" bearing the same reproach that was heaped upon Him.

The application for us is similar: the "camp" today is the entire religious system that teaches salvation by works, ritual, and ordinances. It is the modern church system with its humanly ordained priesthood, its material aids to worship, and its ceremonial trappings. It is corrupt Christendom, a church without Christ. The Lord Jesus is outside it and we should go forth unto Him, bearing His reproach. If Paul summoned Christians of his day outside the "camp" of the only religious system that was ever established by God, then how much more should we today "go forth" from any and every humanly conceived and established religious system "unto Him", gathering according to His appointment upon the ground of the local church alone and around Himself as the magnetic gathering centre!

Day 6

THE MEDIATORIAL CHRIST

Hebrews 13:15

"By him therefore let us offer the sacrifice of praise to God continually …". These Jewish believers had up to this time approached God through the high priest and his mediatorial ministry at the altar of Israel in the temple at Jerusalem. But now a corrupt Judaism and blinded priesthood had rejected their Messiah, put Him outside their "camp" and barred Jerusalem's gates against Him. There is no other course now left for these Jewish believers than to "go forth therefore unto him" in His rejection and embrace Him as their new and exalted High-Priestly Mediator. What are Jerusalem, and the temple, and the unprofitable meats, and the rituals of Judaism now that the Messiah has been cast out of the city and rejected by its religious hierarchy? They have no continuing association any more with the earthly Jerusalem outside of which Christ was made to suffer (v.14). Jerusalem was dear to the hearts of those who worshipped at the temple. It was the very throb of every Jewish heart. It was the geographic centre of their "camp" – but the Jewish believers are outside all that now, citizens of another "country" (cf. 11:16). They have no continuing city on earth; their heart is set on the heavenly city, the new Jerusalem, where the Lamb is all the glory!

But importantly this exhortation is equally applicable to us also as we bring our sacrifices of praise still today to our God and Father through the mediatorial ministry of Jesus, the Son of God (see also Heb 4:14-16). This verse emphasises what is too often forgotten today, that the exalted Lord of the churches has a mediatorial ministry conferred upon Him. It is the high office and dignity of the Great High Priest of all His elect people (4:14). In this church age believers are viewed as a holy priesthood on earth whose place of worship is in the heavenly sanctuary, and whose Lord has ascended on high and holds both the offices of Mediator and Great High Priest. Worship therefore today is 'through' Him rather than 'to' Him, and to forget this vital truth is a denial and abandonment of His mediatorial office. "*Through him* therefore let us offer the sacrifice of praise to God continually" (RV).

Our verse today, as also the overwhelming testimony of Scripture, encourages us to see that God the Father seeks worshippers who will worship Him in spirit and in truth (John 4:23). God the Spirit prompts us to cry "Abba, Father" (Rom 8:15). And God the ever-blessed Son has been appointed the sole Mediator for access "into the holiest", through whom alone we are exhorted to offer our priestly and spiritual "sacrifices of praise to God continually, that is the fruit of our lips giving thanks to his name".

Day 7

THE SHEPHERDING CHRIST

Hebrews 13:20

The seventh title of our beloved Lord comes within the closing doxology – one of the most comprehensive doxologies of the New Testament – of this great epistle. "Now the God of peace, who brought [up] again from the dead our Lord Jesus, that great shepherd of the sheep, through the blood of the everlasting covenant …". God, here termed the "God of peace" (an exclusively Pauline phrase used only by him in the NT and a strong indication of Paul's authorship), has raised our Lord Jesus from the dead: in so doing He has brought in "peace" and become the Author and Giver of it for all who believe in His Son. Peace is the cessation of hostility, the laying down of rebel arms and agreement of reconciliation: it is the harmony which exists on the basis of an accord or covenant of peace. Such is the state now existing between a holy God and pardoned and reconciled sinners. The context of our verse shows it was the substitutionary death of Christ for His sheep as their Shepherd, and the shedding of His covenant-blood, that is the basis of this "peace"! It is an echo of Paul's phrase "And, having made peace through the blood of his cross" (Col 1:20). This is the only place in Hebrews where the resurrection of Christ is mentioned, and in His resurrection He is termed the "great" Shepherd of the sheep. It is in His risen life that He continues His shepherding ministry toward the sheep of His flock. Praise God, He is our great Shepherd even today.

The God of peace, we may say, *planned* peace on the basis, or within the sphere, of an agreement between divine persons called here an "everlasting covenant". That is, before the universe was born, while it still slept as a conception within the mind of God, within His own glorious Triunity He planned the sinner's salvation! The terms of this covenant were that He, the Father, would bring up from among the dead the Lord Jesus, if He on His part would *procure* peace by shedding His blood vicariously for sinners, taking a body prepared to do so (10:5-7) and making Himself lower than the angels (2:7). This is the "new covenant" mentioned in 9:15. The glorious and eternal peace that would result from this divine covenant would then become *perfected* or realised peace in the experience of all who believe. "Make you perfect" literally means "to equip you for service" (Wuest), showing the goal of God's covenant purpose is to have a holy people in this world, and throughout eternity, through whom He can work out His good pleasure, and who are eager to do His will through the enabling agency of Jesus Christ. To whom be eternal glory!

O Lord, make me such a vessel for Thy glory and service today. Amen.

MICHAEL BROWNE

Week 31

7 MENTIONS IN SCRIPTURE OF "THE GOD OF MY SALVATION"

Introduction

God has chosen to reveal Himself in a variety of ways. In the material world we see the fingerprints of His omnipotence right across the universe. In the world of grace the light of Calvary manifests a God who delights in mercy. In time and history we observe a God of providence who places His hand into the glove of human history and shapes our circumstances for the fulfilment of His purpose. In Scripture God had selected many names which display facets of His character and make Him known to His creatures. Some of these names, such as the great Jehovah titles, are uniquely His. In other cases he condescends to be identified with some of the great men of faith and allows Himself to be called, for example, the God of Abraham, the God of Elijah, the God of Daniel. At other times He associates Himself with places and is called, among others, the God of Bethel, the God of Jerusalem, the God of the whole earth.

In the following seven studies we will consider a very intimate, encouraging title of God which occurs seven times in the Old Testament, "the God of my salvation". It is exceedingly personal. How often we have rejoiced in the "salvation of our God", but how much greater it is to contemplate the "God of our salvation".

The salvation we have experienced is a deliverance which only God Himself, in all the vastness of His great being, could provide. The human dilemma was such that a wisdom less than God's could not have devised the plan, and love less than divine would not have been willing for the sacrifice involved.

Employing figurative language, the OT speaks of God as the "Rock of salvation" (Deut 32:15; 2 Sam 22:47); "horn of salvation" (2 Sam 22:3; Ps 18:2); "shield of salvation" (2 Sam 22:36; Ps 18:35). Every one of these blessings derives from the "God of our salvation".

In the following meditations we will examine these seven occurrences of the "God of my salvation", and observe how each reference is located in a different context. We will also see how each mention presents a God who saved us, saves us still, and who can meet and deliver us in all of life's circumstances.

Day 1

THE GUARDIAN OF MY PROTECTION

Psalm 18:25-50

This psalm is a poem of celebration. As the poet confesses, "great deliverance" has been granted (v.50). The dangers had been life-threatening but now, as he looks back, David is in no doubt who deserves the credit. He exclaims, "The LORD liveth; and blessed be my rock; and let the God of my salvation be exalted" (v.46).

In order to reinforce the point he multiplies metaphors that describe the saving power of the God who has rescued him. "The LORD is my rock, and my fortress, and my deliverer; my God, my strength, in whom I will trust; my buckler, and the horn of my salvation, and my high tower". The cumulative effect of this catalogue of colour is to magnify the grace and greatness of His God. No matter how menacing the dangers, or how many and mighty the enemies, there is a God who is all sufficient.

There is an earlier reference in the poem to "salvation", where David acknowledges "Thou hast also given me the shield of thy salvation: and thy right hand hath holden me up, and thy gentleness hath made me great" (v.35). He has been conscious of divine protection when dangers were assailing. He is also grateful for divine power when natural weakness would have allowed him to collapse. The upholding hand of the God of his salvation helped him to stand. In all of this the Lord had dealt with tenderness and gentleness. His present greatness is due to the gentleness of the God of his salvation.

While these deliverances have been indisputably divine, David has nonetheless felt his own responsibility. He sought to be "pure" (v.26) and "righteous" (v.20). He maintained "cleanness of hands" (vv.20, 24) together with humility of mind (v.27). Neither was he passive for, girded with divine strength, he ran through a troop (v.29), leapt over a wall (v.29), used his hands to fight (v.34), broke a bow of steel (v.34) and pursued his enemies until he overtook them (v.37). David was infused with special power, but this did not absolve him from giving of his best endeavours.

We may not have to fight literal battles this day. Nevertheless there will be challenges to face, deadlines to meet, choices to make. Let this be our watchword as we embark on this day: "The LORD liveth; and blessed be my rock; and let the God of my salvation be exalted" (v.46). In a world of death we triumph in the Lord of resurrection; He lives! In a world of change and decay we lean upon a God who is a "rock". In a world of danger we find security in the "God of my salvation".

Day 2

THE GUIDE OF MY PATH

Psalm 25:1-22

Surrounded by enemies, threatened by dangers, subdued by a sense of personal inadequacy, this poet cries with fervency, "Shew me thy ways, O LORD; teach me thy paths. Lead me in thy truth, and teach me: for thou art the God of my salvation" (vv.4-5). We all feel the need of this same control in our lives. The landscape of life is complex and difficult. It is very easy to make a mistake and take the wrong step. The poet is conscious that God does not reveal His path to all indiscriminately, and those whom "He will teach his way" (v.9) will be characterised by:

Prayer: This psalm is filled with petition. Here is a man on his knees and on his face before the Lord. Only those who feel their need and earnestly seek the mind of the Lord in prayer can discover the secret of His will.

Penitence: His prayers are accompanied by a liberal sprinkling of confession. There is no hiding or minimising his sin. He recognises the gravity of personal depravity – "it is great" (v.11). Pardon is enjoyed "according to thy mercy" (v.7) and "for thy name's sake" (v.11). This saint does not engage in a trifling rationalising of sin; neither does he immerse himself in self pity; he relies upon divine attributes of mercy and truth to meet his need. "If we confess our sins, he is faithful and just to forgive us our sins, and to cleanse us from all unrighteousness" (1 John 1:9).

Piety: All his requests are presented in the atmosphere of reverential fear. He assures us that "the secret of the Lord is with them that fear him" (v.14). Discerning the mind of the Lord is not a matter of merely human intelligence or cleverness. "What man is he that feareth the LORD? him shall he teach in the way that he shall choose" (v.12).

Pliability: The human will is also involved here, and there must be a ready submission to the Lord's leading. Often we resent the Lord's will, or assert our own, and only succeed in frustrating the blessing that we could enjoy. 'Meekness' is the beautiful Bible word for this submissiveness of spirit. "The meek will he guide in judgment: and the meek will he teach his way" (v.9).

Patience: Time will also be involved. In a world where we demand instant attention and answers, patience is a hard lesson to learn. This saint recognises the importance of waiting on the Lord. Twice he confesses this: "on thee do I wait" (v.5); "I wait on thee" (v.21).

Persistence: This dependent attitude is not something irregular and erratic. The psalmist looks to the Lord "all the day" (v.5) and every day.

Day 3

THE GOAL OF MY PURSUIT

Psalm 27:1-14

There is a clear division in this psalm when, in the first six and last two verses, the poet is speaking *about* the Lord, and in the intervening verses he is speaking *to* the Lord. The One whom he describes as the "God of my salvation" supplies his every need and is the panacea for every longing of his spirit.

This God of salvation is his **Glory**. Though surrounded by foes he will not be overwhelmed by inner fears. The Lord will be his light. In a world where we have so much man-made illumination it is difficult for us to imagine what a world of darkness is really like. When the ancients spoke of darkness and light they were employing figures of great reality. The Lord can shine with the brightness of His saving and strengthening presence into the most dark and dismal of life's experiences.

The same Lord is also his **Goal**. It is the noblest aspiration of his spirit to enjoy uninterrupted communion with God. When the psalmist expressed his desire to "dwell in the house of the LORD all the days of my life, to behold the beauty of the LORD, and to enquire in his temple" (v.4) he was not expecting to become a perpetual inhabitant of the ancient tabernacle. He cannot become a Levite or a priest. He rather longed for a life of perpetual communion with the Lord. The enjoyment of the presence of the God of salvation was where true security was to be found.

This God was likewise his **Guard**. A consciousness of God's ability to protect encouraged this believer to aver "in the time of trouble he shall hide me in his pavilion: in the secret of his tabernacle shall he hide me; he shall set me up upon a rock" (v.5). Should the situation arise where he would not only be surrounded by foes, but also abandoned by friends, even then "when my father and my mother forsake me, then the LORD will take me up" (v.10).

In addition the God of salvation will be his **Guide**. He will walk a "plain path" (v.11). His communion with God will have practical implications. The term 'enemies' in v.11 is literally 'observers'. He is under surveillance by those who would plot his downfall. In such temptation he is dependent on the Lord to guide his footsteps and he prays "Teach me thy way, O LORD, and lead me in a plain path, because of my enemies" (v.11). This is a path where patience will be learnt, for God's timetable and ours do not always coincide. "Wait on the LORD: be of good courage, and he shall strengthen thine heart: wait, I say, on the LORD" (v.14).

Day 4

THE GIVER OF MY PARDON

Psalm 51:1-19

There is no hiding for David now. Convicted by Nathan's words and gripped by a sense of guilt he turns to the only source of help – "the God of my salvation" (v.14). A dark and complicated web of deceit, intrigue, murder and immorality had been woven by David. Now he takes this garment of guilt apart and thoroughly examines it, thread by thread, in the presence of God. The problem is so encompassing that he begs deliverance from every aspect of its damage.

First, he mentions the **debt** of sin. There is a record which he longs should be blotted out. He had stolen another man's wife and had also robbed a man of his life. Ultimately, all sin is a debt against the Almighty and only according to the multitude of God's tender mercies can the ledger of iniquity be cleared.

Then he laments the **defilement** of sin. Sin had also left a mark. Its stain was upon David's memory and conscience. His character and administration were sadly tarnished by what had happened. In our anaemic society the foulest of deeds are white washed by our permissiveness. David prays to be "washed throughly" and "purged with hyssop". He is leprous, and only by the sprinkling of blood can restoration to a state of holiness be achieved. The problem is deep seated and David confronts the **depravity** of his sin. Genes and environment may each have played some part in what happened, but David sees the problem as stemming from his depraved nature. He acknowledges "Behold, I was shapen in iniquity; and in sin did my mother conceive me" (v.5).

The true penitent plays no blame game. David accepts full responsibility and confesses the **defiance** of his sin. No mention of any lack of caution on Bathsheba's part. The "sin", "iniquities", "transgressions" and "bloodguiltiness" were all his. David did not sin because of ignorance; it was wilfulness. He craves full deliverance from the **dominion** of sin. The slave longs to be free but is conscious of weakness and needs divine help. "Create in me a clean heart, O God; and renew a right spirit within me", he cries (v.10). He fears a repeat of any similar evil so, as he anticipates the future, he asks "Restore unto me the joy of thy salvation; and uphold me with thy free spirit" (v.12).

Restoration is possible for him and us. We have a clearer light than was available to him. The God of his salvation is our God and "if we confess our sins, he is faithful and just to forgive us our sins, and to cleanse us from all unrighteousness" (1 John 1:9). A forgiven man will be a free man. Holiness and true happiness will go together.

Day 5

THE GROUND OF MY PRAYER

Psalm 88:1-18

"Darkness" is the last word of this psalm and it is also its pervading theme. In verse 6 the poet speaks about the darkness of the lowest pit and of the ocean depths. In v.11 he refers to the darkness of death and the grave. A nether gloom hangs over this composition like a heavy cloud of despair. Emotions of "distraction" (v.15) and despair fill the soul of the author. The encompassing troubles of his life have put him in lonely isolation. He is severed from his erstwhile friends and previous contacts (v.18).

His trouble is incessant, but so is his prayer. This sufferer is persistent in his cry to the God of his salvation. He emphasises this fact three times over. "I have cried day and night before thee" (v.1); " I have called daily upon thee, I have stretched out my hands unto thee" (v.9); "in the morning shall my prayer prevent thee" (v.13). This is his only solace as he suffers intolerably, endures loneliness and nears death. He cries to, and clings to, God.

Is there any hope? Will any shaft of light appear to relieve the depressing darkness which envelopes him? There is one and only one. As he opens his lament he acknowledges the Lord as the "God of my salvation". If deliverance will ever come this must be its source. Like Jonah in the darkness of the fish's belly, this saint acknowledges that "salvation is of the Lord".

How often the Lord allows His people to come to this position. Like those sailors in Acts 27:20, we arrive in a place where neither sun nor stars appear in many days. Not only does light disappear but hope also fades. Faith then must rise above the dark clouds of the shadowy day to recognise that, above it all, sits the "God of salvation".

A sombre feature which adds to the gloom of the entire psalm is the sufferer's feeling that he is enduring the displeasure of God. This is the most serious aggravation of his whole situation. He speaks of "Thy wrath lieth hard upon me, and thou hast afflicted me with all thy waves." (v.7); "while I suffer thy terrors I am distracted" (v.15). This has given the psalm a Messianic reference, and we see here the inner agony of the supreme sufferer of Golgotha. Is there also a hint of resurrection in the poem? Surely the six questions of verses 10-12 can only find their fullest answer in the clear resurrection light of 1 Corinthians 15.

Whatever the darkness and distresses of this day may be, let us, like this man, find our refuge in the "God of my salvation" (v.1).

Day 6

THE GUARANTOR OF MY PROSPECT

Micah 7:1-20

Micah lived through the toughest of times. In the land there was poverty; in the street, violence was rampant; in high places, corruption flourished; in society, anarchy reigned; in the family, treachery abounded. It was risky to trust your closest friend, even the wife of your bosom. Confidences were often betrayed; relationships were violated; family loyalties were wilfully overlooked. Indeed, a righteous and good man was as scarce as a cluster of first-ripe grapes would be in a vineyard after the vintage had taken place (vv.1-2). The best of those who remained were no better than a wild brier or a thorn hedge. They would only pierce, tear and injure (v.4). What could one do and where could one look in such times?

Micah has the answer. He must turn to the Lord and trust in Him. The vocabulary of v.7 is instructive, especially the verbs. He will "look" to the Lord. This is a term of expectancy. It is often translated "watchman" and has that meaning in v.4 of this very chapter. Micah will be a spiritual "watchman". When looking *around* yields nothing but disappointment, the only option is to change direction and look *up* to the Lord. Secondly, he will "wait for" the God of his salvation. This verb is most often translated as "hope". When everything seems to be humanly hopeless, Micah will hope in God. It may be some time before a change comes, but Micah is sure that, in His own time, the Lord will act. He will also pray, "My God will hear me" (v.7). Micah has just told us that the days were so treacherous, a man had to "keep the doors of his mouth even from the wife of his bosom" (v.5). There was, however, an ear into which the closest confidences and concerns could be breathed, and this lonely sufferer would employ the avenue of prayer to the relief of his soul.

In these verses, though Micah speaks in the first person, he has others in mind. He represents those who suffer for righteousness' sake in many generations, and especially a remnant of his own people who will suffer acutely during the days of tribulation. They will be days of treachery, apostasy, suspicion, cruelty, but even then the godly will 'look' and 'wait' and 'pray'.

Whatever the difficulties of this day, may we be encouraged to follow the example of the godly prophet Micah and anticipate the attitude of a believing remnant yet to be born. The God of our salvation is the same in every generation and, true to the meaning of Micah's name, we can exclaim, "Who is a God like unto thee?" (Mic 7:18).

Day 7

THE GLADNESS OF MY PRAISE

Habakkuk 3:1-19

A dialogue from agony to ecstasy describes the spiritual pilgrimage of Habakkuk. He begins by wrestling with great questions of righteousness and fairness (ch.1). The awareness of the coming Chaldean invasion has made him writhe in mental pain. To be sure, there was great wickedness in Judah, but how could God use an even more wicked and pagan nation for the discipline of the people of Judah and still be consistent? After standing in his spiritual watch tower (ch.2), Habakkuk now becomes the worshipping man of chapter 3. Chapter 2 concluded with a silence before the majestic presence of the Lord. After a pause, the silence is replaced by a poem of praise recorded in chapter 3. It is essentially a song of salvation. In the earlier parts of the song Habakkuk celebrates the salvation of God. Now, at the end, he rejoices in the God of his salvation.

This is a man buoyant above the circumstances around him. His vision has been so filled with the greatness of God's power and purpose that he no longer depends for his joy upon his surroundings. The fields may be barren, the trees may be bare, the stalls may be empty; nevertheless Habakkuk will rejoice. The source of his joy will be "the Lord" and the "God of his salvation". It is not that the Chaldean invasion has been cancelled. It will happen. Habakkuk trembles and quivers at the very thought (3:16). The invading armies will strip the land of its beauty and fertility. However, it cannot rob Habakkuk of his relationship of joy in the Lord. He will joy in the God of his salvation.

As Habakkuk acknowledges, this is high ground. This is where the hinds can stand far above the valleys and breathe the clear mountain air (v.19). Here he stands upon the mountain peak of spiritual experience and triumphant trust. The valley and vexation of chapter 1 have been exchanged for the victory of chapter 3. The same atmosphere pervades the letter to the Philippians. There the apostle Paul, despite his years in Roman custody, rejoices in the Lord himself and encourages his readers, "Rejoice in the Lord alway: and again I say, Rejoice" (Phil 4:4). Rejoicing in the Lord, like Habakkuk and Paul, is more than emotion. It is a choice. It does not, like happiness, depend upon happenings. It does not come easily or naturally. If circumstances dominate one's thinking we can easily exhaust our mental and spiritual energies on wishing that circumstances would change; such wishful thinking leads to joyless despair. If, however, we perceive God as transcending circumstances, our trust will be in Him and this will give birth to renewed joy.

David Gilliland

Week 32

7 KINGDOM PARABLES IN MATTHEW 13

Matthew 12:22-37, 46-50; 13:10-17, 34-35, 51-52

Introduction

The OT reveals the essential features of the millennial kingdom of our Lord Jesus Christ, so that is a subject which clearly has not "been kept secret" (v.35). What the OT does not reveal is that an entire age would intervene between Israel's rejection and its future reception of the Messiah. This 'secret' period between the two advents of the Lord Jesus is the subject of the parables of Matthew 13. Thus it began while Christ was still on earth, and it extends until His return to the earth in power and great glory. This Kingdom period includes within it 'the Church Age' from Pentecost to the Rapture.

Jesus said, "If I cast out devils by the Spirit of God, then the kingdom of God is come unto you" (12:28). The Pharisees committed blasphemy against the Holy Spirit by attributing His power to Beelzebub (the dung god – Satan) and rejected the kingdom on behalf of the nation. Now relationships change. Natural, physical relationships are replaced by spiritual relationships, and the Lord moves out of the house to sit by the seaside (13:1). Hebrews 8:8 speaks of the "house of Israel", and Isaiah speaks of "the way (vicinity) of the sea … Galilee of the nations" (Isa 9:1). Thus the Lord moves away from His exclusive relationship with Israel and the introduction of a physical kingdom upon earth, to offer a spiritual kingdom to the "whosoever" of every nationality.

Parables are a savour of life to some and death to others, just as the pillar of cloud and fire was darkness to Egyptians but light to Israel. Israel, however, by rejecting the truth, was now to be on the dark side.

Jesus was confronted by a mixed multitude comprising those who had received Him and those that had rejected Him. He did not separate them and then only instruct the believers. He so constructed his teaching that those who had believed would understand, and those who had rejected, even though they heard, would not understand. Believers have the key to knowledge and can interpret His teaching. Unbelievers do not and cannot understand His word. The one who has the key will gain more knowledge, but the one with no key will lose any knowledge he once possessed (13:12). Interpretation must be consistent, using Scripture in its context (2 Pet 1:20). Those who are "instructed unto the kingdom of heaven" (v.52) have a responsibility to properly combine OT scriptural truths with NT doctrine, for use at the appropriate time to accurately preach the Gospel and to teach others.

Day 1

THE PARABLE OF THE SOILS

Matthew 13:3-9, 18-23

This parable appears in three gospels. In Mark, Jesus asks "Know ye not this parable? and how then will ye know all parables?" (Mark 4:13). It seems that the Saviour regarded this parable as the simplest and plainest of parables, and gave an explanation of it that they might understand the general principles of interpreting others.

The seed represents the word of God communicated to the minds of people by the Scriptures, by preaching, or by the direct influence of the Holy Spirit. In natural sowing, the largest proportion of seed will fall into good soil. Sadly, this proportion is not replicated among those who hear the gospel. What determined the outcome of the sowing was the preparation of the soil, because the seed, the sower and the place were all otherwise the same.

The purpose of the seed is that "they should believe and be saved" (Luke 8:12). "With the heart man believeth" (Rom 10:10). The seed must be intellectually received before it will go into the heart, "then opened he their understanding" (Luke 24:45). "He that heareth my word, and believeth on him that sent me, hath everlasting life" (John 5:24). Therefore Satan and his emissaries (the birds) snatch the seed from those with no mental comprehension by the wayside. Consider the importance of simple and clear gospel messages to unprepared hearts!

Shallow professions only last during good times and prove to be rootless when tested. Emphasis on the need for true "repentance toward God" is required (Acts 20:21). "I know whom I have believed" (2 Tim 1:12). Individual conviction "of those things which are most surely believed among us" will ensure that we are "strengthened … in the inner man", "rooted and grounded". Seed among the thorns, already there, necessitates tender gardening by pastors, and a change of desires in a new believer to stop the choking of the word.

If fruit is to be seen, the seed needs to go *on* (heareth), *in* (understandeth), *down* (beareth fruit) and *up* (bringeth forth). There are different levels of fruitfulness from the same seed, with a reverse order in Mark. Peter, narrating the gospel, may humbly feel his return as but thirty-fold. Matthew, the taxman, identifies diminishing returns over time, whereas Luke writes about the perfect man, singularly 100%.

Although related to receiving the gospel, this parable is true of the believer's on-going reception of the word. If the heart is hardened, shallow or crowded, the fruit of the Spirit will not be evidenced, and there will be no return for God's glory. The devil cannot snatch our salvation as a bird, but he can shake our faith "as a roaring lion, walketh about, seeking whom he may devour: whom resist stedfast in the faith" (1 Pet 5:8).

Day 2

THE PARABLE OF THE WHEAT AND THE TARES

Matthew 13:24-30, 36-43

The Lord plants men in good ground where He wants them. The devil immediately sets up men in opposition to thwart, hinder and damage the effectiveness of God's men. It is not obvious who they are. The serpent has never changed his subtlety that led Eve into doubt due to her vagueness about God's word. Ever since Cain slew Abel, Satan has caused brethren, both natural and spiritual, to counter each other to the point of exhausted ineffectiveness for God. Consider Ishmael and Isaac, Jacob and Esau, Joseph and his brethren. Some opposition is blatant; Jannes and Jambres, Elymas the sorcerer and Alexander the coppersmith all 'withstood' God's men: but most opposition is not even recognised.

Tares, or darnel, bears the closest resemblance to wheat till the ear appears, and only then the difference is discovered. "Beware of false prophets, which come to you in sheep's clothing, but inwardly they are ravening wolves. Ye shall know them by their fruits" (Matt 7:15-16). "For such are false apostles, deceitful workers, transforming themselves into the apostles of Christ. And no marvel; for Satan himself is transformed into an angel of light. Therefore it is no great thing if his ministers also be transformed as the ministers of righteousness; whose end shall be according to their works" (2 Cor 11:13-15).

Paul warned the Ephesian elders "after my departing shall grievous wolves enter in among you, not sparing the flock. Also of your own selves shall men arise, speaking perverse things, to draw away disciples after them" (Acts 20:29-30). This planting of wicked men is done "while men slept", so Paul exhorts the Ephesian brethren to watch. The appeal to the Corinthian believers is "Watch ye, stand fast in the faith, quit you like men, be strong" (1 Cor 16: 13). How did Diotrephes gain his position?

Paul left the church the "whole counsel of God". It needs to bear fruit, not just in elders, but in us all so that the unbeliever might be clearly identified. "If any man love not the Lord Jesus Christ, let him be Anathema Maranatha" that is, cursed to the Day of Judgement (1 Cor 16:22).

That old serpent will continue to oppose God right to the end of the Tribulation when an angel will bind him and "cast him into the bottomless pit, and shut him up, and set a seal upon him, that he should deceive the nations no more" (Rev 20:3). Other angels will bind up the living wicked ones who will join all wicked men in Hades awaiting the great white throne judgement. The devil and his agents "transform" (disguise). Our Lord was "transfigured" (changed) and "did shine as the sun". With evil opposition removed "the righteous shine forth" in the reflected glory of their conquering Saviour.

Day 3

THE PARABLE OF THE MUSTARD SEED

Matthew 13:31-32

The grain of mustard seed was deliberately and carefully taken to the place of sowing so that its geographical starting point was determined by the sower. All previous kingdoms had been established by military might. One empire succeeded another by displaying greater might or power. This would not be true of the kingdom in this present age. Obedient to His command "that they should not depart from Jerusalem", the apostles "were all with one accord in one place" when the church came into being in Acts 2. Very soon, the acknowledgement was that they had "turned the world upside down" (Acts 17:6).

Three groups became identifiable; Jews, Gentiles and the church of God. Then great persecution came upon the church, scattering the saints abroad, but still it flourished until the distribution of the seed reached "unto the uttermost part of the earth" (Acts 1:8). This growth was supernatural but not aberrant. Research suggests that the extraordinary growth of the mustard plant came through cultivation, whereas the self-serving interests of men tampering with genetics today creates abnormalities. When Emperor Theodosius, in the 4th century, made Christianity the imperial religion of Rome, with compulsory church membership, a plethora of pagan practices and corrupt individuals were absorbed into what has since been known as 'Christendom'. The prevalence and publicity of evil contrasts with the obscurity of that which is precious and of God.

The empire of Babylon, like Assyria, was described as a tree in which birds lived. All flesh was fed of it, the young were born in its sphere of influence "and under his shadow dwelt all great nations" (Dan 4; Ezek 31). The desire of Christendom is like that of the king of Sodom, "Give me the persons ('souls')" (Gen 14:21). The birds have been identified as the devil's agents, and subtle corruption is best started early. The insistence of religious rites, such as infant baptism, tie biblically ignorant individuals to a lifelong "form of godliness". Religious size and dominance, managed on commercial lines,

gives influence over politics, education and society. Disagreement leads to punishment, torture and death. What a massive distortion from the days of "gladness and singleness of heart, praising God, and having favour with all the people" (Acts 2:46-47).

The psalmist says, "I have seen the wicked in great power, and spreading himself like a green bay tree" (Ps 37:35). Mystery, Babylon the Great, shows the perverted depths to which man's religion sinks whilst constantly professing to represent Christ's interests upon the earth (Rev 17).

May it be said of our local testimony "thou hast a little strength, and hast kept my word, and hast not denied my name" (Rev 3:8).

Day 4

THE PARABLE OF THE LEAVEN

Matthew 13:33; 1 Corinthians 5:6-8

"Leaven" is the first of four important components in Matthew 13:33. The first mention of leaven is linked with the separation of God's people from the world through sacrifice at Passover. "Even the first day ye shall put away leaven out of your houses" (Exod 12:15). The kingdom knew doctrinal wickedness in practice from the first day; "Then Jesus said unto them, Take heed and beware of the leaven of the Pharisees and of the Sadducees" (Matt 16:6). "He bade them not beware of the leaven of bread, but of the doctrine of the Pharisees and of the Sadducees" (16:12). Again, "Beware ye of the leaven of the Pharisees, which is hypocrisy" (Luke 12:1). Leaven is universally used in Scripture as a type of sin spreading its influence, a secret working of evil which may not be outwardly manifest, but which arises from the corruption within. All types of our blessed Lord which refer to Him as the bread of heaven, are without leaven.

"A woman", the first mention of which concerns Eve. She did not acknowledge her husband's headship, mishandled the word of God and actively brought sin into the world because it appealed sensually. Citing this, Paul states "But I suffer not a woman to teach, nor to usurp authority over the man, but to be in silence" (1 Tim 2:12). The woman seen in Revelation 17, Babylon, is the fountainhead of all false religion in the world. That character, which was seen in Jezebel who slaughtered the prophets, was witnessed again in the church at Thyatira which allowed "that woman Jezebel, which calleth herself a prophetess, to teach and to seduce my servants to commit fornication, and to eat things sacrificed unto idols" (Rev 2:20).

"Hid" has its first mention as Adam and Eve, in the garden, broke fellowship with God because of sin. The NT Greek word translated "hid" means 'encrypt.' The parables are encrypted by God then decoded for us. Leaven is Satan's counterfeit exposed by the plumb-line of Scripture.

"Three measures of ... meal" are associated with Abraham's fellowship with God (Gen 18:6). Later, "the LORD said, Shall I hide from Abraham that thing which I do?" (18:17). In view of the blessing to others through him, his own relationship with God in the world, guidance for the upbringing of future generations, and the appreciation of future blessings that God guarantees, the LORD communed with Abraham. Every believer needs this unadulterated fellowship with God, confident that the "Father giveth you the true bread from heaven" (John 6:32). Fed with food convenient, none should ever utter "our soul loatheth this light bread" (Num 21:5).

Sincerity and truth mark out those who appreciate the person and work of "Christ our Passover". Malice and wickedness abound in the kingdom as "the mystery of iniquity doth already work" (2 Thess 2:7).

Day 5

THE PARABLE OF THE HIDDEN TREASURE

Matthew 13:44; Romans 11:7-12, 25-33

There are two dissimilar but inter-linking interpretations of this parable. The first is based on the fact that God twice calls Israel "a peculiar treasure" (Exod 19:5; Ps 135:4). Satan is the owner of the field, Adam having handed over dominion to him. Counting the casting away of Israel a victory, Satan didn't know that God would bury the treasure and then buy the whole field. The council of the Godhead planned Calvary not just for the church but for the whole world (1 John 2:2). The Saviour must become poor to purchase the field yet, "for the joy that was set before him endured the cross" (Heb 12: 2). The treasure is not so much a pot of gold, as more like a richly-seamed mine. God has invested heavily in Israel in the past, and His covenants still stand. However, the field will have to be transformed in order to evidence the wonder of this treasure in the purpose of God. In the physical millennial kingdom, when the King of kings and Lord of lords has total dominion, Satan being bound in the bottomless pit, Israel will be the glorious Nation, the revealed peculiar treasure on universal display. The price to be paid for a field that is to be sanctified to the Lord is according to the projected harvest (Lev 27:16). The participants in the first resurrection (Rev 20:6) will yet worship Him for selling all that He had to buy the field.

The second view is that the treasure in 13:52 is the whole word of God. In this first private parable, the pure deposit of the word of God counters adversarial men, a polluted religious system and corrupt doctrine. "It is hid from the eyes of all living, and kept close from the fowls of the air" (Job 28:21). Satan cannot corrupt this repository of wisdom. The kingdom has within it a wealthy resource of which so many are ignorant. Those who study the Bible are humbled that God should reveal such deep things by the Holy Spirit. This illumination gives such joy that the student is willing to make any sacrifice to claim the full "knowledge of the truth". All the righteousness and truth of God is "more to be desired … than gold, yea, than much fine gold"

(Ps 19:10). Gold is of principal value among men; yet to a believer's mind the revealed truth of God should be esteemed the most valuable of all things.

The riches of the world and of the Gentiles are inextricably linked to Israel (Rom 11), and God's dealings with both Israel and the church demonstrate the depth of His riches of wisdom and knowledge. If Israel's temporary rejection and casting off for a time has already accomplished so much, what will the ultimate blessings be?

Day 6

THE PARABLE OF THE PEARL

Matthew 13:45-46

There is no mention of pearl in the OT (in Job it is 'crystal'). It was not precious to the Hebrews and had no place among the twelve precious stones on the breastplate of the high priest. It was a thing of beauty associated with the Gentiles. Archaeology shows it was used in Egypt and Nineveh for outward display, to show its beauties. A pearl of great price would be acknowledged by all, bringing honour and glory to the one whose wisdom, knowledge, and personal sacrifice had obtained it.

The pearl is the only precious stone to be the direct product of a living organism. It is recovered from the ocean of the world and can only become the displayed adornment by being lifted out of the place in which it was formed. Created through injury to the life that produces it, the pearl is not the hurtful grain of sand but it is the outworking of the injured upon the injury done. The injurious thing is converted into a precious jewel, being beautified by each gradual layer upon it. That which was impure and harmful has been so dealt with by the very life it has injured, that it is transformed into a thing of glorious beauty and stands forever in essential purity.

How readily this beautiful description matches the church. The perspective is from heaven looking upon the scene of time. Christ has seen the church from eternity and, having found the pearl, He departed from heaven and sold all that He had, and bought it. "For ye know the grace of our Lord Jesus Christ, that, though he was rich, yet for your sakes he became poor, that ye through his poverty might be rich" (2 Cor 8:9).

The church is His personal possession by purchase, for "Christ also loved the church, and gave himself for it; that he might sanctify and cleanse it with the washing of water by the word, that he might present it to himself a glorious church, not having spot, or wrinkle, or any such thing; but that it should be holy and without blemish" (Eph 5:25-27). In holiness and purity, a trophy of grace over sin, the church shall yet "shew forth the praises of him who hath called you out of darkness into his marvellous light: which in time past were not a people, but are now the people of God: which had not obtained mercy, but now have obtained mercy" (1 Pet 2:9-10).

Day 7

THE PARABLE OF THE NET

Matthew 13:47-50; 2 Thessalonians 1:3-12

The One who knows the end from the beginning utters the awful explanation of this final parable. He is "not willing that any should perish", but these are actively wicked ones, in effect and influence, who have seriously opposed the development of the kingdom to the day the net is cast. Angelic ministry, witnessed in Scripture when dealing with earthly conditions, is the agency used by God to violently sever the wicked out from the middle of the righteous. The force of casting the net is the same used to cast them into the furnace of fire. Living men will be gathered up as in a seine net, a fishing net which hangs vertically in the water with floats at the top and weights at the bottom, the ends being drawn together to encircle the fish. Not one, high or low, will escape as they are drawn helplessly to individual judgement. When the net was 'crammed full', the same word as used for fulfilment of Scripture, nothing missing or allowed to slip the net, they "drew" it, a unique word meaning 'hauled up'. Men operated as the dark denizens of evil, but God has them hauled up to an equal level, where sea and land meet, so that the selection standard will be just.

These men are principally of the gentile nations since the net is cast into the sea. Those of Israel, "the children of the kingdom", would be seen in the tares. The same word "gathered" (13:40) is employed to demonstrate the grouping together of kinds, essentially good and evil. Even the most practised fisherman cannot judge of his haul till the net is emptied; then the sorting process begins. "Good" contrasts with the corrupt and rotten, as "good seed" differed from "tares". Both confirm the preservation of the "good" for the future, whilst the bad are cast into fire which Mark states three times is "where their worm dieth not, and the fire is not quenched" (Mark 9:44, 46, 48). It is "everlasting fire, prepared for the devil and his angels" (Matt 25:41).

The disciples asked, "When shall these things be?" (Matt 24:3). The Lord said, "When the Son of man shall come in his glory, and all the holy angels with him" (Matt 25:31). This is "when he shall come to be glorified in his saints" (2 Thess 1:10); not to the air *for* His saints, but to the earth *with* His saints.

This spiritual kingdom will conclude with "weeping and gnashing of teeth, when ye shall see Abraham, and Isaac, and Jacob, and all the prophets, in the kingdom of God, and you yourselves thrust out" (Luke 13:28). "And there was given him dominion, and glory, and a kingdom, that all people, nations, and languages, should serve him" (Dan 7:14).

DAN COULSON

Week 33

7 FEATURES OF MESSIAH'S MINISTRY IN ISAIAH 61:1-2

Introduction

Our Lord Jesus has endeared these verses to the hearts of His people by reading them in public in the Nazareth synagogue (Luke 4:16-21). Those were the early days of His ministry, and His introduction as Messiah to His own townsfolk in Nazareth. They must have known Him well in the Nazareth synagogue. He had lived in Nazareth for thirty years and it had been His custom to attend the services regularly. But on this occasion it was to be different. He had been to Judea, and had been baptised by John in the Jordan. He had been identified and approved by the Father from the opened heaven as His beloved Son, and the Spirit of God had descended upon Him in bodily form, like a dove. In the power of that Spirit He had returned to Galilee, teaching in the Galilean synagogues until His fame spread throughout the whole surrounding region.

Now He was in His home town, Nazareth. With what feelings He must have entered the synagogue of His boyhood and youth. When opportunity came He stood up, indicating His desire to read the Scripture portion. Every Jewish adult male had a right to do so. There was handed to Him the scroll of the prophet Isaiah and, without the luxury of chapter and verse numbers in this scroll which would have been rolled on two wooden cylinders or spools, He calmly found the place.

Having read the portion which dealt with the ministry of the Messiah in the acceptable year of the Lord, He abruptly ceased His reading in the middle of a sentence, handed the scroll back to the attendant and sat down to speak to them. It was all now being fulfilled in their ears He told them and, as we shall see in subsequent meditations, He presented Himself to them as the anointed Prophet, Priest, and King for whom they were waiting.

Initially they marvelled at His gracious words, but soon revolted against the application of it to them and thrust Him out. They would have cast Him over the brow of the hill on which Nazareth was built, but He calmly passed through the midst of them and went His way. Was He ever back in Nazareth again?

Day 1

A SPIRIT-FILLED MINISTRY

Isaiah 61:1

"The Spirit of the Lord God is upon me". Prior to the commencement of His Messianic ministry Jesus had been baptised by John Baptist in the Jordan. It was a baptism unto repentance which, emphatically, He did not need. But in grace He identified Himself with those who were obedient to the word preached by John and, as another has said, "He saw His sheep struggling in the dark waters of death and He fain would be with them". It was at that time that the heavens opened and, as the Father spoke His approval and delight in the Son, the Spirit descended and abode upon Him. John had pointed Him out as the Lamb, meek and lowly on His way to sacrifice, and the Spirit came in the form of a gentle dove to rest upon the Lamb.

Soon, that same Spirit drove Him into the wilderness to the confrontation with Satan. After the Dove, the devil! He repelled every proposition of Satan with quotations from the Book of Deuteronomy and, after forty days, He returned "in the power of the Spirit" into Galilee (Luke 4:14). How accurately was the ancient typical teaching of the Levitical offerings being fulfilled in the Saviour's life and ministry. Sometimes the flour of the meal offering was mingled with oil. Sometimes the offering was anointed with the oil. At other times the oil was poured and the offering was saturated (Lev 2). It was by the power of the Spirit that the Lord Jesus was miraculously conceived in the womb of the virgin; the flour mingled with the oil, as it were. At His baptism came the anointing. Now, during the years of His service, His would be a ministry endowed with the Spirit.

When, in the course of that ministry, He cast out demons, the Pharisees charged Him with being in collusion with Beelzebub the prince of the demons. He showed them the fallacy of Satan casting out Satan, and the folly of a divided kingdom or a divided house, and said to them, "But if I cast out devils by the Spirit of God, then the kingdom of God is come unto you" (Matt 12:24-28). By the presence of the King in the power of the Spirit, the kingdom was in their midst.

The charge which they were making was blasphemy against the Spirit of God. It was the unpardonable sin. All other sin and blasphemy could be forgiven, but blasphemy against the Holy Spirit was a rejection of the only means of repentance, and without this there was no salvation.

So it was then, throughout His three busy years of public ministry, an unbroken communion with the Spirit of God.

AN ANOINTED MINISTRY

Isaiah 61:1

"The Lord hath anointed Me". Every Jew knew the meaning and significance of anointing for it was a custom in general use among the Hebrews and other oriental nations. They anointed the hair, head, and beard (Pss 104:15; 133:2). At their feasts and at times of rejoicing they anointed the whole body; but sometimes only the head or feet (Ps 23:5; Matt 6:17; John 12:3). It was also used in hospitality and welcome, as a customary mark of respect to guests (Luke 7:38, 46). The act of anointing was often significant of consecration to a holy or sacred use; hence the anointing of the high priest (Exod 29:29), and of the sacred vessels (Exod 30:26). The high priest and the king are thus called the "anointed" (Lev 4:3; Ps 132:10). Prophets were also anointed (1 Kings 19:16; Ps 105:15), and "Anointed" is an actual title of Messiah (Ps 2:2).

In Acts 4:27 the apostles, addressing God, speak of "Thy holy Servant Jesus, whom thou hast anointed" (JND; ASV) and Peter, speaking to the house of Cornelius, rehearsed how "God anointed Jesus of Nazareth with the Holy Spirit and with power: who went about doing good, and healing all that were oppressed with the devil" (Acts 10:38).

It was in the enjoyment of this anointing that Jesus came to the synagogue in Nazareth in those early days of His ministry (Luke 4:16-30). He read that portion from Isaiah 61 and presented Himself to them as the fulfilment of what Isaiah had written centuries earlier. He was the anointed Prophet, coming to preach glad tidings to the meek. He was the anointed Priest and had come to them with a ministry of healing and comfort. He was too, the anointed King, coming to deliver the captives and liberate men who had been in bondage.

If only they could have recognised Him, He was the Prophet, Priest, and King for whom they had waited but, sadly, they did not know Him. For a while they listened intently, with all eyes fastened on Him. They marvelled at the gracious words which He spoke, until He began to apply the Scripture to them, recalling how, in ancient times, Jehovah had come to their fathers with blessing, only to be rejected, so that

Gentiles like Naaman the Syrian and the widow of Sarepta received the blessing instead.

At this, their wonder turned to wrath and they thrust Him out of the synagogue. They would have cast Him over the brow of the hill on which Nazareth was built but He quietly withdrew from them. Was it a foreshadowing of the brow of another hill on which they would later crucify Him?

Day 3

A PREACHING MINISTRY

ISAIAH 61:1

"The Lord hath anointed me to preach good tidings unto the meek". Messiah's ministry was not all preaching, but preaching was a large part of it and His message was one of glad tidings. The angel of the Lord had indeed brought a foregleam of this on the morning of His incarnation saying, "Behold I bring you good tidings of great joy", and this was, in after years, the burden of our Lord's ministry.

He had, of course, a message for all men, but it is both interesting and important to note that His earliest recorded words of public ministry were, "Blessed are the poor in spirit". This is exactly the meaning of the word "meek" in Isaiah 61.1. Those who would truly profit by His ministry were those who had no wealthy thoughts about themselves, but who would come, devoid of all pride, acknowledging need and humbly trusting Him for everything.

It was, however, a difficult thing for a proud Jew, with all the advantages of Judaism, to come in humility and accept by grace what could not be obtained by works and by human effort. It is similarly difficult for many a Gentile to confess spiritual poverty and come in meekness to the Saviour to hear the good tidings. It was then, the common people who heard Him gladly (Mark 12:37), and on one sad occasion an apparently serious enquirer turned away because of the possible loss of his great possessions. When he had gone Jesus said to His disciples, "How hardly shall they that have riches enter into the kingdom of God" (Mark 10:23-24). He explained that those who were rich were accustomed to trusting in their riches for everything, but entrance into the kingdom could not be bought with money. If this was an encouragement to the poor then it was indeed a deterrent to many who were rich.

It is touching to remember that He who came preaching good tidings to the poor was Himself a poor man. He had voluntarily become so, leaving riches incalculable for depths of poverty, so that others by His poverty might be rich (2 Cor 8:9). There is no record anywhere of His ever handling money, so that when He appealed to the poor in His preaching, the poor could listen to Him appreciatively. He was too, the meek and lowly One, and when He denounced pride and offered salvation to the meek, men could hear Him and acknowledge the sincerity of His preaching.

So He preached good tidings to the poor, tidings of the love and mercy of God, tidings of grace and glory, always mingled with the sweet invitation to come to Him for peace and rest.

Day 4

A COMFORTING MINISTRY

Isaiah 61:1

"He hath sent me to bind up the brokenhearted". Ever since the fall of man in Eden earth has abounded in broken hearts. Sin has brought sorrow, and men of all ages and all parts have mourned for a variety of reasons. There has been sickness and pain, bereavements and burials, poverty, loneliness, toiling and tears. These were all present in the days of our Lord's ministry so that, again and again, we read of Him that He was "moved with compassion". He had come to bind up the brokenhearted.

Many in the Saviour's day were leprous, for whom men had no help to offer. Many others were possessed with demons, beyond the reach of human aid. Blindness too was a common affliction in Israel in those days, and broken hearts were the inevitable result, both of the afflicted and of their helpless families and friends.

Of Jehovah, centuries earlier, the psalmist had said, "He healeth the broken in heart and bindeth up their wounds" (Ps 147:3) and now, in the Person of the Son, that same Jehovah had come to sojourn among men. The ministry of comfort and healing became a practical reality for many who heard the word and felt the touch of Messiah in their midst. Matthew writes of a busy day of such healings, and records the cleansing of a leper, the cure of a grievously ill paralytic, and the deliverance of Peter's wife's mother from a fever. In the evening of the same day they brought to Him many that were demon possessed, and He healed them all. Matthew sees a fulfilment of a prophecy in Isaiah 53 and writes, "That it might be fulfilled which was spoken by Esaias the prophet, saying, Himself took our infirmities, and bare our sicknesses" (Matt 8:17; Isa 53:4).

It is precious to know that the Lord Jesus shared in the sorrows of men. He made them His own, and sympathised in a very real and genuine way with the brokenhearted.

There was, however, another thing. How He longed to see hearts broken in repentance and sorrow for sin. Then that other Scripture could be fulfilled, "The Lord is nigh unto them that are of a broken heart; and saveth such as be of a contrite spirit" (Ps 34:18). How it must have saddened Him to see those who sinned with impunity, with no fear of God. Then, in their self-righteousness they rejected Him and the ministry that reproved them, so that

He could say, "Reproach hath broken my heart" (Ps 69:20). O the sad irony, that He who had come to heal the brokenhearted was Himself brokenhearted, despised and rejected by those whom He had come to heal.

Day 5

A LIBERATING MINISTRY

Isaiah 61:1

"The Lord hath anointed me to proclaim liberty to the captives". Men have ever resisted the suggestion that they are in bondage. On one occasion the Jews indignantly protested, "We be Abraham's seed, and were never in bondage to any man" (John 8:33), yet from the turrets of the Antonia Fortress, on the corner of their temple mount, the flag of Rome must have been fluttering at that very moment. Nationally they were indeed in bondage, to Caesar and to Rome.

But there was a greater bondage, not only of Jews but of all men everywhere. It was a bondage to sin and Satan. Whoever practised sin was indeed the bondservant, the slave, of sin. A fallen nature impelled men to sin. In spite of resolutions, best intentions and noble endeavours, the sinner would sin. Men were sinners by nature and, therefore, sinners by practice. Jehovah had given a law but, such is the state of the human heart, every prohibition actually incites a man to do that very thing and to lust after the forbidden fruit. The Saviour had come to deliver. He had liberty for such captives if only men would first acknowledge the bondage.

Again, there was another captivity. In Luke 13:11 there was a poor woman who had been bent over with some curvature of the spine for eighteen years. Jesus healed her, but it was on the Sabbath day and this angered the ruler of the synagogue who spoke to the people, pointing out that there were six other days when the woman could have been healed. The Saviour denounced his hypocrisy, reminding the people that even their oxen and asses were loosed from their stalls on the Sabbath day and led to the watering. Satan had bound this poor woman for eighteen years. Ought she not to be loosed from her physical bondage on the Sabbath? His adversaries were ashamed and the people rejoiced. Sin had brought sickness into the world and the creatures were in bondage to it. The whole creation groans in this bondage (Rom 8: 22), but Messiah had indeed come to proclaim liberty to the captives and, one day, will come to deliver the creation. During His gracious ministry He demonstrated His power over demons, disease, and death, and again and again He emancipated men from their maladies. With what joy do those who know Him love to sing:

> He breaks the power of cancelled sin,
> He sets the prisoner free!

His promise, and His assurance to men was, "The truth shall make you free", and "If the Son therefore shall make you free, ye shall be free indeed" (John 8:32, 36). This is still His promise in the Gospel.

Day 6

An illuminating ministry

Isaiah 61:1

"The opening of the prison to them that are bound". This expression is not quite the same as "proclaim liberty to the captives". A comparison of Isaiah 61:1 with Luke 4:18 will reveal that something more is intended than just the freedom from bondage, while this is most welcome. The Septuagint Version of the Old Testament (LXX) appears to add, "the recovering of sight to the blind". This, however, is not so much an addition as an expanded explanation. The word "opening" here is a remarkable word, actually a combination of two Hebrew words (*peqach-qooach* Strong 6495).

The following is, in condensed form, as the commentator Delitzsch explains it in his customary scholarly fashion, "*Peqach-qooach* is written like two words. The Targum translates it as if *peqach* were an imperative: "Come to the light," probably meaning 'undo the bands' in the sense of throwing open the prison ... always applied to the opening of the eyes (Isa 35:5; 42: 7 et al), except in Isa 42:20, where it is used for the opening of the ears ... if we understand by *peqach-qooach* the opening up of the eyes (as contrasted with the dense darkness of the prison); ... this is how it has been taken even by the LXX".

The Jamieson-Fausset-Brown commentary explains it similarly, "The Hebrew rather is, 'the most complete opening', namely, of the eyes of them that are bound, that is, deliverance from prison, for captives are as it were blind in the darkness of prison (Isa 14:17; 35:5; 42:7). So Luke 4:18 and the Septuagint interpret it; Luke 4:18, under inspiration, adds to this, for the fuller explanation of the single clause in the Hebrew, "to set at liberty them that are bruised"; thus expressing the double "opening" implied; namely, that of the eyes (John 9:39), and that of the prison".

The dungeons of old must have been dismal places indeed, in which the captives were in perpetual darkness, deprived of light. What an experience it must have been to be eventually released, to emerge into the light of day. So it was with those who, under the ministry of Christ, were set free. It was while He and His disciples conversed about a man who had been blind from birth that He said, "As long as I am in the world, I am the light of the world" (John 9:5). The poor man was delivered from his affliction to see Him who was the light of the world. And as it was with him physically, so it was, and so it is today, with those who are set free from their sins. It is the opening of the prison doors and a coming into the light.

Day 7

PROCLAIMING "THE ACCEPTABLE YEAR OF THE LORD"

Isaiah 61:2

It is often remarked upon, and indeed it is very important to note, that the Lord Jesus, when reading this passage in the Nazareth synagogue, stopped abruptly in the middle of a sentence. He had come to proclaim the acceptable year of the Lord but would not yet introduce the day of vengeance. That belonged to a later period in the programme of prophecy. It was not yet for Him who said, "I came not to judge the world, but to save the world" (John 12:47).

In the "acceptable year of the Lord" there would appear to be an allusion to the year of jubilee. Every Jew would have been familiar with Lev 25:8-13. Those to whom Isaiah 61 was first given, and those who heard it read on that memorable Sabbath day in Nazareth, would alike have known the passage well. "And thou shalt number seven sabbaths of years unto thee, seven times seven years; and the space of the seven sabbaths of years shall be unto thee forty and nine years. Then shalt thou cause the trumpet of the jubilee to sound on the tenth day of the seventh month, in the day of atonement shall ye make the trumpet sound throughout all your land. And ye shall hallow the fiftieth year, and proclaim liberty throughout all the land unto all the inhabitants thereof: it shall be a jubilee unto you". On that fiftieth year when the trumpet was blown, the proclamation was made through the whole land. Hebrew slaves were set free, debts were cancelled, and possessions and properties were restored to their original families. It was indeed a year of rejoicing.

How significant that the proclamation was made on the Day of Atonement in that year. Two young goats had been taken from the people for a sin offering and, as the blood of one goat was carried into the tabernacle and the other, the scapegoat, was led into the wilderness, burdened, as it were, with the sins of the nation, on that very day the shofar was proclaiming liberty throughout the land (Lev 23:7-10). So it is, that on the basis of that great offering at Golgotha, the preacher can sound the notes of the emancipating gospel to all men everywhere.

In that Nazareth synagogue the Saviour announced that He had come to proclaim the acceptable year of the Lord. "Behold now is the accepted time", Paul wrote. "Behold now is the day of salvation" (2 Cor 6:2; Isa 49:8). And still, after two thousand years of gospel preaching, the day of grace yet runs its course. How long now, before the year of jubilee comes to an end and opportunities will be gone?

JIM FLANIGAN

Week 34

7 DOWNWARD STEPS OF THE SAVIOUR IN PHILIPPIANS 2:6-8

Introduction

In dealing with any passage that speaks of the person of the Lord we must be conscious that we are treading upon holy ground. These verses speak of the deity of Christ, "being in the form of God" (v.6), and the humanity of Christ, "being found in fashion as a man" (v.8). Both these truths must be respected and preserved. They have been attacked by ungodly men who are intent on undermining anything that elevates the Saviour.

We need to appreciate the context of these verses. The teaching on the seven downward steps of the Saviour is not given purely to exalt the Lord. Paul's argument is that believers might see in these steps something that they might seek, with the help of God, to emulate. This teaching runs directly opposite to the trend of the world. People amongst whom we live and work have high aspirations. They want to make it to the top, even though many of them do not have the necessary moral or academic right to such status and power. We should appreciate that this thinking often permeates the minds of believers, and we begin to follow the lead of the world.

James and John asked the Lord, "Grant unto us that we may sit, one on thy right hand, and the other on thy left hand, in thy glory" (Mark 10:37). Even those closest to the Lord seemed to have caught, and been drawn along, by the spirit of the age. They thought nothing of their fellow disciples and wanted everything for themselves. However, the Lord taught "whosoever will be great among you, shall be your minister" (Mark 10:43). In the divine estimation, greatness consists of what we make of others rather than what we make of ourselves. It is not gained by effort and endeavour but is conferred by one to whom all our service should be rendered, God Himself.

As we shall see in the meditations that follow, the Lord had the moral right to emphasize this teaching because He had evidenced it in His own life. Paul could teach it here to the Philippians because, as he writes later, "what things were gain to me, those I counted loss for Christ" (3:7).

Day 1

"MADE HIMSELF OF NO REPUTATION"

Philippians 2:6-7

To appreciate the first of the downward steps of the Saviour we need to remind our hearts of who He is. Paul tells us, "Who being in the form of God" (v.6). All the essential attributes of deity are His in His nature and person. They always were His and they will ever remain characteristics of Him. Deity was not something that He claimed falsely, a title that He aspired to and sought to plunder for Himself. He is co-existent, co-eternal, and co-equal with God.

What a wonder, then, to read that He "made himself of no reputation". Whether we take this phrase as a summary of the seven steps in total, or as one of the steps, He came "From the highest in heaven to the lowest on earth; from the Sovereign of all to the Servant of all; from the crown of glory to the cross of Golgotha' (*John Pickford*). It throws into the starkest of contrasts His pre-incarnate glory and the incarnate humiliation that He knew in stepping into humanity.

It is equally remarkable to appreciate that the Lord was active in this step. The apostle does **not** say that He was made of no reputation. It was **not** an action taken by another, imposing its consequences upon the Saviour. Rather, it was something in which the Lord was wholly involved. It was His own voluntary act. Seen positively, it can be stated that the Lord was wholly committed to the great task of saving men. He gave all He was, as well as all that He had.

What did it mean for the Lord to make "himself of no reputation"? When, as in the literal translation, it states that the Lord emptied Himself, He could **not** empty Himself of His deity. He could **not** cease to be what He is eternally. Different expositors offer various suggestions to this vexed question. But all of this is conjecture, for the phrase offers no explanation that can be directly deduced.

However, it is clear, from the context, that He gave up temporarily His place in glory. "When He emptied Himself, it was not a question of plenitude, but one of altitude" (*Fred Stallan*). He stepped from heaven's glory into the midst of earth's shame. He was born of the virgin. His

mother was not a woman of status or wealth. He came to the poverty of the manger of Bethlehem. There were those who, even then, would cast doubts upon the morals of His mother, (John 8:41). He was not associated with the palace or the throne of occupied Judea, but with the carpenter's bench of despised Nazareth. This was not a family or home or occupation of reputation. Truly, he "made himself of no reputation"!

Day 2

"*TOOK UPON HIM THE FORM OF A SERVANT*"

Philippians 2:7

We have stressed in our previous meditation that the Lord was wholly involved in, and committed to, the step that He took. From the wording of the part of our verse for today, it is clear that this is equally true here. He took upon Himself a servant's form as a voluntary act!

We may notice, from the King James version, that He took "the form of a servant". The phrase 'the form of' is one that the apostle has already used in his statement of verse 6, "being in the form of God". It is the translation of one word that is important to this whole passage. The word, *morphe*, describes the essence of a thing, the core qualities that never change. Applied to the Lord, it clearly tells us that He is God for this is His unchanging being and character. But, here in today's verse, it tells us that He became a real servant. This was not the outward show that some assume for the purpose of publicity. The Lord knew what it was to become a true servant, to experience its demands, its rigours, its deprivations, and its humiliations.

We might pause to consider the nature of this service. We know, from our own experience, that there are different levels of service. In human reckoning, the lowest would be that of a slave. A slave is owned by his master, has no rights of his own, and little opportunity to express or carry out his own will or desire. The word that is used here describes the Lord as taking upon Himself the form of a bond-slave. We must be careful not to view this in relation to men, but to acknowledge that the Lord became wholly submissive to His Father's will. He was the willing bond-slave of the Father. The Lord said, "I came down from heaven, not to do mine own will, but the will of him that sent me" (John 6:38). Such was His devotion that it became His sole focus, His very meat and drink (John 4: 34). He was prepared to endure whatever rigours, whatever deprivations, whatever humiliations that were necessary to see the Father's will complete.

There could be no greater demand than that which the Saviour faced in anticipation of Calvary. But we can remember His words in that prayer in Gethsemane, "not my will, but thine be done" (Luke 22:42). The victory assured, the work assumed complete, the Lord could say to His Father, "I have glorified thee upon the earth: I have finished the work which thou gavest me to do" (John 17:4). What a servant!

Day 3

"*MADE IN THE LIKENESS OF MEN*"

Philippians 2:7

It is possible to translate this phrase "becoming in the likeness of men" (RV margin), or "taking his place in the likeness of men" (JND). As in previous phrases, it is important to emphasise that this too was an activity in which the Lord was wholly involved and to which He was committed. Each step was taken as an act of devotion to the Father's will and with the desire to accomplish the divine plan.

It is clear that we have here a remarkable step of condescending grace. At a particular point in time, and from that point onwards, the Lord became what He had never been before. He became man, initially a babe wrapped in swaddling bands and lying in Bethlehem's manger (Luke 2:16).

There were wise men from the east, who came to Jerusalem asking, "Where is he that is born King of the Jews?" (Matt 2:2). But they did not find Him in the palace, they found Him in the house. Again, we need to emphasize that His was not the glorified humanity conferred upon a man of status and power such as a king. He came in lowly guise without any external features that would mark Him out from other men.

The Lord was a real man. The Word became flesh, real flesh and blood (John 1:14). But, in using the word 'likeness', the apostle is telling us that His was a unique humanity. For "great is the mystery of godliness: God was manifest in flesh" (1 Tim 3:16). We must remember that "this likeness to men did not express His whole self" (*Marvin Vincent*). When looking upon men and women we see all that there is to see – mere humanity! When looking upon the Saviour, John had to acknowledge that "we beheld his glory, the glory as of the only begotten of the Father, full of grace and truth" (John 1:14). Here was someone greater than the flesh and blood in which He chose to manifest Himself at that time. Here was the very Son of God!

The apostle teaches us that the Lord Jesus "was made in the likeness of men". We have paid close attention to the words of Scripture, for each one is significant. The use of the word 'likeness' has indicated similarity but not sameness. Men are innately sinful. Since Adam's fall, the will of man has taken him away from God, brought opposition and enmity. How important, then, for the apostle to establish the sinless perfection of Christ! Likeness, but not sameness!

Day 4

"FOUND IN FASHION AS A MAN"

Philippians 2:8

We have noted in our previous meditation that the Lord became "in the likeness of men" (v.7). This is extended by our phrase for today. Here the apostle is considering more than the birth of the Lord. He is thinking of the life that followed on from the time of His birth, the years of His relative obscurity in Nazareth as well as the years of His public ministry.

We have in our phrase an interesting contrast of words. We have mentioned the word *morphe*, translated 'in the form of', and commented upon its significance. Here, the word *schema*, translated 'in fashion as' is introduced and contrasted with its predecessor. This word emphasizes outward appearance in contrast to essential character. When men looked upon the Saviour they could only ever discern the external. Only God looks upon the heart and discerns the thoughts and intents of that heart. Thus, as men beheld the Lord they beheld a man. "But we see Jesus, who was made a little lower than the angels" (Heb 2:9). Not an angel, but a man!

Looking upon the Saviour, men asked the question, "Is not this the carpenter's son?" (Matt 13:55). To outward appearance He looked like any similar tradesman. His teachings and His actions might distinguish Him and set Him apart from others, but His appearance did not. They said of Him, "How knoweth this man letters, having never learned?" (John 7:15). There was no denying that He was possessed of a knowledge and understanding of the Scriptures, and a wisdom in applying them, that was far beyond that of any of their teachers. Their puzzlement was because what He said did not match how He looked, and the assumptions that men made based upon that appearance.

There are many different aspects that demonstrate to us the reality of His humanity. We see Him "wearied with his journey" (John 4:6). He knew what it was to be hungry, (Matt 21:18; Luke 4:2). We see Him thirsty, (John 19:28). He was "a man of sorrows and acquainted with grief" (Isa 53:3). He shared with us the experiences common to humanity, yet sin apart.

But, as we have said, this is more than a mere repetition of what has gone before. This phrase is a necessary forerunner of what is to come. For it is only as a grown man that the Lord could humble Himself as a voluntary act of His own will. It is only as a man that He could become obedient. It is only as a man that He could die.

Each step that the Saviour took was a measured step leading Him inexorably towards the accomplishment of the work of the cross.

Day 5

"HE HUMBLED HIMSELF"

Philippians 2:8

We would emphasize again the voluntary nature of this humbling. "No crisis disturbed the heavenly realm; no demands for abdication range through His kingdom; no Absalom moved to usurp the throne of the greater David. Our Lord did not have to come to earth; no one compelled Him. He humbled Himself" (*John Pickford*).

At this point in the downward steps of the Saviour, it seems strange to find a phrase such as this. He had stepped into humanity. He had come to the manger of Bethlehem and the carpenter's bench at despised Nazareth. He had assumed a servant's status and occupation. He was living out His life amongst the poorest of men. He was bearing the burdens of life and ministering directly to the needs of others. Had He not done enough? No, says Paul, "he humbled himself". It means to reduce oneself to meaner circumstances, to rank oneself below others, or to abase.

It seems that there was no depth to which the Saviour would not stoop to save the souls of men. He had stepped below the rank of angels into humanity. He had stepped below the rank of kings and princes to be called "a Nazarene" (Matt 2:23). He was prepared to sit upon the well at Sychar and talk to the woman there. He was prepared to take a journey across the storm-tossed lake of Galilee to be associated with, and bring deliverance to, a man who had his dwelling amongst the tombs. He was found amongst the sick and dying at the pool of Bethesda in order to heal a man who had suffered from an infirmity for thirty-eight years. In the upper room He was willing to lay aside His garments, to gird Himself with a towel and to wash His disciples feet.

As we ponder these words, "he humbled himself", they appear the more remarkable in the events leading up to the cross. What humiliations were brought upon the Saviour and yet he did not demur or resist. As Peter states, "who, when he was reviled, reviled not again; when he suffered, he threatened not; but committed himself to him that judgeth righteously" (1 Pet 2:23).

What an example the Lord left! He taught His disciples, "he that shall humble himself shall be exalted" (Matt 23:12). As He taught His disciples, so He lived. As Paul asserts, there could be no question as to the reality of the Lord's self-humbling. However, standing in stark contrast to that are Paul's words in v.9, "Wherefore God also hath highly exalted him". As the poet wrote,

> "Every mark of dark dishonour,
> … told in answering glory now" (Centra Thompson).

Day 6

"BECAME OBEDIENT UNTO DEATH"

Philippians 2:8

As we think of the events leading up to the Saviour's crucifixion, we can appreciate that obedience had its price before the cross. The writer of Hebrews reminds us, "Though he were a Son, yet learned he obedience by the things which he suffered" (5:8).

They came with lanterns and staves to take Him in the garden of Gethsemane. He was harangued and falsely accused. He was buffeted and beaten. Their mock trials continued through the night depriving Him of sleep. He became the object of man's ridicule and scorn. He was scourged, crowned with thorns and led to His death.

What makes the Lord's death different from all others is not the manner of His death, but the fact of His death at all. Others have stood falsely accused and have been cruelly treated. Others have been tortured and killed for no reason. But, in the Lord's own words about His life, "no man taketh it from me, but I lay it down of myself" (John 10:18).

When He could have spoken a word in His own defence, Pilate marvelled at His silence. One who had used but three words to still a tempest and calm a storm, did not speak a word. He willingly submitted Himself to the Father's will and went on to the cross and death.

Although in untold physical and mental agony, there was a dignity about the Lord's death. Luke records that He cried with a loud voice, "Father, into thy hands I commend my spirit" (Luke 23:46). As we might lay our head upon the pillow to sleep, John adds that "he bowed his head" (John 19:30) before He finally "yielded up the ghost" (Matt 27:50). The other prisoners were hastened to their death by the hands of the soldiers, but not so the Lord. "Pilate marvelled if he were already dead" (Mark 15:44).

How remarkable that in this extremity of death, the Lord demonstrated that He was in full control of all events. As the Lord was in His life so, in His death, all things were done in accord with the divine calendar and timing.

But the question that Paul asks, as he pens our phrase today, is how far are you prepared to go? For the achievement of a goal, for the accomplishment of a task, as an expression of love and devotion, how far are we prepared to go?

Most people put a very high price upon life. Their own lives in particular. This is what makes these words of Paul so remarkable. The Lord did not count His own life dear. He laid it down in sacrifice to God (Heb 9:14).

Day 7

"EVEN THE DEATH OF THE CROSS"

Philippians 2:8

In but six words (four words in the Greek) the apostle encompasses so much! This was no ordinary death. It was the death of the cross. Today, we need to pause and consider, what did the death of the cross mean?

The prophet Isaiah said of the Lord, "He is despised and rejected of men" (Isa 53:3). This description of the Lord in His life might also be attached to Him in His death. The place of crucifixion was outside the city walls of Jerusalem. John describes it as "nigh to the city" (John 19:20). It indicated that those crucified had no place in the society of the day.

Crucifixion meant shame. Isaiah tells us that "he was numbered with the transgressors" (Isa 53:12). The Lord was exchanged for a common criminal, one who was a robber and a murderer. He was identified with two common thieves on either side of Him on the cross. Over His head on the cross was written "the superscription of his accusation" (Mark 15:26). He was made an open spectacle as if He were the chief of sinners. Even Roman citizens regarded this means of capital punishment with revulsion.

To the Jew the cross meant more. "A sin worthy of death" could be judged by the perpetrator being put to death and hanged on a tree. But a solemn note accompanies such justice, "he that is hanged is accursed of God" (Deut 21:22-23). Paul appreciated the significance of this when he wrote, "Christ hath redeemed us from the curse of the law, being made a curse for us" (Gal 3:13). To be crucified meant to be put outside of the nation of Israel and the divine covenants associated with it. The cross was to "the Jews a stumbling block" (1 Cor 1:23).

The cross was also a death of great suffering, a slow and lingering death. Those crucified would be taken out in the early part of the morning, affixed to the cross, and reared up to bear the heat of the noonday sun. For the Lord, His contact with that rough-hewn wood that formed His cross would be through His nail pierced hands and feet, and through His back that had been "ploughed" with the Roman lash. The hours would pass with no thought of comfort or respite. His prospect was darkness and judgement. What an experience for the Son of God!

As we conclude our meditations we might remember that the cross is history. The Lord is risen, ascended, exalted and glorified! Those that despised and rejected Him will confess Him as Lord. Those that ridiculed and scorned Him will bow the knee before Him. He will be acknowledged as King of kings and Lord of lords!

JOHN BENNETT

Week 35

7 CHURCHES IN ASIA

Introduction

The Apostle Paul wrote to seven churches who were part of the body of Christ on earth, linked to the risen Head in Heaven, whereas the Apostle John wrote to seven churches and showed them to be a responsible body on earth, in public testimony, answerable to their risen Lord who walks amidst the lamp stands.

The letters to the seven churches in Asia can be viewed in three ways; historically, practically, prophetically. **Historically** – The churches all existed in Asia Minor at the time John wrote. **Practically** – In any one of the letters there can be found a suitable message to meet the need of any church, at any time. **Prophetically** – Why these seven churches when others existed in that area? The word 'mystery' (Rev 1:20) seems to indicate 'a meaning not apparent at the time' and, if this is accepted, we observe a panoramic view of the church from the close of the apostolic era to the rapture.

The seven letters can be divided into three and four. The first three are consecutive. The last four are concurrent. The four conditions seem to run side by side until the return of the Lord.

In the first three, the seeds of departure are sown; in the last four, departure is in full bloom. In the first three, the call to hear precedes the invitation to the overcomer; in the last four, it follows after. In the first three, the churches are pointed back to the beginning for recovery; in the last four, they are pointed on to the end when, at His coming, the true will be raptured, and the false, will be spued out of his mouth (Rev 3:16) and will form part of the harlot church described in chapter 17.

Who is "the angel" addressed in each letter? I take the expression to be a reference to the spiritual element in each church. To such believers the Lord Jesus is presented in a way relevant to their particular condition and need but, ultimately, He is the One who stands in all the dignity and glory described in the opening chapter of the book (vv.12-16).

In each case, the invitation to the overcomer is an incentive to encourage those in the particular difficulty to go on. There is no such thing as a 'two-tier' Christianity.

Day 1

THE CHURCH AT EPHESUS

Revelation 2:1-7; Proverbs 23:26

Ephesus means 'desirable'. Many desirable features were found in the church at Ephesus. To them had been imparted the highest principles of divine truth. Paul had declared unto them the whole council of God (Acts 20:27) and his epistle to the church unfolds these great truths to us. Now before us, in this letter, the church at Ephesus is seen as a distinctive witness shining in the darkness of this world. It is a golden lamp stand, indicating its divine origin and constitution. Within it is a spiritual element, held in the Lord's right hand, supported by His power and thus enabled to declare His mind to the church.

We listen now to the Saviour's voice of commendation. Cognisant of every detail of their activities, the Saviour said "I know thy works" – their labouring to the point of exhaustion; "I know thy toil" – their perseverance; "I know thy patience". This was not a church which gave that which cost them nothing.

They also guarded the fellowship against men who were evil, and those only professing to be apostles, so keeping the church morally pure and doctrinally sound. This would be a company we would recommend, with whom we would be happy to have fellowship yet, to this seemingly faultless church, the Lord says, "I have somewhat against thee, because thou hast left thy first love" (v.4). With these words they are exposed. The divine diagnosis was heart trouble; bridal affection had cooled; the love of espousal had been left. No question could ever be raised as to His love for them (Eph 5:25) but He longed for a reciprocal love. The house was in order and He looked with affection on their toil and testimony but, sadly, like Samson, inward reality had gone.

Could the Lord's words to Peter "lovest thou me more than these?" (John 21:15) be a challenge to us? Does our heart beat true to Him? We listen to His exhortation to the Ephesian believers, and to us, "remember", "repent" and return, for the place of departure is still the place of recovery. If these words go unheeded, a church would cease to be a responsible testimony on earth for

Him. In the light of future blessing they are encouraged to overcome, and to enjoy the tree of life, which is life enjoyed eternally in the pristine beauty of the Paradise of God.

Let us then carefully guard our affections, so we can truly say "Lord thou knowest all things; thou knowest that I love thee" (John 21:17). Only then will all other things find their rightful place, for He will brook no rival.

Day 2

THE CHURCH AT SMYRNA

Revelation 2:8-11; Proverbs 17:3

In these four short verses in Revelation we see Christianity in the crucible. The persecution of Christians had become the sport of the masses. As the tarred bodies of some, on stakes around the amphitheatre, would be torched to light up the stadium, others, as the crowds cheered, were torn to shreds as they fought with wild beasts in the arena. How comforting for them to hear the words of the Saviour, "I am the first and the last, which was dead, and is alive" (2:8). Though he was God, he became man, trod faithfully the path that led Him to Calvary, became dead and lived again. He reminds them that He had passed that way before them and He was with them in their trials. "When thou passest through the waters, I will be with thee" (Isa 43:2). He knew their poverty, the awful hatred of the combined forces of religious and political power, satanically inspired, that had stripped Him of every thing, and engineered his crucifixion. Now that same power was operating against the believers in Smyrna.

The Saviour offered no alleviation of their suffering. For some it was to be prison, pain and death, but He speaks words of comfort. "Fear not", "be thou faithful" and, if there was to be no alleviation, there was a limitation of "ten days". All was under divine control; satanic activity was limited, just as Pilgrim found that the lions in his way on the narrow path to the palace Beautiful were chained. As we learn also from Job, Satan's ferocious attack on him was only by divine permission.

We value also the Lord's estimation. Whereas the world saw them as poor, He says they were "rich". There was nothing to censure in this church; all was unadulterated gold, the fires of persecution had purged away the dross. There was no false doctrine to correct, no spurious believers to reprove; all was genuine and pure, a delight to His heart. To them is His voice of encouragement, as to the disciples on the storm tossed lake "Be of good cheer; it is I; be not afraid" (Matt 14:27). On another occasion the Lord said, "fear not them which kill the body", for that is all that they can do.

Here in Smyrna the martyr's crown is held out to those "faithful unto death" and, as overcomers, they will never experience the second death which is the lake of fire (Rev 20:14). So, to all who are suffering for righteousness sake, we are reminded that "weeping may endure for a night, but joy cometh in the morning" (Ps 30:5).

Day 3

THE CHURCH AT PERGAMOS

Revelation 2:12-17; 2 Samuel 23:11-12

In this letter we see the church no longer persecuted but patronized. No longer is Satan the 'roaring lion' but now an 'angel of light' seeking to corrupt what he had failed to destroy.

The seriousness of the danger is highlighted by the threat of the Lord, "Repent; or else I will come unto thee quickly, and will fight against them with the sword of my mouth" (Rev 2:16). The church was now walking hand in hand with the world, receiving its honours and defiled by its practices. Pergamos means 'marriage', so we witness this unholy alliance, called the doctrine of Balaam, whose name means 'devourer of the people'. God had declared Israel was to dwell alone, a separate people, but Balaam by his wickedness linked them with Moab, corrupting the people whom he had failed to curse. This resulted in divine judgment when 24,000 of Israel were slain (Num 25). How careful we should be in our separation to the Lord.

Also in Pergamos were those who held the doctrine of the Nicolaitans, whose name means 'conquerors of the people'. We hear again the hiss of the serpent in this impure sect which indulged in extreme licentiousness whilst professing to be the children of God. Such impurity the Lord hated. We must observe in Rev 2:14-16 the distinction between "thee" and "them". It is against "them" the Lord threatens to fight. Yet, in this stronghold of Satan, there were the faithful who held fast His name (v.13) and had not apostasised from the faith. Such a dear saint was Antipas, "my faithful martyr", who was slain by being roasted alive in a brazen bull.

Maybe as we read again this letter it would challenge us as to our faithfulness and fidelity to the Lord, remembering we are in the same conflict. How encouraging to hear the invitation to the overcomer to eat of the hidden manna, which speaks so eloquently of the Saviour's path down here. The manna (Exod 16) was "round" – the eternal one; "small" – His stoop in grace; "white" – His sinless, stainless purity; the "Bread of God that came down from heaven". The Father found all His delight in Christ, "This is my beloved Son in whom I am well pleased" and, when we are in heaven, He will be our eternal enjoyment in the Father's house.

The white stone was possibly a voting pebble or given to one justly acquitted of a wrong, or victorious in battle, or given the freedom of a city. What a day when justified saints who have fought the good fight are given the freedom of that millennium city, and on that white stone a new name!

Day 4

THE CHURCH AT THYATIRA

Revelation 2:18-29; Galatians 5:9

The one reference in the NT to Thyatira, apart from these verses in Revelation, is in Acts 16:14-15 where we read of Lydia, a seller of purple. She was from Thyatira, the place of its manufacture, a place of industry and commerce. Did she take the message back there? To make progress, and prosper in business in Thyatira, required membership in a trade guild. That membership carried with it an obligation to worship idols and to eat meat offered to idols. Participation in immoral practices, so often linked with idolatry, had now become an acceptable practice. The words of Acts 15:29 are very clear, "that ye abstain from meats offered to idols".

We observe that in this church there is now a serious departure from the NT simplicity of gathering to the name of the Lord Jesus Christ. The whole now comes under divine scrutiny by Him who is described as "the Son of God, who hath his eyes like unto a flame of fire, and his feet are like fine brass" (2:18). "I am he which searcheth the reins and hearts" (v.23). Method and motive are truly assessed by Him.

A woman having control in the church, as a self designated prophetess, is contrary to the divine mind according to 1 Tim 2:11-12 and also 1 Cor 14:34-35. Seduction, fornication and idolatry, whether physically or spiritually, and a refusal to repent, bring upon them the Lord's severe condemnation. He will cast her into the great tribulation and kill with death her offspring as will be the ultimate end of apostate Christendom.

But still in the church, amidst all its failure, there was a faithful remnant who refused to sink to the depths of Satan, and would not subscribe to the false doctrine and practice held by some. The Lord was able to commend this company for their work, their love, their ministry, their faith, their endurance, and for the increase in their zeal, their last works being more than the first. The Lord understood their difficulty and would not suffer them to be tempted above that which they were able to bear. How precious are His words, "I will put upon you none other burden but that ye have already" (vv.24-25), exhorting them to hold fast till He comes, encouraging them to be steadfast to the end, which will bring its own reward, ruling and reigning with Him in His coming kingdom.

But, prior to this, there is the precious promise of the morning star, the rapture of the church. "Even so, come, Lord Jesus" (22:20).

Day 5

THE CHURCH AT SARDIS

Revelation 3:1-6; Mark 14:37

The city of Sardis seemed an impregnable fortress standing 1500 feet (about 500 metres) high, yet history tells us that more than once it had been captured through lack of watchfulness. This would seem to be reflected in the life of this church, outwardly strong and active, but inwardly marked by spiritual lethargy and decay.

They had a name to live; orthodoxy and correctness marked them, outward forms and ceremonies which would satisfy an outsider. They may have had the right words in prayer and worship, but they never reached the throne, or delighted the Father's heart. They may well, behind closed doors, sing lustily words such as "rescue the perishing" when all around them men and women were dying in their sins. There was nothing in this church for God, nothing for Christ and nothing for lost sinners.

Without any word of commendation, the Lord solemnly tells them that they are dead and that the things that remain are "ready to die". Their works are incomplete before God, but the Lord graciously presents Himself to them as the one who can meet their need, for He has the seven Spirits of God, and the seven stars. From this we learn that the Holy Spirit in all His power was available to them to resuscitate them, and the seven stars, a divine fullness of ministry, to meet their spiritual need and strengthen the things that remain. They are exhorted to remember, think back to the ministry they had received and, in the light of it, to repent, to hold fast and be watchful. If they should neglect this solemn counsel and fail to repent, His coming will take them by surprise as a thief and take from them their most prized possessions.

The Saviour now addresses a remnant who, amidst the mass of profession in Sardis, had not defiled their garments, refusing to be associated with what would defile and besmirch their testimony. They are given a promise of walking with Him in white. On civic occasions in Sardis, the families of those honoured would don a white toga and be given the great privilege of walking in procession along with others whose names had been inscribed in the city's roll of honour. As the procession advanced, so their name would be clearly announced before the city's ruler and all the gathered hosts.

So the Lord would encourage the overcomer to look on to a far greater day of pageantry and glory when God's Son will be honoured and all the faithful in shining white garments alongside of Him, reflecting His glory.

These are they whose names are indelibly inscribed in the Lamb's book of life, and announced before His father and all the holy angels. What an honour!

Day 6

THE CHURCH AT PHILADELPHIA

Revelation 3:7-13; Hebrews 13:1

The churches at Philadelphia and Smyrna have the unique distinction of having no word of rebuke, only encouragement, as they seek to be faithful to Him in the midst of religious antagonism called "the synagogue of Satan" (2:9, 3:9). The Philadelphian saints will one day see their antagonists bow at their feet but, in the meantime, though possessing little strength, are bidden to look to the Saviour who is the reservoir of all power.

In 3:7 the Lord is presented to the Philadelphian church in **His official position**, "he that hath the key of David" (cf. Isa 22:22); **His administrative power**, "he that openeth, and no man shutteth; and shutteth, and no man openeth"; **His character**, "he that is holy"; **His conduct**, "he that is true".

What an encouragement, how precious His commendation, "thou hast kept my word", that is, "the faith which was once delivered unto the saints" (Jude v.3). Thou "hast not denied my name", that Name which bespeaks His lovely person, reminding us of His authority. How we should count it our unique privilege to be among those who gather alone to His precious name (Matt 18:20).

An open door of service was given to them, that of making known the Saviour to a world that knows Him not. Do we take advantage of open doors? They also shared His patience, "Because thou hast kept the word of my patience" (v.10). Our Saviour patiently waits, and His heart longs for that moment when He can leave the throne and come to the air to take all His blood-bought people home to His Father's house (John 14:1-3). In the light of His promise, "behold, I come quickly", we also should be marked by that patient waiting for Christ, who will be our deliverer from the coming wrath.

They are exhorted to "hold that fast which thou hast", to remain faithful to His word, continuing to gather to His Name, and to redeem the time, seeking the lost ones for whom the Saviour died. All are encouraged to overcome, awaiting that day when, in contrast to their experience of living in a city plagued by earthquakes, and having to constantly move in and out of it, "they would go no more out". All would be stable there: from little strength, to being weight-bearing pillars in the temple of the new Jerusalem; from refusing to deny His Name here, to the great dignity of bearing their Saviour's new Name up there, and the honour of bearing the name of the city, new Jerusalem.

Day 7

THE CHURCH AT LAODICEA

Revelation 3:14-22; Song of Solomon 5:2

In this last church there is nothing to commend. They had miserably failed in their witness. The Lord presents Himself to them as "the Amen", God's final word, "the faithful and true witness". He was that from the cradle to the crucifixion. "The beginning ('beginner') of the creation of God" (cf. Col 1: 18; John 1:3). He is outside of time, the Eternal One who "spake, and it was done" (Ps 33:9). His assessment could hardly be worse, "thou art neither cold nor hot". Their tepid condition was nauseating to Christ, a church without enthusiasm or compassion, self-centered and indifferent. We hear Him sigh "I would thou wert cold or hot" (v.15).

Their self-assessment was totally different; "I am rich, and increased with goods, and have need of nothing" (v.17). They lived in a wealthy city where gold was refined and stamped as pure. It had its own financial institutions, its own expensive clothing manufactured from the black wool of a rare breed of sheep raised there, and its own medical centres renowned for the production of eye salve. Sadly, such a materialistic atmosphere had affected the church.

The Lord's assessment is one of great pity as He describes their spiritual condition: "thou art wretched" – in need of help; "miserable" – pitiable, abandoned; "poor" – destitute and penniless; "blind" – without spiritual sight; "naked" – without a spiritual garment. His counsel is "buy of me" (v.18). All they lacked could be obtained from Him. In effect, He tells them "You are poor, and I have gold tried in the fire; you need to appreciate again what is divine. You are naked, I have white raiment to give clear evidence of salvation in righteous acts and living. You are blind, I have eye salve that can cure your spiritual myopia and restore lost vision, enabling you to see beyond the present".

What we have down here is not important, but wealth and treasure up there are most important. Because the Lord loves us He bids us to respond to His patient knocking, seeking that we will open to Him, sup with Him. The hour is late; it is the last meal of the day of which He speaks, supper time. If we respond, then in that coming day He will share His throne with us.

As we close our meditation on these seven churches, let us observe: the patriarch Isaac and the priest Eli were blind physically; the last king, Zedekiah, and the last judge, Samson, were blinded by their enemies; the nation of Israel and Laodicea are blind, and ignorant of it!

ERIC HUGHES

Week 36

7 UNCHANGING FEATURES OF CHRIST IN HEBREWS

Introduction

The silent penman of this masterly epistle is not identified since the magnificent theme of Christ eclipses him. The author is the Holy Spirit, a fact confirmed to the heart of the believer in Christ simply by the reading of this majestic masterpiece. It has the ring of authority and truth. It has the voice of dignity and divine majesty. It is the voice of God. The readers could well have been the great company of priests in Jerusalem who were obedient to the faith (Acts 6:7). We know for certain that they were Jews, those specifically of the seed of Abraham.

The writer describes his letter in a surprising way: "And I beseech you, brethren, suffer the word of exhortation: for I have written a letter unto you in few words" (Heb 13:22). It is a confession that he had not even told the half concerning the wonderful person of Christ, though his letter is not short. The purpose of the letter was to encourage the readers who were obviously spiritually downcast and possibly physically weary: "But call to remembrance the former days, in which, after ye were illuminated, ye endured a great fight of afflictions" (Heb 10:32). But, "Ye have not yet resisted unto blood" (Heb 12:4). They were suffering persecution, though not martyrdom, from the apostates among them. 'Apostasy' has the meaning of 'forsake', not the forsaking of salvation once embraced, but a rejecting of salvation once understood. Apostates wished to return to the old order of things in the Old Testament.

The epistle is therefore a blend of encouragement to the believers, interspersed with five distinct warnings to the apostates who were hindering their spiritual progress. We learn that wherever there is blessing to be enjoyed, Satan will do his best to prevent it.

We might ask, why is the epistle included in the New Testament if the ritual Old Testament sacrifices ceased when the Romans destroycd the temple in Jerusalem in AD 70? The answer is simple but profound. It presents the glories of the risen Christ, our Lord and Saviour! It brings the shadow of Christ in the Old Testament into the reality of His person in the New.

Thus, when the letter is patiently studied, it increases our appreciation of Christ and a liberty to express it, whether audibly or silently.

Day 1

THE UNCHANGING KINGSHIP OF CHRIST

Hebrews 1:1-14

Uniquely, the Hebrew epistle begins with "God", and chapter 1 is God's supreme revelation of His eternal Son. In verses 1-2, the Son is **presented**. "God … hath in these last days spoken unto us by his Son". In verses 2-3, the Son is **described**. He is "the express ('exact') image of his person". In verse 3, the Son is **seated**. When He "sat down on the right hand of the Majesty on high", it expressed highest honour to Him because He had put away our sin. This is the high point of the opening sentence of the epistle, and it is easy to see why He is superior to the prophets of the past (v.1). They were good men, but only men at best, and spoke fragmentarily and in various ways. The Son completed a tremendous work.

In the remaining verses, 4-14, the Son is **glorified**, but it may puzzle readers why there is so much reference to angels. The reason is that the law given at Sinai was the centre of the God-given old covenant with man. Moreover, it was given in the presence of myriads of angels on the summit of Sinai's fiery mount (Deut 33:2). Little wonder that the Israelites at the foot of the mount were afraid! Therefore, at the outset, the writer needed to confirm to Hebrew believers that, though the mighty angels had such a prominent part in the giving of the law, they were inferior to the Son who had now spoken. The Son did not make the magnificent Old Testament order of things null and void. Rather, He fulfilled it. The apostates were not convinced of this.

The evidence is presented from several OT quotations – how skilful that choice! – so that by the end of the chapter, the Jewish believers, whose faith had been sorely tested, were spiritually re-energized. Verse 7 is a quotation from Ps 104, a psalm of praise to the God of creation. It reminds us that angels were created to serve. In contrast, verse 8 is a quotation from the royal Psalm 45 in which we read the sublime and majestic statement, "Thy throne, O God, is for ever and ever" (v.6). Jewish expositors regarded it as referring

to Messiah, and Hebrews 1 confirms this. The Son is addressed as God, as king for ever, whose kingdom is marked by perpetual righteousness. It affirms the deity of Christ – His equality, not merely association, with God. No such words were ever addressed to angels who were appointed to serve, whereas Christ was anointed the everlasting king. Though the statement is violently attacked and twisted by heretics, this is the sense indicated by all the ancient versions of Scripture, and a benchmark for other versions.

Day 2

THE UNCHANGING PERSON OF CHRIST

Isaiah 40:21-31; Hebrews 1:10-14

The work of creation is astounding, but its continuous maintenance is equally breathtaking, a fact seemingly overlooked by those who desperately cling to the myth of evolution. The Lord once asked His suffering servant Job two difficult questions: "Where wast thou when I laid the foundations of the earth?" "Whereupon are the foundations thereof fastened?" (Job 38:4, 6).

The questions were unanswerable of course, but when the earth was created, we do know that: "The morning stars sang together, and all the sons of God shouted for joy" (Job 38:7). The angels looked on with joy and sang in that sinless day when earth's foundations were locked into place and the heavens were stretched out "like a curtain" (Ps 104:2). Scripture nowhere records that angels ever sang again after sin struck that fair scene of perfection.

Hanging curtains of even moderate size can be a difficult task, but what tremendous power and skill were needed to stretch out the heavens! Digging the foundations of a building of even moderate size is physically exhausting, but what infinite power was required to lay the foundations of the earth! Hebrews 1 identities the Son as the mighty maker who accomplished this. "Thou, Lord, in the beginning hast laid the foundation of the earth; and the heavens are the work of thine hands" (Heb 1:10).

But the same Lord who constructed them will, in a coming day, also fold them up as an article of clothing. They will perish, wax old as doth a garment, and be changed, but nowhere in Scripture do we read that the heavens and the earth will be annihilated. By inspiration, Peter, the unlearned Galilean, tells us that fire of great intensity will accomplish the taking apart of the elements that form the earth. The atomic building bricks of the universe will be dissembled, purged by fire and reconstructed to form the new heavens and the earth. "The elements shall melt ('be dissolved') with fervent heat" (2 Pet 3:10), possibly by the heat of a mighty nuclear reaction. This must alarm the person without Christ as Saviour, especially as it is He who will perform this mighty work of reconstruction.

The most stable reference point known to man is the planet on which he dwells. Yet it will be folded up as a garment.

The year is the largest time unit used by man that does not exceed his normal life span, but the passing of years does not affect Christ the eternal Son one iota: "They shall perish; but thou remainest; … they shall be changed: but thou art the same, and thy years shall not fail" (Heb 1:11-12).

It is delightfully reassuring to the believer that the Lord who gave the gift of eternal life is Himself eternally the same.

Day 3

THE UNCHANGING PRIESTHOOD OF CHRIST

Exodus 28:1-3; Hebrews 7:23-28

A priest is someone to whom people can go, who can go further than people, and through whom approach can be made to God on behalf of the people. He must also "offer both gifts and sacrifices for the sins of the people" (Heb 7:1,3). A priest in the religious world is a source of comfort to his followers, if he is not feared. What a doctor is in the physical realm, the priest is in the spiritual realm.

The world observes that believers in Christ do not have a visible priest when they meet together. This is perfectly true, for our great High Priest is in heaven. When He had by Himself made purification for sins, He sat down on the right hand of the Majesty on high (Heb 1:3), and it is there that He continues to make intercession for us.

The priesthood of Aaron and his sons in Exodus 28 would have been dearly loved and highly respected by the Jewish readers of the Hebrew epistle. The trouble was, as Hebrews 7 reveals, it was an imperfect priesthood. The writer, now well into his address, gives several reasons for this. One grave disadvantage was that many priests were necessary because they could not continue indefinitely. They eventually died! (Heb 7:23).

It is a good thing to have just one priest because then the priesthood never changes. The character of a new priest is different from that of a deceased priest, and this causes not only sadness to the people but also unsettles them and undermines their security. But death prevented the continuity of the Aaronic priesthood because it overtook every one of its priests. It was also evident that the problem of sin which had brought death had not been conquered. A defective priesthood to be sure! Of necessity then, there were many priests, one after the other.

There is one priest however whose priesthood is unique and perfect: "But this man, because he continueth ever, hath an unchangeable priesthood" (Heb 7:23). The priesthood of Christ is unchangeable because it is eternal, and wonderful blessings flow from this: "Wherefore he is able also to save them to the uttermost ('the greatest possible extent'), that come unto God by him" (Heb 7:25). Through this priest, salvation is total and eternal, and His intercession is perpetual (v.25).

And what sacrifices did this priest offer for sin? Only one. It was a sacrifice for our sins, not His own, for He is sinless. It was no less than the sacrifice of Himself!

Thus in his inspired masterpiece, the writer patiently and skilfully unfolds not only the perfection of the person of Christ, but also the perfection of His eternal priesthood. Thanks be to God for the eternal priesthood of Christ!

Day 4

THE UNCHANGING SACRIFICE OF CHRIST

Hebrews 10:1-18

The writer reaches the pinnacle of his marvellous address in chapter 10. Like a barrister, he summarises the case by underlining the weakness of the old order of sacrifices, but triumphs in the perfect sacrifice that Christ made. The old order of things was imperfect because the sacrifices offered continually year by year under the law could never make those who offered them perfect – the condition they yearned for (v.1); the continual sacrifices offered every year brought back the remembrance of their sins (v.3); the kinds of sacrifices offered were woefully inadequate to take away sins (v.4); those sin offerings brought no pleasure to God (v.6).

What did bring God pleasure was the willingness of His own dear Son to step into humanity and offer Himself a once for all sacrifice for sin. He offered no sacrifice for Himself, for He is sinless, but for sinful humanity it was vitally necessary. By the once for all sacrifice of the body of Jesus Christ, His Son, God assures believers that we are sanctified, free from the guilt of sin and set apart for God.

With a tinge of insecurity and anxiety, someone asks, "For how long is that sacrifice effective?" The beautiful answer is sublime: "For by one offering he hath perfected for ever them that are sanctified" (v.14). "Their sins and iniquities will I (that is, God) remember no more" (v.17). Thus v.18 is the joyful conclusion to the superb presentation of Christ: "Where remission of these is, there is no more offering for sin".

The Aaronic priesthood is therefore totally redundant. The priesthood of Christ is eternal, and the sacrifice that He made on our behalf eternally effective. How then should verse 12 read? "But this man, after he had offered one sacrifice for sins (comma) for ever sat down on the right hand of God"? or, "But this man, after he had offered one sacrifice for sins for ever (comma) sat down on the right hand of God"? In light of our meditation on the chapter, it must be the latter.

Now it is unusual for three negative statements to bring us joy, but Hebrews 10 is an exception. Because of the eternal effectiveness of the sacrifice that Christ made for us, there is no more conscience of sins (v.2); no more remembrance of sins (v.17); no more offering for sin (v.18).

The epistle encourages us to live in the light of the wonderful sacrifice of

Christ by which we have boldness to enter into the holiest by the blood of Jesus (v.19). Therefore, "Let us draw near with a true ('sincere') heart in full assurance of faith" (v.22); "Let us hold fast the profession ('confession') of our faith" (v.23); "Let us consider one another to provoke unto love and to good works" (v.24).

Day 5

THE UNCHANGING PURPOSE OF CHRIST

Hebrews 10:26-39

This part of Hebrews 10 is puzzling, even disturbing, until we realise that the writer is addressing two sets of readers. Verses 26-31 record the fourth warning to the apostates who, having heard the truth, turned away from it. They were guilty of serious contempt, having "trodden under foot the Son of God, and … counted the blood of the new covenant (that is, the shed blood of Christ) an unholy ('common') thing … " (v.29). They were not true believers, though professing to be saved ("sanctified" v.29).

Verses 32-39 record the writer's encouragement to true believers. They were first exhorted to constantly remember their early days of conversion in which they endured, as a contesting athlete, a great conflict of suffering. They were exposed to public contempt, reviled and bitterly persecuted. They were oppressed, not only because they had renounced Judaism, but because they had also given practical assistance to suffering fellow-Jews. For this, their possessions were unlawful seized, but they had joyfully endured because they kept in mind something far better. Though they had lost their earthly wealth, their cheerful courage was not to be lightly regarded since it had "great recompense of reward" (vv.35-36). This was far better because it was in heaven, lasting in quality and eternally enjoyed (v.34).

This encouragement to continue in the difficult pathway of life required endurance, but because "the just shall live by faith", it was not anticipated they would wither, but would do the will of God (v.36). The faith that initially saved them was the foundation of their faith to equip them. Magnificent examples of such faith were witnessed in many valiant OT saints and are recorded in the next chapter. Those who drew back deprived themselves of this marvellous privilege of bringing pleasure to God. The writer then concludes, "We are not of them (the apostates) who draw back unto perdition", an utterly wretched prospect of total and eternal loss.

We must not, however, omit the pinnacle of encouragement in these verses. Severe difficulties often mark the believer's pathway today, though perhaps of a different kind. Many of our hopes and desires never reach the light of day, but are seemingly dashed to the ground. Yet there is one hope that is absolutely sure and steadfast. We do not know its precise timing, but it will be a reality in the fulness of time and, after all, the time of waiting is really only short.

At precisely the right moment, "He that shall come, will come, and will not tarry" (v.37). The Lord will return for His redeemed, and it is this that strengthens the believer's faith and endurance. He whom we love and long to see has an unchangeable date marked for this glorious event.

Day 6

THE UNCHANGING PROMISE OF CHRIST

2 Timothy 4:10; Hebrews 13:5-6

In my father's old Bible, the following note is written in the margin opposite the title verse (Heb 13:5): "A man may leave his wife in the morning to go to his work, but he does not thereby forsake her". It is also encouraging to discover that, in the original language, two negatives precede "leave" and three negatives precede "promise". They combine to emphasise the promise of God: "I will in no wise leave thee, nor will I in any wise forsake thee".

Security is a vitally important ingredient in the life of any person, and it is greatly reassuring to the believer in the Lord that He is always by our side. It is equally reassuring to know that because of His great love for us, He will never let go of us. Security energised by love is exceedingly precious.

I well remember the day we arrived at our new home, having moved some fifty miles to a new area. Packing boxes filled every room and our minds were in a whirl. I was anxious about the effect of this upheaval on our two boys, but I need not have worried. The older one was four at the time, and the picture deeply embedded in my memory is of a little lad happily playing in and out of those boxes. He was happy because he felt secure, even though his surroundings were totally new. Most important to him was that his mother and father had not left or forsaken him.

The context of our verse is, "Be content with such things as ye have", not so much because of the yearning for riches, but reliance on them for security. It is fear of the future, especially when our circumstances are surrounded by dark clouds, that causes us to forget the promise of God and fail to totally rely on Him.

On a wall in our home is a picture of an old man seated at a table and giving grateful thanks to the Lord for the bowl of soup and the loaf of bread before him. The simplicity of the scene is impressive and eloquently witnesses to the utter dependence on the Lord of possibly a poor man. Not to be missed is the Bible on the table, with a pair of spectacles on top. It seems as if the Scriptures have already been read.

The circumstances of our lives can dramatically change in an instant of time, and sometimes for the worse. But if we have learned to completely trust in the Lord in everything, we need have no fear. Rather, because He has promised never to leave us, we can confidently and boldly say "The Lord is my helper, and I will not fear what man shall do unto me" (v.6).

Day 7

THE UNCHANGING CHARACTER OF CHRIST

Hebrews 13:7-21

The remarkable feature about Hebrews 13:8 is its seeming isolation from the preceding and succeeding verses. Yet it is not alone, for throughout this wonderful epistle, we have glimpses of the unchanging, unchangeable God. If Jesus Christ is the unchanging One, and He is, then it is important that we constantly keep our eye on Him. While it is good to remember and follow the godly believers who guided us in the past, their ministry was only for a season, for they are no longer with us (v.7). In contrast, the subtleties of evil and ill-motivated men seek to blow us off course by their varied and strange teachings (v.9). We are warned not to be "carried about with every wind of doctrine, by the sleight ('trickery') of men and cunning craftiness, whereby they lie in wait to deceive" (Eph 4:14). But Jesus Christ is eternally the same. The days of His perfect manhood confirmed this, and now His intercession for us in heaven as our great High Priest amply demonstrates it. His priesthood for us is unchanging. His evident love for us is eternal.

I vividly remember the last time I ever saw my father. He was in a London hospital and we were visiting him on a Sunday afternoon. He was very weak, and I sat at the side of his bed holding his hand. As the afternoon wore on, I became a little anxious about the time since I was due to preach the gospel that evening. My father sensed this, and quietly said, "You carry on my son, the eternal bond is strong enough".

There is so much in those last few words – words that are as true today as when they were uttered thirty years ago. They are as powerful today as ever because the eternal, unchanging God is the bedrock of the reality of that truth. We may safely entrust our lives to Him. The dictionary definition of 'bedrock' is "the solid rock underlying the looser materials of the earth's surface". How spiritually appropriate is that statement! There is no solidity in the things of earth. That is why the Scriptures very wisely tell us, "Set your affections on things above, not on things on the earth" (Col 3:2).

I left the hospital that afternoon, sad in heart at the severing of earthly ties, but rejoicing in the security of the eternal bond with Christ who is our life. Jesus Christ is the unchanging, unchangeable One.

> "We change, He changes not,
>   Though changing years roll by;
> His love, not ours, the resting-place.
>   His truth, not ours, the tie.

ALLAN CUNDICK

Week 37

7 PRINCIPLES OF THE HOUSE OF GOD

Introduction

"Who is like unto the Lord our God, who dwelleth on high, who humbleth himself to behold the things that are in heaven, and in the earth!" (Ps 113:5-6). So the psalmist expressed something of the character of God who, dwelling in the majestic splendour of unimaginable and infinite glory, would yet interest Himself, with loving compassion, in the affairs of a world He had simply called into being by the word of his power. Consider it my soul! The source of every blessing I receive, the origin of the eternal salvation with which I as a poor, repentant, believing sinner am blessed, is the heart of a God infinite in greatness and full of mercy. Well can the believer say with the unknown psalmist, "I love the Lord, because he hath heard my voice and my supplications. Because he hath inclined his ear unto me …" (Ps 116:1-2). He hath inclined His ear unto me! I could never have an audience with a Prime Minister, President or King, but the God of heaven, eternally existent, mighty in omnipotence, the Creator of all things, He hath inclined His ear unto me! What mercy! What compassion! What love! What grace!

The willingness of God to bestow abundant blessings from above upon men on earth is wonderful. But more wonderful still is the desire of God's heart expressed to His servant Moses, "And let them make me a sanctuary; that I may dwell among them" (Exod 25:8). Not content with pouring out his undeserved favour upon His people, God would humble Himself to dwell among them. Ever since Adam's sin cast up a barrier to divine fellowship with man, God has been working out His purpose to righteously restore all that Adam forfeited, and more besides. If the Bible begins with "the Lord God walking in the garden in the cool of the day" (Gen 3:8), then it will finish with "a great voice out of heaven saying, Behold the tabernacle of God is with men, and he will dwell with them …" (Rev 21:3).

The house of God has had various different forms as God has progressively unfolded His great plan of redemption, but the principles concerning His house have never altered. He is unalterably holy, and His dwelling place must be holy too. A house for God must be made according to a divine blueprint, for any design born out of a human mind would fail. If the native dwelling place of God is heaven, then His house must be heaven upon earth. Everything about it must be heavenly. The outcome of God's commandment to Moses, already quoted, was the building of the tabernacle in the wilderness. For the first time, the house of God was tangible and visible, made "according to the pattern shewed to thee in the mount" (Heb 8:5).

But the unfolding revelation of the character of the house of God did not begin with the tabernacle. Important principles concerning the house are first set forth in the book of Genesis, and they hold good for all time. An understanding of, and our submission to, these principles is vital if we are to effectively function for God in local assemblies of believers today. Our first desire must be to honour and glorify our God "whose house are we" (Heb 3:6).

Day 1

THE PLACE OF DIVINE PRESENCE

Genesis 28:10-22

Jacob had just left home. The scene he left behind was one of bad feeling, recriminations and tears. Mother and younger son had deceived father and older son, and the blessings of the firstborn now belonged to Jacob. They would have been his, and God would have been honoured, if he and his mother Rebekah had waited for God to act. Instead, so like ourselves, they thought that God's purpose would unravel unless they did something. It was a sad way for a family to part company with each other, and a sorry outcome to the beautiful story of Isaac and Rebekah's marriage. So much grief was caused by each parent having a favourite son; "And Isaac loved Esau, because he did eat of his venison: but Rebekah loved Jacob" (Gen 25:28). Memories of the altar experience in the land of Moriah had faded for Isaac, and the precious spiritual bond he had enjoyed with his godly father Abraham as "they went both of them together" (Gen 22:6) was not being enjoyed with his own sons. Isaac had become cold and carnal, the clear pronouncement of God concerning his sons that "the elder shall serve the younger" had been forgotten, and he bestowed favoured status upon Esau, the profane man, simply because "he did eat of his venison". The early days of Rebekah's sweet submission, so lovely to recall, were now but

history. Eavesdropping on her husband's conversation with Esau, she said to Jacob "Now therefore, my son, obey my voice…" (Gen 27:8).

Fathers and mothers, as you read these words in the hearing of your children, remember the importance of treating them with godly even-handedness. Remember they are sinners with a fallen nature just like your own. No amount of doting will improve the flesh, but godly instruction, loving discipline and the family altar will help to preserve family unity and instil respect for parents.

Little did Jacob know that his journey would take him from the house of rebellion, deceit and tears to the house of God! As he went toward Haran he settled down for a night's sleep in the desert, gathering warm stones around him to ward off the deep chill of the night. Waking from the wonderful dream concerning millennial conditions, the same scene of which the Lord Jesus spoke to Nathaniel in John 1:51, Jacob said, "Surely the Lord is in this place … this is none other but the house of God" (Gen 28:16-17). Herein lies the first, deeply instructive, principle concerning God's house. We might have said to Jacob, "How is this the house of God? We see no building, nothing but a desert place with a few stones". How solemn his reply would be; "God is here. That fact, and that alone, makes this place the house of God". The house of God, then and today, is the place of divine presence. Never let us forget that!

Day 2

THE PLACE OF DIVINE FELLOWSHIP

Genesis 28:10-22; 1 Timothy 3:14-15

Jacob's recognition of the divine presence at Bethel caused him to declare "this is none other but the house of God" (Gen 28:17). This is the first occasion that "the house of God" is spoken of in our Bibles. Centuries later, Paul would write to Timothy, "These things write I unto thee, hoping to come unto thee shortly: but if I tarry long, that thou mayest know how thou oughtest to behave thyself in the house of God, which is the church of the living God, the pillar and ground of the truth (1 Tim 3:14-15).

The house of God today is the entire church, that is, every believer in the Lord Jesus Christ from the time the church was born on the day of Pentecost (Acts 2:1-4) until the Lord returns to the air to call his believing people home to glory (1 Thess 4:13-17). A local assembly is not "*the* house of God", but it is "house of God" in character. The principles and character of the whole should be evident in the part, and every local assembly should replicate in miniature the features of the whole house.

Implicit in the thought of the house is the idea of fellowship, for houses are dwelling places. On a modern housing development many hundreds of families may be living in identical buildings, but the conditions within those walls will differ vastly. Tastes in décor and furnishing will be different, as will the rules governing the standards of acceptable speech and behaviour. In some of those houses we would definitely not feel 'at home', whilst in others, particularly those where believers were dwelling, the grounds of fellowship would be present. 'Home-making' is a popular concept, and some people spend a lot of time, money and effort on setting their unique stamp upon their dwelling place. Do you, dear saint of God? Do you endeavour to create an atmosphere of godly contentment, order and spiritual serenity in your home? Is the word of God prominently displayed for the instruction of your family, the encouragement of fellow-believers and the challenge of those unsaved?

The house of God is a place of divine fellowship. God has set his stamp upon the place, and it displays His holiness, His glory and His pleasure. Into that house, by wonderful grace, He brings redeemed sinners to enjoy fellowship with Himself. If courtesy demands that you and I submit to the rules and ways of each other's houses when we come to stay, how much more should godly fear and reverence cause us to bow in submission to the order of the house of God? Fellowship has to be on God's terms, and His word declares "holiness becometh thine house, O Lord, for ever" (Ps 93:5).

Day 3

THE PLACE OF DIVINE GOVERNMENT

Genesis 28:10-22

As the knowledge that he was in the divine presence pressed upon his soul like a great weight, Jacob recognised not only the privilege of fellowship in the house of God, but also the responsibility to acknowledge the principles of the government of God. He said "this is the gate of heaven" (Gen 28:17). The careful reading of this verse will remind us that Jacob did not say "this is the gate *to* heaven". The gate *to* heaven is our Lord Jesus Christ who said "I am the way, the truth and the life: no man cometh unto the Father, but by me" (John 14:6). No, Jacob was speaking of Bethel as "the gate *of* heaven", and Scripture will show that the thought of government and administration is in mind. When order had to be restored in the camp after the golden calf had been made, "Then Moses stood in the gate of the camp, and said, Who is on the Lord's side? let him come unto me" (Exod 32:26). The unwitting manslayer could flee to a city of refuge, "And when he that doth flee unto one of those cities shall stand at the entering of the gate of the city, and shall declare his cause in the ears of the elders of that city, they shall take him into the city unto them, and give him a place, that he may dwell among them" (Josh 20:4). The rebellious son would be brought "unto the elders of his city, and unto the gate of his place" (Deut 21: 19). How sad it is to read "and Lot sat in the gate of Sodom" (Gen 19:1), his testimony for God non-existent and his family ruined.

If the house of God is the gate of heaven, then it is the place of divine government, divine administration and divine rule. Man's thoughts, ways and innovations have no place there. The practical outworking of this solemn truth is

that every local assembly of God's people is nothing less than an outpost of divine rule in a thoroughly godless world. In just the same way that a Roman colony in a foreign land was a place where the rule, currency, customs and language of Rome were observed, so a local assembly, house of God in character, is a colony of heaven upon earth. It is a place where divine rule is acknowledged and the precious twin truths of the Headship and Lordship of Christ are not only taught but practised. For men to tamper with divine order, and displace it with their own notions of what is right and suitable, is nothing short of breathtaking arrogance, absolute folly and the provocation of God to move in judgment against them. Submission to divine order, as revealed in the word of God, is acknowledgment that the house of God is truly "the gate of heaven".

Day 4

THE PLACE OF DIVINE TESTIMONY

Genesis 28:10-22

It would not be an exaggeration to say that Jacob owed his life to the stones he set up as a pillar at Bethel. The desert can kill a man with its heat during the day and with its cold during the night. As he settled for the night, Jacob would have taken stones about the size of his head, or slightly larger, stones that had absorbed the heat of the sun all through the day. As the sun set and the night air became suddenly and dangerously cold, Jacob would draw the stones close into his body so that their heat might keep him warm and alive. His subsequent dream and the realisation that God had not only preserved him but also brought him to His house, prompted Jacob to raise a pillar of testimony in that place. It might seem from a reading of verses 18 and 22 that there was only one stone involved but, in the same way that we might speak of a house being built of a lovely Cotswold stone, meaning the kind of stone rather than its number, so the stone that Jacob used was singular in kind but multiple in number. Hence "the stone" was used "for his pillows" in verse 18.

The stones of the pillar were the stones of the pillows, teaching us that Jacob's testimony was that on which he rested. Thus the house of God was a place of divine testimony, the pillar drawing attention not only to the place but also to the character of the God of that place. The pillar marked God's house (v.22) and testified to Jacob's personal experience of His goodness and grace. Having raised the pillar of testimony, Jacob then did two further things. He "poured oil upon the top of it. And he called the name of that place Beth-el" (vv.18-19).

There is practical instruction for us in these things. A feature of the house of God is that it is a place of testimony to divine grace, and every local assembly should, therefore, be a centre for the presentation of the Gospel. The church at Antioch was the first proper New Testament assembly, in that it was made up of both Jews and Gentiles saved by the grace of God. It had been planted as the result of the eager testimony of believers who had been "scattered abroad upon the persecution that arose about Stephen" (Acts 11:19) and who travelled "preaching the word" and "preaching the Lord Jesus" (11:19-20). Such preaching, in the power of the Holy Spirit (typified in the pouring of oil upon the pillar of testimony) resulted in souls being saved, an assembly being established, and the disciples being "called Christians first in Antioch" (11:26).

Day 5

THE PLACE OF DIVINE LIGHT

Genesis 28:10-22

It is interesting to note that the place Jacob named "Beth-el", "was called Luz at the first" (Gen 28:19). It is possible that Jacob slept amongst the ruins of an old city that had borne that name. The meaning of the word "Luz" is 'almond tree', and as we explore the significance of that name we learn more of the features of the house of God.

The gold lampstand that shed its gentle light in the holy place of the tabernacle is described as having "Three bowls made after the fashion of almonds in one branch, a knop and a flower; and three bowls made like almonds in another branch, a knop and a flower: so throughout the six branches going out of the candlestick. And in the candlestick were four bowls made like almonds, his knops, and his flowers" (Exod 37:19-20). We should note that this lovely piece of furniture in the tabernacle was not a candlestick but a lampstand. A candlestick is simply a receptacle for a candle, and has no part in the process of producing light. The lampstand in the tabernacle, however, had bowls in the shape of almonds into which olive oil was poured and, from them, light emanated to bring the beauty and order of the house of God into relief. The oil, as always in relation to the tabernacle and its service, speaks of the Holy Spirit whose gracious ministry is to shed divine light on divine things so that they might be seen and appreciated by a priestly people.

The Lord Jesus, speaking to His own in the upper room, taught them "the Comforter, which is the Holy Ghost, whom the Father will send in my name, he shall teach you all things, and bring all things to your remembrance, whatsoever I have said unto you" (John 14:26). Thus the Gospel records were given to us through the inspiration of the Spirit.

Later in the same discourse the Lord said "But when the Comforter is come, whom I will send unto you from the Father, even the Spirit of truth, which proceedeth from the Father, he shall testify of me" (15:26). So through the inspired writing of the book of the Acts, and the epistles, the person and work of the Lord Jesus in relation to the church is recorded.

Then, in John chapter 16, the Saviour said "Howbeit when he, the Spirit of truth, is come, he will guide you into all truth … and he will shew you things to come" (16:13). The Scripture record was filled up by the apostle John who, guided by the Holy Spirit, gave us the last of the Gospels, the last of the epistles and the final word of prophesy in the Revelation.

The house of God is illuminated by divine light as the Holy Spirit graciously reveals Christ "in all the scriptures" (Luke 24:27).

Day 6

THE PLACE OF DIVINE LIFE

Genesis 28:10-22; Numbers 17:1-13

As well as being associated with light, the almond tree ("Luz") is linked with life. The events recorded in Numbers 16 make very sombre reading and, by the end of that chapter, more than 15,000 of the children of Israel are lying dead in the wilderness. Such is the outcome of rebellion and murmuring against God. In chapter 17 the matter of who is to bear priestly responsibility in the nation will be settled once and for all. Would the Levites, discontent with their own dignified office, presume upon the priesthood also? (Num 16: 9-10). If so, God will not only visit His wrath upon the pretenders and make the earth to swallow them up, but He will also destroy with a plague those who subsequently murmur. But, if God will judge in His wrath that which dishonours Him, He will also show in His grace how His people may please Him. Thus, in Numbers 17, God commands something to be done that will "quite take away their murmurings from me, that they die not" (17:10). Truly, judgment is "his strange work" (Isa 28:21).

"And the LORD spake unto Moses, saying, … take of every one of them a rod according to the house of their fathers … write thou every man's name upon his rod … lay them up in the tabernacle … and … the man's rod, whom I shall choose, shall blossom: and I will make to cease from me the murmurings of the children of Israel … and … on the morrow Moses went into the tabernacle of witness; and, behold, the rod of Aaron … was budded, and brought forth buds, and bloomed blossoms, and yielded almonds" (Num 17:1-2, 4-5, 8).

It was "on the morrow" that Moses beheld a wonderful foreshadowing of the resurrection life of the Lord Jesus. The dead rod with Aaron's name upon it had lain still and quiet all through the night, lying in the darkness alongside the tokens of Israel's rebellion. But all was under the watchful eye of God and, in the light of a new morning, Aaron's rod "budded, and brought forth buds, and bloomed blossoms, and yielded almonds". Resurrection life! What a glorious vindication of Israel's high priest! And how should that great truth remind us, today, that in the "house of God" we serve a risen Saviour whose resurrection life we share. The church is not an organisation, it is an organism, possessed of divine life. Aaron's rod would subsequently be kept in the ark (Heb 9:4), figuratively "hid with Christ". "If ye then be risen with Christ, seek those things which are above, where Christ sitteth on the right hand of God. Set your affection on things above, not on things on the earth. For ye are dead, and your life is hid with Christ in God" (Col 3:1-3).

Day 7

THE PLACE OF DIVINE LEADERSHIP

Genesis 28:10-22; Numbers 17:1-13; 1 Samuel 8:1-22

We must understand that spiritual leadership is not based upon politics but priesthood. In their dealings with other nations Israel had a king to lead them. In their dealings with God, however, they were led by priestly men. The sad thing about Israel's monarchy is that it came into being through the failure of its priests. What dark days spread over the land when blind Eli's wicked sons abused their priestly office! Did a glimmer of light show when godly Samuel "opened the doors of the house of the Lord"? (1 Sam 3:15). Would there be an early fulfilment of God's promise "I will raise me up a faithful priest, that shall do according to that which is in mine heart and in my mind: and I will build him a sure house; and he shall walk before mine anointed for ever"? (2: 35). Alas, no. "It came to pass, when Samuel was old, that he made his sons judges over Israel … and his sons walked not in his ways, but turned aside after lucre, and took bribes, and perverted judgment" (8:1, 3). Divine order was not upheld and, consequently, the people demanded a king. Eli's failure to censure his sons became Samuel's failure, warning us that men do think differently in old age from the way in which they once thought. Determination to cling to perceived position in old age, and to manoeuvre unqualified men into a place of leadership on the grounds of family ties, has been the cause of so much distress amongst the saints over the years.

Distress also comes when fleshly men challenge those who are rightfully leading in the house of God. Such was the situation in Numbers 16. The abundant fruitfulness of Aaron's rod was not only the vindication of him as high priest standing before God, it was also the confirmation of his authority in standing before the people. The authority that was challenged was that of the priestly family, and divine order in the house was the issue. The challenge to Moses and Aaron was rightly identified to Korah, "Both thou and all thy company are gathered together against the Lord" (Num 16:11). The nation's insistence on a king caused God to say to Samuel "they have not rejected thee, but they have rejected me, that I should not reign over them" (1 Sam 8:7). Leadership in the house of God is by divine appointment alone, and is to be recognised by every believer. "Obey them that have the rule over you, and submit yourselves: for they watch for your souls, as they that must give account …" (Heb 13:17).

PHIL COULSON

Week 38

7 SAYINGS FROM THE CROSS

Matthew 27:46; Mark 15:34; Luke 23:33-46; John 19:25-30

Introduction

Perhaps the most precious words in Scripture are the seven recorded occasions when the Lord Jesus spoke from the cross. They form a wonderful pattern, their order displaying something of His perfect character, and offering comfort and encouragement to His people.

Their pattern is similar to many of the other sevens of the Bible. Matthew and Mark record only the central cry, "My God, My God, why hast thou forsaken me"; it alone is recorded twice. It comes at the close of three hours of darkness and declares the words of **the Sin-bearer**, abandoned by God as He "bore our sins" alone. In contrast to this Luke records the first and last sayings, "Father forgive them…" and "Father into thy hands I commend my spirit". How appropriate the sayings begin and end with the words of **the Son** who is "ever in the bosom of the Father". Luke also records the second saying, to the dying thief, which seems to match the second last, "it is finished", recorded by John. In both of these we hear the words of **the Saviour**, confirming salvation to an individual and completing the work of salvation for the "whosoever". John also records the two sayings on either side of the central cry; these are the words of **the perfect Servant** as he completes His final responsibilities, firstly His last domestic duties as He provides for His mother, committing her to "that disciple … whom he loved", and then fulfilling Scripture as he cries "I thirst".

The chronological order is also most appropriate as the Lord Jesus speaks on behalf of His enemies, a dying thief and His mother, before ever He refers to His own situation. Truly He looked not on His own things but also on the things of others.

The sayings also demonstrate His ability to sympathise with us, as He is wronged, encouraged, separated from loved ones, asks "why", suffers, completes His work and even goes through death. Well might the Hebrew writer proclaim "we have not an high priest which cannot be touched with the feeling of our infirmities…" (Heb 4:15).

Day 1

"*Father, forgive them* … "

Luke 23:26-37

How appropriate that the opening words of the Lord on the cross are addressed to His Father. In Luke's Gospel His first recorded words refer to His "Fathers business" (Luke 2:49), and His last recorded words in this Gospel refer to "the promise of my Father" (24:49). Yet while the object of His words, His Father, is no surprise, perhaps the subjects are. The Saviour prays for the people carrying out the greatest injustice there ever has been, or ever will be. It is from this that we can learn some very practical lessons.

The one who asks forgiveness for His enemies is the one who instructs us to "forgive one another". Sometimes we find this hard if we believe we have been wronged, but never could we be as wronged as was the Lord, whom they "hated … without a cause". We do well to reflect on this as we hold grudges and bitterness against each other, never mind our enemies.

Then we must remember that these words are indeed a prayer. Prayer is sadly a much undervalued form of service. Maybe someone is reading these words and you are discouraged as you can no longer carry out the service you once did. Perhaps ill health or advanced years prevent you from tract work, children's work, preaching, giving hospitality or making things for the Lord's people? Well, here is a great service still open to you. Many servants of God and local assemblies owe much to the prayers of saints who are prevented from other service. The Lord had healed, preached, comforted, raised the dead, cast out demons and "gone about doing good". But now those avenues of service have closed, so He prays. In fact while on earth He tells us that He had the power "to forgive sins" but now, "lifted up" from the earth, He asks the Father to forgive them.

A question arises as to who exactly are the "them". The context, the fact that "they know not what they do" (notice this does not remove the need for forgiveness), and the subsequent events of Acts chapters 2 and 3 lead us to conclude it is the people of the nation of Israel who are in view. In these passages we see this prayer answered when, in response to Peter's preaching, thousands of that guilty company repent (an essential prerequisite) and receive forgiveness. Notice this takes place sometime after the Lord's death and return to heaven. Maybe someone today has prayed for loved ones for many years and still awaits an answer. Well, be encouraged that the answer to your prayers may be like that of the Lord's – after your home call.

Day 2

"Verily I say unto thee, To day shalt thou

be with me in paradise"

Luke 23:32-43

The incident that precedes these words, like others in this series of seven, involves the fulfilling of Old Testament Scripture. Isaiah wrote prophetically of the Lord "… he was numbered with the transgressors" (Isa 53:12). Indeed, here we see the Holy One being crucified between, and with, two common criminals. However, in addition we see a little fulfilment of the previous verse in Isaiah 53, "He shall see of the travail of his soul and shall be satisfied …" The words of the Saviour confirm the eternal security of the most hopeless and helpless of sinners. The dying thief had no past virtues to commend him and no future to offer making amends. He is stripped of all reliance on self or others, so he casts himself in faith on the mercy of the man on the centre tree. What consolation, in the midst of suffering, this must have given the blessed One "who for the joy that was set before him endured the cross, despising the shame …" (Heb 12:2).

What an example also of the sovereignty of God. Only moments before, this man had joined his fellow and the rest of the throng railing upon the Saviour. Suddenly, we see a complete change in an instant. He had witnessed no great miracle nor heard any great sermon, other than the words of the first cry, but nevertheless a complete transformation occurs. Surely this can only be the intervention of the Sovereign. Notice the remarkable understanding the man has, in his own few short statements. He clearly appreciates the judgment of God and his own personal guilt. On the person of Christ he acknowledges His deity; sinlessness; Lordship; resurrection; Kingship; second coming and ability to save. How true the words written by John to new born saints in Christ; "… ye know all things" (1 John 2:20).

Finally, we can enjoy the way in which the Saviour's response exceeds the sinner's request, "Lord, remember me when thou comest into thy kingdom". The man had asked to be remembered, but the Saviour says he would be "with me", better than merely being remembered. The man had looked to a then distant coming, but the Saviour assures him of blessing "today". The man hoped for prospects in a future earthly kingdom, but the Saviour promises him "paradise". Much has been debated as to exactly where and what this paradise is, as with the dwelling place of the dead in Christ now. We would do well to simply rest on the truth illustrated in this incident, and confirmed by later

Scripture: for the dying thief, as for departed loved ones, it is "with Christ" and it is "far better". What a wonderful Saviour we have!

Day 3

"WOMAN, BEHOLD THY SON! ...

BEHOLD THY MOTHER!"

John 19:25-27

Our narrative now moves to John's Gospel for this beautiful incident which we will consider from three standpoints.

First, we see the Servant's perfection as He fulfils His responsibilities to this blessed woman. As a babe He had graciously entrusted Himself to her care; as a boy of twelve, in Luke 2, He had subjected Himself to Joseph and to her; as a man, in John 2, at the commencement of His public ministry, He had responded to her request at the wedding in Cana. Now, on the cross, His provision is in perfect keeping with Scripture. He demonstrates obedience to the fifth commandment as He honours His mother, something He had condemned the Jews for failing to do in Mark 7:9-13. He goes beyond the instructions Paul would write in 1 Timothy 5:3-15, as He provides for this widow. His brethren, her sons, did not yet believe, so He entrusts her to John the beloved disciple.

Second, it is recorded of the men "they all forsook him, and fled" (Mark 14:50), but here we see the devotion of Mary and, indeed, this little group of four women who took a stand by the cross. How in keeping this is with John's Gospel. In chapter 2 He performed His first sign for His mother and an unnamed bride; in chapter 11 He performs His seventh sign by raising the brother of two distraught sisters. In chapter 4 He reveals new truth regarding worship to a Samaritan woman and, in chapter 11, does the same regarding resurrection to Martha. It was Mary His mother who most appreciated His life, and she confirmed it with the words "whatsoever he saith unto you, do it" (John 2:5). Another Mary prepared for His death and burial by anointing Him in chapter 12, and another, Mary Magdalene, sees Him on resurrection ground in chapter 20.

Finally note His provision for John. John too had forsaken Him in the garden, but now recovery is confirmed as, standing by the cross, in the right place at the right time, he is entrusted with this responsibility. Mary would tell John much of the unrevealed life of the Lord Jesus, perhaps contributing to John's writing that the world itself could not contain the books if all was written, and his reference to the "hidden manna" (Rev 2:17). Mary is removed from the scene, before the hours of darkness, to John's "own house", thus sparing her from further distress. One day, John would suffer great distress as his beloved brother James would be murdered (Acts 12:2), but the Saviour had graciously entrusted to him one who could sympathise from her own experience. How beautifully all things work together when He is in control!

Day 4

"ELI, ELI, LAMA SABACHTHANI?

THAT IS TO SAY, MY GOD, MY GOD,

WHY HAST THOU FORSAKEN ME?"

Matthew 27:45-49; Mark 15:33-36; Luke 23:44-45

When approaching this central cry, we must realise at the outset that we are on holy ground and cannot fully enter into these events. Up to this point man has been highly involved in the events of the crucifixion. Wicked men have accused, tried, sentenced and tormented the Saviour. All the words spoken by Him so far have concerned men and women. But now the world is shrouded in darkness, mankind is shut out and His words are between Him and His God. Even the language used is foreign to the hearers and is interpreted for us, while they are kept in confusion thinking He called for Elijah.

It is not the first time God has altered the Sun's light. In Joshua 10 the Sun had stood still while a great victory was won. In 2 Kings 20 it had been moved back ten degrees to confirm healing. In Exodus 10 darkness had descended on Egypt as God delivered His people, but there was no darkness in Goshen where Israel dwelt. But here we believe the darkness, from noon to 3pm, extends everywhere as Christ brings about victory, healing and deliverance from sin for a fallen creation.

This cry had been clearly prophesied in Psalm 22, where the accuracy is so astounding. It details that the cry was in the time of day, but the season, or circumstances, of night. The psalm also gives the key to the event: the holiness of God (v.3). This is not, as some have said, an "orphan cry"; the relationship of Father and Son is not in view, but that of God and the Man who is bearing sin. The holy God forsakes the Sin-bearer as He is "made ... sin (sin offering) for us" (2 Cor 5:21). Having suffered at the hands of man, He now suffers at the hand of God as prophesied in Isaiah 53:4-5.

Here Christ experiences in these hours of darkness the abandonment which we, who deserved the second death of eternal judgment, will never experience if we are trusting in Him. Here God "spared not his own Son, but delivered him up for us all" (Rom 8:32), and the Saviour "bare our sins in his own body on the tree" (1 Pet 2:24). He who was so near was forsaken so that we who were far off might be brought near. The Holy One was made sin so that sinners like us could be made righteous.

Thankfully we will never be called upon to enter into these extremities, but perhaps in our circumstances there is something of comfort from His example.

Maybe today some reader finds themselves in seemingly inexplicable circumstances and would cry "Why?" from a burdened heart. Remember that the Saviour knows better than any what it is to cry "Why?".

Day 5

"I THIRST"

John 19:28-30

In keeping with the character of John's Gospel, it alone carries no record of the hours of darkness. The words "after this" pass over those hours and bring us to the fifth cry, "I thirst". As outlined in our previous study the Lord Jesus suffered at the hand of a holy God to atone for sin. This cry now shows the reality and extreme nature of his physical sufferings at the hands of men detailed in Psalm 22:15. Now, while the present writer does not believe these sufferings atoned for sin (that would infer man played a part in the atonement), he does believe these physical sufferings were essential and real. Like the emotional and psychological suffering caused by man's hatred and rejection, they enable Him to sympathise with us and be a "merciful and faithful high priest" (Heb 2:17).

This cry was "that the scripture might be fulfilled" (John 19:28) and, of course, there is a specific Scripture, Psalm 69:21, in view. However, the manner of fulfilling shows that this One fulfils all Scripture perfectly. The Lord had had two previous opportunities to fulfil this Scripture. In Matthew 27:34 (and Mark 15:23) we find He had rejected the stupefying mixture of vinegar (wine) and gall just before the crucifixion, in keeping with priestly restrictions (Lev 10:9). In Luke 23:36 the soldiers, mocking Him with a king's regalia, also offered Him wine prior to the hours of darkness. But, "Jesus knowing that all things were now accomplished", sin having been dealt with, the greatest *Priestly* act completed in the hours of darkness, only now will He say "I thirst". Only now does the rejected *King* shows He is also "that *Prophet*" and perfectly fulfils the Scripture. If the detail is so important to Him, should it not be to us? Should we not also ensure that all Scripture is adhered to, in detail?

Having considered this saying in relation to His **Sufferings** and the **Scriptures**, we will now suggest it might also be **Symbolic**. Every other mention of thirst in John's Gospel is, in fact, symbolic of something more than just physical thirst (see John 4:14; 6:35; 7:37). So what did our Saviour thirst for? Perhaps the answer is found in Psalm 42. Verse 7, "Deep calleth unto deep at the noise of thy waterspouts: all thy waves and thy billows are gone over me" makes it clear the psalm refers to the Lord Jesus. Verse 2, "My soul thirsteth for God, for the living God" shows that His thirst is for God. In John 13 He tells the disciples He is going to "His Father's house", but it is going to be by way of the cross. Now, the separation of the hours of darkness over, He thirsts "for the living God" as the moment of His returning home draws near.

Day 6

"IT IS FINISHED"

John 19:28-30

John closes his account of the crucifixion with this, the sixth, saying. Before considering it further, it is perhaps worthwhile making clear what it does not mean. Some have tried to suggest it refers to the vinegar just received. This is a ridiculous suggestion which, apart from anything else, can be dismissed grammatically. Others think of the last feeble words of a man whose life was being taken. However, we must remember the Lord's life was not taken, it was given (John 10:18). In addition to this, it appears that while only directly recorded in John, this saying is referred to in the other Gospels where they record Him crying "with a loud voice" prior to giving up His spirit. No, this is not the whimpering last breath of a dying man, but the triumphant cry of victorious accomplishment!

Throughout this Gospel we are reminded that Christ always had a specific task before Him. This great work was announced by John the Baptist when the Lord first appeared in His public ministry, and John said "Behold the Lamb of God, which taketh away the sin of the world" (John 1:29). This confirmed the angelic utterance before His birth, "thou shalt call his name JESUS: for he shall save his people from their sins" (Matt 1:21). The Lord Himself acknowledged his task with the words "My meat is to do the will of him that sent me, and to finish his work" (John 4:34). He relentlessly "set his face" to pursue this work and, in His prayer on the eve of the crucifixion, anticipated its completion: "… I have finished the work which thou gavest me to do …" (John 17:4). But only now, after the hours of darkness and the fulfilling of Scripture, could He cry "it is finished", as "all things were now accomplished". Hebrews 12:2 confirms that the work of the "author and finisher of our faith" has been accepted, and He "… is set down at the right hand of the throne of God".

These wondrous words have significance for all concerned with the events of Calvary. For Christ, we have seen they confirm a completed task. For God, they announce His satisfaction with what is done; He requires nothing more, but will accept nothing less. For the wicked one, it signifies his defeat, "the prince of this world is judged" (John 16:11), although the sentence still remains to be carried out.

Finally, for all who trust in Christ, it means we have finished with our own efforts, finished with our old life, finished with sin. We are now resting everything on the glorious completed work of the One who cried in victory from the cross, "it is finished"!

Day 7

"Father into thy hands I commend my spirit"

Luke 23:46-56

For the final cry we return to Luke's Gospel where the first two were also recorded. As we noticed, the cries, like all His words in Luke, begin and end by addressing, or referring to, His Father. How sweet these final words must have been as He anticipated returning to His Father's house.

Notice He commends His spirit into "the hands" of His Father. In the hours of darkness He had been judged on account of sin at the hands of a holy God, but now He anticipates the loving hands of His Father. Similarly, His body also would experience a change of hands. It had been roughly treated at the hands of wicked men. It would now be taken down and wrapped by the loving hands of a "good" and "just" man, Joseph of Arimathaea.

Our passage mentions His spirit and body, but what of His soul? The Lord Jesus, as to His manhood, like all mankind, was tri-partite, that is, body, soul and spirit, with all three referred to in Scripture. Some quote Psalm 16: 10, repeated in Acts 2:27, "… thou wilt not leave my soul in hell (Sheol), neither wilt thou suffer thine Holy One to see corruption", to suggest that the Lord's soul descended to Sheol while His body was in the tomb. However, the present writer concurs with the authorities, including the RV in Psalm 16 which renders the phrase "to Sheol", who suggest the idea is 'in the direction of hell'. The soul and spirit, though distinguishable, appear to be generally inseparable, except by the governmental action of God (Heb 4:12). In the previous cry recorded in Luke, the Saviour assures the dying thief he would be "with me in paradise". Here now is the fulfilment of this as the Lord commends His spirit (and soul) to His Father. This is the pattern for all His people; the body is laid to rest awaiting resurrection, but the believer, soul and spirit, goes to be "with Christ", which is "far better". How blessed, should we be called upon to go through death, as with many of the other experiences seen in the seven sayings, to know that He has been before us.

Finally though, we see that He "commends" his spirit. In this He is unique. These words could never be cried by another; only He could "commend" Himself. We, like Stephen, may ask "receive my spirit" (Acts 7:59), but in ourselves we have nothing to commend us. He, however, as the centurion in our verses declares, is "a righteous man". Well might we, along with the people, His acquaintances, and the women that followed Him, be found "beholding these things" (Luke 23:49).

Alastair Sinclair

Week 39

7 *"PRECIOUS"* THINGS IN THE EPISTLES OF PETER

Introduction

Peter uses the word "precious" on seven occasions in his two epistles and it can be legitimately translated in several different ways. However, in the Greek language the force of the word is the same wherever it is used. It has the idea of that which is costly or of great value and, in using the word, the writer implies that he has had some personal experience which has prompted him to appreciate the value of what he is writing about. As we look closely at those things Peter describes as precious, we may well be able to identify certain experiences and situations in his own life which have led to his practical understanding of their value, and caused him to draw on them when looking back both to the Gospel period and his later service for God after Pentecost. He uses these experiences to assist him in fulfilling the shepherd ministry given to him by the Saviour to "strengthen thy brethren" (Luke 22: 32) and "tend the flock" (John 21:5-17; 1 Pet 5:1-4). This is a pattern for our own Christian lives, because one of the reasons we go through circumstances of severe trial and testing is so that we might use the experience gained to be a comfort and encouragement to others (2 Cor 1:4). It is God's strategy to use saints to minister to saints and, in His sovereignty, every circumstance of daily life is designed to equip us for that goal.

As we go through these seven references it is also worth comparing the things that Peter deems to be of value with those things which mean most to us. This will enable us to examine them in the light of that future review at the judgement seat of Christ (1 Cor 3:12-13). Because Peter wrote by divine inspiration, his value judgements are God's value judgements. This should provoke us to serious self-examination, for His standard must be the measurement of all that we say, think and do.

Peter is not the first inspired writer to use the word "precious". We discover in Luke 12:7 that the people of God are of "more value (precious) than many sparrows"; indeed, the psalmist records that "Precious in the sight of the Lord is the death of his saints" (Ps 116:15). We learn from the Old Testament as a whole that Israel is especially precious to God (Isa 43: 4), a truth confirmed by other clear Scriptures which teach that the nation still features in His plans for the future. But the climax of all preciousness is Christ Himself. We shall see later that the Lord Jesus is pre-eminently precious to God, when Peter quotes from Isaiah 28:16 describing Him as "a precious corner stone". All God's purposes find their centre and their fulfilment in His Son.

Day 1

"THE TRIAL OF YOUR FAITH, BEING MUCH MORE PRECIOUS THAN OF GOLD THAT PERISHETH ..."

1 Peter 1:6-9

Peter commences his first epistle by reminding the suffering saints of the *past* (1:2), looks to the *future* (v.3) and encourages them by highlighting their *present* resource (v.5). What wonderful assurance it is for the saints of God to know that, not only does He have the power to save (Heb 7:25) but also to keep and, ultimately, to present us "faultless before the presence of his glory with exceeding joy" (Jude 24). Having reminded those scattered believers of their inheritance both past and future, he acknowledges their present sufferings and the trial of their faith, which is precious.

Rejoicing in suffering (v.6). J.B.Nicholson describes this as "one of the great paradoxes of the Christian faith". That is to say, that gladness can co-exist side by side with sadness. It is also one of the hardest principles to put into practice! Peter acknowledges that trials are not easy; indeed, the word "heaviness" acknowledges they are difficult (see Matt 26:37; 1 Thess 4:13). Joy can only be achieved by faith that God will fulfil His promises (v.8) and the understanding that our afflictions are a preparation for glory (Rom 8:17-18). "While we may not be able to rejoice as we look around in our trials, we can rejoice as we look ahead" (Wiersbe).

Refining in suffering (v.7). The refining process, to remove the dross and impurities from the raw gold or silver ore by heating it in the furnace, has a two-fold function; to prove its genuineness and to reveal its value. When faith has been put into the red-hot crucible of trials the result is a treasure much

more valuable than gold. God uses trials to prove the reality of our faith and to remove from our life that which is dross (Job 23:10; Prov 25:4). It has been said that the goldsmith of old would know that the impurities had all gone when he could see his face reflected in the molten gold! It is God's purpose that the beauty of His Son be reflected in the lives of suffering saints.

Resignation in suffering (v.9). We do not give in, but intelligently accept that the suffering we go through now will end one day when the final instalment of our salvation is revealed in accordance with God's great plan (vv.4-5). It is one of the great principles of Scripture that suffering always precedes glory (Rom 8:18; Heb 2:9; 1 Pet 1:11), and we can experience, even in the midst of suffering, a taste of that future glory by "loving Christ (v.8), trusting Christ (v.8), rejoicing in Christ (v.8), and receiving from Christ (vv.9-12)" (Wiersbe).

Day 2

"NOT REDEEMED WITH CORRUPTIBLE THINGS …

BUT WITH THE PRECIOUS BLOOD OF CHRIST"

1 Peter 1:13-23

The second "precious" thing Peter refers to in his epistles is the "precious blood of Christ". This he also contrasts with the passing worth of gold or silver which, ultimately, gets tarnished and destroyed. As an apostle, Peter appreciated that what he had in Christ was far more valuable than this world's wealth. To the lame man who asked for alms at the temple gate he gladly gave something better than financial support; the power of Christ to heal and save (Acts 3:6). If the opening section of the epistle focuses mainly on the faith of the persecuted saints and their walk in hope, then this section emphasises their fidelity, and their walk in holiness. What can these verses teach us?

Present sanctification (vv.13-17). How often it is said that 'privilege brings responsibility'? Paul highlights in writing to the Ephesians, where he gives the reason for our election, "that we should be holy and without blame before him" (Eph 1:4). Peter teaches that the recipe for a holy life is: knowing God's *will* (v.13), obeying God's *word* (v.16) and doing God's *work* (v.17).

Past sacrifice (vv.18-20). It has been said that the Lord's sacrifice for us is the highest motive for holy living. How often have the words of verses 18-19 been quoted at the Lord's Supper – yet what do they really mean to us? Have we become so familiar with them that they have lost their freshness and become stale and routine? Has the substitutionary work of Christ ceased to be "precious"? Can we really still sing "the blood has always precious been, 'tis precious now to me" and mean it? We were in bondage to sin yet, unlike a slave of old, we could not pay for our freedom. The ransom price could only be paid by the "blood of Jesus Christ his Son", which "cleanseth us from all sin" (1 John

1:7). He was God's lamb, not only without blemish in His holy life, but also without spot. He is absolutely perfect and pure, without and within.

Prospective salvation (vv.21-23). Looking back, Peter shows us the *redeeming work of the Son*, not an accident but a divine appointment (Acts 2: 23); the present *refining work of the Holy Spirit* who indwells every believer (Rom 8:9) and who will, if allowed by us, use the word of God which should be dwelling richly in the heart of every saint (Col 3:16), to purify the soul; and the *rewarding work of the Father*, who raised the Lord Jesus from the dead and gave Him glory, has opened the way for each believer, through faith, to approach Him, knowing full and eternal life in Christ.

Day 3

"A LIVING STONE, DISALLOWED INDEED OF MEN,

BUT CHOSEN OF GOD, AND PRECIOUS"

1 Peter 2:4-10

In this little section Peter uses the word "precious" three times, on each occasion referring to the Lord Jesus, once by quoting from Isaiah 28:16. The Lord Jesus is precious to God (v.6), and to those who believe (v.7). Peter uses the metaphor of a stone to bring out some lovely truths about Christ. By association with Him, we who believe become living stones in that great "spiritual house", the Church, of which the Lord Jesus Christ is the "head of the corner". Peter seems to be teaching something that he himself once learnt from the Saviour when he confessed that Jesus was "the Christ, the Son of the living God" (Matt 16:16), and the Lord responded that Peter was a stone who would be one of the building blocks of the Church. In verse 5 Peter uses the same word for "built up" that the Lord used for "build" in Matthew 16:18.

"A living stone" (v.4). Peter has already referred to a living hope (1:3) and a living word (1:23). Now he speaks, not of an inanimate dead stone, but of One who lives in the power of an endless life (Heb 7:16). The stone would remind us of that which is reliable, true and faithful (Rev 19:11).

"disallowed" (rejected) (v.4). It seems incredible that this "living stone" was discounted by men, having been tested and deemed to be of no value. Thirty pieces of silver, the price of a slave, was their estimation of Him. How sad that today men are still prepared to build the fabric of their lives on a foundation of sand and will not turn to the only solid, sure foundation for human existence.

"chosen" (v.4). The Messiah, elected by God, not as one out of many, but as the only One who could accomplish the divine work and occupy the place of divine honour. He is the chosen servant of Jehovah (Matt 12:18).

"precious" (v.4). As far as God is concerned there is no one like His beloved Son. The word here in verse 4 means 'held in honour', and the same word is found in Luke 7:2 in relation to the centurion's servant. When used in verse 7, the word means 'much more precious', and is used of the "very costly" spikenard ointment in John 12:3. We know something of what Christ means to God, and Peter also appreciated that (Acts 2: 22-36), but the challenge today is what does He really mean to us? Can we honestly say that He is our 'preciousness'? If so, we'll accept God's valuation of Him and obey, love, honour and serve Him until He comes to take us home to glory.

Day 4

"A CHIEF CORNER STONE, ELECT, PRECIOUS: AND HE

THAT BELIEVETH ON HIM SHALL NOT BE CONFOUNDED"

1 Peter 2:4-9

The Jewish builders rejected Christ but that did not stop God from laying His choice Stone in Zion. Indeed, in spite of them, He has founded and built His church comprising those upon whom He has set His love and mercy in Christ, those who, through grace, now constitute His people (Hos 2:23; Matt 21:42-43). These are the people who count the Lord Jesus as 'precious'. In verse 9 Peter outlines four great facts about them which would be of great encouragement in their period of suffering.

"A chosen generation (race)". As Adam was the federal head of the human race, here a new race has been formed with Christ as its Head. Since the members of this new humanity are chosen by God's love and grace, all human pride is excluded (John 15:16; Eph 1:4-6).

"A royal priesthood". Unlike those in the Old Testament priesthood, all New Testament believers function as priests. This is a spiritual privilege (v.5; Heb 13:15) and we exercise it as kings (Rev 1:6). God wanted His people Israel to become "a kingdom of priests" (Exod 19:6) yet they failed. What an encouragement to despised saints that, like the Lord Jesus, we bear the titles of both king and priest! As holy priests we offer up to God; as royal priests we show forth His character to the world.

"An holy nation". Our priesthood is also to be holy (v.5). As the children of God we have been "set apart to belong exclusively to God" (Wiersbe). This expression parallels the Lord's description of Israel in Exodus 19: 6. Israel failed again in this as they wanted to break down the God-given walls of separation which made them distinct from the other nations. We must ever remember that "our citizenship is in heaven" (Phil 3:20) and that whilst we are "in the world", we are not "of" it (John 17:11,14).

"A peculiar people". This phrase is better translated 'a people for a possession', and it is linked with Ephesians 1:14 "which is an earnest of our inheritance unto the redemption of God's own possession, unto the praise of His glory" (RV). This gives a clearer understanding of what Peter was saying. Used also in the OT and translated 'jewels' or 'special treasure', it "goes beyond the thought of 'peculiarity' to convey tones of the redemption, of singular value and beauty, and of affectionate possession" (Nicholson). So God's people are "a people for God to clasp to His heart, to live in His love, to dwell in His presence" (Lincoln).

Day 5

"A MEEK AND QUIET SPIRIT, WHICH IS IN

THE SIGHT OF GOD OF GREAT PRICE (PRECIOUS)"

1 Peter 3:1-7

This particular passage is included in our study of 'precious things' because the NKJV translates the expression "great price" relating to "a meek and quiet spirit" in verse 4 as "precious", and also because Peter's teaching is so antagonistic to twenty-first century thinking that it deserves our consideration. The same teaching which relates to governments and masters, Peter brings into the home, specifically dealing with wives married to unsaved husbands. However, these principles are applicable to all marital relationships today, providing very practical and necessary guidance.

Stridency versus submissiveness. "God has given to the man the place of headship, and it is His will that the woman should acknowledge the authority of the man" (McDonald). What does it mean for the wife to be in submission? Peter outlines two essential elements in marriage; obedience (v.6) and respect (v.2). One speaks of action (what the wife does) and the other of attitude (how she does it). Both are important, for "the absence of one will cancel out the effect of the other" (Adams). Of course, the husband's responsibility is so to act towards his wife that it will not be difficult for her to submit, and he should display those features of consideration, chivalry and companionship (v.7).

Cosmetics versus character. In verses 3 and 4 Peter is contrasting inner and outer beauty. One is artificial, something added, and the other is real, a result of a change within. What is truly valuable to God, and more likely to influence a husband, is inner character not external decoration. Of course, this does not mean that a woman should neglect her appearance, but her concentration should be on cultivating a quiet and gentle demeanour. Any godly husband will want in his wife what God wants, and not set too much store on external beauty.

Carer versus career. Interestingly, Peter uses Sarah as an example of what he is teaching. She obeyed Abraham calling him "lord", but Genesis 18:12 indicates that she did that "within herself" and not loudly so that all would hear. Women who follow her example are her "daughters", for "children should carry the family likeness" (McDonald). The influence of a godly mother is indispensable in a child's formative years because she can both teach, and exemplify, the truths which Peter describes. The need for making ends meet financially is readily understood, but Christian mothers are kindly urged to be at home for their children's sake whenever that is possible.

Day 6

"LIKE PRECIOUS FAITH"

2 Peter 1:1

Having spoken much about faith in his first epistle, Peter commences his second with the same subject. He teaches us that faith involves God's *person* (vv.1-2), His *power* (v.3) and His *promises* (v.4). It is a faith which is:

Obtained. This is an uncommon word which refers to something being obtained by lot. It is often translated "received" and can mean "attaining by divine will" (Macarthur). In the Scriptures we read that God, on occasions, did use the casting of lots as a way of revealing His will (Acts 1:17). Again Peter is emphasising that our faith in the Lord Jesus is not a result of personal effort, skill, worth or anything else to do with ourselves. Rather it is everything to do with His grace, and comes to us "through the righteousness of God and our Saviour Jesus Christ" (v.1).

Identical. The word for "like precious" was generally used to denote equality in rank, position, honour, standing, price or value. In biblical times it was often used of strangers and foreigners who were given equal citizenship in a city. In context it could have a two fold meaning, in that our standing with God is based upon a faith which has two great characteristics. First of all, it is the same as that of the apostles' centuries ago who had the wonderful privilege of talking, walking and sharing fellowship with the Lord (1 John 1:1). We do not have to see Him with our eyes to enjoy what they enjoyed, because through the written word we, by faith, can enter fully into "the knowledge of our Lord Jesus Christ" (v.8).

Second, it is the same kind of faith as that exercised by believing Jews in NT times. Peter himself was able to make this point to the church at Jerusalem when he rehearsed his experience at Joppa (Acts 11:1-18). The wonderful news that Gentiles had been gifted with the same faith made them glorify God saying "Then hath God also to the Gentiles granted repentance unto life".

There are no first and second-class Christians whether we think of spirituality, race or gender. All who are saved by the grace of God enjoy equal acceptance before Him. All have come, with an equally precious faith, into equally precious privileges.

Valuable. This is a faith which glorifies and honours God. Paul speaks of Abraham as being "strong in faith, giving glory to God" (Rom 4:20). To be saved by works would cast the spotlight on man's achievements, but a salvation received simply by faith magnifies the God who provided it.

Day 7

"… EXCEEDING GREAT AND PRECIOUS PROMISES"

2 Peter 1:4

As we conclude our series it is obvious that the apostle Peter liked the word "precious". In his epistles he has already brought before us "precious faith" (1 Pet 1:7); "precious blood" (1 Pet 1:19); "precious stone" (1 Pet 2:4,6); "precious saviour" (1 Pet 2:7); "precious beauty" (1 Pet 3:4); "like precious faith" (2 Pet 1:1) and now, "precious promises". John Bunyan once said that "the pathway of life is strewn so thickly with the promises of God that it is impossible to take one step without treading upon one of them". Peter, without listing any, states the character of these promises. They are:

Great. According to William McDonald, "it is estimated that there are at least 30,000 promises in the Bible", so they are certainly great in number. They are also great because of whom the promissory is, God Himself. We know that the promises of men are 'like glass, so easily broken', yet God must and will keep His promises whether they are to the nation of Israel (Rom 9: 4-5) or to us as the people of God today, for all His promises are bound up in the person of the Lord Jesus.

Valuable. The promises of God are precious to us in every circumstance of life. Here are some of them just to enjoy! He has promised us life, all blessings in the heavenlies, abundant grace upon grace, joy, strength, guidance, help, instruction, wisdom, the Holy Spirit, heaven, and eternal rewards. You can think of many more and they are all ours. No wonder Peter sees them as precious!

Ours. The purpose behind the promises, the purpose of God's goodness through Christ, is that we can become partakers of the divine nature. When we come to the Lord Jesus Christ we receive everything we need for life and godliness, we receive all the promises of God in time and eternity, and we become a partaker of God's nature (Gal 2:20; Col 1:27). The word "partaker" is 'koinonos', a word often translated as 'fellowship', meaning 'sharer' or 'partner'. We partake of God's life in us; we are partners in the same life.

There are various reasons why we may fail to keep our promises. We can forget, we may be unable to do what we have said, or we may wilfully change our mind. None of this can apply to our God. "For all the promises of God in him are yea, and in him Amen, unto the glory of God by us" (2 Cor 1:20). The promises of God never fail despite their astonishing abundance!

PAUL RICHARDSON

Week 40

7 EXHORTATIONS IN GENESIS TO "FEAR NOT"

Introduction

Fear is a very human emotion. It is something we all experience in varying degrees, from childhood days and on throughout life. Fear is that feeling of anxiety, distress, apprehension or alarm caused by impending danger, pain or loss. Sometimes our fears are unfounded, or the cause is quickly removed, and we feel a great sense of relief. On other occasions fear can become a heavy burden which affects both mind and body.

It was Adam who first experienced fear when, having sinned in the Garden of Eden, he tried to hide himself from the presence of God. His reason for such action is clearly given in Genesis 3:10, as he admits "I was afraid". He knew instinctively that his disobedience was a good reason to be fearful, as God walked to meet him in the cool of the day. Communion between God and man was broken. But there was no "fear not" of comfort and assurance on this occasion. Adam was brought face to face with the enormity of his deed, the far-reaching consequences of his sin, and the inevitable return to the dust from whence he came. Yet there was a glorious shaft of light which pierced through the fearful darkness. A promised Deliverer, the Seed of the woman, a Saviour; "A way back to God, from the dark paths of sin". A great plan of salvation whereby God could remain just (He would not compromise His holy character) yet, because of the work of Calvary, He could become "the justifier of him which believeth in Jesus" (Rom 3:26).

The plan of salvation, conceived in the eternal mind, motivated by divine love, assures us that God's heart goes out to fallen man. The psalmist David took comfort in the knowledge that "he knoweth our frame; he remembereth that we are dust" (Ps 103:14). And, because He is aware of our frailty, He whispers to His own in the anxieties of life – "fear not".

Of the seven occurrences in the book of Genesis, four times the voice of God is heard. Once, the words are spoken by Joseph's steward and, later, by Joseph himself; and once by the midwife to Rachel. On each occasion it is a ministry of assurance, of comfort and of promise. May we too hear His tender "fear not" in the trying circumstances of life.

Day 1

THE "FEAR NOT" OF DIVINE PROMISE

Genesis 14:17 - 15:6

Abram was facing a crisis. The great man of faith had a choice to make and weighty issues rested upon his decision. Abram had known the conflict of choice before. When the God of glory first appeared to him some years before, he had left the comfort of home, friends and family and took the journey as God directed, "not knowing whither he went" (Heb 11:8). The pathway had not been easy. He had abandoned city life to become a tent-dweller, moving from place to place. He had known famine in the land, suffered embarrassment in Egypt, and faced strife in his own family.

Lot, the nephew of Abram, had never journeyed with the conviction that so characterised the patriarch. Always a follower, never able to make a stand without Abram as his 'prop'. When he finally did make a decision for himself, it was to prove disastrous (Gen 13.11); and now he had become embroiled in the political conflict which engulfed the cities of the plain. He was taken captive with all his possessions, and little or no chance of recovery. Until, that is, word came to Abram. It is encouraging to note that although Lot and Abram had separated as a result of disputes between their servants, Abram maintained a constant interest in Lot's welfare. He could have taken a dismissive attitude and ignored Lot's plight but, no, he arms his own servants and, with just a handful of men, by God's grace a great victory is won.

Now in the moment of triumph, the crisis comes. Returning from the battle, Abram is met by the king of Sodom. As the victor in the battle, Abram had first claim on all the spoils of war. The king of Sodom, however, offers Abram a compromise which will remove his responsibility to the released captives, and ensure great material riches for him. A tempting prospect. It is significant that just at this moment another person appears, Melchisedec. He blesses Abram, and refreshes him with bread and wine. Thus strengthened and blessed, the choice is made; he refuses the offer from the godless king.

It is in light of this, when having turned away from a lucrative prospect, albeit one which would have offended his conscience, and with questions in his mind regarding the future, the word of the Lord comes to him "Fear not, Abram: I am thy shield", to protect against enemies both physical and spiritual, "and thy exceeding great reward". In contrast to the transient wealth offered by an earthly monarch, Abram can lay hold of the eternal promise of reward from the great "I am".

God never needed to repeat these words to Abram; he believed God and continued his pilgrim walk in the assurance of divine protection, provision and blessing.

Day 2

THE "FEAR NOT" OF DIVINE COMPASSION

Genesis 21:1-21

How wonderful are the ways of our God! Nothing was further from the mind of Hagar than the realisation that her circumstances would be used by the Spirit of God, through the apostle Paul, to illustrate God's great purposes of grace toward man (Gal 4:19-31) and to show that the law given at Sinai, just and good though it was, depended essentially on man's own ability if any were to benefit from it. It would be the child of promise, Isaac, foreshadowing Christ, the ultimate promised one, through whom blessings would flow. In Ishmael, the son of Hagar, we see but the results of man's efforts to accomplish the will of God. Good intentions, admirable motives and sincerity of purpose alone, can never bring any man into the blessing of salvation. It must be faith in the word of God, based on the work of Christ. All else will fail.

We are taken back in thought today to the wilderness of Beer-sheba, a barren, inhospitable place. Hagar had every reason to be fearful: alone, with only the bare essentials on which to survive. Water spent, and her fifteen year old son apparently dying of thirst in the meagre shade of a desert shrub where in her desperation she had left him. Now "she sat over against him, and lift up her voice, and wept", a picture of abject misery and despair.

Hagar's tears are the first to be mentioned in Scripture; there would be many more as time ran its course. But we have a God who is mindful of tears. The psalmist David appreciated this when, in his distress, he cried, "put thou my tears into thy bottle" (Ps 56:8). When the Lord Jesus met the funeral procession at the gate of Nain, it was a mother's tears for her only son which arrested His steps (Luke 7:13). At Bethany, as Mary cast herself down at His feet, it was when He "saw her weeping" (John 11:33) that tears began to flow down the cheeks of that lovely compassionate man.

Yet, attentive as God was to the anguish of Hagar, it was the "voice of the lad" which touched the divine heart. Notice how intimately God knew their circumstances. He called Hagar by name, and assured her that He knew precisely where Ishmael lay. Then came the word of comfort and assurance, "fear not; for God hath heard".

The promise made to Hagar concerning Ishmael (Gen 16:10-12) had dimmed in her memory, but God had not forgotten. Now, together with the word of reassurance, a well of water is given, and with the "fear not" from heaven in her ears, Hagar passes off the record of Scripture.

Day 3

THE "FEAR NOT" OF DIVINE PROTECTION

Genesis 26:12-33

It was Solomon who posed the question "who is able to stand before envy?" (Prov 27:4). In our chapter today, we see the admirable response of Isaac to the envious attention of the Philistines. They saw the material blessings which Isaac had received at the hand of the Lord, and resentment filled their hearts.

It has often been noted that, as altars are associated with the life of Abraham, so wells are frequently seen in connection with Isaac. In those days, to a man with flocks and herds, wells were a source of life, essential to the wellbeing of Isaac and his family. "Wells digged, which thou diggedst not", were part of the inheritance of Israel as they entered the land (Deut 6:11). They speak to us of the blessing and refreshment which we enjoy within that abundant inheritance "prepared for them that love him" (1 Cor 2:9). The Philistines had no appreciation of these things, and filled with earth the wells which Abraham had dug. We are not surprised at this, because "the natural man receiveth not the things of the Spirit of God: for they are foolishness unto him … they are spiritually discerned" (1 Cor 2:14).

Isaac sought to recover the wells and to lay claim to them by right of inheritance, calling them by the same names as had Abraham. But the Philistines dogged his steps, striving and contending. Isaac seems to have been by nature a very placid man. Rather than engage in conflict, even though he was "mightier than" them (v.16), he moves on, doubtless disappointed, until he is brought to the place that God would have him to be. It is then that he receives the word of compensation from the Lord, "fear not, for I am with thee, and will bless thee".

The response of Isaac on receiving this assurance is commendable. "He builded an altar … called upon the name of the Lord … pitched his tent there: and … digged a well" (v.25); all the essential features which marked out a man of pilgrim character. This is in fact the only time we read of Isaac building an altar. Some years before, he had been bound and laid upon one! Altars would have a particular significance to this man.

No sooner had Isaac become settled than the Philistines returned. Isaac's heart must have sunk as he saw them approaching. Were they to rob him of another well? No, on the contrary, they sought only reconciliation! How true the words of the wise man, "When a man's ways please the Lord, he maketh even his enemies to be at peace with him" (Prov 16:7).

Day 4

THE "FEAR NOT" OF COMFORT

Genesis 35:1-20

The midwife who attended Rachel at the birth of her second child was a true professional. Like so many of her calling, she sought to calm the distress of the mother for the sake of the child. Comforting and encouraging, even though she must have known that the situation for Rachel was critical, still she gave support and reassurance, "Fear not; thou shalt have this son also".

Some years before, as Rachel had witnessed the family of Jacob and Leah steadily increasing in number, envy had taken root in her heart. At last she could restrain herself no longer and, with a cry of anger and frustration, she confronted Jacob with "Give me children, or else I die" (Gen 30:1). Rachel's immediate solution to the problem, involving her maid Bilhah, started a whole chain of events which over the years would cause sadness and difficulty in Jacob's family.

Eventually, and in God's good time, "Rachel … conceived, and bare a son … Joseph". Such was her elation that she immediately spoke in anticipation of another son. Some years were to pass before her desire was realised, and it was on the journey back to Canaan that events overtook her. It is in these verses that we have the first mention of Bethlehem, and that in connection with the birth of a child. A sovereign God already had His eye upon that place! We note also that for Jacob, it was "but a little way" from Bethel, 'the House of God', to Bethlehem, 'the House of Bread'. How much greater that journey undertaken "when the fulness of the time was come", from the inner sanctuary of the House of God, to the outside place at Bethlehem's inn!

Twice over, the Spirit of God records that "she had hard labour", but the child is born even as Rachel dies. As her strength fails she names her son Ben-oni, 'Son of my Sorrow'. Jacob has no intention of allowing such a legacy for his beloved Rachel, and quickly re-names him Benjamin, 'Son of my Right Hand', the only occasion in which we read of Jacob naming any of his sons!

For the believer in the Lord Jesus, the application is simple and clear. The One who took that great journey to Bethlehem long ago, who willingly became "a man of sorrows, and acquainted with grief" (Isa 53:3), that very same One is now "by the right hand of God exalted" (Acts 2:33)! And, because He has sojourned in this vale of tears, He is able to minister comfort and assurance to His own, even in the face of death itself: to take firm hold of a weak and trembling hand, and whisper "Fear not, I am with you".

Day 5

THE "FEAR NOT" OF PEACE

Genesis 43:1-25

The story of Joseph is, without doubt, one of the most interesting and instructive in the whole of Scripture. We are told by some that there is no direct reference in the New Testament to Joseph as a type of the Lord Jesus. However, we would surely be the poorer in our appreciation of the word of God, if we failed to see and enjoy the many parallels between the Lord Jesus and the experiences of Joseph. It is the psalmist who sums up so much of this teaching in two brief statements, "He sent a man . . . He made him lord" (Ps 106:17, 21).

In chapters 42-45 of Genesis, the scene changes several times between the home of Jacob in Canaan and the house of Joseph in Egypt. The sons of Jacob do not appreciate that the one whom they despised and sold is now in a position of supreme authority in Egypt. Joseph, meanwhile, having immediately recognised his family, and seeing in their behaviour the fulfilment of his dreams, seeks now to probe their conscience before revealing himself to them.

In this present time, the once rejected, now exalted, Man is unrecognised by the chosen earthly nation. Yet He is far from unmindful of them. Through the prophet He says, "For mine eyes are upon all their ways: they are not hid from my face, neither is their iniquity hid from my eyes" (Jer 16:17).

The actions of Joseph were designed to bring his brothers to a full acknowledgement of their sin. We see the progression of this in their thoughts and words. Initially they would justify themselves, "we are true men" (42:11). Then, having been three days in prison, they confess, "we are verily guilty concerning our brother" (42:21). Later, after further testing, they cry, "what shall we say …? what shall we speak? or how shall we clear ourselves? God hath found out the iniquity of thy servants" (44:16). Throughout this process, which inevitably brought anxiety and heart searching, Joseph's purpose is to bring them ultimately into blessing. His heart is tender towards them. After their first visit he instructs his steward to return their money, resulting in words of assurance to the bewildered brothers. "Peace be to you", he says, "fear not: your God … hath given you treasure".

There is coming a day when the nation who once cast out their promised deliverer will "look on him whom they pierced" (John 19:37), and will "mourn for him, as one mourneth for his only son" (Zech 12:10). How the nation will need that "fear not", as they pass through the crucible of trials before their final restoration and blessing.

Day 6

THE *"FEAR NOT"* OF DIVINE ASSURANCE

Genesis 45:17 - 46:7

There are some defining moments in Scripture, when we feel "I would have loved to have been there when ...". The occasion when Jacob was told "Joseph is yet alive" must surely be one of those moments!

The behaviour of Jacob, with its resultant problems, does not always evoke sympathy, particularly in his early years. It would, however, be a callous heart that could not feel for the old patriarch as, doubtless with tears of grief, he cries "Me ye have bereaved of my children: Joseph is not, and Simeon is not, and ye will take Benjamin away: all these things are against me" (42:36). There is no doubt that Jacob deceived both his father and his brother, only to be deceived himself later by Laban and by his own sons.

It is noteworthy that when the brothers brought to Jacob the bloodstained coat and cruel lies, that Jacob believed them; "Joseph is without doubt rent in pieces" (37:33). When, however, word comes that in truth Joseph lives, "Jacob ... believed them not" (45:26)! Such is ever the heart of man, more prone to believe the lie and reject the truth!

The light of truth begins to dawn in Jacob's mind as his sons then tell of all Joseph's glory in Egypt. It was when he saw the wagons, the means prepared to transport him, every provision for his blessing made by Joseph, that faith comes to the fore, "and Israel said, It is enough ... I will go".

At Beer-sheba, Jacob pauses in his journey. It was here that his father Isaac built his altar and dug his well. Jacob was remembering. Many years before, Abraham had journeyed down into Egypt, and that experience brought no value to his spiritual development. Faced with similar circumstances, Isaac headed off in the same direction as his father. Before he stepped outside of the land however, the Lord appeared to him with a clear word of direction, "Go not down into Egypt ... sojourn in this land, and I will be with thee" (26:2-3).

What should Jacob do? Anxiety prevailed. The precedents set by his forefathers did not bode well for a journey to Egypt. Jacob needed something more than the word of his sons; after all, they had a fairly dubious record when it came to telling the truth!

Then, for the first recorded time in many years, "God spake unto Israel" the word of assurance that he needed. "Fear not to go down into Egypt; for I will there make of thee a great nation". That was sufficient for the aging patriarch; if God was directing his journey, all must be well. And Joseph would be there at the end of the journey!

Day 7

THE "FEAR NOT" OF FORGIVENESS

Genesis 49:33 - 50:26

The closing chapters of Genesis record for us the passing of two of the most influential characters in OT history, Jacob and Joseph. Although both accomplished much in their lifetime, it is in death that their faith in the purposes of God shines through, and merits a place in Hebrews 11. Both men grasped the importance of the land which God had given to the children of Israel. Jacob's instruction was "bury me not … in Egypt" (Gen 47:29). Joseph gave the commandment "carry up my bones from hence" (50:25).

There is a significant time pointer on God's calendar found in Genesis 47: 29; "The time drew nigh that Israel must die". The purposes of God are moving on and Jacob, having blessed his sons, and the sons of Joseph, with remarkable prophetic vision, "was gathered unto his people". With the burial over, Joseph and his brothers return to Egypt. There is no doubt that God could have preserved Jacob and his family in the land of Canaan. But in His sovereign plan He would form them into a nation in Egypt, to then teach the value of redemption by blood, deliverance by power, and all the attendant lessons, before bringing them back to the land as promised to Abraham (Gen 15:13-16).

Some seventeen years had elapsed since the whole family had moved down to Egypt, and Joseph's care for them was evident. Now, with Jacob no longer there, conscience begins to work. Would Joseph seek retribution? Had he really forgiven them? Sadly, they did not know their brother and benefactor as they should. It remains a moot point as to whether Jacob actually gave the instruction as rehearsed to Joseph in 50:17, but the very suggestion to Joseph that he might exact revenge moves him to tears. The "fear not" of Joseph to his brethren finds an echo for the believer in the assurance that our sins have been forgiven, they will be "remembered no more". Any lingering doubts are but evidence that we are not acquainted with Him as we ought to be! Had the brothers known Joseph better, they would have trusted him more.

In all the trials which had befallen the family over the years, Joseph looks back and sees God's hand in it all. He "meant it for good". It is precisely because Joseph knows his God, that he is able to forgive his brethren, to comfort them, and speak kindly to them (lit. 'to the heart'). If we too hear the "fear not" that assures us of our forgiveness, may we likewise be "kind one to another, tenderhearted, forgiving one another, even as God for Christ's sake hath forgiven you" (Eph 4:32).

JOHN SCARSBROOK

Week 41

7 TITLES OF THE
ARK OF THE LORD

Introduction

The days had long since passed when the Garden of Eden had seen man enjoying communion with his Creator. Sin severed this fellowship, and Adam was driven out of the garden. Yet we learn something of the desire that lay in the heart of God as He would "devise means, that his banished be not expelled from him" (2 Sam 14:14). On Mount Sinai, Moses was given the pattern for a sanctuary through which God would enjoy fellowship with His redeemed people.

Having told Moses which materials were to be collected from the people, God then used three simple statements to describe the purpose of the tabernacle and, in particular, the ark. The first of these is found in Exodus 25:8, "that I may dwell among them". God longed to be in the midst of His people, not just to visit them as He had done in times past. He wanted His people to enjoy His presence amongst them, and that He might be the focus of their lives.

The chapter then unfolds the instructions for the making of the ark, until we come to verse 22. Here we find a second purpose that God intended through the means of this golden ark: "there I will meet with thee". In this expression God is drawing a little nearer to His people. From between the two cherubims, on the basis of the blood-sprinkled mercy seat, God would meet with His people. The final one of these three phrases is also found in verse 22: "I will commune with thee". Thus we find that God was seeking to restore something of the conditions that were lost through the disobedience of the first man. We proceed from enjoying His presence to meeting Him face to face and, ultimately, we commune heart to heart with our God. The use of the singular word "thee" in verse 22 teaches us that God seeks to enjoy this fellowship with us individually.

We know that the ark would speak to us of Christ. He is the basis of our fellowship with God today. Do you appreciate the sweetness of His presence? Do you enjoy a daily meeting with Him? Do you value those precious moments of communion with Him?

Day 1

THE ARK

Exodus 25:16

When God introduces the subject of the tabernacle in Exodus 25, the very first description He gives is that of the ark. He issues very clear instructions to Moses as to the materials that are to be used in its construction, as well as the exact dimensions to which it will be made. God states that the testimony that He would give was to be placed inside it, and that there would be a lid comprising a mercy seat with two cherubims. Yet as we read these detailed instructions, there is still much of a mystery that surrounds this golden vessel. This mystery is apparent from the many differing illustrations drawn by those who have tried to give us an impression as to what it would have looked like.

As we turn to consider the One of whom this ark speaks, we realise that God has given us many Scriptures that reveal to us something of the glory and beauty of our Lord Jesus Christ, yet there is a great mystery that accompanies our study. We know that when He came into the world the angel spoke to Mary saying, "that holy thing which shall be born of thee shall be called the Son of God" (Luke 1:35). We understand that the babe that lay wrapped in swaddling bands, so dependent, in the arms of Mary was, at the same time, the One who was "upholding all things by the word of his power" (Heb 1:3).

"Thy word have I hid in mine heart" may have been the experience of the psalmist (Ps 119:11), but surely the complete fulfilment of such sentiments could only be found in the heart of our Lord. He alone could "magnify the law, and make it honourable" (Isa 42:21). We bow humbly in the presence of God to think that the righteous remission of our sins could only be effected because God has set forth this lovely man "to be a mercy seat (propitiatory) through faith" (Rom 3:25). Just as the basis for communion between God and His people in the wilderness was by means of a blood-sprinkled mercy seat, so too today, apart from the work of Christ, there can be no fellowship with heaven.

The writer to the Hebrews would remind us that God may have spoken in various ways before, but has only in these last days given the fulness of revelation, and that through His Son. In holy wonder we ponder the words penned by Paul to Timothy, "great is the mystery of godliness: God was manifest in the flesh" (1 Tim 3:16).

God gave both prominence and pre-eminence to the ark in the function of the tabernacle. In what measure have we placed similar value on our Lord Jesus Christ?

Day 2

THE ARK OF SHITTIM WOOD

Exodus 25:10

"They shall make an ark of shittim wood" are the words that God uses as He begins to reveal to Moses His pattern for this holy piece of furniture. With careful detail God describes the materials that are to be used, not just any wood, but shittim wood; not just gold, it must be pure gold. Nothing of the ark would be left to the imagination of Moses. On a number of occasions God would remind him, "see … that thou make all things according to the pattern shewed to thee in the mount" (Heb 8:5). It is also important to note the words recorded in Hebrews 9:23-24. The tabernacle, this ark included, was to be a pattern "of things in the heavens"; they were "figures of the true". We must ever remember that however beautiful and detailed the ark might appear, it is only a shadow of the glory and beauty of Christ.

The shittim wood overlaid with the pure gold brings to our mind the perfect humanity and glorious deity of our Lord Jesus Christ. This wood, sometimes referred to as acacia wood, (although not in the Scriptures) is said to have grown in the dry, arid, conditions of the wilderness. Immediately our minds turn to the words of Jehovah concerning His Servant, "He shall grow up before him as a tender plant, and as a root out of a dry ground" (Isa 53:2). Amidst all the sinful barrenness and corruption that marked the conditions around Him, this blessed man lived and walked bringing great delight to the heart of His God.

This chest of wood was then to be overlaid within and without with pure gold. This turns our mind from the glorious life of our Lord Jesus to the glory of deity that is essentially and eternally His; from scenes of earthly humility and lowliness to scenes of heavenly regal splendour that now surround His person. In this pattern of the heavens we are not thinking of pure gold encased in shittim wood; this is not the earthly life of our Lord Jesus Christ in which He veiled His glory in human flesh. Here, God is revealing an ark of shittim wood overlaid with pure gold. He is seeking to teach us concerning the One who has carried that perfect manhood back into heaven, right into the holiest and is there viewed in resplendent majesty as the glorified man. The throne of God, the mercy seat, rested upon this ark. How instructive to our minds today, that we rest where God rests; on the risen, glorified, Lord Jesus Christ.

It was on another mount that Moses saw something of the radiant beauty of which this ark was only a picture. There he beheld the glorious outshining of the inherent majesty that belongs in the holiest of all.

Day 3

THE ARK OF THE TESTIMONY

Exodus 26:34

One of the instructions that God gave to Moses concerning the ark was "And thou shalt put into the ark the testimony which I shall give thee" (Exod 25:16). Those tables of stone, engraved by the finger of God, would be laid up in the "ark of the testimony". In committing this testimony unto His people Israel, God was marking them out as His peculiar treasure; for "what nation is there so great, that hath statutes and judgments so righteous as all this law, which I set before you this day?" (Deut 4:8). Also in this ark of testimony were "the golden pot that had manna, and Aaron's rod that budded" (Heb 9:4). All through their wilderness journey the children of Israel experienced daily the faithful provision of God. In spite of their rebellion they witnessed the almighty power of God, typified in the rod that, although cut off from its branch, had budded, blossomed and yielded almonds (Num 17:8-10).

On one particular day each year the minds of the people would be focused on this one spot in the midst of their camp. In silent apprehension they would wait to see a solitary goat being led out from the precincts of the tabernacle, out beyond the camp, into the wilderness, to a land not inhabited. With a sense of relief they would know that, once again, blood had been sprinkled upon the mercy seat, atonement had been made for their sins. This was surely a continual testimony to the mercy of their God!

As they dwelt in their tents all these things were hidden from their view by boards and coverings, yet arising from off the mercy seat and standing over the tabernacle was the cloud that could be seen from every corner of their camp. When the camp set forward, there in the midst of their procession could be seen the ark of the testimony with its conspicuous veil of blue. What a testimony to the constant presence of their God!

It is interesting to notice that after God instructed Joshua to "command the priests that bear the ark of the testimony, that they come up out of Jordan" (Josh 4:16), we never read this description again. God, who had brought them out of bondage, leading them through the wilderness, had now seen them safely cross over into the Promised Land.

In Christ we find the fulness of all these things: the Word that became flesh; the true Bread that came down from heaven; the blood that has put away sin; the One who was cut off out of the land of the living and raised out from among the dead in mighty power; the One who has promised to be with us to the end of the age. "Being confident of this very thing, that he which hath begun a good work in you will perform it until the day of Jesus Christ" (Phil 1:6). What a testimony to the faithfulness of our God!

Day 4

THE ARK OF THE LORD

Joshua 4:11

The wilderness wanderings of the children of Israel were now behind them, and they had crossed over the Jordan to the land flowing with milk and honey. They had tasted the manna for the last time, having newly enjoyed the old corn of the land. It was on this momentous occasion that "the ark of the testimony" became "the ark of the Lord". Mr.. Newberry defines the divine title "the Lord", or Jehovah, thus; "He that always was, that always is, and that ever is to come". The circumstances might have changed: their desert journey was past; the land lay before them; they must now fight to possess it; but their God remains the same. He is the unchanging One. As He had been with Moses, so now would He be with Joshua.

On the tenth day of the first month the Passover lamb was selected. On that same day, forty years later, we have this first reference to "the ark of the Lord" as it is seen emerging from the midst of the Jordan. From this particular day we project our minds forward, almost fifteen hundred years, to come upon another scene. We behold the perfect Servant of the Lord, whom John has proclaimed as "the Lamb of God, which taketh away the sin of the world" (John 1:29). We watch as this lovely man, without spot or blemish, steps down into the river to be baptised, and see Him emerging from the Jordan as the voice from heaven declares; "Thou art my beloved Son" (Mark 1:11).

The final occurrence of the title "the ark of the Lord" is found in the days of Solomon. All the journeys and battles are past and the people dwell in peace. The staves have been drawn out; the ark is at rest, surrounded by majestic beauty and splendour. Such a scene would direct our thoughts to that glorious coming reign of our Lord Jesus Christ. The King of glory has ascended to the throne to reign in righteousness and regal grandeur. His people are enjoying a sweeter peace; swords have been beaten into plowshares and they are not learning war any more. The earth is "filled with the knowledge of the glory of the Lord, as the waters cover the sea" (Hab 2:14).

From the euphoria of entering the land through to the days of Solomon, Israel's God proved to be the One who was constantly faithful. In their days of triumph and joy, as well as in the days of defeat and despair, the word that came through the prophet rang true "I am the LORD, I change not" (Mal 3:6). From the banks of Jordan to the throne in Jerusalem, yea from eternity to eternity, the Hebrew writer reminds us that Jesus Christ is "the same yesterday, and today, and forever" (Heb 13:8).

Day 5

THE ARK OF THE COVENANT

Numbers 10:33

In its various forms throughout the Scriptures, this is the most frequently used title that has been given to the ark. It speaks of the covenant that was made between God and His people. In Deuteronomy 28 we read these words: "If thou shalt hearken diligently … blessings" (vv.1-14); "If thou wilt not hearken … curses" (vv.15-68). Therefore this covenant held out the prospect of blessing where no such favour was deserved.

When the children of Israel were preparing to move from Mount Sinai, we read that "the ark of the covenant … went before them in the three days' journey, to search out a resting place for them" (Num 10:33). This is the first of only two occasions recorded when the ark went before them. With delightful contemplation of these words we consider the One who has gone before us. It was those three days' journey that saw Him rise from the dead, thus bringing us into a place of rest.

Moses the servant of the Lord is dead. Joshua, his successor as leader of the children of Israel, has received words of encouragement and consolation from the Lord, "I will be with thee" (Josh 1:5). Only the river Jordan now stands between them and the land of their possession. For the second time the ark of the covenant will go before them. The feet of the priests that bear the ark will stand firm on dry ground in the midst of Jordan until all the people are passed clean over. What a contrast from the One who sank in deep mire, who knew the anguish of the waves and billows of judgment that relentlessly buffeted His soul until, at last, the storm was exhausted. Yet there is a sense in which we see Him standing firm in judgment and death until, in the mind of God, all His redeemed have passed safely over. Through the death of our Lord Jesus Christ we are introduced to a life that lies on the other side of death.

Jericho and Ai lie conquered, and the people come to the valley spoken of by Moses. All the people stand, half of them over against mount Gerizim and half of them over against mount Ebal. The ark of the covenant is in the valley in their midst. The blessings resound from Gerizim, followed by the cursings from Ebal. In holy wonder we bow before our God in thankfulness for a Redeemer who, in the valley, silenced forever the voice of cursing, "being made a curse for us" (Gal 3:13). Our souls thrill at the

glorious language from the pen of the apostle Paul: "Blessed be the God and Father of our Lord Jesus Christ, who hath blessed us with all spiritual blessings in heavenly places in Christ" (Eph 1:3).

Day 6

THE ARK OF GOD

1 Samuel 3:3

It is during a dark period in the history of the children of Israel that we are introduced to the expression "the ark of God". Eli, the priest, was going blind, and his sons were indulging in immoral and profane behaviour. Communication from God to His people had all but ceased, and we are told that there was no open vision.

The Philistines smote the Israelites in battle but, rather than look to their own failure, they blamed God. "Wherefore hath the Lord smitten us today …? Let us fetch the ark … out of Shiloh unto us, that, when it cometh among us, it may save us out of the hand of our enemies" (1 Sam 4:3). Instead of turning to God they looked to the ark, like some kind of lucky charm, to deliver them from their enemies. They might shout, the earth might ring, but God will not associate with their sin. He would sooner deliver "his strength into captivity, and his glory into the enemy's hand" (Ps 78:61). The symbol of His presence was in the camp, but God was not amongst them. In the ensuing battle the ark was captured and spent seven months in the land of the Philistines, but it was about a century later before it once again occupied its rightful place. It is only during this hundred-year period that the ark is called "the ark of God". There is no thought of relationship with His people, simply divine ownership.

During this time we notice some disturbing events, all triggered by this failure of God's people. In Ashdod, the Philistines set the ark in the temple of Dagon, just another idol to be placed alongside the others. But they would witness the power of God, for not only did Dagon lie prostrate before the God of Israel, but it was also broken in pieces. The men of Beth-shemesh dared to look into the ark, and with a lack of reverential fear they defied the command of the LORD and many of them died. Years passed before David sought to bring the ark to Jerusalem. This was also marked by failure in the beginning. The God-appointed means of transporting the ark was forsaken in favour of the method used by the Philistines, and the judgment of God was the result.

In these days of ever increasing darkness, can we learn these fundamental lessons? We can't blame God for the lack of blessing; we need more than just the symbol of His presence. In the minds of some, Christ is viewed as one among many. His glorious person is questioned and modern ideas replace the word of God. May we ensure that He is given His rightful place, so that we might know the blessing that was enjoyed by the house of Obed-edom (2 Sam 6:11).

Day 7

THE HOLY ARK

2 Chronicles 35:3

Not until the reign of Josiah, towards the closing days of the kingdom of Judah, do we read of the ark so described. Yet it is a truth that is impressed upon our minds by the very place in which it was found, not in the court of the tabernacle, nor even the holy place, but through that second veil, in the most holy place. Ere Aaron could ever enter through that veil he must put on the holy linen garments, and even then it could only be once each year. The psalmist has captured the sentiment so profoundly; "Holiness becometh thine house, O Lord, for ever" (Ps 93:5).

By the time Josiah came to the throne, years of neglect and departure had taken its toll on both the people and the house of God. As a youth of sixteen, he "began to seek after the God of David" (2 Chron 34:3). This resulted in the purging of the temple from all the idolatrous filth that had been brought within its confines. He then turned his attention to repairing the house of God. The solemn truth behind all this is that none of the damage was inflicted by the attacks of the godless nations around them, but it was rather the result of the actions of the kings and people of Judah. It was in these conditions that we hear the command "Put the holy ark in the house which Solomon … did build". The ark must be restored to its rightful place and the holiness of God, though a truth long since forgotten, must be freshly appreciated by His people. It may be the twilight years of the kingdom, yet through the guidance and exercise of this godly man there would be an appreciation of the Passover that hadn't been known since the days of Samuel, almost 400 years before.

The temple had been defiled, but not the ark: it remained holy, even though it had been removed from its place. How significant that, chronologically, this last mention of the ark in our Old Testament should be linked with a man who esteems its worth and restores it to its rightful place. In turning to the Revelation we find that it is the last of the seven churches where Christ is outside the door. In the wretchedness of their state He isn't even missed. Sadly, these conditions are found in some places today. Are you willing to be one who will seek after God and, through His power, endeavour to cleanse and repair the damage that has been wrought through years of neglect and departure from the truth of His word? May God grant us the grace to esteem the preciousness of Christ and enthrone Him in His rightful place as Lord, both personally and collectively.

AINSLIE PATERSON

Week 42

7 THINGS IT "PLEASED GOD"
TO DO

Introduction

"Who art thou that repliest against God?" is the question raised by Paul in Romans 9:20 in respect of the man who questions the divine will. The apostle teaches us by the Spirit that whilst God is not in any sense arbitrary or capricious, He is free to act as He wills, in accordance with His nature, in respect of the universe He has made and everything in it. He is truly the one who "worketh all things after the counsel of his own will" (Eph 1:11). All glory is thus to be ascribed to God, and honour and praise rightly belong to Him.

The will and pleasure of God are not things that can be understood by the rationalising mind. Human intellect is inadequate to understand His purpose and ways. "Canst thou by searching find out God?" (Job 11:7). Nevertheless, by faith we understand, and the renewed mind will bow to His wisdom, power and love and acknowledge that all His ways are right and true.

This is a recurring theme of many poets, and the writers of the Bible, but perhaps the apostle Paul expresses it most fully; "O the depth of the riches both of the wisdom and knowledge of God! how unsearchable are his judgments, and his ways past finding out! For who hath known the mind of the Lord? or who hath been his counsellor? Or who hath first given to him, and it shall be recompensed unto him again? For of him, and through him, and to him, are all things: to whom be glory for ever. Amen" (Rom 11:33-36).

In the course of this week we shall be considering that God, from eternity to eternity, does all His pleasure. At the very heart of this is His Son.

Remarkably, God's pleasure in relation to Him involves both suffering and glory, both the bruising of Calvary and the fact that in all things He has the pre-eminence. However, it also involves those who belong to His Son: their salvation, preservation and glorification are due to divine pleasure. What a day it will be when all His pleasure is fulfilled and His people surround His throne to give Him the honour and praise that is due to His name.

Day 1

A PEOPLE FOR HIMSELF

1 Samuel 12:22

"For the LORD will not forsake his people for his great name's sake: because it hath pleased the LORD to make you his people" (1 Sam 12:22). There is great comfort in knowing that God is sovereign, not least in times of failure. The people had sinned against God in the matter of desiring a king: the ideal government of God had been rejected and a desire to be like the nations round about had taken hold. However, God would not forsake them. He had made them His peculiar people and would not forsake them for His name's sake, because of all that He is. Deuteronomy 7:6-8 lies behind the statement of our verse: "Thou art an holy people unto the LORD thy God: the LORD thy God hath chosen thee to be a special people unto himself, above all people that are upon the face of the earth. The LORD did not set his love upon you, nor choose you, because ye were more in number than any people; for ye were the fewest of all people: but because the LORD loved you, and because he would keep the oath which he had sworn unto your fathers, hath the LORD brought you out with a mighty hand, and redeemed you out of the house of bondmen".

It is establishing to faith to recognise that what was true for Israel nationally is similarly true in the case of each individual believer. I am justified because He called me: I am called because He foreknew me (Rom 8:29-30). When I came to Christ He did not refuse me, for those who come are drawn by the Father (John 6:37,44). Bartimaeus called to Christ, but how beautiful that he only actually came to the point of blessing when the Saviour called him. Again, Zacchaeus "sought to see Jesus who he was", but had to learn that before ever he did that Jesus was seeking him, for "the Son of Man is come to seek and to save that which was lost" (Luke 18: 35-19:10).

We do well to enquire as to the purpose God had in saving us. If we think merely in terms of salvation from hell, or for heaven, or towards the betterment of our lives as being recipients of blessings bestowed by grace, we miss the larger truth. He has made us His own that we might be His "peculiar people", a people that belong uniquely to Him. Four times in the Old Testament this is stated of Israel, and twice in the New Testament of

saints in this dispensation. This will elevate our thinking relative to salvation so that we no longer think of it in a selfish way, but realise that God desired a people for Himself that they might "shew forth the praises of him who hath called you out of darkness into his marvellous light" (1 Pet 2:9).

Day 2

HE WAS BRUISED

Isaiah 53:10

"Yet it pleased the LORD to bruise him; he hath put him to grief" (Isa 53:10). It "pleased the Lord" in that it was His will that His Son should be bruised at Calvary. This bruising took place as our Saviour became answerable for sins that were not His own. God dealt with Him as He must deal with sin, and on the tree the Lord Jesus was

> "crushed beneath the load
> of the wrath and curse of God".

The Servant Song of which Isaiah 53 forms part details the sufferings of the Lord Jesus both at the hand of man and at the hand of God. His suffering at the hand of man was because He was holy: His suffering at the hand of God was because of sin. Man's activity was to give to Him the cross, but God laid on Him our sins. In the action of men we see the world's condemnation: in the action of God we see the world's salvation.

Two verses have often been juxtaposed: "He bearing his cross went forth" (John 19:17) and "who his own self bare our sins in his own body on the tree" (1 Pet 2:24). He was helped in the bearing of His cross by Simon of Cyrene, but in bearing our sins He stood alone. God "spared not his own Son" (Rom 8:32). He was delivered up by Pilate to be crucified (Matt 27: 26) but He was delivered up by God to unsparing justice as He became the bearer of sins. Men did nothing further to Him once they had impaled Him on the tree: He did not bare our sins *until* He was on the tree.

These separate aspects of the sufferings He endured are important to keep in mind. When this chapter speaks of His being bruised, in verses 5 and 10, it is not referring to the bruising He must have endured at the hand of man as He was struck by fist and reed, and as He was scourged. Rather, it intimates what He suffered for our sins. "He was bruised for our iniquities". He was forsaken by God as He was there "made ... sin" (2 Cor 5:21).

The first and last cries from the cross were addressed *to the Father*. He said, "forgive them" and "into Thy hands I commend my spirit". The middle cry, however, "Why hast Thou forsaken me?" was addressed *to God*. Great mystery of Calvary! Always the Son of the Father's bosom (John 1:18), He was nevertheless forsaken by God and endured His hot displeasure against sin (Ps 6:1). In time, which is by its nature finite, He suffered infinitely; sufferings unknown to man because he is God. "It pleased the Lord to bruise Him".

What love and service we should render to Him as we contemplate all that our salvation cost!

Day 3

THE FOOLISHNESS OF PREACHING

1 Corinthians 1:21

"For after that in the wisdom of God the world by wisdom knew not God, it pleased God by the foolishness of preaching to save them that believe" (1 Cor 1:21). It is not foolish to preach, of course. Indeed, Christ had sent the apostle to Corinth *to* preach (1:17). Preaching is a divinely appointed way to communicate the message of "Christ and him crucified", a fact that ought to be remembered in our day and generation in which emphasis is being placed elsewhere.

However, Paul recognised that to those who gloried in signs or human wisdom, the content of the message which he preached was foolishness. Imagine what many of the Greeks thought after assembling to hear the apostle preach the wisdom of God, only to discover that he preached a crucified Saviour. The Jews likewise listened to the preaching, longing for a sign, only to hear that the unsearchable riches of Christ involved His being rejected and made a curse.

We do not have a message that is appealing to human ears, for the message of the cross is one that speaks of the total depravity of man in the flesh. He cannot please God, being insubject to His law and hostile to His person (Rom 8:7-8). That order of man to which he belonged was thus terminated in judgment by God, by the cross (Rom 6:6). To seek to make it appealing by presenting it in a manner which entertains or amuses the man in the flesh is to negate the very message which we present, a fact which Paul recognises in that he determined not to preach the gospel with "wisdom of words" (1:17). That would make it of none effect. After all, the cross slays men and leaves them with nothing before God, cast upon His mercy and grace.

In this the gospel stands distinct from every other message in the world. These all say that man must do something, or be somebody or pay somewhat. The message of the cross empties man of all pretension and arrogance, and every thought of human merit, and insists that salvation is by grace alone, through faith alone, in Christ alone.

The wisdom of this world, whether philosophical, cultural or ecclesiastical will never lead a person to the knowledge of God. Indeed, such wisdom leads a person away from God. But it has pleased God by the preaching of the message of the cross to save them that believe. Such faith acknowledges that God's verdict on man in Adam is correct, and that there is no hope in self or anything else that this world might promote. Accordingly, faith abandons itself to a risen Saviour who alone is able to save. To the believer that message is indeed the wisdom of God. Let us not pander, then, to the modes and trends of this world, but faithfully preach the word of truth.

Day 4

MEMBERS SET IN THE BODY

1 Corinthians 12:18

"But now hath God set the members every one of them in the body, as it hath pleased him" (1 Cor 12:18). The fact of design in creation is far from the vain imaginings of the atheist and evolutionist who postulate that everything is here by a string of statistically impossible coincidences over unimaginable periods of time. Whether we think of the eye handling half a million messages at the same time; the ear which, if it is compared to a grand piano, has 24,000 strings and 20,000 keys; or the heart with its 100,000 beats per day, pumping blood through 80,000 miles of blood vessels, with the result that daily the aggregate distance covered by blood cells is in the region of 168,000,000 miles, we stand in awe of the greatness of the wisdom of the Creator!

Not only is each individual organ of the body brilliant in its concept and design, but the relationship of one member of the body to all other members is evidently appropriate. We are all glad that we do not have a foot on the end of our arm or, for that matter, a hand on the end of our leg. The eye would not be a lot of help on the side of the head, but we see that that is the perfect place for the ear. God has set the members in the body as it has pleased Him, for the benefit of the whole body.

Paul's interest in this, of course, is that an application might be made in respect of believers in fellowship with others in the local church. All are not the same. God has made each with distinct character and personality but, more especially, with differing gifts. He has not saved us so that we might all be replicas of each other, but that we might fulfil His purpose for us which, in this chapter, is connected to the local church. As there is both unity and variety in the human body, so there is also in the assembly.

Two possibilities arise. One member of the body, apparently superior in function, might say to another member, "I have no need of you". Again, a member of the body might think that it has no value because of the perceived superiority of another member. The apostle reminds the believers at Corinth that all members of the body are important: they differ in function but are interdependent and part of a single whole.

Each believer is important in the local church, having been placed there by God Himself. If one decides not to exercise one's gift, the spiritual health of the whole is jeopardised and the assembly is not what it might otherwise be. Let us be what God wants us to be, and do what He wants us to do for the benefit of the whole and for His glory.

THE RESURRECTION BODY

1 Corinthians 15:38

"But God giveth it a body as it hath pleased him, and to every seed his own body" (1 Cor 15:38). Two questions in particular are answered by the apostle in this great resurrection chapter. In verse 12 he asks how it is that, despite all the evidence which he has adduced, some at Corinth said that there was no resurrection. Others, in verse 35, sceptically ask how the dead are raised up and, in the event that it does actually happen, with what body do they come from the dead?

A feature of Paul's writings by the Holy Spirit is that he anticipates the questions of sceptics and answers them in devastating fashion. No doubt these sceptics thought that no body could ever be raised again, especially if the person has been dead for many years, or they died as martyrs at the stake or in the arena, but the apostle indicates the vanity of their objection by asking them to look at something commonly observed. A seed is sown. It is not quickened except it dies (v.36), and when the sowing takes place it is not the body that shall be that is sown but "bare grain". In fact, God gives it a body as it pleases Him. The objection is invalid.

The bodies of believers are also sown in the ground. To the Christian, death is not the grim reaper. When a believer goes to be with Christ, an event which as far as the body is concerned is spoken of as the believer falling asleep, his body is sown as a seed in springtime. The harvest is when the Lord returns to the air, when that which has been sown shall be raised. Incidentally, the Bible never speaks in terms of the believer's body being cremated, but always of it being buried. Just as God in His creation gives bodies to seeds as it pleases Him, so it is in the resurrection.

The body that is sown in the ground is the same one that is raised. Note that in verses 42-44 "it" is sown and "it" is raised. However, if we keep in mind the analogy of the seed, we will realise that that which is raised is not the same in resurrection as it was in mortality. Corruption, dishonour and weakness give place to incorruption, glory and power. It is sown as a body suited to earth but it is raised a body suited to heaven, a redeemed body at one with a redeemed spirit.

Best of all, however, is the fact that whether our bodies are quickened or raised at the rapture (depending on whether we are living or not at the time it occurs) they shall be changed, and we shall have a body which is like unto His body of glory. Perhaps today!

Day 6

HIS SON REVEALED IN ME

Galatians 1:15-16

"It pleased God, who separated me from my mother's womb, and called me by his grace, to reveal his Son in me, that I might preach him among the heathen" (Gal 1:15-16). The apostle Paul had a great sense of divine intervention in his life. He spoke of this in different ways and at different times, always acknowledging that his salvation was not brought about by anything in himself. He had no testimony of seeking after Christ and eventually finding Him: rather, he was glad to acknowledge that his being found in Christ was all to do with God. "I am apprehended of Christ Jesus" is the language he employs in Philippians 3:12. Christ Jesus pursued and overtook him, laying hold on him that His purpose might be fulfilled in his life.

Christ did not reveal Himself to Paul's companions on the Damascus road. This revelation was for Paul alone of all who were with him. They heard a voice but saw no man (Acts 9:7), and from another standpoint saw the light that shone but heard not the speaker's voice (Acts 22:9). But whatever the nuances of the way the incident is described, it was Paul alone to whom the Lord revealed Himself. Further, the apostle had profited in Judaism above many of his equals, but it was not to these either that the Lord made Himself known. Why was this? Some might think it unfair or unjust that this should be, but the answer is simply that "it pleased God". Paul was a vessel of mercy whom God had "afore prepared unto glory" (Rom 9:23), a "chosen vessel" unto Him (Acts 9:15). Accordingly, God revealed His Son in Paul's case (though not in the case of the others who were his companions) and did so in accordance with His own will and to accomplish His own good pleasure and purpose.

This all goes to the heart of salvation. God did not act in this way for the mere purpose of saving Paul from wrath or fitting him for heaven but, because it pleased Him to do so. And what was true in the case of the apostle is no less true in the case of all His own. God's purpose centres in His Son rather than in His people. His people have been brought into the sphere of His purpose for the greater glory of the Lord Jesus. Salvation is thus seen to be God centred, not man centred; it is for His glory more than for any other reason.

It is a good thing to render the thanks that is due to God that our salvation is sourced and centred in Him who alone is worthy of our heart's adoration and praise. Not only will this honour Him as He should be honoured but it will also assure the heart of the believer, secure in the knowledge that He will never fail in the accomplishment of His will.

Day 7

CHRIST PRE-EMINENT

Colossians 1:19

"For it pleased the Father that in him should all fulness dwell" (Col 1:19). This first chapter of the Colossian epistle is full of Christ. He is altogether and incomparably glorious. As the Son (v.13) He is the object of the Father's love and was so to all eternity. As the Redeemer (v.14) His blood has secured the redemption of His people and in Him they have forgiveness. As the Divine equal (v.15) He alone manifests and represents God. As the almighty creator (v.16) He stands apart from, and is superior to, all created things for, in Him, by Him and for Him all things were created: He therefore predates it and, adds the apostle, He upholds it. Furthermore, if attention is directed towards the new creation rather than the old, material one, our Lord Jesus Christ is the glorious Head of the church, the beginning, and the firstborn from among the dead (v.18).

In all of these things God has purpose, and the fulfilment of that purpose is that to which all His ways are directed. His Son is the very centre of all His counsels. Truly, He is the one who by divine design has the pre-eminence in all things, "for it pleased the Father that in him should all fulness dwell".

The expression "it pleased the Father that in him should all fulness dwell" is thus to be distinguished from that in 2:9 which says that "in him dwelleth all the fulness of the Godhead bodily". There our attention is directed to the person of the Lord Jesus who is possessed of deity and all its attributes. This was no less true of Him while He was here on earth, having become flesh, as it was to all eternity and, indeed, as it is so now. In 1:19 however, it is not so much the thought that it pleased the Father that all the fulness of deity should dwell in Him, rather the "fulness" is connected with the fact that in all things God has purposed that He might have the pre-eminence. In this connection the significance of the word "for" at the beginning of the verse should not be lost. The verse amplifies and expands that which has previously been stated, and it indicates why it is that the Lord Jesus has the pre-eminence.

God delights in His Son but He is desirous that His people should also delight in Him. It is as we are taken up with the greatness of His person, His pre-eminence, dignity and glory and the beauty of His character that we begin to find in Him that which satisfies the Father's heart.

> "O fix our earnest gaze so wholly, Lord, on Thee,
> That with Thy beauty occupied we elsewhere none may see".

IAN JACKSON

Week 43

7 ETERNAL THINGS IN
THE EPISTLE TO THE HEBREWS

Introduction

The epistle to the Hebrews stands out as one of deep significance and value to the Lord's people. While there is a veil thrown over such things as the author and the destination, there is no such veil over the subject. The glorious Person, sacrifice and priesthood of our Lord Jesus Christ are the major themes.

The original readers had been brought up in the Jew's religion and, having heard the gospel, professed faith in Christ. They received this epistle a few years prior to the Roman conquest of Jerusalem in AD 70, which effectively destroyed the last semblances of the old covenant and its system of worship. Surrounded by increasing persecution, a hardening of Jewish attitudes to Christ, the unexpected delay of His return, the passing of their leaders, and the ever-widening gulf between Judaism and Christianity, these Hebrews were being severely tested.

The writer felt these matters to be serious, and thus the epistle contains not only glorious words but also grave warnings. He was confident that most of these Hebrews were truly Christ's, but was concerned that some would turn back and prove to be otherwise. Some were wavering amidst all the difficulties, and needed confirmation and encouragement. To set forth the supremacy of Christ would best achieve this. The epistle impresses us with a sense of finality and, in connection with our present meditations, eternality. Key words are 'better', 'perfect', 'eternal'. The writer shows that the aging, decaying Old Testament system has been superseded by what is permanent. The age of foreshadowing has given way to the age of fulfilment, the external to the internal, the earthly to the heavenly, the temporal to the eternal. There were two main reasons why the old Jewish system was set aside. First, it had degenerated so much that its leaders rejected and crucified Christ. Second, with the advent of Christ it was no longer required, since He was its fulfilment.

Along with the seven eternal things, we notice, in passing, associated ideas: Christ "remains" (1:11); He is the same "forever" (13:8); He has a throne that is "forever" (1:8); He will have glory ascribed to Him "forever" (13:21). Truly, as 12:27 puts it, these are "things which cannot be shaken". May these considerations refresh us, and produce worship from our hearts.

Day 1

"*Eternal salvation*"

Hebrews 5:1-10

The theme of salvation is a common one in this epistle. We are familiar with the expression "so great salvation" and, as the writer develops the subject, this greatness becomes very clear. Christ Himself is the Pioneer of this salvation (2:10), opening up and leading the way. He is able to "save" continuously and completely because of His unending priesthood (7:25). At His return, salvation will be known in its fulness (9:28), angels in the meantime being sent forth as servants to minister to those about to inherit this full salvation (1:14). On a practical note, there are things that accompany salvation (6:9). There is a poignant touch added concerning Noah, that his entire family was saved (11: 7). In 5:9 we have the reassuring truth that this salvation is "eternal".

The Lord Jesus, being divinely called, truly human, acquainted with trial and suffering, and finally offering Himself, is entirely fitted to meet the needs of mankind. Moral perfection is not in the question in 5:9, but rather the completing of His qualification to be the Saviour and High Priest of His people. Christ has become 'the source of "eternal salvation" to all them that obey Him'. The Saviour obeyed in sacrifice (10:7-10) and, in doing so, made salvation possible for the sinner who obeys. This obedience is the initial obedience of faith. Such obedience will then become characteristic of a true Christian life.

Throughout this epistle a contrast is repeatedly drawn between the effectiveness of the old system and that of the new. This contrast is true regarding salvation. Those who obeyed the Old Testament laws of sacrifice (with repentance and faith) enjoyed only a temporary salvation from retribution. There was a constant feeling of uncertainty about it. But Christ, by His one offering, "hath perfected for ever them that are sanctified" (10: 14). No further sacrifice is required. What He has accomplished at Calvary provides eternal security for all those who obey Him. He Himself was 'saved' out of death (5:7). For a risen Christ, judgement and death are past. Our salvation is thus linked to His, and can never end.

Some Christians, sadly, neither grasp nor enjoy their eternal security. This leads to introspection and loss of vitality in service. It is pointless to look to human reasoning or experience to give settled peace. God's word is confirming and clear to all who believe on Christ. To deny eternal salvation is to deny Bible teaching on eternal life (John 3), sheep never to perish (John 10), divine purpose (Rom 8), Holy Spirit sealing (Eph 1), Christ's intercession (Heb 7), membership of His Body (1 Cor 12), the unconditional terms of the new covenant (Heb 10), to mention only a few. May we rejoice today in this "uttermost" salvation, and remember the cost at which it was provided.

Day 2

"ETERNAL JUDGMENT"

Hebrews 6:1-2

The contrast between this subject and the previous one is beyond words. Judgment is another common theme in the epistle, and especially the fact that God is the judge (9:27; 10:27, 30; 12:23; 13:4). This present expression occurs in the third warning passage of the epistle, which includes a censure for immaturity (5:11-14), a call to perfection (6:1-3), a caution about apostasy (6:4-8) and a challenge to fruit bearing (6:9-12).

In verses 1-3, the Hebrews are encouraged to advance from the foundational truths, six of which are mentioned in verses 1 and 2. These six truths were firmly believed in Judaism, and were not distinctively Christian. A person may have held all these and yet fall short of the perfection which was in Christ. We should note that 'perfection' in Hebrews always refers to what results from the work and priesthood of Christ, and not merely Christian growth. However, maturity (5:11-14) would be an outcome of properly grasping this perfection that Christ brought. These six truths had their foundation in the Old Testament but are now given fuller meaning in this Christian era. The last one mentioned is eternal judgment.

As already noted, the advent of Christ has brought this serious subject into clearer light. Who ever taught it more forcibly than He? Christ Himself will be the Judge, rightly assessing every case and giving sentence according to each person's works. Very clear in Scripture is the fact of degrees of punishment (Matt 11:20-24; Luke 12:47-48; 20:47; Rom 2:2-16; Rev 20:12), the verdict upon each sinner's life being arrived at by the strict justice of an impartial Judge. God will not only be righteous, but will be seen to be such by means of a great Tribunal. We should understand that His judgments are firmly based upon His holiness and justice, and not merely upon reactionary impulses of revenge that human emotions often display. As R. M. McCheyne once said, "the eternal hell is closed in and surrounded by the attributes of God". Down the centuries men who have been most faithful in preaching this truth have been most fruitful.

It is probably true that many Christians are weak on this subject, not because they doubt the letter of Scripture, but rather have not let the awesome import of it grip their hearts with life-changing effects. Certainly a fuller understanding of the reality of everlasting punishment, the fire that never shall be quenched, the great gulf fixed between two destinies, and the ceaseless existence of all people, would make necessary changes upon us. Everything would be put in true perspective. Perhaps today we will give greater thanks to God for ever saving our souls, remembering that Calvary alone made this possible. May we feel like debtors to those who are perishing, that they too will be rescued.

Day 3

AN ETERNAL PRIESTHOOD

Hebrews 7:20-28

The priesthood of Christ is the outstanding theme of this epistle. Such is its vastness and depth, the author was not sure if he could fully expound it to those who were spiritually immature. Yet he goes on to give some precious details, recalling that even in Old Testament days a high priest was selected from among men, representing them in things pertaining to God and offering gifts and sacrifices for sins. The high priest had to be divinely called, and taken from the tribe of Levi and the family of Aaron. He must be compassionate, remembering the weakness of the people. He was also conscious of sin and frailty in himself. Eventually he would die, and the priesthood pass on to his lawful successor.

As the Lord's people in this era, we too need a high priest. It is not merely a nice thought that Christ now appears in heaven for us, but His ministry there is as vital to our well-being as was the cross. Without it our pilgrimage would never have begun, much less continue. We should distinguish some of the offices of Christ which, to many, appear similar: as Mediator He meets our need as sinners; as Advocate He functions for us as children of the Father when sin has interrupted communion; as Great High Priest He deals not with our sins, but graciously ministers to us as pilgrims in the trials, difficulties and infirmities that we experience along the way.

It is a source of wonder and worship to think of how Christ became fully qualified to be such a High Priest. He became true yet sinless man, endured trials and reproach, learned experimentally the cost of obedience and, by such things, became perfectly fitted to minister to our present needs. "He knows what sore temptations are, for He endured the same" (Isaac Watts). He too offered a sacrifice, after Aaron's pattern, but infinitely greater.

"But", the Hebrews would ask, "was He called of God"? Yes, and their own Scriptures had the vital proof: Jehovah had sworn "Thou art a priest forever after the order of Melchizedek" (Ps 110:4). Hebrews 7 shows the greatness of this man of Genesis 14:18, and that he excels Aaron. Thus we learn that Christ's priesthood is vastly superior to Aaron's and, indeed, excludes it. If Christ then as priest can never die, it is obvious that His official priesthood could not begin until after His death on the cross. When He ascended to glory, the great ceremony took place as Psalm 110 had foretold. He will soon, like Melchizedek, be seen as the King Priest, as Zechariah 6:13 also states. Meanwhile, He ever lives to make intercession for us, and as forerunner (which Aaron never was) is bringing many sons to glory.

Day 4

"ETERNAL REDEMPTION"

Hebrews 9:1-15

Having considered the eternal priesthood of Christ, it is appropriate now to ponder the excellence and effectiveness of His work. To do this, we limit ourselves to 9:11-12, where the day of atonement is in the background (Lev 16). In verse 11 we have Christ so named for the first time since 6:1. What a difference now that He has arrived on the scene! Truly this Messiah is the great High Priest of the good things now come. In these verses we have three important contrasts with Aaron. First, Christ serves not in an earthly sanctuary but in heaven itself. Second, His sacrifice was not of blood of animals, but His own blood. Third, there was no need to offer Himself often, as the Old Testament priest offered animals year by year. Once was sufficient, and the results are permanent.

When reading Hebrews, we should not belittle the OT system as though it was worthless and vain. Rather, it was God ordained, and provided forgiveness of sins for all who truly repented and had faith. It was not the blood of the animal sacrifices that accomplished this, but the blood of Christ's sacrifice which they foreshadowed. Yet, at best, the blessings that OT believers enjoyed were temporary, and when sins were again upon the conscience, more sacrifices were required. There was no permanency of forgiveness, or purging of the conscience, under this old system. Sins were remembered repeatedly, meaning that Israelites were never sure of being fully and finally accepted of God. To summarise, it may be said that they enjoyed the same forgiveness that we enjoy, but a forgiveness continually being updated.

What a contrast we have in Christ! He has entered in once into the holy place, the heavenly sanctuary, having already obtained eternal redemption. (The words "for us" in verse 12, are italicised; the results of Calvary touch not only us, but the whole universe). He entered, not "with" His own blood, but 'through' it, that is, through His blood-shedding at Calvary. The securing of redemption did not await His arrival in heaven, but was the basis of His entry and taking His seat at God's right hand. This redemption has the idea of deliverance, or setting free by payment of a price. This basic word was used by Zacharias in Luke 1:68, and concerning Anna's testimony in Luke 2:38. Well might we use it still to those around us! It has a broad reference to all that the Cross has provided. While we are yet in our bodies here, sin, Satan and death are enemies. But we look for the "fullness of redemption, pledge of endless life above" and, in the little while between, may our hearts be stirred to genuine praise and consecrated lives.

Day 5

"The eternal Spirit"

Hebrews 9:1-15

In addition to those seen in our study of eternal redemption, Hebrews 9: 13-14 has further great contrasts. The blood of bulls and goats, and the ashes of the heifer, refer to two of the most lasting of the Old Testament provisions, that of the annual day of atonement and that of the red heifer whose ashes were available for many years. Yet even these had meagre duration when viewed in light of Christ's eternal redemption. In addition, these provisions had reference to ceremonial and external purity, whereas Christ's sacrifice deals with the very conscience and deepest realities of our sin. A liberated conscience was impossible until the matter of sin was brought to a closure. Only Calvary ensured this. Further, while animals died passively and unwittingly, Christ offered Himself with full understanding and willingness. Dead works marked the old order, but vitality marks the new, for example, "*eternal* Spirit … *living* God" (9:14).

Perhaps some Hebrews, when hearing about all the limitations of the Old Testament sacrifices, would begin to wonder if their Jewish ancestors were saved at all. This brings us to consider the context of this passage. We read that Christ offered Himself without spot to God, and this was done through the eternal Spirit. It is not said that this was Christ's own spirit. Nor is it suggested that it was His human nature as distinct from His divine nature. We know that it was His whole Person that was offered in sacrifice, not His humanity only. Neither is there any hint of an eternal spirit of priesthood that then became active as He offered this sacrifice. Rather, it is much more consistent with other Scriptures to see that just as Christ was begotten by the Holy Spirit, was anointed by the Holy Spirit, led by the Holy Spirit, preached and performed miracles by the Spirit, so likewise, in death as in life, He offered Himself to God in the consciousness of the power and sustenance of the Holy Spirit. It is worth noting in Hebrews the instances where the 'Trinity' is brought together, for example, 2:3-4; 6:4-6; 9:14; 10:12-17; 10:28-31.

But if this is the Holy Spirit in 9:14, why is He referred to as "eternal"? We are learning in these verses that whether men lived in the days of Moses or the days of the Millennium or any other day, the sacrifice of Christ has an eternal, all-embracive efficacy, and all who ever will be redeemed will owe it to His work alone. The writer even goes on to assure them that those who died long before the new covenant came into being, have had their sins dealt with, on credit so to speak, awaiting the Cross (9:15).

Let us not miss the practical note: we can only "serve the living God" in the measure that we reflect our holy standing in the conduct of daily life.

Day 6

"*THE EVERLASTING* [*ETERNAL*] *COVENANT*"

Hebrews 13:20-21

A covenant is simply an arrangement or agreement between parties. So prominent is this theme in Hebrews, that one writer has called it "the epistle of the diatheke" (covenant). We are told it is "everlasting" (13:20); "new", that is, in form or character (as in 8:8; 8:13; 9:15); "new", a different word (only used of this covenant in 12:24) meaning new in time, recent; "better" (8:6); "second" (8:7). This shows that five different words are used to describe its superiority. "But", we ask, "which covenant is it being compared with"? There can only be one answer, the Mosaic covenant of Sinai, that is, the law. There is no hint in Scripture that the covenants with, for example, Abraham or David, will ever be consigned to the waste-bin of history to be replaced by others or enjoyed by other peoples. No, the covenants made with Israel as to their people, place and potentate will be literally fulfilled. Matters concerning Israel's identity, territory, and royalty are secure for the future. But the law covenant of Sinai with its ritual has proved ineffective, and caused faithful Israelites to look for something better. It made nothing perfect. All the limitations we have considered in recent pages stemmed from this. The fault lay with the people, and this fault then reflected upon the covenant. There were obligations on both God and the people, but the people failed. In the days of this epistle, the last traces of its externals were soon to vanish away in the destruction of Jerusalem under Titus.

How precious then to consider this new, eternal covenant, ratified by the blood of Christ (13:20). It was spoken of in the very Scriptures that the Hebrews revered, in Jeremiah 31. To know that their own prophets had spoken of a new covenant to come was a weighty appeal to their minds. While this new covenant is with the nation (ultimately uniting the two houses of Judah and Israel, 8:8) and awaits full realisation in the future, yet many have already been blessed under its gracious terms, including us. This eternal covenant has been active since Calvary, and continues to bless every repentant sinner in at least a three-fold way: a new birth that enables joyful obedience; a personal knowledge of God; and a full remission of sins (see 8:10-12). Assuring the Hebrews of a present share in these blessings is one of the main points of the epistle, while for us all there is a serious reminder of our responsibilities before God and to one another.

The cup we receive at the Lord's Supper is the emblem of the precious blood of this new covenant (Luke 22:20). Paul was a minister of it (2 Cor 3:6). Thus, even now, Christians enjoy great and lasting blessings. Not our faithfulness, but God's, underlies this eternal relationship. The knowledge of this gives peace.

Day 7

AN "ETERNAL INHERITANCE"

Hebrews 9:13-28

The concept of an inheritance provokes interest with most people, but with the Hebrews for very particular reasons. Many of them, on receiving Christ, had been disinherited, and their goods had been spoiled. But awaiting them was a better country, a heavenly city, and a better and enduring substance. It would far surpass the earthly inheritance of Canaan. They were now linked with "the heir of all things", and just needed patience and faith in the meantime.

In the world generally, a person may be due to inherit great wealth. The will-maker may have vast amounts of money and property. But one thing must happen before the inheritance can be claimed – the man who made the will must die. Upon death, someone is ready as the appointed executor. It is hoped that the estate has been wisely divided (not always the case), and also that the executor will act fairly and transparently. Then the heir enjoys what has been bequeathed, keeping in mind that even a fortune can be frittered away. Even at best, the time for him to die will come too. Christ, in Luke 12: 13-21, forcefully teaches the transience of earthly things. As Christians, one of the greatest tests is our attitude to possessions. It is possible to be scrupulous in many things, and yet fall down in this important area of stewardship.

With this background, let us ponder Hebrews 9:15-16. The word used for "covenant" now has the idea of a will or testament. Reasons for this change may be to emphasise God's sole responsibility in this new order of things, and also that it could not be implemented apart from death taking place. Note how often death and blood are mentioned in this part of the chapter. Christ's death was vital. The question then arises, "if Christ is dead, who is going to distribute the riches"? But the fact is, He lives again! Thus, the testator in this unique case is also the executor. Nothing can ever be mishandled by such a righteous One, for He is the perfect Mediator. No fear of losing out should alarm His people, for He is the perfect Surety, guaranteeing the outcome. Even the Hebrews' ancestors would not lose out, because Christ's death has value retrospectively, meaning they too would receive the inheritance. Everything to them seemed so distant, but will some day be realised. Peter describes this inheritance, which all the saints will enjoy, as "incorruptible, and undefiled, and that fadeth not away" (1 Pet 1:4). In measure we are already partakers of this inheritance, but its fulness awaits the return of Christ. Until then, may we revel in the great wealth to which we are heirs, assured that eternity itself will never diminish its vastness.

JOHN FLECK

Week 44

7 MINISTRIES OF THE HOLY SPIRIT TO THE CHURCH

Introduction

"When the Comforter is come, whom I will send unto you from the Father, even the Spirit of truth, which proceedeth from the Father, he shall testify of me" (John 15:26). "When he, the Spirit of truth, is come, he will guide you into all truth: for he shall not speak of himself: but whatsoever he shall hear, that shall he speak: and he will shew you things to come. He shall glorify me: for he shall receive of mine, and shall shew it unto you" (16:13-14). The full import of these lovely words of the Saviour to His own in the upper room was, at that time, beyond their understanding. Their minds were more occupied with the perplexity of the imminent departure of the One in whom was all their trust. They knew Him, they had left all to follow Him, they needed Him, they loved Him. The thought of being left alone was too much to contemplate. How well the Saviour knew their thoughts and anxieties. Was it not for that very reason he had said to them "Let not your heart be troubled"? (14:1).

As He unfolds His tender ministry to His disciples, the Lord shows them that, for two reasons at least, they should not be despondent but glad. The first reason concerned His own comfort; "Ye have heard how I said unto you, I go away, and come again unto you. If ye loved me, ye would rejoice, because I said, I go unto the Father: for my Father is greater than I" (14:28). The Saviour was longing for home, knowing that the cross stood between Him and His return to the Father. His loved ones should have rejoiced that His sojourn as the man of sorrows was soon to be over.

The second reason for gladness concerned their comfort; "It is expedient for you that I go away: for if I go not away, the Comforter will not come unto you; but if I depart, I will send him unto you" (16:7). The Lord Jesus clearly testifies to the Personality, co-equality and gracious ministry of the Holy Spirit. To the natural mind, nothing could replace the presence of the Lord in their lives. Yet, if they would believe, they would find through the Spirit's ministry a deeper, fuller knowledge of the Lord than they could ever have obtained while He was with them!

Day 1

THE BAPTISM OF THE SPIRIT

Acts 1:1-5; 2:1-4; 1 Corinthians 12:13

The baptism of the Holy Spirit was an event that happened just once, in Jerusalem, on the day of Pentecost. It was a corporate, representative act that will never be repeated. The baptism of the Spirit was that event which brought the Church into being, bringing divine life corporately and individually to those who "were all with one accord in one place" (Acts 2:1). These believers in the Lord Jesus were in the house when, suddenly, the place where they were was filled by the presence of the Holy Spirit. They were in the house, and the house was filled, so they were quite literally baptised (immersed) in the Holy Spirit. It was a literal baptism where those baptised were the disciples, the baptiser was the Lord Jesus (as he had promised), the medium in which they were baptised was the Holy Spirit, and the purpose of it was that in one Spirit they would all be baptised into one body (1 Cor 12:13). Not only that, but "they were all filled with the Holy Ghost" (Acts 2:4), so the corporate life they received in the baptism of the Spirit was accompanied by individual divine life as each of them became the abiding place of the Holy Spirit. Thus was fulfilled the Lord's promise "for he dwelleth with you, and shall be in you" (John 14:17).

Immediately they "began to speak with other tongues, as the Spirit gave them utterance" (Acts 2:4), so there was a divinely enabled demonstration of the significance of this event. Why this sudden ability to speak in other languages? It was, of course, a means of communicating "the wonderful works of God" (2:11) to those proselytes from other nations, and it was also an irrefutable evidence of a divine work. It showed also that the judgment upon Babel in Genesis 11 was being divinely reversed. The world of men had endeavoured to establish a unified, godless system centred on Babel and that forerunner of the man of sin, Nimrod. In judgment God said, "Go to, let us go down, and there confound their language, that they may not understand one another's speech" (Gen 11:7). But now, on the day of Pentecost, the time had come for God to unite men of all nations in one body under Christ, and he signified that this work was of Himself by reversing, temporarily, the judgment He had imposed at Babel.

Every believer today came into the good of the baptism of the Holy Spirit the moment they were saved. There is no such thing as an individual baptism of the Holy Spirit; we were all represented by those who were in the upper room on the day of Pentecost. None of us were in Eden, but we all came into the effects of the Fall. None of us were at Calvary, but by grace we have been brought into all its blessings. None of us were there at Pentecost, but salvation has brought us into the body of Christ and we are personally indwelt by the Spirit of God.

Day 2

THE GIFTS OF THE SPIRIT

1 Corinthians 12:1-13; 13:8-11

The early church was made up of Jews and Gentiles, gloriously saved by divine grace and united in Christ. Those steeped in Jewish ceremony were united with believers from Gentile stock who, for the most part, had been idolaters. None of them had any knowledge or experience of the distinctive character and activity of the church. They had all to learn things immensely different from everything they had previously known. Whether Jew or Gentile, each was familiar with a priesthood made distinctive by special garments. Each had had their temples, sacrifices and rituals. Holy days, auspicious times, feasting and fasting were understood by all.

But now! Now, in Christ, they were dead to everything that had once demanded their devotion and, as believers, they gathered unto One whom they could not see. The only temple was that of their bodies, the dwelling place of the unseen, unfelt, Holy Spirit. They themselves constituted the new priesthood, responsible for offering sacrifices that were no longer tangible but spiritual. How could they possibly function as local assemblies of Christians when the only Scriptures available were those of the Old Testament in which nothing of the Church and its principles was revealed? True, there was "the apostles' doctrine" (Acts 2:42), but the full revelation of Church truth was going to come through the ministry of the apostle Paul alone (Eph 3:1-12).

So that the early churches could function, and have confidence that they were possessed of divine life and light, the Holy Spirit bestowed special gifts that would meet the need of the saints until the full revelation of truth had been given and taught (1 Cor 13:10). The nine sign gifts of 1 Corinthians 12 were all of a temporary nature, and none of them is in existence today. The nine gifts divide into three groups; two, five and two, the distinctive features of which can be summarised as "knowledge", "prophecies" and "tongues". Paul goes on to show that "… prophecies, they shall fail; … tongues, they shall cease; … knowledge, it shall vanish away. For we know in part, and we prophesy in part. But when that which is perfect is come, then that which is in part shall be done away" (13:8-10). "That which is perfect" speaks of something complete, and it refers to the full revelation of church truth, as delivered by Paul. The Holy Spirit inspired the record of that truth and we have it all today in the word of God, the Bible. The sign gifts, having served their purpose, have "vanished away". Paul uses his own infancy to illustrate this point. "When I was a child, I spake as a child (tongues), I understood as a child (prophecies), I thought as a child (knowledge): but when I became a man, I put away childish things". As he grew, the features of his infancy vanished, and so it was with the early church.

Day 3

THE INDWELLING OF THE SPIRIT

1 Corinthians 6:19-20

The Lord Jesus promised His disciples that the Holy Spirit "dwelleth with you, and shall be in you" (John 14:17). The sheer enormity of all that this implies was not only difficult for them to comprehend, but it is equally difficult for us. The Holy Spirit is not a force or an influence, as some suggest. He is a distinct Person of the eternal Godhead, co-equal with the Father and the Son. Which of us has not wished at times that we could have known the precious company of the Saviour as He walked for God in this world? Do we think that such an experience of Christ would have made us know Him more, and made us more devoted to Him? Yet there were things concerning the Lord that the disciples never knew whilst He was here. It was only after the Lord had gone back to heaven and the Holy Spirit had come down at Pentecost that the disciples not only had a divine Person with them, but also in them.

What a wonderful day it was in Israel's history when God graciously deigned to dwell amongst them in the tabernacle. Many years later, as the temple was being prepared, Solomon said "Behold, I build an house to the name of the Lord my God, to dedicate it to him … and the house which I build is great: for great is our God above all gods. But who is able to build him an house, seeing the heaven and heaven of heavens cannot contain him?" (2 Chron 2:4-6). Let us feel the weight of Solomon's words, beloved, "the heaven and heaven of heavens cannot contain him". Then, with holy wonder, we should meditate upon Paul's words, "know ye not that your body is the temple [the inner shrine] of the Holy Ghost which is in you" (1 Cor 6:19). The One whom heaven cannot contain is pleased to make His abode not just with us (as He did in the tabernacle, the temple and the Person of the Lord Jesus in His earthly sojourn) but in us!

When we consider the holiness of the conditions in which God must dwell, what does that tell us about the standing we have in our Lord Jesus Christ? What a thorough work He has accomplished so that sinners might not only be saved from wrath but also made fit for the indwelling presence of a divine Person! And what more do these things tell us about the necessity of practical holiness on the part of the child of God? Every place to which I go, every deed I perform, is with the company of the Holy Spirit, a divine Person. An understanding of this immense and precious truth would regulate every aspect of our lives. "For ye are bought with a price: therefore glorify God in your body, and in your spirit, which are God's" (1 Cor 6:20). Think about it.

Day 4

THE SEAL OF THE SPIRIT

Ephesians 1:1-14

There are three thoughts that are particularly precious concerning the seal of the Holy Spirit set upon the believer. A seal can be a mark of authenticity, a legal declaration of ownership, or a guarantee of security.

Is there a foe who would challenge the effectiveness of the soul-saving work of the Lord Jesus? Praise God, we have His stamp of authenticity that guarantees His eternal satisfaction with the work the Saviour has done, "Nevertheless the foundation of God standeth sure, having this seal, The Lord knoweth them that are his" (2 Tim 2:19). None in earth, heaven or hell may tamper with that which God hath decreed: He has set His seal upon it. Remember the incident recorded in the book of Esther, "Then the king Ahasuerus said … Behold, I have given Esther the house of Haman, and him they have hanged upon the gallows, because he laid his hand upon the Jews. Write … in the king's name, and seal it with the king's ring: for the writing which is written in the king's name, and sealed with the king's ring, may no man reverse" (Esther 8:7-8). If the seal of an earthly potentate carried such weight, how much more the divine seal?

A seal was used as a proof of legal ownership. When Jeremiah recalled the purchase of the field in Anathoth he said "And I bought the field of Hanameel … and weighed him the money …and I subscribed the evidence, and sealed it, and took witnesses, and weighed him the money in the balances. So I took the evidence of the purchase, both that which was sealed according to the law and custom, and that which was open: And I gave the evidence of the purchase unto Baruch the son of Neriah" (Jer 32:9-12). The seal declared that the purchase price had been fully paid. Legal ownership was beyond dispute. Lift your heart in worship, dear saint of God! You have been sealed to demonstrate that the full purchase price demanded for your freedom has been paid, and you can confidently declare "I am thine" (Ps 119:94).

Security can be guaranteed by a seal. What unchallengeable authority and power was vested in king Darius! "Then the king commanded, and they brought Daniel, and cast him into the den of lions … And a stone was brought, and laid upon the mouth of the den; and the king sealed it with his own signet, and with the signet of his lords; that the purpose might not be changed concerning Daniel" (Dan 6:16-17). The seal of Darius was worthless before God, as was the seal of Rome upon the Saviour's tomb. But His seal can never be broken. An official seal can only be broken by one of higher authority than the person who set the seal. It is God himself who has sealed us, and the Holy Spirit Himself is the seal. There is no higher authority in the universe than God our Saviour! Upon believing "ye were sealed with that Holy Spirit of promise" and truly saved, for ever, because the purchase price has been paid. Hallelujah!

Day 5

THE EARNEST OF THE SPIRIT

2 Corinthians 1:21-22; 5:1-5; Ephesians 1:1-14

In modern language the word "earnest" means 'sincere' or 'genuine', but it once had the meaning of 'a pledge' or 'guarantee'. A person who wished to buy an article for which they did not immediately have the money would leave a reasonable sum as a down payment, thus securing the article for a period of time. Providing the remainder of the purchase price was paid within the specified period, the article was 'redeemed' and became the full property of the purchaser. Whilst this illustration helps us understand the use of the word "earnest", we need to be very clear about one thing. As far as our redemption is concerned, the price has been fully paid in the precious blood of Christ, and we are as secure for heaven today as we shall ever be. The idea we want to draw from the example is that of a pledge securing the article against the day of redemption. On that day of redemption the article, which already belongs legally to the purchaser, is collected and comes into his full possession. He can take it to his home, set it in its place, and enjoy it for ever after.

Such is the wonderful truth concerning God's purpose for the Church. He has purchased it with the blood of His own (Acts 20:28) and it belongs to Him legally by reason of the price paid. The "earnest" (or pledge) that He will take His loved ones home to glory is the Holy Spirit. His presence within us is the divine guarantee that on a coming day of redemption God will call us home to heaven. Paul expresses this very thought as he speaks to the Roman believers about creation's future deliverance: "For the creature was made subject to vanity, not willingly, but by reason of him who hath subjected the same in hope, because the creature itself also shall be delivered from the bondage of corruption into the glorious liberty of the children of God. For we know that the whole creation groaneth and travaileth in pain together until now. And not only they, but ourselves also, which have the firstfruits of the Spirit, even we ourselves groan within ourselves, waiting for the adoption, to wit, the redemption of our body" (Rom 8:20-23). "The firstfruits of the Spirit" is another expression for "the earnest of the Spirit". As the harvest ripened and the time drew near to gather it in, a sample sheaf was cut and presented to the Lord. The firstfruits were the evidence of a much greater ingathering that was soon to be brought home. So the presence of the Holy Spirit in us is God's gracious assurance that, in His own time, He will gather us all home to glory and to the glorious inheritance that is ours in Christ Jesus.

Day 6

THE FILLING OF THE SPIRIT

Ephesians 5:8-21

"And be not drunk with wine, wherein is excess; but be filled with the Spirit; Speaking to yourselves in psalms and hymns and spiritual songs, singing and making melody in your heart to the Lord; Giving thanks always for all things unto God and the Father in the name of our Lord Jesus Christ; Submitting yourselves one to another in the fear of God" (Eph 5:18-21). In this extremely practical section of his letter to the Ephesians, Paul makes his point clear by using a very obvious comparison and an equally evident contrast. The believer who is filled with the Spirit can be compared with the person who is filled with wine, in that both are under the influence of a powerful, life-changing force. The stark contrast lies in the effects produced by the Holy Spirit on the one hand, and by strong drink on the other. The contrasting effects are displayed in speaking, singing and attitude.

Dear saints of God, we should have nothing whatsoever to do with strong drink. Red wine can have a beneficial medicinal effect as Paul instructs Timothy (1 Tim 5:23), but note that Paul was speaking only of wine and only within very clear medical constraints. Social drinking in all its forms should be shunned by every believer. How utterly degrading and godless are the speaking, singing and attitude of the drunkard! Speech becomes slurred and inarticulate, loud, vulgar, abusive and foul. What part does the child of God have in that? The singing of those intoxicated with drink is bawdy, discordant, vacuous and coarse. In that poignant psalm which describes so much of the sufferings of Messiah, the Saviour Himself was the subject of "the song of the drunkards" (Ps 69:12). Those who belong to the Lord should never be near even the perimeter of such things. And what of the attitude of the drunkard? Inhibitions gone, he will reel to and fro with belligerent words and behaviour, fighting, swearing and defiling himself and others with all the products of his own wasteful and disgusting excess. Dear young ones, keep away from alcohol totally, in all its forms, for those who name the name of our Lord Jesus Christ have no fellowship at all with these works of darkness.

Thank God for the holy language of the sanctuary! How does the believer speak? Of the Lord and His ways. How does he sing? With sweet melody in his redeemed heart. What is his attitude? Thankfulness to God in the name of our Lord Jesus Christ, and deference to his brethren and sisters as he lives in the reverential fear of God. To be filled with wine is to give oneself over to drink and all its effects. To be filled with the Spirit is to submit to Him, and let Him produce Christ-likeness in us.

Day 7

THE UNCTION OF THE SPIRIT

1 John 2:18-20, 26-27

John's epistles were the last to be written, and the concern of the apostle for the family of God lies evident on the page. A particular burden to him was the knowledge that there were unsaved men moving amongst the saints, and they were claiming to have a knowledge of divine things superior to that possessed by ordinary believers. The heresy taught by these men particularly attacked the Person and work of the Lord Jesus. Some were teaching that the man Jesus was not truly divine but had merely been endowed with a divine presence from the time of His baptism until He went to the cross. At the cross the divine presence left Him and He died as any other man. Others denied that Jesus Christ was come in the flesh so, on the one hand some denied the Lord's deity and, on the other, some denied His humanity. The devil's attacks on the Lord Jesus have not diminished, and we have a great responsibility to teach, learn and be assured of those precious truths concerning His unrelinquished eternal deity, His unchanging co-equality with the Father and His wonderful, impeccable, true humanity.

What defence did the simple believers of John's day have against these blasphemous heretics, pompous and arrogant in their claims of superior knowledge? Those dear saints had the same protection as you and I enjoy: "But ye have an unction from the Holy One, and ye know all things" (1 John 2:20). An "unction" is an anointing, something poured out upon another. John was saying, "ye have an anointing from the Anointed One". The Lord Jesus, the perfect, dependent man, was anointed by the Holy Spirit at His baptism as He commenced His public ministry to the nation. The abiding of the Spirit on Christ was a declaration of heaven's delight in Him, but it also demonstrated that this man would move for God under the guardianship of the Holy Spirit. Now the Anointed One, in accordance with His own promise in the upper room, has anointed His loved ones with a view to our guardianship in a hostile scene.

Believers new to the faith, faced with false teaching, can know instinctively that it is wrong. How? Because the indwelling presence of the Holy Spirit affords protection for the believer and gives the potential to "know all things". That statement should not be understood as "all things" in an absolute sense, meaning that there is nothing else to know. Rather, it is telling us that "all things" necessary for the preservation of the believer from false teaching will be afforded by the Spirit of God.

PHIL COULSON

Week 45

7 FEATURES OF DAVID OBSERVED BY AN UNKNOWN SERVANT

Introduction

"Provide me now a man that can play well, and bring him to me" were the words of Saul in 1 Samuel 16:17. The response to this royal command leaves us suddenly listening to the words of a young man, a servant of Saul, an unnamed servant – one of a number in the word of God. If an unnamed servant is a picture for us of the Holy Spirit, then this young man is no exception as he unfolds to Saul some of the remarkable features of David the son of Jesse.

As to when, how and where he had come to appreciate these virtues of David we are not told, but it seems that very early on in David's life the servant had recognised and come to value the one that God had chosen. As a servant of Saul he would have known all about the man after the flesh, the people's choice, but David was a man who was different and the servant describes him in detail.

Saul said "Provide me a man" and, in the next chapter, Goliath said "Give me a man". But before either Saul or Goliath found David, God had his eye upon him and said, "I have provided me a king" (1 Sam 16:1). How fitting that God's man was one who "keepeth the sheep" (16:11). He was unnoticed and unknown by most, but chosen of God, "a man after mine own heart" (Acts 13:22). Truly "man looketh on the outward appearance, but the Lord looketh on the heart" (1 Sam 16:7).

If only we could live our lives before God who knows and sees all, rather than seek the favour and praise of men. A life lived for Him will not go unnoticed and, as David rejoices in the greatness and glory of His creator, God takes note of him. This servant of Saul had noticed him too, and we note he also was "a young man" (JND). It is wonderful to think that we do not have to wait until we are old to get an appreciation of Christ, One far greater than David, who can occupy our hearts here and now. This is the work of the Spirit of God, to reveal Him to us in His word and in His wonderful work of creation. Let us make it our ambition to know Him whom to know is life eternal.

Day 1

"A SON OF JESSE THE BETHLEHEMITE"

1 Samuel 16:17-19

Perhaps one of David's greatest virtues in the midst of so much fame and prominence was that he never ceased to be the "son of Jesse the Bethlehemite". This was true right up to his dying day, even in his last words in 2 Samuel 23: 1, "Now these be the last words of David. David the son of Jesse said …". May God help each of us "not to think of himself more highly than he ought to think" (Rom 12:3).

We remember that David's great grandmother was Ruth the Moabitess, and the law forbade a Moabite to "enter into the congregation of the Lord; even to their tenth generation shall they not enter into the congregation of the Lord for ever" (Deut 23:3). Then we think of Ruth's words, "Why have I found grace in thine eyes, that thou shouldest take knowledge of me, seeing I am a stranger?" (Ruth 2:10). We might well ask "why?". It is all of God's grace that we have been brought in, and we might also join with David in Psalm 122 and say "I was glad when they said unto me, Let us go into the house of the Lord".

The one whom God raised up on high and anointed, the sweet psalmist of Israel, was the one who was first of all prepared to go down into the valley. When David returned with the giant's head in his hand, Saul said, "Whose son art thou, thou young man? And David answered, I am the son of thy servant Jesse the Bethlehemite" (1 Sam 17:58). Jesse himself is described as a man who "went among men for an old man in the days of Saul" (17:12). His name means 'gift', and what a gift his youngest son was – David (beloved) from Ephrath (fruitful) of Bethlehem (house of bread) Judah (praise). This son of Jesse seems the answer to all of these meanings, coming from the place of obscurity into the very centre of attention, yet never seeking recognition, fame or prominence. It all brings before us Another, with whom no mortal can compare. We think of God's gift to a world, great David's greater Son, the Son of God, coming forth from Nazareth, the despised city, from a place of obscurity. God could break the heavens and declare concerning Him "My beloved Son in whom I am well pleased". He was One who was the fruitful vine, One who was the bread of life and One whose life continually brought

praise and glory to God. At the end of it all, having ascended into heaven, this blessed man could say to Saul on the Damascus road, "I am Jesus of Nazareth" (Acts 22:8). Well might we rejoice in Him daily and seek grace to be more like Him (Phil 2:5).

"CUNNING IN PLAYING"

1 Samuel 16:17-19

"Cunning in playing"; and so he was! The son of Jesse could take his harp and not just constantly pluck one string but play on an instrument of ten strings (Ps 92:3), and what results came from his music as we see the effect that it had on Saul. He was both refreshed and restored (1 Sam 16:23).

How many since have found refreshment and restoration from the lovely psalms of David. So many have been refreshed and found peace to sleep; "I laid me down and slept; I awaked; for the Lord sustained me" (Ps 3:5), and "I will both lay me down in peace, and sleep: for thou, Lord, only makest me dwell in safety" (Ps 4:8). What confidence the psalmist had in his God. Not only refreshed but restored, and it is just as if he gives a big sigh of relief as he pens Psalm 32 and says "Blessed [Happy] is he whose transgression is forgiven, whose sin is covered". He remembers the days and nights of departure, misery and barrenness of soul, but now it is all over and he is forgiven and restored. In the 23rd Psalm he brings both thoughts together and rejoices in the green pasture which makes him full, satisfied, refreshed, and thereby his soul is restored.

> "Pastures abundant doth his hand provide,
> Still waters flowing ever at my side".

If we could only take David's harp and through these lovely psalms bring a ministry of refreshment and restoration to others, what a blessing it could be! It is only a ministry of Christ that will heal the broken-hearted and bring the wanderer back. As we contemplate Him in all the Scriptures, and see Him here in this world delighting the heart of God and bringing gladness and joy to so many, we remember Him

> "By the Galilean waters, in the busy city street,
> On the highways, in the deserts, or where congregations meet;
> In the house of Simon Peter, sitting wearied at the well,
> 'Mid disciples on the hillside with the truth of God to tell.
>
> Cleansing here the pleading leper, opening there the darkened eye
> Of the beggar by the wayside – He a stranger passing by.

Standing radiant on the mountain, meeting unbelief below,
Bearing grief, sustaining sorrow, calming fear, dispelling woe".
(H J Miles)

We are reminded of Onesiphorus of whom Paul said "he oft refreshed me" (2 Tim 1:16). "The house of Stephanus … addicted themselves to the ministry of the saints … they have refreshed my spirit and yours" (1 Cor 16:15, 18). And Paul speaks not just of refreshment, but also restoration: "If a man be overtaken in a fault … restore such an one in the spirit of meekness" (Gal 6:1).

Day 3

"*A MIGHTY VALIANT MAN*"

1 Samuel 16:17-19; 17:1-58

"A mighty valiant man"; and so he was! It seems that even before David had gone out to meet Goliath that this young servant of Saul had come to appreciate that he was a mighty, valiant man. We remember that when everyone's hearts were failing them for fear, when they saw Goliath and fled from him, that David said, "thy servant will go" (1 Sam 17:32). It was not until Saul said "Thou are not able" (v.33) that David recounts the story of the lion and the bear, and it is here we see the secret of the ability of this mighty, valiant man.

After saying "Thy servant slew both the lion and the bear", he said "moreover, The Lord that delivered me … he will deliver me" (vv.36-37). What tremendous confidence he had in God. He had proved God in a way that few ever have, out there on the hillsides of Palestine, looking after his father's sheep, alone and yet occupied with the Lord of Hosts. Both day and night he rejoiced in the glory of God as it was revealed in silent wonder and, as he meditated in the law of the Lord, it became precious to him, more precious than fine gold and sweeter than the honeycomb (Ps 19:10). The greater his appreciation of the Almighty, the less he thought of himself, and his strength was made perfect in weakness.

Nobody else seemed to have noticed David, but God had. It was God who said "I have provided me a king" (16:1), and He "took him from the sheepfolds" (Ps 78:70); it was God who said "I have found David my servant" (Ps 89:20), one who was mighty yet had a shepherd heart. It was a shepherd they saw go down into the valley, prepared to take his life in his hands for the people of God.

Oh for mighty, valiant men with shepherd hearts, believers who, out of love for Christ and his people, are prepared to give themselves for what they know to be of God!

There was only One, our blessed Lord, who truly and absolutely lived down here for God. Thank God He lived and died for others that "he might destroy him that had the power of death, that is, the devil; and deliver them who through fear of death were all their lifetime subject to bondage" (Heb 2:14-15). We rejoice in a far greater than David who slew a far greater than Goliath, and may we, like those in Hebrews 11:34, "out of weakness" be "made strong". "I can do all things through Christ which strengtheneth me" (Phil 4:13). "God is our refuge and strength, a very present help in trouble" (Ps 46:1).

Day 4

"*A MAN OF WAR*"

1 Samuel 16:17-19

"A man of war"; and so he was! David was always fighting battles and his secret of success was undoubtedly summed up in his words "the battle is the Lord's, and he will give you into our hands" (1 Sam 17:47). He had proved God and could confidently say "the battle is the Lord's" before it was fought. It is almost as if faith can see the end from the beginning.

It seems there are at least three battles in chapter 17. Perhaps the first was the hardest, because it came from his family as he listened to the taunts of his eldest brother, but the man who had come from the presence of God knew how to respond. Eliab did not know David's heart, and accused him falsely of pride and just coming to see the battle. We might well ask, "What battle?". The battle at that moment must have been going on in David's heart, and with God's help he wins the victory. It is hard to be falsely accused, but we remember One who "when he was reviled, reviled not again" (1 Pet 2:23).

The second battle for David must have been among the people of God as he put on the king's armour. If ever there was a time for pride and a display of the flesh it must be then. But the man who had proved God put it all off. He knew he could do nothing, but "with God all things are possible".

It was a shepherd that they saw go down into the valley of Elah with a staff in his hand, a shepherd's bag, five smooth stones and a sling. There is no room for pride here. It is unlikely that any in Israel were boasting in their champion. As he went to fight his third battle, he was all alone with the hosts of the Philistines and their formidable champion Goliath, but the man who had proved God rejoiced in the power of God and ran towards the army to meet the Philistine.

We think of a far greater than David who came unto His own and His own received Him not. One to whom Satan could come and find nothing in Him that responded to promised fame and glory, One who went alone, all alone, to meet the foe and return victorious.

We remember Paul's exhortation to Timothy to "fight the good fight of faith", and some of his own last words, "I have fought a good fight". Again, to the church at Ephesus, he said "Put on the whole armour of God", but we remember that we can only "be strong in the Lord, and in the power of his might" (Eph 6:10).

Day 5

"PRUDENT IN MATTERS"

1 Samuel 16:17-19

"Prudent in matters" (or, 'skilled in speech' JND); and so he was! His first recorded words show his concern at the reproach of Israel as the giant defied the armies of the living God. "What shall be done to the man that killeth this Philistine, and taketh away the reproach from Israel? for who is this uncircumcised Philistine, that he should defy the armies of the living God?" (1 Sam 17:26). Again, as he responds to Eliab's taunts with "What have I now done? Is there not a cause?" (v.29), it is a "soft answer" that "turneth away wrath" (Prov 15:1). "I said, I will take heed to my ways, that I sin not with my tongue: I will keep my mouth with a bridle while the wicked is before me. I was dumb with silence, I held my peace" (Ps 39:1-2); "I waited patiently for the Lord; and he inclined unto me, and heard my cry … he hath put a new song in my mouth" (Ps 40:1, 3); "My heart is inditing a good matter: I speak of the things which I have made touching the king … grace is poured into thy lips" (Ps 45:1-2).

We think of One even greater than David, and when He spake, "they were astonished at his doctrine: for he taught them as one that had authority, and not as the scribes" (Mark 1:22). "They were all amazed … for with authority commandeth he even the unclean spirits, and they do obey him" (1:27). Again, when He came to Nazareth in Luke 4, "as his custom was, he went into the synagogue on the sabbath day, and stood up for to read" (Luke 4:16). He stood and took the book. He knew where to start and where to finish, and as He read and taught "the eyes of all … were fastened on him … And all bare him witness, and wondered at the gracious words which proceeded out of his mouth" (4:20, 22). The officers in John 7 could say when He spake "Never man spake like this man". Poor Peter, we remember his speech betrayed him and we can all identify with him only too well. If only we could learn the lessons of James in relation to our speech. Moses was slow in speech; Absalom was fair of speech and subtle with it. Apollos was eloquent in speech, but not always right. We might well envy Stephen, whose tongue is "the pen of a ready writer" as he pours out his soul in defence of the gospel, intelligently, faithfully and yet with grace.

We thank God for One who never had to take back a word and whose words were full of grace and truth, beautifully balanced. The two on the road to Emmaus could say "Did not our heart burn within us, while he talked with us by the way" (Luke 24:32). We challenge our own hearts, and remember the words of Paul, "Let your speech be alway with grace, seasoned with salt, that ye may know how ye ought to answer every man" (Col 4:6).

Day 6

"A COMELY PERSON"

1 Samuel 16:17-19

"A comely person" ('of good presence' JND); and so he was! From the very first time we see him brought in before Samuel "ruddy, and withal of a beautiful countenance", he was pleasant to look upon. His personal appearance, his behaviour, the very way he presented himself was appealing and attractive to Saul's servant, to Samuel and to God. What a contrast to Saul, whose countenance was so often that of a morose, angry and selfish man. What a contrast to Goliath, a great lumbering lump of boasting flesh, disdaining and cursing, and full of his own strength and ability. What a contrast this youngest son of Jesse is as we read through these wonderful well-known chapters. You can almost hear him singing and rejoicing in the living God whom he had proved and had come to know; "Every day will I bless thee; and I will praise thy name for ever and ever" (Ps 145:2).

In Proverbs 30:29 there are four things that are comely in going, and we remind ourselves of the lion's strength, the greyhound's speed, the steadfastness of the goat and the supremacy of the king. We think of this young son of Jesse who slew the lion, who "hasted, and ran toward the army to meet the Philistine" (1 Sam 17:48), whom Saul sought in vain to find in the mountains of the wild goats (1 Sam 24) and eventually became sovereign, being crowned king of all Israel. Again, it all reminds us of a far greater than David. So often David's courage failed and, instead of running, he turned and fled, his feet slipped, and his crown was taken by another. Thank God for the Lord Jesus who never had to retrace a step, steadfastly setting His face toward Jerusalem, there to be crowned with thorns; but "the head that once was crowned with thorns is crowned with glory now". That crown is unfading and will never be relinquished to another.

> "Fairer than all of earth-born race,
>   Perfect in comeliness Thou art;
> Replenished are Thy lips with grace,
>   And full of love Thy tender heart.
> God ever blest, we bow the knee
>   And own all fulness dwells in Thee."

> "All beauty may we ever see in God's beloved Son,
> The chiefest of ten thousand He, the only lovely One."

As those who belong to Him, representing Him here in the world, may we display something of the comeliness of Christ, in our countenance, our appearance and in our lives before others. "For what shall the world see of Jesus, if they cannot see Jesus in me?".

Day 7

"THE LORD IS WITH HIM"

1 Samuel 16:17-19

"The Lord is with him"; and so He was! If ever there was a man who seemed to be in the enjoyment of the conscious knowledge of the presence of the Lord, it was David. It is almost as if this young servant of Saul had recognised the fact that the Lord was no longer with Saul, but he was with David, and what a difference it made. Here are the carnal man and the spiritual man, the one only thinking about himself, the other thinking about others and God's glory. The Lord meant everything to David and, as we read his psalms, we know that from an early age his delight was in Him and in His law. Rejoicing in the glory of God seen in the heavens, David feels so small and undeserving as he considers "the work of thy fingers, the moon and the stars, which thou hast ordained". Again, in Psalm 19, he is rejoicing in the way the heavens declare the glory of God. Twenty-four hours of every day and night, a silent testimony to the whole world. He finishes the psalm by saying He is "my strength, and my redeemer" (Ps 19:14).

David seemed constantly to enjoy the Lord's presence. It brought him such peace, strength and security, whether it was night or day, morning or evening. He also realised that he could not hide from God, and said "Whither shall I go?", finishing with "Search me, O God, and know my heart" (Ps 139:7, 23). What a constant challenge it was to him, knowing that if there was a hand to hold and to lead, and arms which gathered and carried, there was also an eye that sees everything.

We remember the last words of our Lord in Matthew's gospel, "Lo, I am with you alway, even unto the end of the world" (Matt 28:20) and it is just as if He has never left the world at all. God said to Moses in Exodus 33, "My presence shall go with thee". David prayed in repentance "Cast me not away from thy presence" (Ps 51:11). We remember the last words of Paul, "All men forsook me … notwithstanding the Lord stood with me, and strengthened me" (2 Tim 4:16-17). David says in his lovely shepherd psalm "Though I walk through the valley of the shadow of death, thou art with me … and I will dwell in the house of the Lord forever". We rejoice in the Lord's own words "I will never leave thee, nor forsake thee … The Lord is my helper" (Heb 13:5-6).

> "I must have the Saviour with me
> For I dare not walk alone
> I must feel His presence near me
> And His arm around me thrown"

HAROLD HATT

Week 46

7 MENTIONS OF "IN THE LORD" IN EPHESIANS

Introduction

The apostle Paul wrote this divinely inspired epistle to the saints at Ephesus, conveying truth relating to their exalted blessings and privileges as believers in our Lord Jesus Christ. The title "Lord Jesus Christ" occurs three times in chapter 1, with other appropriate references to our Lord Jesus. Reading and meditating upon this chapter will remind us that we owe everything to Him.

"The God and Father of our Lord Jesus Christ … hath blessed us with all spiritual blessings in heavenly places in Christ". This infinite, divinely given wealth of blessing belongs equally and alike to every Christian. We enter upon it fully upon believing, and thereafter it can neither increase nor diminish.

Of course we have never deserved or merited such blessings, but God, according to the riches of His grace, hath bestowed them upon all who are in Christ. The phrase "in Christ" denotes the sphere or place of privilege, and every Christian will readily acknowledge that to be "in Christ" is indeed a wondrous privilege in contrast to being "in Adam" (1 Cor 15: 22) in unconverted days. There ought to be, however, an equal readiness to appreciate Paul's teaching in Ephesians that Christians are not only "in Christ" but also "in the Lord" or, to put it another way, we not only have blessings and privileges, but also duties and responsibilities.

In our modern society emphasis has been placed upon rights to the detriment of recognition of responsibilities. As Christians we should be careful not to be influenced by the thoughts, opinions, and maxims of this age "wherein in time past ye walked" (2:2). We all have secular responsibilities but, more importantly, we have spiritual responsibilities, and it is salutary to realise that in an epistle in which Paul writes so much of the Christian's exalted privileges as being "in Christ", he also writes of the Christian's responsibilities as being "in the Lord".

In our meditations upon this recurring phrase in Ephesians we shall be confronted with a variety of Christian duties and responsibilities. As we seriously address the issues involved, may we acknowledge the claims of the Lord upon us and endeavour to bring Him glory. To do so is really to do honour to the glorious One who is Lord of all.

Day 1

"... FAITH IN THE LORD JESUS"

Ephesians 1:15-23

It is Luke, that worthy companion of Paul, to whom we are indebted for the story of that day when the parents of the child Jesus brought Him into the temple to do for Him after the custom of the law. His narrative vividly describes Simeon taking the child up in his arms and, as we read, we marvel – the child Jesus – an infant in the arms of an old man but, "a light to lighten the Gentiles, and the glory of thy people Israel" (Luke 2:32).

Of course the child grew, and how His earthly parents must have marvelled at the perfection of those boyhood days of His flesh, throughout which He was subject unto them. At length, in full grown manhood, He entered into His public ministry, leading on to His sufferings and death at Calvary. Each of the Gospels tells us of Joseph, who went unto Pilate and begged the body of Jesus so that it might with dignity be laid in a sepulchre wherein never man before was laid.

To that sepulchre upon the first day of the week, very early in the morning, the women came. Finding the stone rolled away they entered in and, as Luke tells us, they found not the body of the Lord Jesus. It is the first occurrence in our Bibles of the title "Lord Jesus", and how fitting that it is on resurrection ground. He was born, and lived and died, and now He is risen from the dead, He is Lord. That eternally blessed One who, in infant days, was the "child Jesus", is now the "Lord Jesus".

Paul learned that glorious truth on the road to Damascus, the glory of that light (Acts 22:11) making manifest that the Lord Jesus raised from the dead is exalted, a man in the glory of heaven. This very truth is set forth in the reading recommended above. Wherever Paul went he was faithful in the ministry which he received of the Lord Jesus to testify the gospel of the grace of God. When he continued in Ephesus for two years "all they which dwelt in Asia heard the word of the Lord Jesus" (Acts 19:10).

The epistle was, of course, written to those who believed the gospel, and whose faith was in the Lord Jesus. He was their Lord and Saviour. They had acknowledged His supreme authority, and the corollary, namely the submission of their wills in obedience to the word of the Lord Jesus. Submission of the will to the Lord Jesus is an axiom of Christianity and ought to be practised by the believer from the outset. After all, our faith is "in the Lord Jesus".

Day 2

"... AN HOLY TEMPLE IN THE LORD"

Ephesians 2:19-22

In our previous meditation we recalled the words of Simeon, "a light to lighten the Gentiles, and the glory of thy people Israel". We may feel it was gracious of Simeon to mention the Gentiles first but, of course, he was speaking by the Spirit and thus in accord with Isaiah, who refers to the Gentiles more often by far than does any other prophet. Isaiah alludes to the Gentile as "him that is far off", and to the Jew as "him that is near" (57:19), using the same order as does Simeon.

Centuries later Paul takes up the same theme and, in Ephesians 2:17, quotes from Isaiah. The glad tidings of peace have been preached to Gentile and to Jew, and the blood of Christ is the secure basis of that peace. Paul, however, is able to go so much further, and by revelation make known truth previously hidden. Not only are poor Gentiles to be blessed but the enmity between Jew and Gentile is annulled. God has now before Him "one new man", the universal church, Jew and Gentile, reconciled both unto God in one body. The thought of oneness and unity pervades the passage.

This great universal church, in which distinction of Jew and Gentile is lost, is spoken of in four ways. (1) a citizenship (v.19); (2) an household (v.19); (3) an holy temple (v.21); and (4) an habitation of God (v.22). These may be considered as two couplets, so that we understand that we now share with all saints of this dispensation the privileges of citizenship, all being the family (household) of God, and that the saints comprise an holy temple which is an habitation of God.

What an exalted privilege to be, by divine grace, a stone in this building "fitly framed together" (v.21). The phrase occurs only twice in our New Testament, here reference the church as a building and, at 4:16, reference the church as a body. The construction of Solomon's temple illustrates the truth. It "was built of stone made ready before it was brought thither" (1 Kings 6: 7). The temple presently growing, or increasing (JND), is holy, sanctified and suitable for the worship and praise of God, and therein the supreme authority of the Lord is acknowledged. Jesus Christ is Lord not only of the saints individually but corporately too. Only a spiritual house of this character, as seen in divine purpose, is suitable to be the dwelling place of God.

We are challenged by v.22, "in whom ye also are builded together". Do our lives reflect our being part of this great purpose which can neither fail nor falter? We would surely wish them to!

> "So shall no part of day or night
>   From sacredness be free,
> But all my life, in every step,
>   Be fellowship with Thee."   (Bonar)

Day 3

"I ... TESTIFY IN THE LORD"

Ephesians 4:1, 17-18

The letter to the Ephesians is one of the 'prison epistles' written by Paul whilst a prisoner in Rome. Outwardly he was a prisoner by imperial authority but Paul really considered himself to be a prisoner of, or in (JND), the Lord. That is, Paul recognised that his being in prison was not in consequence merely of the whim or hostility of men, but according to the Lord's will. In this, as in all other matters, he was subject to the authority and dominion of the Lord. This conviction must have been of great comfort to Paul, and a source of strength in testimony.

Coming to v.17, at which point the practical part of the epistle commences, we note that Paul testifies in the Lord. Elsewhere (1 Tim 1:12) we learn that the Lord counted Paul faithful putting him into the ministry. Today we are grateful for brethren who are faithful in their ministry to the saints, whose teaching or exhortation is spiritual and, therefore, authoritative.

The apostle's word and witness refers to the nature of their walk, that is, their lives. Conversion, by its nature, is a radical event, and things cannot be the same as before. The word "henceforth" just means 'no longer'. They were to live no longer as other Gentiles. Once they had done, as described so vividly in 2:1-3, but no longer would it be so. Other Gentiles walk "in the vanity of their mind" or aimlessly, with no real purpose. Sadly, lack of purpose or direction is evident in many lives today.

Two reasons are given in verse 18 for this vain, empty life. First, the understanding is darkened, that is, the thinking capacity, the intellectual discernment of the unregenerate, is in a continually darkened state. Second, there is alienation from the life of God. What a sombre scene of darkness and death on account of ignorance (lack of knowledge), and because of blindness or, more accurately, hardness of heart. Perhaps the ignorance is mental, the hardness moral.

Reflecting upon verse 18 we cannot expect the unregenerate to understand the nature of Christian life. There may be appreciation of kindnesses shown, love expressed, generosity of spirit, but no sympathy for a conviction to live

for the Lord's glory. This is why men, even though religious, were hostile to Christ.

That lovely verse concerning our Lord often comes to mind, "he stedfastly set his face to go to Jerusalem" (Luke 9:51). Luke reveals steadfastness at a particular moment, but we know that the Lord's whole life was one of purpose, of fixed intent. We may ensure that we no longer live aimlessly by heeding the exhortation of Barnabas to Gentile converts at Antioch, "that with purpose of heart they would cleave unto the Lord" (Acts 11:23).

Day 4

"… NOW ARE YE LIGHT IN THE LORD"

Ephesians 5:1-14

We find these verses to be deeply searching as we read them thoughtfully and prayerfully, because Paul's exhortations rest upon the very essence of Christian life. In verse 2 we read "walk in love" and, in verse 8, "walk as children of light". Love and Light! Both are in the nature of God Himself.

Children, beloved of God, are to imitate Him by walking in love which is sacrificial, as was the love of Christ. God delights when our lives are pervaded by such love, when we breathe its atmosphere. The result will be that things abhorrent to God will have no attraction for us. In verses 3 and 4 are things now prevalent in our society but which are not to be "once named among you". To speak of such things with approval would be unbecoming in those who are sanctified, for they who practise them have no inheritance in the kingdom of Christ and of God. We are not to be deceived (v.6) by the empty talk of men who neither believe nor understand that the things in which they may delight incur divine judgment. Neither are we to partake with them in the lusts and passions of this age.

In verse 8 we find the past and the present of our lives contrasted in a way similar to chapter 2, and the contrast is equally stark. It is not that we were *in* darkness but now are *in* light, rather we *were* darkness but now *are* light in the Lord. What marvellous change wrought by divine grace, that Gentiles who were spiritually dead and dark, are now alive and light! Praise God for the import of the words "sometimes" and "now". Saints are light in the Lord. That is, they are brought into a sphere where the Lordship of Christ is paramount, and are made suitable to that place.

But then an injunction comes, yea a command. "Walk as children of light". For we ought to be in practise what God has made us. We are children of light, it is the Christian's native sphere, and that fact must characterise our lives. Thus we prove or find out by experience what is well pleasing to the Lord. In verse 11 Paul further exhorts them to "have no fellowship with the unfruitful works of darkness, but rather reprove them". The context suggests reproof by life rather than by lip. The life of the Christian ought to stand as a reproof of the lives of the ungodly, as did the life of Christ. Did not our Lord say "Ye are the light of the world. A city that is set on an hill cannot be hid"? Let us therefore resolve to let our "light so shine before men" (Matt 5:14,16).

Day 5

"CHILDREN, OBEY YOUR PARENTS IN THE LORD"

Ephesians 6:1-4

Whilst we may fail to live up to our responsibilities, being Christians we instinctively recognise that no part of our lives is outwith the authority of the Lord. We are therefore not surprised to discover that our Bibles contain guidance and instruction for every facet of life.

"God setteth the solitary in families" (Ps 68:6). This verse affirms the wise providence of God in establishing the family for the mutual comfort of its members, and for the stability of nations. The weakening of family life and ties is acknowledged as a major cause of our society's ills but, regrettably, not as a consequence of the disastrous abandonment of the Christian ethic.

Within a family of Christians, however, the divine ideal should be realised. The husband's love for his wife will create a home environment conducive to the happy submission of the wife to her husband, and the willing obedience of the children to their parents. Paul addresses believing children who are "in the Lord", the sphere of submission to the supreme authority of Christ within which is required recognition of human authority including that of parents. That modern trends may run counter to this should not influence the attitude of believing children to their parents.

Siblings can be remarkably diverse in personality and behaviour. Esau and Jacob are an example, and their habits and demeanour appealed to Isaac and Rebekah respectively to the extent that preferences were shown to the detriment of both sons. Parents must be even handed so as not to undermine encouragement and discipline (the meaning of nurture and admonition, v.4). Ultimately, Esau gave both his father and mother "grief of mind" but Jacob obeyed the voice of his parents. Interestingly, both statements are in the context of their marrying, suggesting that in adulthood sons and daughters still ought to honour their father and mother and, further, reminding us of the vital importance of marrying "only in the Lord" (1 Cor 7:39). Isaac and his family lived prior to the law, we in a later dispensation, but the commandment quoted expresses the mind of God in regard to children and their parents for all time.

How precious and deeply significant are Luke's brief allusions to the boyhood of our Lord Jesus. "He went down with them, and came to Nazareth, and was subject unto them" (Luke 2:51). How satisfying His behaviour to Joseph and Mary! What infinite pleasure to God in His condescension to fill a subject place! The filial devotedness of our Lord continued until, when upon

the cross, He commended His mother to the care of the disciple whom He loved. Such an example is surely an adequate incentive for children to do right by obeying their parents. Happy the home where such honour and love are shown.

Day 6

"BE STRONG IN THE LORD"

Ephesians 6:10-17

Paul draws to the end of his letter, though he has important things remaining to tell us. "Be strong in the Lord". We could not otherwise be strong. It is the passive "Be strengthened", meaning that we are naturally weak and will only find strength in Him. There is an infinite resource, "the power of his might". This power is a divine attribute, the strength by which God raised His Son from amongst the dead. The might is the measure of it – irresistible!

The exhortation of verse 10 is illustrated by the history of Joshua. Three times he is told "Be strong and of a good courage". Once it is "very courageous". Joshua needed to be strong to lead Israel to victory against its enemies, but he was assured "As I was with Moses so shall I be with thee". The Lord would be with him and no man would be able to stand against him.

Joshua's enemies were flesh and blood. Ours are neither tangible nor visible but are nevertheless real (v.12). The equipment essential to wage this spiritual warfare is "the whole armour of God", and so we are to have it put on. This armour provided by God is sufficient against every deceit of the devil. The only other occurrence of this word "armour" in the New Testament is at Luke 11:22 where our Lord is referring to the power by which He cast out demons. He is stronger than the strong man (Satan), and has overcome him, taking from him all his armour wherein he trusted, and divided his spoils. What resource then we have. Our confidence is in the Lord who has overcome.

We must not, however, minimise the conflict or, worse, imagine it does not exist. Paul has reminded the Ephesians that "in time past ye walked according to the prince of the power of the air". Millions still do and spiritual wickedness abounds, witness the occult, astrology, new age philosophy, even devil worship. Sadly, some aspects are treated lightly, for example horoscopes, but the devil and demons are behind every manifestation of these evils. The believer must abhor all such, and gain victory in wrestling, in the close combat of hand to hand fighting.

The armour is described in verses 14-17. Notice the one offensive weapon provided, "the sword of the Spirit, which is the word of God". We recall how Jesus was led up of the Spirit into the wilderness where he would be tempted of the devil. To each temptation he replied "it is written". In perfect wisdom he used Scripture to answer. In perfect knowledge he employed with precision the suitable portion of Scripture. May we too employ the word of God in the power of the Spirit.

Day 7

"Tychicus, a beloved brother ... in the Lord"

Ephesians 6:21-22

Tychicus would have been well known to the Ephesians. From Acts 20: 4 we learn that he was of Asia, the Roman province of which, Ephesus, was the principle city. Indeed it is possible that Tychicus was himself an Ephesian. At a later date Paul sent him to Ephesus (2 Tim 4:12). From these verses and others it is clear that he was one of Paul's trusted fellowservants.

We rightly esteem Paul as an apostle, on account of his labours, the revelation of truth given to him and, not least, the epistles he was inspired to write. However, we must appreciate that there were other brethren and sisters, contemporary with Paul and the other apostles, who did a valuable work and were greatly esteemed. We find frequent instances in the Pauline epistles of others being commended. Paul had a noble and generous spirit. There remain servants today, like Tychicus, who perhaps are less well known than others, but who do a work for the Lord.

He was a beloved brother. There were features that endeared him to the saints and indeed to Paul. Now it is fundamental to Christianity that we love one another, but how good it is when there is that of Christ in us that endears us to our fellow believers. He was also a faithful minister in the Lord. He felt himself responsible to the Lord for the ministry (diakonia) entrusted to him, and it is important that we too see our service as "in the Lord" so that all will be done as before Him, with a desire to please Him. Thus the minister, servant, deacon (the same word) will be reliable or trustworthy.

The saints at Ephesus were no doubt anxious about Paul in prison, and he wanted to let them know of his affairs and how he was doing. It is a lovely example of mutual comfort and love which we do well to emulate. So he sent Tychicus, a reliable messenger who carried the epistle with him. What a privilege that was, to become the bearer of an inspired document! When he arrived he told them all things concerning Paul so that they could pray more intelligently, for the apostle certainly valued and desired their prayers for him (v.19). He comforted their hearts – a gracious ministry for which he was well suited, being one of them. He would have been close to them, speaking words of warmth, encouragement and cheer, a faithful minister in the Lord.

Paul valued such men whom he could send to various assemblies, confident that their ministry would be a blessing to the saints. May we value and encourage men of that calibre today.

JAMES BROWN

Week 47

7 "GAINS" THAT PAUL COUNTED "LOSS" FOR CHRIST

Introduction

Approximately thirty years have passed since Saul met the Lord on the Damascus road with such life transforming results. He can never forget the day and the circumstances when the Lord Jesus intervened in his life. The light from heaven and the accompanying voice still grip his being, as he makes clear on other occasions (Acts 22:6-7; 26:13-14). That was the day when he yielded to a new master (Acts 9:5-6), received a new commission (Acts 9:15) and a new name (Acts 13:9). The God of glory, who centuries earlier appeared to Abraham whilst he was as yet an idolater and changed his outlook on this world for ever (Acts 7:2), now appears to Saul of Tarsus in the person of Jesus!

Having received the highest degree in education and religious training at the feet of Gamaliel (Acts 22:3), this young Pharisee was head and shoulders above his contemporaries in intellect and religious zeal (Gal 1: 14). Now, as he writes to the Philippians from prison in Rome, he recounts the things which he once held dear, but has gladly renounced for the sake of Christ. He does this, not for the purpose of self gratification, but because no one is better qualified to deal with those who still cling to Judaism, and who would, by their false teaching, adversely affect those whom God has graciously delivered from that system.

It is clear that Paul consistently and repeatedly taught the Philippians the fundamental doctrines of the Christian faith. He had not found this an irksome task, but regarded it necessary to safeguard the testimony (Phil 3:1). So, as he reaches this section of the letter, Paul calls upon his readers to be joyful – "rejoice in the Lord" (v.1) – and then to be careful, as three times he urges them to "beware" (v.2). As to the first, the Lord Jesus taught that his disciples should be filled with joy (John 15:11; 16.22, 24), and this is also a key feature of the Philippian letter. As to the second, Paul urges them against having any confidence in the flesh (v.3). It is this latter point that leads Paul to write of those things which he once prized, but now regards as dung (v.8).

Day 1

"CIRCUMCISED THE EIGHTH DAY"

Philippians 3:4-7; Acts 15:1-11

Instructions for circumcision were first given by God to Abraham to mark God's covenant with him concerning his seed and their inheritance (Gen 17: 10-13). All males born into his house were to be circumcised when eight days old. Jews later referred to Gentiles as "uncircumcised" and, particularly in our New Testament, "circumcision" became synonymous with the Jewish race. However, the term was also used in a moral sense, such as when Stephen charges the Jewish religious leaders as being "uncircumcised in heart and ears" (Acts 7:51).

In his unconverted days, Saul of Tarsus would boast in such a mark as a token of his pedigree connecting him with the father of the nation of Israel. Elsewhere he argues that there was an advantage in being a Jew, and profit in circumcision, for it marked them as a people of special privilege, albeit with accompanying responsibility in which, alas, they failed. (Rom 3:1-2; 9:4-5). The emphasis here is on the "eighth day", his meaning being 'as to circumcision eight days old'. By this he asserts that "he was not a proselyte to Judaism (and so circumcised as an adult), neither was he from Ishmael (whose descendants were circumcised at age thirteen). Saul belonged to the covenant race from his infancy" (See H.C.G. Moule – Philippians).

Should there be any ground for natural boasting in religious or national prowess, Paul had that right, but following his Damascus road experience, and the transforming power of Christ, he had learned "that in me (that is, in my flesh,) dwelleth no good thing" (Rom 7:18). Now from a spiritual standpoint he teaches that the true circumcision are they "which worship God in the spirit, and rejoice in Christ Jesus, and have no confidence in the flesh" (Phil 3:3). This was one of the main features of Judaism that caused so much havoc in the early church, for its adherents taught that unless a person was circumcised he could not be saved (Acts 15:1).

Paul confirms that circumcision is now a spiritual matter affecting the hearts and minds of believers, as identified with our Lord Jesus Christ in his death (Col 2:11-13).

The apostle carries another mark of a different kind in which he may now glory. It was more costly and more precious than that carried by the Judaising teachers which he describes as but a "fair shew in the flesh"! He says, "I bear in my body the marks (lit. 'brand marks') of the Lord Jesus" (Gal 6:12, 17). This may well refer to the scars left on Paul arising from his sufferings out of loyalty to Christ. Those who continue to boast in circumcision, glory in something that has been rendered obsolete by the cross!

Day 2

"OF THE STOCK OF ISRAEL"

Philippians 3:4-7; Romans 9:1-13

Here Paul focuses upon what he was nationally or racially, and he links himself directly with the stock of Israel. The word "stock" is the Greek word 'genos' and is used to denote a family, an offspring, or a race (W. E. Vine), so here he is tracing back his family roots.

In the epistle to the Galatians Paul reminds them that Abraham had two sons, Isaac and Ishmael, and that the promised seed was to come through Isaac (Gal 4:21-25). However, Isaac also had two sons, namely Jacob and Esau and, in the purpose of God, even before they were born, it was decreed that Jacob should predominate (Rom 9:10-13). The twelve tribes came from Jacob, but here Paul uses the name "Israel" rather than "Jacob". This carries our thoughts to that night of wrestling at Peniel when God said, "Thy name shall be called no more Jacob, but Israel [a prince with God]" (Gen 32:28). It was this new name that was later conferred upon the nation of Israel, so Paul can rightly link his pedigree to its origins.

Paul had a deep love for that nation who were his brethren according to the flesh, and he wrestled in prayer that they might be saved (Rom 9:1-5). He reminds his readers, however, that together with other believers in the Lord Jesus he now belongs to a new Society which, in the epistle to the Galatians, he calls "the Israel of God" (Gal 6:16).

In addition to his Jewish pedigree, Paul was a citizen of Tarsus which he describes as "no mean city" (Acts 21:39). He was a free-born Roman citizen, a privilege which one of the Roman chief captains had to purchase at great price (Acts 22:28). However, in this epistle to the Philippians, he takes great pleasure in the fact that now he, with all who are in Christ, has a heavenly citizenship, and all his present interests are of a heavenly character. His destiny lies in heaven, and from there he waits for a Saviour, the Lord Jesus Christ (3:20).

Paul is happy to consider his national prestige as nothing when compared to that which he has gained in Christ. It leaves us with a challenge as to how much we esteem earthly things when weighed against our heavenly citizenship. As Moses reached maturity, he faced this challenge when he "refused to be called the son of Pharaoh's daughter; choosing rather to suffer affliction with the people of God, than to enjoy the pleasures of sin for a season" (Heb 11: 24). After all, both Moses and Paul were sacrificing temporal things for things eternal, and in this both could anticipate abundant recompense.

Day 3

"OF THE TRIBE OF BENJAMIN"

Philippians 3:4-7; Romans 11:1-12

The genuineness of Saul's pedigree is such that he now narrows his focus from a nation to a tribe, the tribe of Benjamin (See Rom 11:1). There was something special to Jacob about his youngest son Benjamin. Like Joseph, Benjamin was the son of Jacob's much loved wife Rachel, and amongst all Jacob's sons, Benjamin alone was born in Palestine. The circumstances of his birth are very moving. As the family journeyed towards Ephrath, which is Bethlehem, Rachel died in child-birth. Having already been assured by the midwife that her son was to be born, she named him "Ben-oni", meaning "son of my sorrow". His father, however, called him "Benjamin", meaning "son of my right hand" (Gen 35:16-19).

Later on in Israel's history, when the nation was sadly divided in the reign of Solomon's son Rehoboam, Benjamin remained steadfast with Judah (1 Kings 12:20-21) making up the southern kingdom. After the Babylonian captivity the tribe of Benjamin is regarded as part of Judah (Ezra 4:1; 10:9).

As Paul here traces back his ancestry, he may well have in mind the Saul of the Old Testament, Israel's first king. It is possible that Saul of Tarsus was in fact named after him. He too was of the tribe of Benjamin (1 Sam 9: 1), and in stature he was head and shoulders above his fellows (1 Sam 9:2). What king Saul was in physical appearance, Saul of Tarsus was in religious achievement (Gal 1:14).

When the old man Jacob rallied his sons before his death in order to bless them regarding the latter days, he said of Benjamin that he "shall ravin as a wolf: in the morning he shall devour the prey, and at night he shall divide the spoil" (Gen 49:27). This is very much in keeping with the picture of Saul of Tarsus presented in Acts 9, and in his own later testimony. "He persecuted the church and made havock of it (Gal 1:13 RV). To Timothy he writes, I was "a blasphemer, and a persecutor, and injurious" (1 Tim 1:13).

However, Paul obtained mercy, and the association he now has with the Lord Jesus puts everything in perspective. Divine grace has linked him with another man, the man Christ Jesus, "a man of sorrows, and acquainted with grief" (Isa 53:3), who has been invested with glory as the Son of the Father's right hand (Heb 1:3-13). Like Benjamin at the beginning, Paul owes his life to the death of another, and his greatest desire is to "know him, and the power of his resurrection, and the fellowship of his sufferings, being made conformable unto his death; if by any means I might attain unto the resurrection of the dead" (Phil 3:10-11). May we emulate Paul in this exercise!

Day 4

"AN HEBREW OF THE HEBREWS"

Philippians 3:4-7; Acts 21:37-40; 22:1-16

There is deep significance in the expression "Hebrew of the Hebrews" as Paul's thoughts now turn to his aristocratic parentage and the purity of his ancestry connected with Judaism. "Hebrew" is the most ancient term for the Jewish race, and Paul here is claiming something radical in his pedigree.

The title "Hebrew" is first used by the tribes of Canaan to describe Abram when he crossed the Euphrates to sojourn among them in the land that God promised him (Gen 14:13). The word means 'from the other side'. It distinguished the patriarch as someone different from the society around who, no doubt, regarded him as a foreigner amongst them. Something similar happened in the early Church age when the people first called the disciples Christians at Antioch (Acts 11:26). It is interesting to notice the derogatory use of the Hebrew title by Potiphar's wife concerning Joseph (Gen 39:14-17).

In our New Testament, the term Hebrew is used only of Jews who spoke the Hebrew language and retained the Hebrew customs. In this they proudly distinguished themselves from the Hellenists who were Greek-speaking Jews. When reading the Scriptures, Hellenists would use the Septuagint, the Greek version of the Old Testament, as distinct from the Hebrew Scriptures.

So, although Saul belonged to that illustrious city of Tarsus in the province of Cilicia in Asia Minor, he was always well able to defend himself against his Jewish critics. When, having been taken into custody, he was given leave by the Roman chief captain to speak to the people, he addressed them in the Hebrew tongue (Acts 21:40; 22:2). Later he tells King Agrippa that the Lord, when appearing to him on the Damascus road, spoke to him in the Hebrew tongue (Acts 26:14); and he challenges the false teachers of Judaism with the words, "Are they Hebrews? so am I. Are they Israelites? so am I. Are they the seed of Abraham? so am I" (2 Cor 11:22).

The epistles confirm that he does regard such boasting as folly, but he makes these claims to emphasise the value of the work of grace in his soul, and for the purpose of confuting those who would seek to undermine his stewardship in the Gospel. We learn from the Philippian epistle, perhaps more than any other, that this faithful servant of Christ no longer regards these attributes, which he once held so dear, as anything worth holding on to. The elite status into which he was born no longer holds any appeal for him, and he now consigns it to a place amongst the other things once esteemed as gains but now willingly counted loss for Christ.

Day 5

"AS TOUCHING THE LAW, A PHARISEE"

Philippians 3:4-7; Acts 26:1-23

Paul here weaves another strand into his elitist background; it is now what he was religiously, particularly connected with the ceremonies and ordinances of the Mosaic Law. Pharisees do not appear in the Old Testament. Their origins are somewhat obscure, but seem to date between the Old and New Testament periods. As a sect they are prominent in the Gospel records, often linked with the scribes. Their name is thought to be derived from a Hebrew word meaning 'to separate', and this exclusivism is seen in their professed superiority over others in matters of prayers, fasting, tithing, and in an outward sanctimonious demeanour (Luke 18:11-12). Their conduct brought scathing criticism and condemnation from the Lord, who saw under the outward veneer and knew exactly what was in their hearts.

In his defence before the Sanhedrin, Paul described himself as "a Pharisee, the son of a Pharisee" (Acts 23:6). Gamaliel, the well known Pharisee, was his mentor, and this devoted young student of the law was educated and groomed at his feet (Acts 5:34; 22:3). When appearing before king Agrippa, Paul testified that he lived "after the most straitest sect of our religion" (Acts 26:5). There can be no doubt, therefore, that from childhood Saul of Tarsus was totally immersed in Judaism and possessed the most detailed knowledge of the law of Moses and the Old Testament Scriptures that any man could have. This is seen in his masterly ability to debate matters of the law with his fiercest opponents. His skill in this area is demonstrated in the logical way he develops the Roman epistle.

Yet following his conversion and call to apostleship, he confesses that it was that very law that gave him the knowledge of sin, and made sin appear "exceeding sinful". He freely confesses that the law could never give him life, but rather put him under the sentence of death (Rom 7:7-13).

Now, in Christ, he lives a life of separation of a very different kind (Gal 1: 15). He is "separated unto the gospel of God" (Rom 1:1). Under the Lordship of Christ, he is free from condemnation and controlled by the indwelling Holy Spirit. By divine grace, he strives to fulfil the stewardship in the gospel which has been committed to him by the risen Lord. He therefore forgets his religious past, and his many achievements, counting them all but loss "for the excellency of the knowledge of Christ Jesus my Lord" (Phil 3:8).

The knowledge for which he now continues to thirst is the ongoing personal knowledge of Christ (v.10). Such should be the ambition of each of us as we compete in the race of faith.

Day 6

"Concerning zeal, persecuting the church"

Philippians 3:4-7; Galatians 1:1-24

Up to this point, Paul has concentrated on what he was by race, religion and rearing. Now, however, he gives an insight into how, in his youth, he pursued the cause of Judaism with relentless fervour. From the point at which he consented to the death of the first martyr, Stephen, (Acts 8) he was possessed of an inner enthusiasm and dedication, ignorantly thinking he was doing God service. As his testimony in both the Acts and his epistles reveals, he had a burning energy in the pursuit of the objective to which he was so committed.

Alas, however, Saul's zeal was misplaced in being directed against the disciples of the Lord Jesus (see Acts 8:1; 9:1; 26:9-11). Elsewhere he refers to his own nation Israel as having "a zeal of God, but not according to knowledge" (Rom 10:2), and he would understand exactly from his past life what that meant. He warns the Galatian believers against those who, with similar zeal, would again entangle the saints in bondage to Judaism. "They zealously affect you, but not well", then adding, "it is good to be zealously affected always in a good thing" (Gal 4:17-18). In that zeal, Saul of Tarsus persecuted the church.

In this letter to the Philippians, Paul emphasises that he is better qualified than most to warn of the dangers from false teachers, for he had been there before having his eyes opened by the risen Lord. He also knew that he was called to suffering for the sake of Christ. The persecutor of Christians was now himself persecuted by his fellow Jews (Acts 9:16).

In Philippians 3, Paul shows that he has lost none of that fervour which he had when causing havoc in the church. However, by God's grace, it has now been redirected. The word "persecuting" in verse 6 is the Greek word 'dioko', and Paul also uses the word in verse 12 where it is translated "follow after", and again in verse 14 where it is translated "press". So, as he competes in the stadium of faith, he testifies that he has not yet attained his goal, but he will "follow after" and, "forgetting those things which are behind, and reaching forth unto those things which are before", he will "press toward the mark for the prize of the high calling of God in Christ Jesus" (vv.13-14).

We who belong to Christ should ask ourselves whether the keenness and enthusiasm we once directed towards the things of the world, are now applied to the things of God. It was ever a marvel to Paul that the grace of God had brought him to where he was, from persecutor to apostle (1 Cor 15:9), and this chapter reflects how he feels as he writes of his experience.

Day 7

"TOUCHING ... RIGHTEOUSNESS ... BLAMELESS"

Philippians 3:4-7; Romans 7:1-25

This lofty claim by Paul touching the law reminds us of the rich young ruler who, when questioned by the Lord about the commandments, said "all these have I observed from my youth" (Mark 10:20). How touching that at his reply, "Jesus beholding him loved him". Tragically, however, at the decisive moment the young man renounced Christ for his gains, "for he had great possessions". In contrast, after the Damascus road experience, Paul gladly renounced his gains for Christ.

Saul of Tarsus had lived up to his religion in such an impeccable manner that, however closely he was scrutinised, no one could find fault with his diligent compliance with all that the law demanded. Yet, whilst closely adhering to every "jot and tittle" of that ceremonial system to which men had added so much tradition, he became aware that it could never provide him with true righteousness so essential before God. Jesus taught that "except your righteousness shall exceed the righteousness of the scribes and Pharisees, ye shall in no case enter into the kingdom of heaven" (Matt 5:20). Saul belonged to that very class until the Lord completely changed his life.

He argues with the Judaising teachers who were infiltrating the Galatian churches that, were it possible for man to attain righteousness by the law, then Christ died to no purpose; and again, "if there had been a law given which could have given life, verily righteousness should have been by the law" (Gal 3:21). Man's sinful heart makes it impossible for him to acquire true righteousness by this means.

Paul encourages the Philippians by stating that his prize now is to be found "in him (Christ), not having mine own righteousness, which is of the law, but ... the righteousness which is of God by faith" (v.9). The vital truth of justification, being reckoned righteous before God, is expounded in the epistle to the Romans where Paul teaches that true righteousness comes to us freely by God's grace (3: 24); it is secured for us by Christ's blood (5:9), and personally appropriated by faith (5:1). Every believer in the Lord Jesus has a standing before God because of having been reckoned righteous through the death of His Son.

So, as Paul sums up his schedule of achievements by reason of both ancestry and religion, he writes them off with a single stroke of the pen, for his greater prize, the knowledge of Christ. This example of self renunciation is left on record, not just for the saints of Paul's day, but also for us today, so that we too may go in for the more profitable thing.

ALEX WISEMAN

Week 48

7 ALTARS IN GENESIS

Introduction

The word "altar" literally means 'slaughter place', and was used primarily for sacrifice to God or gods. The construction of the early altars was most probably of earth, although the law given to Moses introduces us to the concept of stone. There was, however, a prescription for the stone. It could not just be any stone, it could not be hewn stone; "for if thou lift up thy tool upon it, thou hast polluted it" (Exod 20:25). In the book of Exodus, the revelation to Moses for the construction of the tabernacle gives much detail with regard to specific altars, namely those of brass and of gold. The dimensions, material, construction and foundation are great types of the person of Christ, that lovely man who brought infinite pleasure to the heart of God. An altar could be built as a means to offer sacrifice, or simply as a memorial to a place where the individual enjoyed a particular experience with God. The key to our spiritual progress and development lies in our daily raising of an altar, a daily relationship with God, and no other factor will influence and effect what we will, or will not, be for God more than this daily experience. Sadly there were other altars erected to false gods, a timely reminder that the enemy's threat is ever present, and how easily the devotion of the people of God can be divided and distracted from the worship of the only true God. Every soul saved should immediately erect an individual altar, by determining to set aside a time and a place, every day, to be alone with God, to read his word and to pray. Every family should do the same; pray together, read God's word together, and the raising of a family altar will help us and guide us in the way to honour God. The objective of the consideration of the altars of Genesis is to show the circumstances surrounding, and the experience leading to, an altar being built for God. May God help us to follow such example, and raise daily something for God's pleasure and glory.

Day 1

A NEW BEGINNING

Genesis 8:1-22

Over one thousand years had passed since Abel placed the first of his flock upon the altar and, subsequently, on account of his obedience to God, died prematurely at the hand of his brother. Throughout the years after Abel's death, few lived with any regard for God until Lamech begat Noah. In the birth of this child there was the beginning of a movement of God. It is worthy of note that the days of Noah were those when men indulged themselves in whatever brought gratification to themselves, having no regard for God. The Holy Spirit's commentary on these men was: "they took them wives of all which they chose" (Gen 6:2) and "God saw that the wickedness of man was great in the earth, and that every imagination of the thoughts of his heart was only evil continually" (Gen 6:5).

In the midst of all this moral darkness, a ray of light shines through; "Noah was a just man and perfect in his generations, and Noah walked with God" (Gen 6:9). Noah was only one man in the midst of an evil generation, but what pleasure he brought to God. The commandment came from God to build the ark, and Noah, his wife, his sons and their wives were shut in when the judgment of God fell on that godless generation.

Then came the moment of new beginning, and in these conditions Noah built an altar. What a background to the first mention of the altar in Scripture. A new day, a fresh start, a purged earth and clean beasts to offer upon the altar. The man who had lived righteously in the midst of all the evil that surrounded him, would now build an altar unto the Lord.

Herein lies the secret of bringing pleasure to God. It is to reserve the first place for Him, the first exercise of our souls being to offer to God that which will speak to Him of His lovely Son. The fact that Noah's offering was of clean beasts reminds us that not everything is suitable for the altar. Godly discernment is necessary with respect to what is offered to God. The stench of man's evil had risen to God for years, but Noah, the man of obedience, now brought that which would ascend to God as a sweet savour.

How precious it would be to the heart of God if He saw in our lives today not only the features of a man like Noah who was just and blameless among men as he walked close to the Lord, but also those features of Christ in all the loveliness of His obedient and submissive walk down here. Such a walk would ensure that from our individual altar there would ascend "a sweet savour" unto God. This would truly be an altar erected for the pleasure of God.

Day 2

THE CALL OF GOD

Genesis 11:27 - 12:7

The raising of an altar brought to a climax one of the most unsettling and disorientating periods of Abram's history. The appearing of the God of glory (Acts 7:2) had brought a revelation of the divine mind which necessitated movement and change. God had a great plan for this man, but to follow it would require a level of dependence upon God hitherto not known. The divine instruction was clear, but demands were high to leave behind all he knew and trust God for the future. This may account for his apparent reluctance to move, reflected in Terah being the one credited with the act of taking them out of Ur (Gen 11:31), and for the fact that Lot was still with Abram when he came out, despite God's command to leave "thy kindred" (Gen 12:1).

Subsequent experience will teach him that complete and unqualified obedience to the will of God is that which will secure the greatest of divine blessings. Once Abram had come into the land of Canaan God appeared to him again, teaching him, and us, that further revelation of God's purpose will be determined by obedience to his previous command. An additional dimension to Abram's circumstances is given to us in Psalm 105:12 where we learn that "they were but a few men in number; yea, very few, and strangers in it (that is, the land of Canaan)". These were difficult days as they came into new territory, and there must have been feelings of uncertainty. But, in their apparent weakness, they stood in the full current of the divine will as there, stretched out before Abram, lay a path full of the richest of divine blessings and the abundance of divine grace.

Take courage in days of weakness and uncertainty that, if the child of God is walking according to the divine mind, there is no greater position of strength. His passing through Shechem (meaning 'shoulder') is a picture of strength, and this is supplemented by Moreh (meaning 'instruction'). These are two great pillars on which to lean; divine strength and divine instruction. At this point in Abram's experience a little warning bell rings, in that the Canaanite is still in the land. The enemy was ever present but, sad to note, the early difficulties in this pilgrim journey arose not from the ranks of the enemy, but from among the herdsmen of Abram and Lot. The trouble came from within.

Abram's first altar reflects the state of a man desirous to reciprocate something for God. It was raised as an opportunity to give God something back by way of appreciation for the divine call and the way in which God had led. Abram was moving in the good of all that God had proved Himself to be to his soul. This altar was an altar built out of true spiritual experience.

Day 3

RECOVERY AND SEPARATION

Genesis 13:1-18

Two altars are presented in this chapter, one at the beginning and the other at the end. The first altar is connected with Abram's recovery from the backslidings of Egypt, and the second altar shows Abram in full fellowship with God. There can be times in our Christian experience when we drift away from the Lord and we can be occupied with the things of Egypt but, thankfully, there is always a way back. Abram returned to the place where his tent had been at the beginning, and the point at which he returns to the place of the altar is the time he calls on the name of the Lord.

A warning is then sounded out. Days of recovery are immediately followed by days of strife. How sad it is to see the herdsmen of Abram and Lot fighting together when God is blessing as He is. Lot was a man who lacked conviction. He would most likely have stayed in Egypt but for Abram's movement. The offer of a choice presented him with the opportunity to possess land similar, in his eyes, to "the garden of the Lord, like the land of Egypt" (13:10), a road which led him to spiritual ruin. Such is the plight of a man driven by that which appeals to his eye rather than that which has been dictated by God. Abram's actions, on the other hand, demonstrate the attitude of a man in touch with God, not intent on striving about earthly things but demonstrating the spirit of peace towards his nephew. Lot made his choice and, with this decided, there is added a further dimension of Abram's obedience to God which brings a further communication from the Lord. As noted before, obedience will bring further revelations of the divine mind. The man who gave another the choice of whatever land he chose to dwell in, as he himself trusted God, now surveys the scope of divine reward for his obedience; all the land that his eye could see. At this point he journeys to Mamre (meaning 'vigour') and he dwelt there. Mamre was in Hebron ('fellowship') and a lovely picture develops of a man enjoying fellowship with God. These things hold great lessons for our soul. The route to spiritual vitality and fellowship is separation from Egypt and abstinence from strife. This is the man who, only a chapter before, had drifted out of the right path, but under the hand of God was now enjoying renewed fellowship with God. It was at this point that he built an altar. May God give us grace to emulate his example and raise an altar out of the enjoyment of such a relationship.

Day 4

THE ULTIMATE TEST

Genesis 22:1-19

Never was there a time in Abraham's life when the demands of the altar were felt so keenly as on the day when God wanted Isaac. This mighty man of God had known the pangs of separation from the comforts of Ur. He had buried his father, journeyed further, separated himself from Lot and put out Ishmael, but this was a new height of experience; to place Isaac upon the altar. This demand necessitated the surrender of his dearest affection on earth, the son of promise, the totality of all his hopes, in whom was invested all of divine promise and purpose in Abraham's experience. When Abraham put out Ishmael God told him to hearken unto Sarah's voice but, in this trial, he stood alone, a man totally relying upon his God. Three times over in the Scriptures we read of Abraham rising early in the morning. Following the judgment of Sodom he rose early and went to the place where he had stood before the Lord, and he surveyed the devastation of divine judgment. He rose early on a second occasion, equipped Hagar with bread and a bottle of water and, with a sad heart, sent away "the bondwoman and her son" (Gal 4: 30). Thirdly, in this, the greatest of all his trials, he rose early in the morning in order to go to the place of divine instruction. Every command of God was obeyed in every detail thus demonstrating the extent of this man's submission to the divine will. Having reached the place, he built an altar, laid the wood in order and bound Isaac his son, placing him on the altar and taking the knife to slay his son. In all these traumatic events Abraham did not reckon on Isaac being spared but, rather, that God would raise him from the dead. An altar built, a son bound, and a father taking the knife to slay his son in absolute obedience to the mind of the God whom he had come to know and trust. This demonstration of obedience was enough to satisfy the demands of God, and the angel of the Lord called unto him out of heaven and Isaac was spared. The late Jack Hunter once said, "God didn't want Isaac's life, he wanted Abraham's heart". Few altars will touch the hearts of the people of God like this altar of Abraham, the altar which calls us to sacrifice that which means more to us than anything else in life, the surrender of our best for God. "And Abraham called the name of that place Jehovah-jireh", having learned by experience of the richness of divine provision, that "In the mount of the Lord it shall be seen" (Gen 22:14).

Day 5

THE UNFOLDING OF DIVINE PURPOSE

Genesis 26:1-25

Famines in Scripture were crisis days in the experience of the people of God. In each famine, however, we can see much evidence of the hand of God at work. In the days of Joseph, a famine arose in the land of Egypt and God was at work in this famine to bring about the reconciliation of Joseph and his brethren. In the days of David a famine arose, and this famine was a sign of divine displeasure over an issue relating to the Gibeonites which, although it happened during the reign of Saul, was still an offence to God. In the days when the judges ruled there was a famine in Bethlehem-Judah, so even the 'house of bread' did not escape this plight. From there Elimelech "went to sojourn in the country of Moab" (Ruth 1:1), never to return.

The famine in Isaac's life was no less significant. God was at work to bring his servant to the place he wished him to be, and a famine would bring an unsettling period into Isaac's life which would culminate in God appearing to him. Gerar was a mixed experience, and the Philistine a strange enemy. The Philistine was both a host and a hindrance to the man of God. Isaac was commanded by God to stop short of going to Egypt but to sojourn in Gerar. The fear of man caused him to compromise the truth, and it took a rebuke from an unregenerate king to remind him of his obligations. This was a chapter of slow progress, digging wells, re-discovering some of the things his father had enjoyed, but constantly plagued by the enemy of the Philistine. This reminds us that the man or woman making progress in the things of the Lord will find themselves constantly under attack from the enemy.

Eventually, Isaac arrives at Beersheba where the Lord appears to him with a three-fold promise: "I am with thee, and will bless thee, and multiply thy seed" (26:24). At this point Isaac builds his altar, pitches his tent and digs his well. These things are most instructive. The place where he lived was the place where he worshipped, and this was the place where he found his refreshment. Isaac had arrived at the place of divine appointing and responded by building his altar, but not before facing the perils of enemy attack.

The man or woman under the hand of God must expect the pathway sometimes to be rough, but a confidence in the purpose of God will be

rewarded with a deeper revelation of his will. In the building of this altar we see a man settled in the place appointed by God, and in such a state Isaac can present something for divine pleasure.

Day 6

RECONCILIATION AND REUNION

Genesis 32:24 - 33:20

The prospect of meeting Esau presented Jacob with one of the greatest crises of his life. The loss of his firstborn blessing to Jacob caused Esau to resolve in his heart; "The days of mourning for my father are at hand; then will I slay my brother Jacob" (Gen 27:41). The blessing, according to divine purpose, was to be given to Jacob (25:23) but the deceptive means whereby it was accomplished could not have been according to the divine way, and had produced hatred in the heart of Esau towards Jacob. The early verses of Genesis 32 record Jacob's initiative to secure peace with his brother, but the only response he received was news that "Esau … cometh to meet thee, and four hundred men with him" (32:6). This news made Jacob "greatly afraid and distressed" (v.7).

At this point Jacob prays and, as the chapter unfolds, we witness a movement of God in his life which confronts him with an issue he had escaped from in the past, namely his lie to Isaac that he was Esau and not Jacob. Jacob is left alone, and a man wrestles with him until the breaking of the day. It should be noted that the initiative in the wrestling lay with the man and not with Jacob. The lesson therefore lies in God's purpose in the adjustment of Jacob. There were certain changes necessary in Jacob, and this chapter will instruct us as to the way in which God might confront his servants with unresolved issues of the past (v.27).

This experience on Penuel left Jacob with a changed walk and deepened his understanding of God. From this experience Jacob took confidence; "I have seen God face to face, and my life is preserved" (v.30). With these things in his heart and a confidence in God, the crisis is solved and he goes out to meet Esau. How lovely it is when feuds among brethren are resolved in the secret of the presence of God! Two men previously in conflict with one another, now with changed minds and hearts, being reconciled. Even the greatest of difficulties can be resolved when God is brought into the circumstances. With reconciliation now complete Jacob builds an altar, and the name he gives to it reflects the depths of his most recent experience; "El-Elohe-Israel", God, the God of Israel. These two great truths must combine in the building of an altar. It must be built in a place of peace, and the altar must be erected by a changed man; "a prince … with God and with men" (32:28). May God exercise us to seek peace on the ground of reconciliation and prove more deeply the greatness of the God we serve.

Day 7

THE JOURNEY TO BETHEL

Genesis 35:1-15

The mention of Bethel must have cast Jacob's mind back many years to the day he left home for the first time, leaving behind him a divided home, a father out of touch with God and a brother who had little regard for spiritual value or virtue and a complete disregard for anything eternal. A divine impression was stamped upon Jacob's soul in the earliest days of his experience; it was the awesomeness of Bethel, a place to be revered, and the place where God dwelt (Gen 28:17). In these early days he received a promise from God which he never forgot, "I am with thee" (28:15).

When we come to chapter 35, well nigh thirty years have passed and, with God having kept his promise, Jacob will return to Bethel where, in obedience to the command of God, he will build an altar. In the course of his journey to Bethel there were some matters which had to be resolved, because condition is critical in the place where God dwells. Rachel, his wife, had brought from her father's house things which could not co-exist with the God of Bethel, namely false gods, and these had to be put away. His household had to change their garments and they had to be clean. Jacob knew God, and this godly man was re-capturing in his soul the holiness of the God of Bethel and, as a result, was making necessary adjustments. With these adjustments made in his household, he journeyed, the presence of God in evidence by the fact that "the terror of God was upon the cities that were round about them" (35:5).

With the journey now complete, he arrives at Bethel and builds the altar. Names in Scripture are always significant, especially in the Old Testament, and we should note that Jacob re-names the place 'El-Bethel'. Jacob not only knew the house of God but he also knew the God of the house. The passage of time had brought him to discover the depths of the divine way, knowing that God had answered his prayer in bringing him back to "this place" (28:17). It is prudent for every child of God to re-acquaint themselves (in spirit) with the place where first they met the Lord, the place where things began in earnest, and examine whether or not there has been a deepening of spiritual appreciation, greater knowledge of God, that elevation of spiritual experience, "let us go up to Bethel" and, if necessary, renew our devotion to God. This chapter with all its blessedness is not without its dark clouds; Jacob buries Deborah the nurse, Rachel his wife and finally Isaac his father. How greatly he needed 'the God of Bethel'.

COLIN HUTCHISON

Week 49

7 SABBATH DAY MIRACLES OF THE LORD JESUS

Genesis 1:31 - 2:3; Exodus 20:8-11; Hebrews 4:3-11

Introduction

When God rested on the original Sabbath day we must not think that He was tired or exhausted. God rested in the sense of taking pleasure and satisfaction in His work. He blessed the seventh day and sanctified it – that is, He set it apart for Himself. In a sense it was for Him. In the New Testament, however, the Lord stated that the Sabbath was made for man, and not man for the Sabbath (Mark 2:27). We learn that God had man in mind when He set apart the Sabbath. He wanted man to enjoy His rest; to share His satisfaction and pleasure in His work. And Adam did.

The entrance of sin into the world changed everything. Instead of finding pleasure in His work, it repented God that He had made man at all. Significantly, the Sabbath is not mentioned again until Exodus 16, that is, after Israel had been redeemed. Neither God nor man could rest in a world so corrupted by sin.

The obligation to remember the Sabbath day was revived in the Ten Commandments. The redeemed Israelites were expected to enter into the rest of God. Sadly, they failed to do so. The Sabbath day became a dreary restriction, a joyless imposition. They lost sight of the true significance of the day.

When the Lord was here, the Pharisees continually accused Him of breaking the Sabbath. Nothing could be further from the truth. He magnified the law in every respect. What He did was to break the man-made rules which the Pharisees had bolted on to the commandment. While He never broke the

Sabbath, He did state "My Father worketh hitherto, and I work" (John 5:17). The Father could not rest until the matter of sin was dealt with. Neither could the Son. The seven Sabbath day miracles display His perfect ability to provide rest for both God and man.

The Christian is under no obligation to keep the Sabbath day. The Sabbath was a symbol of something which the believer now enjoys in reality. Hebrews 4 explains that we rest in Christ through faith in Him. We have come into the benefit of His Sabbath day works!

Day 1

PEACE TO THE POSSESSED

Luke 4:31-37

Privileged Capernaum, what blessed Sabbath days of teaching you enjoyed! Never had such a Teacher been heard before. Accustomed to the powerless sermons of the Pharisees, the people were astonished at the authoritative teaching of Christ. Truly Capernaum had been lifted up to heaven. It was too good to last. As the Son of God teaches, Satan interrupts with a loud voice. Wherever God is at work the enemy will soon make his presence felt.

So it was in the beginning. How many Sabbath days were enjoyed by Adam before Satan interrupted that blessed state? It is fitting that on this first Sabbath day miracle the Lord should demonstrate His power over the very source of evil.

Notice that the man was in the synagogue. It would appear that he was habitually there. Tolerated, perhaps even unnoticed, by the religious leaders, but exposed by the voice of Christ. He had the spirit of an unclean demon. The purity of the place where God's word was read and revered had been sullied. Only the living Word of God preached with moral authority can expose the true conditions in any congregation.

The cry of the possessed man is striking. Firstly, the demon wants to remain undisturbed. Secondly, he fears destruction at the hand of Christ. Thirdly, he identifies the Lord in two ways: as Jesus of Nazareth and the Holy One of God. Satanic forces fear our blessed Lord, have a premonition of final doom at His hand and are aware of the uniqueness of His person.

Although the cry of the unclean spirit correctly identified Christ, the Lord will not accept publicity from such a polluted source (cf. Acts 16:17-18). God demands that the moral condition of the messenger correspond with the holiness of the message.

And so they face each other on the Sabbath day – the Holy One teaching – the unclean spirit shouting. Our Lord can deal with the situation. At the rebuke of Christ the spirit must leave, and the man is left unharmed in the midst. No wonder they were all amazed! The people had already recognised the Lord's authority – now they see that authority combined with awesome power.

The defeat of Satan was an essential part of the work of our Lord Jesus. He was manifested to undo the works of the devil. The believer experiences God's rest today because the power of Satan was broken at the cross. One day Satan and his hordes will be banished from the universe totally and finally. Eternal rest will be enjoyed in a sphere where evil will never raise its head again.

> "In vain doth Satan now oppose
> For God is stronger than His foes!"

REST IN SERVICE

Luke 4:38-41

The Lord moves from the synagogue to the house; from the public to the private scene. If the religious sphere is in a state of unrest, so the domestic scene is marked by fever. Dr. Luke diagnoses "a great fever". He states that Peter's mother-in-law was "taken" or 'holden' by it, indicating the sudden onset and tenacious grip of the complaint. The symptoms of fever are excessive heat and involuntary action, combining to prostrate the victim.

The home is often the place where fever is known. Was Martha suffering from this complaint? Had she lost the calm of divine service? How often anxiety produces fever conditions which render us incapable of rational and acceptable service! How strange to be feverish on the Sabbath – the day when a holy calm should have been enjoyed.

The synoptic gospels all have their own inspired comment on how this lady was brought to the Lord's notice. Matthew tells us that the Lord saw her (Matt 8:14). Mark records "anon they tell him of her" (Mark 1:30). Luke tells us that "they besought him for her" (Luke 4:38). The Lord is aware of our needs before we tell Him or beseech Him.

The Lord stood over her. He assumes the position of power and authority. He then rebukes the fever – animate and inanimate matter respond to the Creator's voice. He rebukes Satan and demons; He rebukes the wind and the sea; He rebukes illness. All matter derives being from Him and must obey His voice. The results were immediate and effective. No period of convalescence was required. The fever left her, "and immediately she arose and ministered unto them" (v.39).

It is encouraging to note that there was a company of women which ministered to the Lord of their substance (Luke 8:3). The practical needs of the Lord and His disciples were met by a devoted band of women, most of whom are unnamed. We can be sure that this ministry was appreciated by the Lord and will be rewarded. The practical ministry of godly women through the years has brought pleasure to the Lord and great blessing to His people.

It may seem a contradiction in terms, but service can only be fully effective by resting – not resting *from* service, but resting *in* service. The Lord Himself said "Take my yoke upon you, and learn of me; for I am meek and lowly in heart: and ye shall find rest unto your souls" (Matt 11:29). Our blessed Lord was the perfect Servant. He served in calm, tranquil dependence upon God. May we enjoy that restful service today.

> "Drop Thy still dews of quietness
> Till all our strivings cease;
> Take from our souls the strain and stress,
> And let our ordered lives confess
> The beauty of Thy peace".

RESTORING THE RIGHT HAND

Luke 6:6-11

In this incident the Lord actually provoked a confrontation with the Pharisees. He could have healed the man on another day. He could have done it privately. However, in His wisdom the Lord made this healing a public demonstration. He brings the man into the limelight, then poses the searching question: "Is it lawful on the sabbath days to do good, or to do evil? to save life, or to destroy it?" (Luke 6:9). In the sullen silence that greeted His question the Lord looked round about Him with anger (Mark 3:5). They would rather see the man left deformed than lose face. The Lord majestically ignores them and turns to the man – "Stretch forth thy hand". How the man would rather have concealed it! How shameful to expose our weaknesses and shortcomings, but sometimes this is necessary. As he obeys, the miracle occurs; his hand is restored a perfect match to the other.

The withered right hand was not just a physical tragedy, it was also a symbol of the spiritual health of the nation. Reverently speaking, Israel was meant to be God's right-hand man. The right hand in Scripture denotes authority, power, skill and dignity. Israel was a withered right hand, powerless, deformed, useless, and clumsy, an object of shame and pity instead of glory and dignity. One day the nation will stretch forth its hand – it will publicly lay bare its shame and acknowledge its true condition. Israel will confess her sin and repent openly (Zech 12:10-14). Only then will they know the transforming and restoring power of God. Only then will they enter the Sabbath rest.

Perhaps today we too need to stretch forth our hands in the presence of God and experience His power to restore. David thought he had kept his withered hand well concealed, but eventually came to recognise the need of laying it bare before God: "I said I will confess my transgressions unto the Lord; and thou forgavest the iniquity of my sin. Selah" (Ps 32:5). Sin must be exposed and confessed before forgiveness and restoration can be enjoyed.

The withered right hand restricted the ability of this man to serve effectively. It is certain that unconfessed sin will have the same effect in our lives.

The principle of doing good or evil, saving or destroying, goes to the very heart of the Sabbath day. It is a general principle that the commands of God must always be on the side of good and saving. If we find a command that seems to hinder good, or prevent saving, then we do well to re-examine our understanding of the word of God. We too can be concerned with "straining at gnats" of our own invention whilst hindering the progress of good and salvation.

Day 4

LOOSING THE BOUND

Luke 13:10-17

The context of this miracle is interesting. At the beginning of chapter 13 the Lord speaks of the need for Israel to repent, and underlines this with the parable of the barren fig tree. The chapter closes with the Saviour lamenting over Jerusalem and stating that they would not see Him until they said "Blessed is he that cometh in the name of the Lord". A crisis has been reached in the Lord's dealings with Israel. Their refusal to repent has shut them out of divine blessing. This Sabbath day miracle reveals the hardness of Israel's heart, represented by the attitude of the ruler of the synagogue, despite the gracious ministry of the Lord.

This woman "was bowed together". Man was created to represent God, and his erect posture and liberty of movement are not the least symbols of his dignity. Here was a woman who had been stripped of creatorial dignity through the direct action of Satan. It is significant that after the Lord had called her, spoken to her and laid His hands upon her, "she was made straight, and glorified God". For 18 years Satan had robbed God of the glory due to His name. Creation exists for the glory of God and, on the basis of the Saviour's work, will one day radiate that glory as never before.

The words of the ruler of the synagogue revealed the state of his heart. He was a coward; he spoke to the people, but the rebuke was intended for the Lord. He was a hypocrite; he would loose his ox or ass on the Sabbath, yet cavilled at a human being loosed! He was hard-hearted; the fact that this woman had been bound eighteen years meant nothing to him. He was blind; the miracles performed by the Lord identified Him as Messiah. The ruler was more concerned with legal regulations than the stupendous fact that people were being healed before his eyes! May the Lord preserve us from similar features today!

The Lord describes her as "a daughter of Abraham". Zacchaeus is the only other named individual in the New Testament called a child of Abraham. She could trace her descent from Abraham and yet be bound by Satan. So could the entire nation. Abraham was noted for the dignity of his walk. This poor woman would be noted for her tortured gait. However, there is reason to believe that she was not only a daughter naturally, but spiritually as well. She shared the faith that Abraham exercised. She had met the Liberator and regained liberty and dignity through His Sabbath-day ministry. Little wonder His adversaries were ashamed!

Day 5

RAISING THE FALLEN

Luke 14:1-6

The Lord not only ate with publicans and sinners, but such is His grace that sometimes He ate with Pharisees too! As was so often the case, their motives in inviting the Lord were wholly bad. "They watched him" is the language of the ambush, not the attentive host.

Whether the man with dropsy had been planted in the company or not, we can imagine the electric atmosphere as he stands before the Lord. The Lord again initiates the confrontation by asking them a direct question, "Is it lawful?" (v.3). No question asked by the Lord was ever to supply Him with unknown information: rather it was designed to awaken in the hearers a spirit of inquiry and consideration. Notice the Lord did not ask about working on the Sabbath. Their answer to such a question would have been a direct "no". He asked about healing. This was a question they had never had to face, simply because healings did not ordinarily happen. The Lord is not merely asking about their interpretation of Scripture. He is drawing their attention to the fact that there is a Divine Healer in their midst! In the silence that follows, the Lord, in an almost matter-of-fact manner, takes the man, heals him and lets him go.

The ass and ox had already been referred to by the Lord in the previous Sabbath-day miracle (Luke 13:15). In that case the Lord spoke of loosing animals that were bound; here He speaks of raising animals that had fallen. This has significance, as the disease 'dropsy' was so named because of a dropping or falling sensation due to the collection and retention of body fluids. He also speaks of a pit, possibly a man-made pit for the entrapment of animals. They had hoped He would fall into the pit that they had dug, but that could never happen.

The ass represents the self-will of man. The ox represents the natural strength of man. Self-will led to a fall in man's history, and all man's natural strength could never raise him up. There is, however, One who can raise the fallen, whether sinner or saint. And such ministry is entirely consistent with the spirit of the Sabbath.

Do we share the Saviour's concern for the fallen? In this, and the previous Sabbath-day miracle, the Lord exposes the fact that the Pharisees cared

more for their animals (and possessions) than for their fellow human beings. Perhaps today the Lord will use us to raise the fallen, and so participate in His Sabbath-day ministry of grace.

Day 6

Strength for the helpless

John 5:1-15

The naming and positioning of the pool of Bethesda is significant. It was the 'House of loving-kindness'. It was situated by the sheep gate, the gate through which the sacrificial animals were brought to the temple. The loving-kindness displayed that day was truly on the basis of the sacrifice soon to be offered.

The details of this incident have been the subject of some debate. Did an angel actually come down and disturb the water, or did the people merely believe that such was the case? The present writer leans towards the latter interpretation. It would seem a most arbitrary and unusual way for God to dispense blessing. However, those around the pool firmly believed in the angelic visitation and, from the words of the man healed, it would appear there were times when he himself had tried to enter the water. Whatever the truth of the matter was, the impotent man was beyond both human and angelic aid. Some have seen the incident as a picture of the inability of the law to save due to man's impotence. A method of salvation that depends in any way on man's efforts is doomed to failure.

Why did the Lord command him to take up his bed? Surely the Lord knew this would attract the anger of the Pharisees. The prohibition of carrying burdens on the Sabbath was clear, and the very fact that this man, after 38 years of powerlessness, was now carrying his bedding down the street must have excited comment and amazement.

The Lord's design was to draw their attention, through the man, to Him. When questioned, the man healed points the Jews to the Lord (vv.11, 15). He instinctively knew that if this Man had authority to heal him, then He also had authority to determine Sabbath observance. He had told him to carry his bed, and that was enough!

The anger of the Jews at the perceived desecration of the Sabbath led to a wonderful declaration by the Lord: "My Father worketh hitherto, and I work" (v.17). The Father was working in view of a Sabbath-day yet to come. The Son, in perfect fellowship with the Father, is found working towards the same glorious end. The Jews rightly understood this statement to claim equality with God. In one sense the purpose of the sign healing had been achieved – they were brought face to face with the claims of the Lord. Sadly, their response was one of unbelief and rejection. Today we rejoice in a Saviour who is divine.

The Lord later found the man in the temple (v.14). No doubt he had returned to offer the sacrifice of thanksgiving to God. May this be our response today.

Day 7

LIGHT IN DARKNESS

John 9:1-11

At the very commencement of their national history, Israel had light not given to other nations: "the children of Israel had light in their dwellings" (Exod 10:23). That light characterised all God's dealings with the nation; the pillar of fire; the supernatural light in the holiest of all; the lampstand in the holy place. Israel was a nation blessed with light from God. However, the light that was in them had become darkness, and "how great is that darkness!" (Matt 6:23).

Light is a leading theme in John's gospel because God Himself is light. This was the message that was imprinted on John's mind by the Spirit: "… that God is light, and in him is no darkness at all" (1 John 1:5). In John 9 the Lord speaks of Himself as "the light of the world". This title was used in chapter 8 where the blazing searchlight of His holiness exposed the sin of the Pharisees. That same light now shines on one sitting in darkness and brings illumination.

His method of healing the blind man is significant. He spits on the ground and makes clay of the spittle. In chapter 8 He also touches the dust, writing with His finger. His actions recall the creative power when man was formed out of the dust of the ground. Healing this man was not a work of restoration (the man had never enjoyed sight in the past) – it was a work of creation.

The first seven verses of this chapter relate to the man's physical sight; the remaining verses relate to his spiritual perception. Notice his growing enlightenment regarding the Person who had healed him: "a man that is called Jesus" (v.11), "a prophet" (v.17), a sinless man (v.31), a unique man (v.32) and finally, Son of God (v.38). This progression of understanding should have marked the nation as a whole. They should have progressed from seeing the Lord as a man to recognising Him as Son of God. Sadly, they had chosen not to believe and, therefore, the Lord warns of judicial blindness (v.39), a judgment which Paul would see implemented in his day (Rom 11).

God can only enjoy Sabbath-rest when His intentions for man have been fulfilled. These intentions include a renewed mind and an enlightened understanding, producing a being capable of intelligent fellowship with Him. That has been achieved through the work of Christ. The epistle to the Ephesians is the epistle of the new creation, and of the illumination of the heart and mind. The light revealed in chapters 1-3 has its practical counterpart later in the epistle where we are to "walk as children of light" (Eph 5:8). We too have been enlightened by Christ. May our conduct today reflect this great fact!

DOUGLAS MOWAT

Week 50

7 THINGS THAT ARE "*IN HIM*" IN COLOSSIANS

Introduction

It will be evident to the reader of this epistle that the person of the Lord Jesus was under attack at Colosse, so Paul was in "great conflict" on their behalf that they might not come under the baneful influence of men with impure motives who would hinder their spiritual progress, and undermine in their souls the greatness of the person of Christ. He warns that such men would try to: "beguile you with enticing words" (2:4); "spoil you through philosophy and vain deceit" (2:8); "judge you in meat, or in drink ..." (2: 16); "fraudulently deprive you of your prize" (2:18 NTr) through the evil of mysticism.

Thus, to preserve them from the danger of false teaching, he presents to them in chapter 1 a most remarkable treatise, unveiling to them the unrivalled glory of the indispensable Christ. Such a ministry of the person of Christ is both instructive and a bulwark against the error of false teaching.

It is to be noted that there is only one mention of the Holy Spirit in the epistle (1:8) where Paul speaks of their "love in the Spirit". How blessed to see that when Christ's person is under attack the Holy Spirit recedes into the background to bring into relief the person of the Lord Jesus, thus fulfilling His blessed ministry as spoken of by the Lord, "he shall not speak of himself", (John 16:13) and, "He shall glorify me" (John 16:14). This contrasts with Ephesians, which could be considered a parallel epistle, where the Holy Spirit is mentioned twelve times.

The Lord Jesus is viewed in this epistle as the indispensable Christ. He is indispensable to Creation (1:15-17); indispensable to the New Creation (1:18) and indispensable to the believer in a sevenfold way in chapter 2.

All that we are and have is "in him", who is the fountainhead of all spiritual blessing to God's people:

"So walk ye in him" (2:6).

"Rooted and built up in him" (2:7).

"And ye are complete in him" (2:10).

"In whom (him) also ye are circumcised" (2:11).

"Buried with him in baptism" (2:12).

"Risen with him through the faith of the operation of God" (2:12).

"Quickened together with him" (2:13).

Day 1

"SO WALK YE IN HIM"

Colossians 2:6; Ephesians 4:1,17; 5:1-16

Since we have received Christ Jesus our risen Saviour or, as the word "received" signifies, 'to take to oneself', it is incumbent upon us to bow to His sovereign lordship, putting us under a moral obligation "to walk in him". High ground it is indeed for the believer to walk in Him, and live a life under His absolute control, expressing in some little measure the features that characterised Him as a man here. The apostle Paul lived such a life, "For to me to live is Christ, and to die is gain" (Phil 1:21).

God has from the beginning been deeply interested in the walk of His saints, and records it for us in His word. "And Enoch walked with God: and he was not; for God took him" (Gen 5:24); "and Noah walked with God" (Gen 6:9); "The Lord appeared to Abram, and said unto him … walk before me, and be thou perfect" (Gen 17:1).

The New Testament epistles teach, in a systematic way, the doctrine of Christ which is so vital for our spiritual education, but before they close they bring to us sound guidance for our practical walk. In the epistle we are considering, instruction is given as to how we should walk, "walk worthy of the Lord unto all pleasing" (Col 1:10), walking in such a way as to bring pleasure to the heart of Christ. We have also the word to the Thessalonians, "That ye would walk worthy of God, who hath called you unto his kingdom and glory" (1 Thess 2:12).

The epistle that has much to say about the Christian's walk, however, is that to the Ephesians. In the early chapters of the epistle Paul unfolds to them the glory of divine purpose as centred in the Lord Jesus, and the great blessings that are theirs as being in Christ. Such a glorious revelation demands a practical response, so he exhorts them to "walk worthy of the vocation wherewith ye are called" (Eph 4:1), because Scripture teaches us it is a holy calling, a high calling, and a heavenly calling. He then reminds them in the same chapter, "that ye henceforth walk not as other Gentiles walk, in the vanity of their mind" (Eph 4:17). How then were they to walk? And how are we to walk? This epistle tells us, "walk in love, as Christ also hath loved us" (Eph 5:2) and "walk as children of light" (5:8). What an example, the love of Christ!

Love and light are the very nature of God, as John teaches in his first epistle. Thus, as God's children, our walk should manifest in some measure the character of our father.

"ROOTED AND BUILT UP IN HIM"

Colossians 2:7; Psalm 1:1-6; Matthew 7:24-29

"Rooted and built up in him, and stablished in the faith" (Col 2:7). The words Paul uses in this verse, "rooted", "built up", and "stablished in the faith", are all suggestive of a believer who, standing upon a firm foundation, would not be easily moved by the false teachings of men.

Similar language is used in Ephesians 3:17, "being rooted and grounded in love". The Christian so established in Him would not be "tossed to and fro, and carried about with every wind of doctrine" (Eph 4:14). The word to the Corinthians would ring out loud and clear "be ye stedfast, unmoveable, always abounding in the work of the Lord" (1 Cor 15:58).

The first figure Paul uses in Colossians 2:7 is that of a tree, and then he speaks of a building, built upon a sure foundation. God speaks of His people as trees, "as the trees of lign aloes which the Lord has planted, and as cedar trees beside the waters" (Num 24:6). Trees planted by the Lord can stand against the winds of adversity.

Two further Scriptures come readily to mind as we think of being "rooted and built up in him": "Blessed is the man who walketh not in the counsel of the ungodly … his delight is in the law of the Lord … he shall be like a tree planted by the rivers of water" (Ps 1:1-3). Drawing his resources from the river, this man will be fruitful and fresh, with no withering leaves. His great prosperity lies in his great love of, and obedience to, the word of God.

Matthew 7 also comes to mind in relation to being built up in Him, where the Lord Jesus teaches us that a wise man is he who "heareth these sayings of mine, and doeth them". He says, "I will liken him unto a wise man, which built his house upon a rock: And the rain descended, and the floods came, and the winds blew, and beat upon that house; and it fell not: for it was founded upon a rock" (Matt 7:24-25).

The lesson that we learn from these Scriptures is that if we have a desire to be established in the faith, and be rooted and built up in Him, we need to have a love for the word of God, and a deep desire to be obedient to its precepts.

There is a great reward for such an exercise, as the psalmist reminds us in Psalm 92: "The righteous shall flourish like the palm tree: he shall grow like a cedar in Lebanon. Those that be planted in the house of the Lord shall flourish in the courts of our God. They shall bring forth fruit in old age; they shall be fat and flourishing" (Psalm 92:12-14).

Day 3

"AND YE ARE COMPLETE IN HIM"

Colossians 1:19; 2:9-10; John 1:1-18

"For in him dwelleth all the fulness of the Godhead bodily. And ye are complete in him, which is the head of all principality and power" (Col 2:9-10). These are most interesting verses of Scripture, disclosing to us the eternal and essential glory of the Son of God and, marvel of marvels, telling us that we are complete (or, 'filled full') in Him. Surely such truth should bow our hearts in adoring worship to His God and Father!

The footnote in the New Translation by JND gives an enlightening interpretation of verse 10. "The word "complete" is the Greek word 'pleroo' which can be rendered "filled full," referring to all the fulness being in Him. The fulness of the Godhead is in Christ, as towards us; and we, as towards God, are complete in Him. "Godhead" here is 'theotes' – Godhead in the absolute sense – not 'theiotes', merely divine in character."

"For it pleased the Father that in him should all fullness dwell" (Col 1:19). Paul is speaking of what was characteristic of the Lord Jesus here as man, all the fulness of the Godhead dwelling in Him, and so he records in 1 Tim 3:16, "And without controversy great is the mystery of godliness: God was manifest in the flesh", and John, in his Gospel, records "He that hath seen me hath seen the Father" (John 14:9).

In Colossians 2:9, "For in him dwelleth all the fulness of the Godhead bodily", Paul is now speaking of a risen man in glory, sitting upon the throne of the universe, in whom all the fulness of the Godhead dwells. This statement is being made to counter the error of those at Colosse who would deny the bodily resurrection of Christ.

How blessed to understand that all the fulness is in Him and not in us. We are but empty vessels, who have been brought into the light of the knowledge that all the fulness of the Godhead is toward us in Him. God has come near to man in the person of His Son, and the attributes of His glorious person are now made known to us in Him, "who hath blessed us with all spiritual blessings in the heavenly places in Christ" (Eph 1:3).

And we, as towards God, are complete in Him: "Wherein he hath made us accepted in the beloved" (Eph 1:6), that is, fully furnished and accepted in Him. The word from John, in his Gospel, is "and of his fulness have all we received, and grace for grace" (John 1:16).

It is most interesting to note that in those Scriptures that reveal the eternal and essential glory of Christ, they also disclose to us the fulness that the saints have received as being in Him. This is most precious, and tells us of the wonderful place the saints hold in the affections of divine persons.

Day 4

"*In whom (him) also ye are circumcised*".

Colossians 2:11; Romans 2:28-29; Genesis 17:1-14

"In whom also ye are circumcised with the circumcision made without hands, in putting off the body of the sins of the flesh by the circumcision of Christ". When man's sin had reached a climax, as recorded in Genesis 6:6 "and it repented the Lord that he had made man", God said to Noah, "The end of all flesh is come before me" (6:13). He then moved in judgement to purge the earth by water, and save only those who sheltered in the ark.

God has never changed His mind about the flesh, so when He called Abraham, and gave him the promise of seed as recorded in Genesis 17, He made a covenant with him that every male child should be circumcised.

The word "circumcised" means 'to cut around' and, typically, would teach us that the flesh is to be cut off completely. This is very different from the asceticism that marked "the concision" ('the cutting of the flesh') of which Paul speaks in Philippians 3:2, and which was carried out by the prophets of Baal on mount Carmel in 1 Kings 18, and is so prevalent in the religious orders of our day.

God's word states that before Israel entered into the land of their inheritance, those who had not been circumcised by the way were circumcised at Gilgal, the meaning of which is 'a wheel', so typically the flesh was completely cut off. However, it is evident from the word of God that Israel never understood the spiritual import of the physical act, for Stephen charged them with being "stiffnecked and uncircumcised in heart and ears" (Acts 7:51).

What in a past era was a typical cutting off of the flesh is now, by the Spirit of God, a deep spiritual exercise. No longer is circumcision an external mark in a man's flesh, but an inward work of the Spirit affecting the heart. Paul puts it so succinctly, "For he is not a Jew, which is one outwardly; neither is that circumcision, which is outward in the flesh: but he is a Jew, which is one inwardly; and circumcision is that of the heart, in the spirit, and not in the letter; whose praise is not of men, but of God" (Rom 2:28-29).

It is a different circumcision now, a circumcision done without hands, not the work of a man, but a deep, inward, spiritual work, effected by the Holy Spirit of God, which results in the putting off of the body of the flesh, by the circumcision of Christ. The circumcision of Christ is the death of

Christ, so that the means of our circumcision is the crucifixion of Christ when He was "cut off out of the land of the living" (Isa 53:8). Christ's death has therefore removed forever from before the eye of God the man after the flesh.

Day 5

"BURIED WITH HIM IN BAPTISM"

Colossians 2:12; Romans 6:1-23; 1 Corinthians 12:13

"Buried with him in baptism, wherein also ye are risen with him through the faith of the operation of God, who hath raised him from the dead" (Col 2:12). Scripture teaches that the subsequent step for a soul repenting of their sins, and exercising faith in the Lord Jesus, is to be baptised. When Peter preached on the day of Pentecost, some "were pricked in their heart, and said unto Peter and to the rest of the apostles, Men and brethren, what shall we do? Then Peter said unto them, Repent, and be baptised every one of you in the name of Jesus Christ for the remission of sins, and ye shall receive the gift of the Holy Ghost" (Acts 2:37-38). "Then they that gladly received his word were baptised" (2:41). It is obvious from this passage of Scripture that those who were baptised were those who had believed, thus establishing the principle that it is believers who should be baptised.

The narrative in Acts 8 highlights another important principle in relation to baptism. After the Gospel had been preached by Philip to the Ethiopian eunuch, he believed, "And as they went on their way, they came unto a certain water: and the eunuch said, See, here is water; what doth hinder me to be baptised?" (8:36); "and they went down both into the water" (8:38); "And when they were come up out of the water" (8:39). This scriptural sequence establishes the principle that believer's baptism is by immersion.

There are various baptisms in the word of God, but we will consider those that belong to the Christian era; the baptism of the Holy Spirit, and water baptism by immersion. The baptism of the Spirit was a once-for-all act as 1 Corinthians 12:13 teaches, "For by (in) one Spirit are we all baptised into one body". It is of note that JND and the RV render the verse, "For by one Spirit *were* we all baptised into one body", thus making it an act of the past, effected at Pentecost. In Matthew 3:11, John the Baptist baptised with water, but he spoke of a coming one who would baptise them in the Holy Spirit.

In water baptism, as our text tells us, we are "buried with him in baptism". He has died and been buried, and we have died with Him, "Therefore we are buried with him by baptism into death" (Rom 6:4). Colossians 2 and Romans 6 are therefore teaching the same baptism, that is, water baptism, and the distinction between the two baptisms of the Christian era is that the baptism of the Spirit baptises into the body of Christ, whereas the baptism in water of believers in the Lord Jesus Christ baptises into death. "Know ye not, that so many of us as were baptised into Jesus Christ were baptised into His death? Therefore we are buried with him by baptism into death: that like as Christ was raised up from the dead by the glory of the Father, even so we also should walk in newness of life" (Rom 6:3-4).

Day 6

"RISEN WITH HIM THROUGH THE FAITH OF THE OPERATION OF GOD"

Colossians 2:12; 1 Corinthians 15:1-20; Ephesians 1:17-23

The doctrine of resurrection is one of the cardinal pillars of the Christian faith, the faith of which Paul speaks in Ephesians 4:5, "One Lord, one faith, one baptism". It forms part of the foundation of the Christian Gospel which was given to Paul by divine revelation, "how that Christ died for our sins according to the scriptures; and that he was buried, and that he rose again the third day according to the scriptures" (1 Cor 15:3-4).

The resurrection of the dead is incomprehensible to the human mind. This was clearly demonstrated by the philosophers of the city of Athens who said of Paul, "What will this babbler say? other some, He seemeth to be a setter forth of strange gods: because he preached unto them Jesus, and the resurrection" (Acts 17:18). We apprehend by faith alone not only the fact of Christ's resurrection, but the vital necessity of it. "Who was delivered for our offences, and was raised again for our justification" (Rom 4:25). We cannot be saved without believing in our heart that God raised Him from the dead (Rom 10:9).

Paul, under the enabling control and power of the Holy Spirit of God, proves conclusively the resurrection of Christ from the dead, and extrapolates from it the certainty of the resurrection of the saints. It is with a note of triumph that he states so emphatically, "But now hath Christ been raised from the dead, the firstfruits of them that are asleep" (1 Cor 15:20 RV). He has died and risen again, and from His death and resurrection there will be a mighty harvest.

The Scriptures teach, apart from a few exceptions, that resurrection is in relation to the body. In our text, however, Paul is speaking about a spiritual resurrection, a resurrection by faith. The word "risen" is in the aorist tense, and so is an accomplished fact, that is, we are presently risen with Him.

Resurrection connects us with another world, for nothing of it is known in this world, "For ye are dead (or have died), and your life is hid with Christ in God" (Col 3:3). Believers, therefore, live a life on earth, fulfilling their responsibilities, but they also live in another scene where all is of God, and where Christ is the Sun and centre. How then should we live in this world, since we are "risen with Christ"? "Seek those things which are above, where Christ sitteth" (3:1); "Set your affection on things above, not on things on the earth" (3:2); "Mortify therefore your members which are upon the earth" (3:5).

Day 7

"Quickened together with him"

Colossians 2:13; Ephesians 2:1-22

The opening words of Colossians 2:13, "And you, being dead in your sins" are most interesting when we consider the closing words of verse 12, "who hath raised him from the dead". He is alive, as Peter reminds us, "being put to death in the flesh, but quickened by the Spirit" (1 Pet 3:18). The One who said, "I am he that liveth, and was dead; and, behold, I am alive for evermore" (Rev 1:18), now lives in "the power of an endless life" (Heb 7:16). But we were all dead in trespasses and sins, Jew and Gentile alike, as we learn in Ephesians 2, and there is a similar thought in this Colossian passage. "And you, being dead in your sins and the uncircumcision of your flesh", is obviously a word to the Gentile. But he then immediately speaks a word concerning the Jew. "Blotting out the handwriting of ordinances that was (stood) against us" (2:14) is a reference to Exodus 24 where God made a covenant with Israel and ratified it by the blood which was sprinkled upon the altar and upon the people. As Gentiles we were not signatories to this covenant, but Paul speaks about "us", the Jew, bound by it until Christ died and released them from its bondage.

Although Paul shows to the Romans that both Jew and Gentile are alike condemned, "For all have sinned and come short of the glory of God" (Rom 3:23), he now speaks to the Colossians of two wonderful truths into which divine grace has brought both elements; we are "quickened together with him" and we are "forgiven … all trespasses" (Col 2:13).

The meaning of the words "quickened together with him" is 'to make one alive together' (of Christians with Christ). We are living now in Christ's life. The word "together" brings in the thought of nearness, and reminds us of the words of Joseph unto his brethren, "Come near to me" (Gen 45:4). In our dead state we heard the voice of the Son of God, "Verily, verily, I say unto you, The hour is coming, and now is, when the dead shall hear the voice of the Son of God: and they that hear shall live" (John 5:25). "And when I passed by thee, and saw thee polluted in thine own blood, I said unto thee when thou wast in thy blood, Live; yea, I said unto thee when thou wast in thy blood, Live" (Ezek 16:6). How wonderful that we have experienced the mighty regenerating power of the Holy Spirit of God to bring us into the life of Christ.

Let us therefore live in the enjoyment of the life of Christ, and the forgiveness God has granted.

Drew Meikle

Week 51

7 TITLES OF JEHOVAH

Introduction

What's in a name? In modern Western culture perhaps not very much. The choice of name for a newborn child is influenced by many factors, but the purpose God has for the child is, generally, not one of them. Names in Scripture, however, are often full of significance for they are not merely a means of identification but, rather, are a form of description.

Think of the first naming ceremony recorded in our Bibles: "And out of the ground the Lord God formed every beast of the field, and every fowl of the air; and brought them unto Adam to see what he would call them: and whatsoever Adam called every living creature, that was the name thereof" (Gen 2:19). And what was the purpose of this exercise? As each unique and beautiful creature came before Adam so he, using the vast knowledge, wisdom and understanding that God had given him, assessed the whole character of each in a moment. According to his assessment, so he named them. The Scripture goes on to say, "And Adam gave names to all cattle, and to the fowl of the air, and to every beast of the field; but for Adam there was not found an help meet for him" (2:20). Herein lies the main purpose of naming all the living creatures God had made. Suitability of character to be a fitting companion for Adam was being assessed and, wonderful though every animal was, none answered to his physical, emotional and spiritual needs. For that reason, God formed Eve from Adam's rib and, the moment she was made and he awoke, he named her. He called her "Woman, because she was taken out of Man" (2:23), thus pronouncing the lovely principle of headship and providing the first illustration in Scripture of Christ and the Church, the bride that was brought out of the wounded side. "Woman" is the generic name that Adam bestowed upon his wife but, after the Fall, he gave her a specific name, unique to herself, and it was "Eve; because she was the mother of all living" (3:20).

When God was preparing Moses for the deliverance of Israel from Egyptian bondage, "Moses said unto God, Behold, when I come unto the children of Israel, and shall say unto them, The God of your fathers hath sent me unto you; and they shall say to me, What is his name? what shall I say unto them? And God said unto Moses, I AM THAT I AM: and he said, Thus shalt thou say unto the children of Israel, I AM hath sent me unto you" (Exod 3:13-14). Thus God explained to Moses the meaning of His Name, Jehovah. It is a Name that expresses personality, self-existence and eternality. It is Jehovah, the great "I AM". Every other name and title gives further revelation of this one great Name, "I AM".

Day 1

"JEHOVAH JIREH" – THE LORD PROVIDES

Genesis 22:1-14; Proverbs 4:18; Romans 4:1-25

The setting of this lovely title is like the setting of a precious stone. To be shown to best advantage, a jewel needs two things: it needs a dark background and a bright light shining upon it. The dark background in Genesis 22 is the altar upon Moriah's mount, an altar upon which Abraham must yield his beloved only son in obedience to the will of God. Things had been uncertain, anxious, demanding, and even bleak in Abraham's previous experience, but never had there been a test like this! His beloved Isaac, the child of promise, God's gift to himself and Sarah in their old age – God wanted him back, and his clear instructions had brought father and son together to this dark scene in the loneliness of the land of Moriah.

But there was a bright light shining in Moriah that day as well. "But the path of the just is as the shining light, that shineth more and more unto the perfect day" (Prov 4:18). "What shall we say then that Abraham our father, as pertaining to the flesh, hath found? For if Abraham were justified by works, he hath whereof to glory; but not before God. For what saith the scripture? Abraham believed God, and it was counted unto him for righteousness" (Rom 4:1-3). Abraham was justified by faith, and it was faith that made him walk so confidently to the altar when every natural fibre of his body and soul was screaming at him to turn back.

And what of your own experience, dear fellow saint? Even as you are reading, is your mind preoccupied with anxiety and fear? Perhaps retirement is looming and you are not sure how you are going to manage financially. Perhaps the mum or dad reading this passage to carefree children knows that redundancy is possible, and little mouths still have to be fed. These cares are real, and it is so

difficult to keep bright for the Lord, for the family, for the saints, for each other, when the background is so dark and lowering. Dear child of God, shine the light of faith upon the scene and, as you do so, you will discover a hitherto unnoticed gem lying upon the dark backcloth of your fears. Shine the light of faith, and suddenly the brilliant flare of this precious title of our God will flood your heart with its radiance: "Jehovah-Jireh" – the Lord provides!

We cannot match the faith of Abraham, can we? But notice, "it came to pass after these things" (Gen 22:1). God did not impose a test on Abraham for which the man was unprepared, and neither will He do that to you. Look to God in faith. You have trusted Him with your soul for eternity, so trust Him with your life and all its circumstances as well. It was when Abraham was totally occupied with the altar that God made provision for him, but that provision was "behind him" (22:13). Cast yourself and your need today upon "Jehovah-Jireh" – the Lord provides!

Day 2

"Jehovah Rophe" – the Lord heals

Exodus 15:22-27

From delight to despair, so quickly and unexpectedly. From singing to sighing and from triumph to tears: how like our own wilderness experience! The children of Israel had seen God's power exercised for them in the most signal and remarkable way. The awesome military might of Pharaoh and his army had been swallowed up by the waters of the Red Sea, and the path that had been death to their erstwhile master and his forces had been the means of their own deliverance and separation unto God. What a God was their's! With a light step and a song on their lips the people of God confidently followed Moses into the wilderness of Shur (Exod 15:22).

Then thirst set in. Uncomfortable at first, then demanding and, finally, all-consuming. The little fresh water they carried was soon consumed by the children and the elderly, and there was no relief from the heat of the sun and the scorching barrenness of the wilderness. The light step had become a stumbling gait, the song had long since ceased. Three days! Perhaps as you are reading this you have a drink at your side and plenty more in the kitchen. Think of three days in the heat of the desert and finding no water. What you might be able to tolerate for yourself becomes heartbreaking as the children have no moisture left with which to weep. The Red Sea and all its triumph is a hazy, distant memory now. All there is today is thirst, thirst, relentless thirst. As the third day with no water runs its agonizing course there comes, from those in the lead, a hoarse cry through parched lips, "Water, water"! Suddenly it becomes clear, they are not crying *for* water but because they can *see* water. An oasis! New reserves of strength are found, the step quickens and God's people offer Him thanks as they rush upon the object of their dreams.

Oh the disappointment! Oh the heartbreak! Oh the tears of frustration and hopelessness! The water is bitter, undrinkable, tantalising in its appearance and foul to the taste. Do we dare to think reproachfully of these dear folk as they murmur "against Moses, saying, What shall we drink?" (15:24)?

Say, beloved, have you not been at Marah? Are you there now? Some long trial that was wearing you down seemed to be at an end and, just as you thought your own strength had seen you through, you found that the waters were bitter. What hopes have been dashed! What dreams have evaporated! Was it the new job, the romance, the recovery from ill health, the longing to see a loved one saved? Is there now frustration, hopelessness, anger against God? If so, the answer is the same today as it was at Marah. Moses "cried unto the Lord; and the Lord shewed him a tree, which when he had cast into the waters, the waters were made sweet" (15:25). The tree made the difference, and the Tree will make bitter water sweet to your taste today. Look at all your disappointment and lost hope in the light of Calvary, and the God who brought you to Marah will make the bitter sweet, and then bring you to Elim for rest. "Jehovah-Rophe", "I am the Lord that healeth thee" (15:26).

Day 3

"JEHOVAH NISSI" – THE LORD IS MY BANNER

Exodus 17:1-16; Galatians 5:17

After God had revealed Himself to His people as "Jehovah Rophe" at Marah (Exod 15:26), He proved His faithfulness and power in providing manna for them in chapter 16. In so doing He not only met the physical need of the children of Israel, but He also furnished us with a delightful picture of the Lord Jesus as the Bread of heaven. Now, in chapter 17, we have another deeply instructive passage where the Lord Jesus is typified by the smitten rock. The result of the rock being smitten by the rod of government and justice was the outflowing of life-giving water to the people of God. In this is illustrated the Person and ministry of the Holy Spirit, by whom life is begotten in men and women who, by nature, are "dead in trespasses and sins" (Eph 2:1). The believer in the Lord Jesus has two natures, the one begotten of the flesh and contrary to God and His ways, and the other begotten of the Holy Spirit and desirous of those things that honour and please God. The flesh cannot abide the presence of the Spirit and, consequently, there is a perpetual war going on in the child of God (Gal 5:17). It is this struggle that is illustrated for us in the actions of Amalek in Exodus 17.

Amalek was spawned by the flesh (Gen 36:12) and became the inveterate enemy of the children of Israel. His character was as profane and fleshly as that of Esau, his grandfather. Notice, it was only when the water flowed from the smitten rock that "then came Amalek, and fought with Israel" (Exod 17:8). So it is with the work of the flesh today. Only those indwelt by the Holy Spirit know the inner conflict produced by the 'Amalek flesh'. The unregenerate person is

under the domination of the devil, but the believer has a new nature which is ceaselessly attacked by the flesh. The battle with Amalek was the first conflict faced by the Israelites, and they only prevailed through the ministry of Moses on their behalf. In Exodus 32 Moses will stand as a picture of Christ in His mediatorial work but here, in chapter 17, Moses is a picture of the praying believer. All the time his hands are upraised in supplication and intercession, the people of God prevailed. When, through weariness, his hands were lowered, Amalek prevailed. In his weakness Moses was helped by Aaron, figurative of the Lord Jesus in His High Priestly ministry in heaven, and Hur, a picture of the Holy Spirit in His prompting of a believer's prayer life (Rom 8:26).

Victory that day was marked by the building of an altar, and Moses called it "Jehovah Nissi" – the Lord is my banner. The banner is the ensign or standard that is carried into battle and marks the rallying point for an army. The rallying point in the believer's conflict with the flesh is Christ, our ever-victorious Lord. Near to Him I need fear no foe, and Amalek will be discomfited. Dare I forget "Jehovah Nissi"? Dare I wander aimlessly amid the perils of the battlefield? "Remember what Amalek did unto thee by the way, when ye were come forth out of Egypt; how he met thee by the way, and smote the hindmost of thee, even all that were feeble behind thee, when thou wast faint and weary; and he feared not God" (Deut 25:17-18).

As Barnabas urged the new church at Antioch to "cleave unto the Lord" (Acts 11:23), he was teaching them about "Jehovah Nissi" – the Lord is my banner.

Day 4

"JEHOVAH MEKADESH" – THE LORD WHO SANCTIFIES

Leviticus 11:42-44; 19:1-4; 20:7-8, 23-26; 1 Peter 1:13-16

With each new self-appointed title, Jehovah revealed more of Himself to His people. It is significant that He revealed Himself as "Jehovah Mekadesh", the Lord who sanctifies, in the book of Leviticus, for that is the book which details how sinners can be made acceptable before a holy God. Holiness is an essential characteristic of God, and holiness pervades His house.

Of all the imperatives that Peter describes as coming from an appreciation of salvation, the first is a call to holiness. "As he which hath called you is holy, so be ye holy in all manner of conversation; because it is written, Be ye holy; for I am holy" (1 Pet 1:15-16). Sanctification and holiness are virtually interchangeable words, coming as they do from a common source. Our God-given title of "saints" simply means that we are sanctified ones, positionally holy in the sight of God. He demands that we practice what we are, and holiness should characterise every believer's life.

It is interesting to notice that, in the Lord's ministry, new life was evidenced differently in the three people whom He raised from the dead. In the case of Jairus' daughter it was by *new appetite*, "he commanded to give her meat" (Luke 8:55). With the son of the widow it was by *new affections*, "And he delivered him to his mother" (Luke 7:15); and with Lazarus it was by *new activity*, "Loose him, and let him go" (John 11:44). These three features of new life are echoed in the three calls to holiness in the book of Leviticus. In Leviticus 11 the whole context is one of *appetite*; in chapter 19 the call to holiness is in connection with purity of *affections* (the gross misuse of which is dealt with in chapter 18); and in 20:26 the demand for holiness is in relation to separation from the nations round about and their *activities*.

Beloved, practical holiness should mark us in our appetite, affection and activity as believers. Peter teaches us that, as believers, our appetite should be for "the sincere milk of the word" (1 Pet 2:2), our affection should be centred on Christ (2:7) and our activity should be to "shew forth the praises of him who hath called you out of darkness into his marvellous light" (2:9). Are we living as those who know "Jehovah Mekadesh" – the Lord who sanctifies?

Day 5

"Jehovah Shalom" – the Lord is peace

Judges 6:1-24

The occasion when Gideon recognised "Jehovah Shalom" marked another spiritual crisis in the experience of Israel. The people of that nation were no different from ourselves and, in spite of God fulfilling His promise to bring them into their promised land, "they ceased not from their own doings, nor from their stubborn way" (Jud 2:19). So we read "And the children of Israel did evil in the sight of the Lord: and the Lord delivered them into the hand of Midian seven years" (6:1). God will sometimes use the agency of the ungodly to chastise His people, and He did so repeatedly with Israel.

The effects of the Midianite coming into the land were truly disastrous. Midian was a son of Abraham, through Keturah (Gen 25:2), so was brother to those whom his offspring now afflicted. His name means "strife" and the dark setting of Gideon's days is now revealed. They were days marked by strife between brethren. How telling it is that, as soon as Midian entered the land, the Amalekite joined him (Jud 6:3). For the character of Amalek see our study of "Jehovah Nissi" on p.414. The lesson is stark: where strife arises between brethren it will not be long before the flesh is in evidence. The consequences are always dire. Those seven years of Midianite oppression saw the people fearful, divided and hungry. They could do no work and there was nothing for the altar. But God had His man! Humble, fearful, hesitant Gideon who, because of his burden of heart, was not only useable by God but was described by the angel as "thou mighty man of valour" (6:12). God was about to demonstrate the abiding principle that "not many wise men after the flesh, not many mighty, not many noble, are called: but … God hath chosen the weak things of the world to confound the things which are mighty … that no flesh should glory in his presence" (1 Cor 1:26-29). The angelic appearance (was it a pre-incarnate appearance of the Lord Jesus?) and the word from God "Peace be unto thee; fear not" (Jud 6:23) caused Gideon to build an altar and call it "Jehovah Shalom" – the Lord send peace, or, the Lord is peace.

Ought not every local assembly to be a haven of peace and tranquillity? How it must grieve the Lord to see strife amongst His people! The devastation caused today by "Midian" and "Amalek" is immense, and those who should be enjoying the land are found languishing under oppression. Recovery begins with men like Gideon, an altar, and the acknowledgment of our God as "Jehovah Shalom".

Day 6

"Jehovah Tsidkenu" – the Lord our righteousness

Jeremiah 23:1-6; Proverbs 14:34; Isaiah 51:1-7

By now we will not be surprised to find that this further lovely title of our God is found against a dark backdrop. Undeterred by the disappearance into Assyrian captivity of the northern kingdom of Israel some 100 years before, the two tribes forming the southern kingdom of Judah persist in their rebellion against their God. A sequence of wicked kings has left its mark on the nation, relieved only briefly by the short reign of godly Josiah. Through the prophet Jeremiah, God speaks to Zedekiah, king of Judah, and warns him that He is going to use the Babylonians as the instrument of His judgment. The warning falls on deaf ears, and Judah teeters on the brink of an abyss of suffering and judgment.

What a comfort it must have been to the godly remnant to know that, in God's purpose, the nation would eventually have a king who was righteous! "I will raise unto David a righteous Branch, and a King shall reign and prosper, and shall execute judgment and justice in the earth" (Jer 23:5). Is the world today not crying out for such a ruler? Corruption and self-aggrandisement are endemic in every nation. Natural justice has gone by the board: the poor are still oppressed, the voiceless millions still go hungry. When will it end?

The humanitarian agencies of this world, laudable though their efforts are, will never make a real difference. Only One can make a difference, the One who "shall be called THE LORD OUR RIGHTEOUSNESS" (23:6). This title looks forward to the millennial reign of our Lord Jesus Christ and the restoration of Israel, but we look back to when the Lord Jesus walked amongst men and proved the words of the psalmist, "Thou lovest righteousness, and hatest wickedness: therefore God, thy God, hath anointed thee …" (Ps 45:7). We think of Him too as the One who was "made sin for us, who knew no sin; that we might be made the righteousness of God in him" (2 Cor 5:21). The Lord Jesus is the manifestation of perfect righteousness, and He is the provision and ground of our righteousness. Whether the Jew, the Gentile or the church of God, all will ultimately have cause in a coming day of glory to praise "Jehovah Tsidkenu" – the Lord our Righteousness.

Day 7

"Jehovah Shammah" – the Lord is there

Ezekiel 48:30-35; Psalm 137:1-9

The last of these great Old Testament titles of Jehovah is found against a backcloth that is not just dark, it is coal black. The dire warnings of the prophets had all gone unheeded, and the experience of the northern ten tribes had had no effect upon the behaviour of the southern kingdom of Judah. Their favoured status as the chosen people of God had been taken for granted by the children of Israel, as had the tokens of God's presence among them. Did they not have the glorious temple that Solomon had built, and was not the Levitical system with all its ornate ritual a manifest evidence that the God of heaven presenced Himself with His ancient people? Not any more. As Ezekiel spoke to them, some fourteen years had elapsed since the unsparing army of Babylon had sacked the temple, carried off the sacred vessels and reduced the glory of Solomon's days to a smoking heap of rubble. The people of God were now in captivity, far from their promised land, and they wept.

Tragedy, time and tears are so often needed to turn the hearts of God's people back to Himself, and so it was in the Babylonian captivity. The same will be true in a more severe way during the great tribulation, still to come, and the same is also true in the individual lives of many saints today. But as the children of Israel wept in Babylon, so Ezekiel began to prophesy concerning another temple that would be built. We know from our vantage point in history that the temple built after the captivity would also be destroyed, but Ezekiel's temple is yet future, and will be in the land during the millennial reign of the Lord Jesus. The crowning beauty of the temple in that glorious day, and the thought with which Ezekiel's prophecy concludes, is that it will be a temple-city called "Jehovah Shammah", the Lord is there!

The Lord Jesus once graced the courts of Herod's temple in Jerusalem: He was there, but they threw Him out. Now He graciously grants His presence in the midst of His believing people, and as a local assembly gathers in His Name, He is there. When, one day soon, the Church is taken home to glory and all the ransomed of this age are surrounding the Saviour, the highest bliss of heaven will be, He is there. And when he returns to establish His kingdom, Israel restored will gather unto the city where once they crucified Him, and they will rejoice because He is there. The nations will rejoice as a great voice from heaven declares, "Behold, the tabernacle of God is with men, and he will dwell with them, and they shall be his people, and God himself shall be with them, and be their God" (Rev 21:3). "Jehovah Shammah" – the Lord is there!

Phil Coulson

Week 52

7 GARMENTS OF ISRAEL'S
HIGH PRIEST

Introduction

The garments in Scripture are a most interesting subject. What a contrast there is between the references in the first book, Genesis, where we read of the effort of man to cover his sin (Gen 3:7), and in the last book, Revelation, where the bride, the Lamb's wife, is clothed "in fine linen, clean and white: for the fine linen is the righteousness [lit. 'righteousnesses'] of saints" (Rev 19:7-8). In the next seven articles we shall look at the garments of the High Priest of Israel. We shall see that every colour, every stone, every thread, every pomegranate and bell brings forth something of the beauty, the grandeur, the glory and the greatness of the Christ of God, our Great High Priest.

You will notice that the quality of the whole of these vestments, whether its texture, material or workmanship, was the very best: fine linen, pure gold, precious stones, costly ointment, cunning workmanship, all used by wise-hearted ones. This was because nothing but the highest quality will do to portray Him who is indeed "altogether lovely" (Song 5:16).

Aaron was clothed with these garments, fitting him for the office to which he was called. The garments gave him a dignity that he did not possess in himself. What a contrast to our Lord! It is character, not the clothes, that fitted Him for the office. His glory was essentially His from all eternity.

You will observe that the colours and material of these garments are in keeping with the tabernacle, as this would be the sphere of Aaron's service. As in the tabernacle, so in the garments, every whit speaks of Christ's glory.

Just as there are seven vessels in relation to the tabernacle, there are seven garments in relation to the High Priest (Exod 28:4,36). Both these subjects tell us of the perfection of Christ. You will notice that Aaron's garments are described before the garments of the priests. The anointed eye can easily discern the reason for this. "In all things he must have the pre-eminence" (Col 1:18).

These garments come between the brazen altar (Exod 27) that speaks so eloquently of the sacrifice of Christ, and before the altar of incense (Exod 30) that prefigures Christ as the Great High Priest in heaven (Heb 4:14).

How good to appreciate that the One who has been to the cross, now is engaged for us in the glory.

Day 1

THE LINEN COAT – HIS SINLESSNESS

Exodus 28:39; 39:27-28

This garment was the first to be put on by Aaron (Exod 39:27; Lev 8:6-7). It was the innermost garment, and so reminds us of what Christ is in Himself. It reached right down to the feet, with sleeves down to the hands, thus showing from head to feet His absolute purity.

It was in this coat that the high priest went in before God on the Day of Atonement. He did not go in with the ephod and breastplate which were his official vestments, but with the linen coat, the girdle and the linen mitre. The linen mitre reminds us that He knew no sin (2 Cor 5:21); the linen coat and girdle that He did no sin (1 Pet 2:22); and the linen breeches (not seen) that in Him sin is not (1 John 3:5). The high priest was robed only in spotless white, speaking of the holiness of the Lord Jesus which fitted Him to undertake the stupendous work of dealing with sin.

Looking at this coat from a distance, and in contrast with the other garments, it would seem quite ordinary, but upon closer examination there is displayed a skill and a beauty in the fabric. To many who took a casual glance at 'Jesus of Nazareth' they saw an ordinary man but, as we look closer at His life and scrutinise His walk and listen to His words, we see that there was that which reveals Him as the Son of God. This garment was all of embroidered damask, "woven work" (Exod 39:27), and the beauty lay not so much in what was worked *on* it, but what was skilfully worked *into* the material.

You will notice the description by the Shulamite of her beloved in the Song of Solomon. The first thing she states is that "My beloved is white …" (5:10). If that was not true, all else was in vain. When we consider this linen coat we hear the words of the psalmist in Psalm 132:9, "Let thy priests be clothed with righteousness …". It reminds us of 1 John 2:1, " … if any man sin, we have an advocate with the Father, Jesus Christ the righteous".

The coat was of fine linen, which reminds us of the fine flour of the shewbread (Lev 24:5), and the fine flour of the meal offering (Lev 2). In Leviticus 16:4 it is spoken of as "the holy linen coat".

We rejoice in the fact that the Lord Jesus was holy before He came (Isa 6), in His birth (Luke 1:35), in His life (John 8:46), in His death (Lev 6:25), in His burial (Ps 16:10) and in His ascension (Heb 7:25).

Day 2

THE GIRDLE – HIS SERVICE

Exodus 39:29

Having looked at the Garment of Linen, now let us consider the Girdle of Love. This girdle was not "the curious girdle of his ephod" (Exod 39:5) which was not really a girdle but rather a moveable belt to keep the ephod in place.

You will notice this girdle was made "of fine twined linen, and blue, and purple, and scarlet, of needlework" (Exod 39:29). When we find these colours elsewhere in our study of the garments, for example the ephod, curious girdle, breastplate and pomegranates, they always come in the order, blue, purple, scarlet and fine-twined linen. But, in this girdle, the linen comes first.

Interestingly, in the study of the tabernacle there is one exception as well. In the gate, door and veil the blue is mentioned first. The exception is with the ten curtains over the boards. Why should this be? The answer is to understand that the emphasis is always on the first item. When the blue is mentioned first it speaks of the One who came from the orbit of blue – Heaven. When the linen is mentioned first it tells of the One who was here in all His holiness and perfection, and is now in the glory in the fulness of perfect manhood. He has carried true humanity back to the throne room of God.

This girdle reminds us of Christ's *humanity* as seen in the gospel of Luke; the blue reminds us of His *authority* as seen in the gospel of John; the purple would tell us of His *royalty* as seen in the gospel of Matthew; and the scarlet would remind us of His *sufficiency* as seen in the gospel of Mark.

And so, in this girdle, we remind our hearts of the fact that the blessed One who lived here, now lives for us in heaven. As we think of this our mind goes to John chapter 13. You will notice in verse 1 of that chapter He is about to depart out of this world unto the Father. So it is not His coming in that is pictured in what He was about to do, but His leaving. So He rises from supper (the Passover supper) that speaks of His death (1 Cor 5:7) and lays aside His garments (cf. John 20:5-8). He then takes a towel and girds Himself. How good to appreciate that the Man who was once here, and has known the trials of life, now lives in heaven to serve His own; a minister (servant) of the sanctuary (Heb 8:2). He is the girded Christ of Revelation 1:13, walking in the midst of the seven golden lampstands.

Day 3

THE ROBE OF THE EPHOD – HIS SPHERE

Exodus 28:31-35

This is the first reference to a robe in our Bible. So we have God's first thoughts of a robe. Coats are for our covering, as seen in Genesis 3, but a robe speaks of dignity, office and authority. The robe is often associated with the apparel of a king, as in 1 Samuel 24:4. Perhaps, therefore, there is a hint here of a priest whose office is superior to that of Aaron, One after the order of Melchizedek the King-Priest. Other priests had linen coats, but only the high priest had a robe of blue.

This robe did not reach to the ground, so it speaks of a heavenly Man. The linen coat speaks of Christ's *holy* character, and the robe speaks of His *heavenly* character. The perfect Man who once was here, now represents us in that heavenly sphere. We will look at:

1. The Stateliness of the Blue – its Hue. We are not told what the high priest's robe was made of, the emphasis is on its colour. It was all of blue. The Saviour could say "I am not of the world" (John 17:16). The world has produced some great men and women, but it never produced Christ. He came from another world. Paul spoke of Him as "the Lord from heaven" (1 Cor 15:47).

2. The Strength of the Binding – its Hole. The robe of the ephod was woven in one piece, "And there shall be an hole in the top of it, in the midst thereof: it shall have a binding of woven work round about the hole of it, as it were the hole of an habergeon, that it be not rent" (Exod 28:32). The hole in the robe enabled it to be passed over the head of the high priest, and was edged in such a way that it would not be rent. The edge was "as it were the hole of an habergeon", which means that it was as strong as that on a coat of mail. No matter what the pressure, it would not be rent. We remember the Scripture concerning our blessed High Priest who "was in all points tempted (tested) like as we are, yet without sin" (Heb 4:15). As we think of our Saviour, our mind goes to the scene of Calvary when "the soldiers, when they had crucified Jesus, took his garments … now the coat was without seam, woven from the top throughout. They said therefore among themselves, Let us not rend it …" (John 19:23-24). John tells us that His title was unchanged – the true King (v.22), and His garment was unrent – the true High Priest (v.24).

3. The Sound of the Bells – its Hem. This is the only mention of a hem in relation to the garments. It would speak of that which is complete. Around the hem were pomegranates of blue, purple, scarlet and twined linen, and bells of pure gold between them. Pomegranates speak of fruitfulness, as they are full of seeds contained in a red fluid. Golden bells speak of faithfulness, and they produced the only music heard in the sanctuary courts. In Christ we see a beautiful balance when we think "of all that Jesus began both to do (pomegranates) and to teach (bells) (Acts 1:1).

Day 4

THE EPHOD – HIS SUPPORT

Exodus 28:6-14

The ephod was the outer garment of the high priest, a sleeveless tunic coming below the waist. It was made up of two pieces, a front and a back, fastened together on the shoulders with clasps of onyx stones. It was belted together at the waist with a curious (embroidered) girdle of the same material and colours. It is helpful to see the relationship between the ephod, the breastplate and the girdle:

The Ephod – the Authority of the High Priest (Heb 4:14)
The Breastplate – the Affection of the High Priest (Heb 4:15)
The Girdle – the Activity of the High Priest (Heb 4:16)

Three things to be considered in our study regarding the ephod are

1. The Clarity of the Colours. The ephod was made by beating gold into thin plates, cutting them into wires and weaving them into the fine twined linen. Although it was one garment, when seen in the light it appeared as a golden garment speaking of Christ's absolute deity, and when seen in the shadow it appeared as a linen garment speaking of His true humanity. The two were intrinsically linked together. Gold is not made but discovered; the fine linen is prepared, "a body has thou prepared me" (Heb 10:5).

The ephod was all of "cunning work", which means 'the work of a thinker'. How good it is to think on these things and see:

The Glory of the Gold – His Deity (John 1:1).
The Loveliness of the Linen – His Humanity (John 1:14).
The Beauty of the Blue – His Authority (John 1:15,18,30).
The Power of the Purple – His Royalty (John 1:49).
The Significance of the Scarlet – His Sufficiency (John 1:29).

2. The Setting of the Stones. Two onyx stones were set one on each of the shoulders, a place of strength (Isa 9:6). The names of the children of Israel were engraved on them according to their birth. It is the new birth that put us on Christ's shoulders. When the lost sheep was found by the shepherd it was placed upon his shoulders (Luke 15). The journey home depended on the power of the shepherd, not the sheep. We are kept by the power of God (1 Pet 1:5).

3. The Grandeur of the Girdle. "And the curious girdle of the ephod, which is upon it, shall be of the same" (Exod 28:8) shows that the girdle was part of the ephod and closely linked with it. The girdle was like a belt to keep the ephod in place, thus speaking of support. In all the colours of the girdle we see the One who supports the saints today. He does so in all the glory of His Deity – the Gold, the tenderness of His Humanity – the Linen, the Authority of His Lordship – the Blue, the Royalty of His Kingship – the Purple, and the Sufficiency of His Sacrifice – the Scarlet.

Day 5

THE BREASTPLATE – HIS SYMPATHY

Exodus 28:15-30

The breastplate is the first item of the garments of the high priest to be mentioned, hence showing its importance. It speaks of the Lord's heart, his sympathy and affection for his people (Exod 28:29-30). There are five things to be considered regarding the breastplate:

1. Its Similarity. The breastplate was inseparably linked with the ephod and girdle as it was made of the same cunning work and displayed the same beautiful colours. In the ephod we see something of His authority, in the girdle His activity, and in the breastplate His affection. He has feelings for His own – He knows, He loves, He cares.

2. Its Shape. "Foursquare it shall be …" (Exod 28:16). Each side was the same, showing there is no partiality with Christ. That truth is seen as well in the foursquare brazen altar (Exod 27) on which the priest would place the continual burnt offering, and the foursquare golden altar (Exod 30) on which he would burn sweet incense.

3. Its Size. The breastplate was a span both in length and breadth. A span is the distance from the tip of the little finger to the end of the out-stretched thumb, approximately ½ cubit, 9 inches or 23 centimetres. It thus covered the whole of the high priest's breast.

4. Its Stones. The twelve precious stones were placed in the order of the tribes, so Judah would be first and Naphtali would be last (Num 2). There are four things we notice about these stones:

    a) Their equality. Every stone was precious. God's people are called his precious jewels (Mal 3:17; 1 Cor 6:20).

    b) Their security. They were all set in gold (cf. Eph 1:4), and not just written but engraved. Their removal is therefore impossible (John 10:28).

    c) Their beauty. These stones came from different countries, some from the depths of the ocean, and others from the darkest mines. Similarly, believers come from all walks of life, cultures and ethnic backgrounds.

    d) Their variety. No two stones were the same. They were different in their colour and brilliance, yet they were all equally precious. We too are all very different, yet precious to Him.

5. Its Stability. The breastplate had a golden ring at each corner. The two top rings were joined to the onyx stones on the shoulders by wreathen chains of gold, and the two lower rings were joined by blue laces to two golden rings

attached to the ephod, just above the curious girdle. The breastplate therefore could not rise above his heart nor fall below.

May we appreciate the place that is ours upon the heart of our Great High Priest.

Day 6

THE URIM AND THUMMIM – HIS SKILL

Exodus 28:30; Leviticus 8:8

Having looked at the breastplate, its similarity, shape, size, stones and its stability, we now come to think of what I would call its secret. There does seem to be a mystery surrounding the subject of the Urim and Thummim. Both words are in the plural, which is a Hebrew way to emphasise their importance and dignity. The breastplate was doubled to form a pouch into which the Urim and Thummim were placed. They were used when a certain decision had to be made where there was no Scripture to guide.

Their Name. The two words mean Light and Perfection. As the people of God today we do not want visions, but we do need light and a knowledge of God's will which is called "good, and acceptable, and perfect" (Rom 12:2). In Christ is light. "I am the light of the world: he that followeth me shall not walk in darkness" (John 812). In Christ "are hid all the treasures of wisdom and knowledge" (Col 2:3). He is indeed the Wonderful Counsellor (Isa 9:6) and God's last and final word (Heb 1:1-2). Today we do not have two stones but we do have the Scriptures, Old and New Testaments, which are indeed profitable for every situation (2 Tim 3:16). May we continue to use them, and may the Spirit of God reveal His will, through them, to us.

Their Position. The Urim and Thummim were placed behind the stones on the breastplate. Behind the selecting, setting and security of the stones we see the wisdom and perfection of our God. You will notice that there is no command to make the Urim and Thummim, but simply instruction as to where to place them, an act carried out not by the workmen but by Moses (Lev 8:8).

Their Use. "The lot is cast into the lap (or, bosom)" (Prov 16:33). The Urim and Thummim may possibly have come in the form of black and white stones, the black stone being negative and the white positive (cf. Rev 2:17). (There are seven other references to the Urim and Thummim, worthy of further study: Lev 8:8; Num 27:21; Deut 33:8-10; 1 Sam 28:6; 1 Sam 30:7-8; Ezra 2:63 and Neh 7:65).

In the upper room, when Peter wanted to know who would betray Christ he signalled to John who was leaning on Christ's breast. He was just where the Urim and Thummim were in all their fulness, and to him was the answer given (John 13:23-26).

May we too avail ourselves of such a provision (James 1:5; Prov 3:5-6).

Day 7

The mitre and crown − His submission and supremacy

Exodus 28:36-38

Very little is known concerning the mitre, and no details are given as to its shape. Yet what God has revealed is most instructive. We shall see in the mitre of fine linen, the Humble One; in the plate of pure gold, the Holy One; and in the lace of blue, the Heavenly One.

The mitre of fine linen. There is a distinction between the head dress of the high priest and that of the priest. In the case of the high priest it was the mitre, and in the case of the priests, bonnets. The word "bonnet" comes from the word to 'lift up' or 'elevate'. We, as sons in the priestly family, have been lifted up to heavenly places (Eph 1:3). Christ as the Son of God came down, taking the submissive place that we may be exalted. The covered head speaks of subjection as 1 Corinthians 11:1-16 clearly shows. The Lord Jesus was ever subject to His Father (John 6:38).

The plate of pure gold. Upon the mitre was a plate of pure gold (no alloy or mixture), and upon the plate an engraving, "Holiness unto the Lord". It is indeed an appropriate finish to the attire of the One who is our High Priest. He is the supreme One (Phil 2:9-11). Four times in Exodus 28 we read, "Aaron shall (or may) bear"; he had a four-fold burden as a high priest: *the burden of our security* (v.12) − I'm glad he bears that responsibility; *the burden of our sorrow* (v.29) − on His heart the names of the children; *the burden of our guidance* (v.30) − the Urim and Thummim; *the burden of our acceptance* (v.38) − the mitre. Aaron shall bear the iniquity of the holy things (v.38). It does seem strange to find these two words together, "iniquity" and "holy", but it is showing that our best gifts to God are defiled by the iniquity of the giver. Our purest worship is mingled with infirmity, our most devoted acts are tainted with self-pleasing, but He bears the iniquity of the holy things.

The lace of blue. We have seen in our studies a robe of blue, and some threads of blue in the ephod, breastplate, curious girdle and pomegranates. Now our study ends with the lace of blue. This lace of blue undoubtedly speaks of our Lord Jesus Christ who has entered into heaven "now to appear in the presence of God for us" (Heb 9:24).

> For us he wears the mitre
>   Where holiness shines bright
> For us his robe is whiter
>   Than Heaven's unsullied light. (Mary Peters)

Malcolm Radcliffe

Scripture Index